A HISTORY OF THE HABSBURG EMPIRE
1700–1918

A History of the Habsburg Empire 1700–1918

JEAN BÉRENGER

Translated by
C. A. Simpson

Longman
London and New York

Addison Wesley Longman Limited
Edinburgh Gate,
Harlow, Essex CM20 2JE,
United Kingdom
and Associated Companies throughout the world

*Published in the United States of America
by Addison Wesley Longman Inc., New York*

Originally published as *Histoire de l'Empire des Habsbourg 1273–1918*
© Librairie Arthème Fayard, 1990

English translation © Addison Wesley Longman 1997

All rights reserved; no part of the publication may be
reproduced, stored in a retrieval system, or transmitted
in any form or by any means, electronic, mechanical,
photocopying, recording, or otherwise, without either the
prior written permission of the Publishers or a licence
permitting restricted copying issued by the
Copyright Licensing Agency Ltd.,
90 Tottenham Court Road, London W1P 9HE.

First published 1997

ISBN 0 582 09007 5 PPR
ISBN 0 582 09008 3 CSD

British Library Cataloguing in Publication Data

A catalogue record for this book is
available from the British Library

Library of Congress Cataloging-in-Publication Data

Bérenger, Jean, 1934–
[Histoire de l'empire des Habsbourg. English]
A history of the Habsburg empire / Jean Bérenger; translated by
C. A. Simpson.
p.   cm.
Includes bibliographical references and index.
Contents: 1. 1273–1700.
ISBN 0–582–09009–1. — ISBN 0–582–09010–5 (pbk.)
1. Austria—History. I. Title.
DB36.3.H3B4713   1994
943.6—dc20   93–7777   CIP

Transferred to digital print on demand 2001
Printed and bound by Antony Rowe Ltd, Eastbourne

Contents

CONTENTS

List of Maps and Tables

MAPS

TABLES

GENEALOGICAL TABLES

Introduction: The Habsburg Inheritance (1273–1700)

by C. A. Simpson

Rudolf IV (1218–91), count of Habsburg, was elected king of the Romans in 1273. The Habsburgs were then a family of minor significance possessing lands in Alemannic Switzerland and Upper Alsace. It was Rudolf's relative power-lessness and obscurity which had commended him to the electors. His election marked the beginning of the Habsburg family's long association with the imperial crown of the Holy Roman Empire which in time was to become *de facto* a possession of the dynasty.

As Rudolf I, king of Germany and king of the Romans, he added a second enduring element to the Habsburgs' patrimony. He challenged the right of the Bohemian king Otakar II to the Austrian provinces and by his victory at the Battle of Dürnkrut in 1278 destroyed the Bohemians' hope of a great Slav empire in Central Europe. The Austrian provinces were secured for the Habsburgs and would remain in their possession until 1918 and the end of the monarchy.

Rudolf I had placed the Habsburg family at the centre of the German world and of European affairs. It was the emperor Frederick III (1415–93) who gave voice to the dynasty's wide vocation. In 1452 he became the first Habsburg to make the journey to Rome to receive the crown of the Holy Roman Empire from the pope. He adopted the device AEIOU (*Austria est imperare orbi universo*; it is for Austria to rule the whole world).

Maximilian (1459–1519), Frederick III's eldest son and heir, contracted a series of fortuitous marriage alliances, the outcome of which might indeed have suggested that the dynasty was destined to achieve his father's dreams of empire and world leadership. By his marriage to Maria of Burgundy, the daughter of Charles the Bold, Maximilian secured, albeit precariously, the Netherlands for the House of Habsburg. For his eldest son and daughter, Philip the Fair and Margaret, he arranged marriages to the Spanish *infante* and *infanta*, Juan and Juana, the children of Ferdinand and Isabella and so heirs to the crowns of Castile and Aragon. The *infante* died young and without issue, but his sister's marriage was more fruitful and her children by Philip the Fair became the emperors Charles V (1500–58) and Ferdinand I (1503–64).

Charles V inherited from his mother Spain and the Castilian overseas empire. In 1519, at the age of nineteen, he secured his election as Holy Roman

Emperor by using the wealth of the Fugger family of bankers to buy votes. The other two candidates, Francis I of France and Henry VIII of England, did not have such secure financial resources at their disposal. Francis I's candidacy was a further move in the continuing rivalry between the Valois and Habsburg dynasties which had intensified since the issue of the Burgundian succession and evolved into the Franco-Austrian rivalry which in one form or another endured to the very end of the Habsburg monarchy.

The Habsburg family's hold over the Iberian peninsula expanded yet further when the Portuguese king Sebastian died fighting the Moors at the Battle of Alczarquivir and Philip II (1527–98) made good his claim to the Portuguese throne through his mother and his wife. In 1580 Portugal and the Portuguese empire came under Habsburg rule.

Ferdinand I extended the family's possessions in Central Europe and is credited with being the true creator of the Austrian monarchy. In 1515 the emperor Maximilian had concluded a pact of mutual succession with the House of Jagiellon whereby the archduke Ferdinand married Anne Jagiellon and his sister Maria married Louis Jagiellon, son of the king of Bohemia and Hungary. In 1526 Louis Jagiellon died in the marshes at Mohács during battle with the Turks. Ferdinand's election as king of Bohemia and Hungary, although not uncontested, was secured and the Bohemian and Hungarian crowns were to remain in Habsburg hands until the dissolution of the monarchy in 1918.

The Habsburgs saw the extraordinary growth of their empire not only as a sign of divine favour but also of their having been entrusted with a mission. As emperors of the Holy Roman Empire it was their duty to defend Christendom from the infidel and from the heretics. Charles V wanted to unite Christendom under the pope and emperor and to wage war against the infidel. To his mind, this God-given task fell upon him as emperor but also as king of Spain and heir to the Catholics kings Ferdinand and Isabella who had prosecuted so vigorous a campaign against both Islam and heresy, driving the Moors from the Iberian peninsula. The rest of Europe, though, felt threatened by the growing power of the Habsburgs and fear of the dynasty and its possible imperial programme outweighed any enthusiasm for a crusade.

Charles V declared that he would be steadfast in defending the Catholic faith. He realized that the Church would have to reform if its supremacy were to withstand the challenges and threats from Protestantism. It was the duty of the emperor, as he, but not the papacy, understood it, to advance the task of Church reform.

In both aspects of his mission, Charles V saw himself as having failed. This failure in his duty as emperor was compounded by the challenges to his power and authority from France, England and from his German vassals. After a series of resounding defeats, in 1556 he surrendered his powers and withdrew to the monastery at Yuste.

His son, Philip II, as king of Spain, took up the banner of militant Catholicism. In Central Europe, the cadet branch of the House of Habsburg was prepared to accommodate confessional pluralism and the Austrian monarchy at the time of Ferdinand I's death was a bastion of Protestantism. The emperor

Rudolf II (1552–1612), grandson of Ferdinand I and son of the emperor Maximilian, defended the position of the Catholic Church but was not a champion of the Counter-Reformation as practised by his Spanish cousin. It was with the accession of the Styrian branch of the family in the person of Ferdinand II (1578–1637) that the full intolerance of the Counter-Reformation was unleashed in Bohemia, Hungary and Austria. The traditional *pietas austriaca* became identified with the House of Habsburg's determined and unswerving championship of Catholicism.

The acquisition of Hungary had brought the Habsburgs into the position of being directly threatened by the infidel Ottomans. During the sixteenth century, the Ottoman armies had advanced further into Central Europe, conquering most of Hungary, and in 1529 the armies of Süleymân the Magnificent had laid siege to Vienna. When the Ottoman advance came to a halt, it was not because of the concerted efforts of the European powers but because of instability within the empire and the recurring threat from Persia. Under the grand viziers Ahmet and Mehmet Köprülu, the sultan was able to resume his programme of conquest. By the terms of the 1664 Treaty of Vasvár, the Ottoman empire reached its greatest extent in Europe. In 1684 the Ottoman armies were again at the gates of Vienna but in the long ensuing war were forced back. In 1699, by the terms of the Peace of Karlowitz, the Ottomans lost territory. Hungary had been liberated and Vienna governed as far east as Belgrade. The monarchy recovered most of the Hungarian crownlands and the Venetian republic, while Venice gained the Dalmatian coast. At one stage it had seemed as though the Turks might be driven from Europe. The imminent death of Charles II of Spain, however, forced the Habsburgs to divert all their energies towards the future of the dynasty.

The armies of the Ottoman empire, as restricted in range as they were by the length of the annual campaign season, had come close to capturing the heart of the Habsburgs' Central European empire and posed by far the greatest threat to their hegemony. The Habsburgs, though, had been continuously challenged throughout their rise to power and their history is characterized by remarkable resilience in the face of internal and external threats.

In the sixteenth century, the Habsburgs found themselves ruling a vast and diverse agglomeration of territories, the only common bond among which was the dynasty in the person of the ruler. The emperors Maximilian I and Charles V had maintained a peripatetic existence, the court moving with them, and by travelling through their domains they had maintained a sense of personal rule. Charles V, though, was the last emperor to travel regularly. Philip II preferred to rule his vast empire from the Escorial, the great palace he had built almost in the centre of the Iberian peninsula, some miles distant from Madrid.

Philip II and his successors on the Spanish throne and the cadet branch of the House of Habsburg were beset by rebellion within their territories. The Netherlands rose in revolt in 1566. A sense on the part of the Dutch that the Spanish were excluding them from the government of their own country combined with discontent over the conditions under which they could practise their religion and grew into a national war of liberation. The ardently Protestant northern provinces were lost to Spain and became the United Provinces. The remaining provinces, the core of modern Belgium, continued under Habsburg rule as the Spanish and then the Austrian Netherlands until the Peace of Campo-Formio in 1797. There were rebellions too in the Iberian peninsula. In 1640 Catalonia rose in a revolt which rumbled on until 1652 and which at its peak raised the prospect of the Spanish Habsburgs being left simply as rulers of Castile. Portugal also rose in 1640 and as in the Netherlands, discontent and dissatisfaction grew into a national war of liberation.

The Habsburgs ruling from Vienna suffered challenges to their authority no less than those ruling from Madrid. The elective character of the imperial crown and the crowns of Bohemia and Hungary meant that they were obliged to uphold and respect the institutions and traditions of the lands they had been elected to govern. As a consequence, when raising taxes or troops, the Habsburgs often found themselves all but at the mercy of the estates within their lands. During the seventeenth century, the nobilities of Bohemia and of Hungary rose in what they argued was legitimate rebellion because the Habsburgs had broken the promises made at the time of their election. As in the Netherlands, the rebels were typically members of the reformed churches and so confirmed Charles V's worst fears as to the consequences of the division of Europe into Protestant and Catholic camps.

In 1618 the estates of Bohemia rose against Ferdinand II and the following year elected the Calvinist Frederick of the Palatinate as king of Bohemia. What started as a confessional dispute and began with the infamous 'defenestration' of Prague, evolved into a German civil war. The Bohemian rebels were crushed at the Battle of the White Mountain in 1620. Other European powers, bent on weakening if not destroying the Habsburgs' great empire, had become engaged in the long and wide-ranging series of conflicts known as the Thirty Years War (1618–48). The Viennese Habsburgs kept Bohemia and took measures to strengthen their control there, but in Germany they were never again to regain their former influence.

After the Treaty of Westphalia (1648) which marked the end of the war, the Spanish Habsburgs still remained at war with France for more than a decade. The Peace of the Pyrenees signed in 1659 arranged the marriage of Louis XIV to the Spanish *infanta* and laid the ground for the Bourbon dynasty's claim to the Spanish throne. For the remainder of the century, Louis XIV would continue to prepare to challenge the Habsburgs' right to inherit Spain and its empire and to encourage those prepared to make trouble for the Habsburgs; the Hungarians who were involved in a series of revolts and rebel plots throughout the seventeenth century found in Louis XIV, as in the Turks, a ready source of moral if not military support.

At the beginning of the eighteenth century, the Habsburg dynasty was preparing to face a further sustained challenge to its position in Europe.

CHAPTER ONE

The War of the Spanish Succession (1665–1713)

Charles II of Spain, on 2 October 1700, a month before he died and already in a much weakened state, named his successor in his will and so achieved the most significant act of his thirty-five-year reign. The king had yielded to pressure from cardinal Portocarrero and the Castilian national party and by disinheriting his uncle, the emperor Leopold I, he had barred the cadet branch of the Habsburg family from what it saw as its rightful inheritance and distanced himself from the House of Habsburg. The Spanish nation wanted to preserve the Spanish monarchy of Charles V and Philip II and would not countenance any division of Spanish territories. The Council of Spain knew that the Austrian monarchy, for all its recent victories in Hungary, was incapable of successfully defending its Madrid ally in the war which then seemed inevitable.

The great powers had completed the final stages of their plans directed against the Habsburgs. Louis XIV of France and William of Orange, as king of England, elaborated a compromise solution which found no favour with the Castilian patriots. They proposed that Leopold I should receive the Spanish crown and compensate his Bourbon cousins, the descendants of Maria Theresa, the Spanish *infanta* and wife of Louis XIV, by giving them the House of Austria's entire Italian patrimony. Since Philip IV's death, the Madrid government had been firmly opposed to any division of Charles II's possessions and had advocated the alternative plan of making the heir the duke of Anjou, Louis XIV and Maria Theresa's grandson, on sole condition that he guaranteed the integrity of the Spanish monarchy. Charles II's decision in his will was surprising and marked the subordination of the dynastic principle to the idea of the nation. It had a decisive effect on how the Habsburgs in the future maintained the balance of power in Europe. The interests involved were so great and so conflicting that to find a peaceful settlement was a great challenge, even though the question of a successor to Charles II had exercised the chancelleries of Europe since the signing of the Peace of the Pyrenees in 1659. Why this was the case becomes clearer when all the negotiations relating to the Spanish succession are examined.[1]

THE DYNASTIC PROBLEM

Philip IV, immortalized by Velazquez's portraits, had not, for all his manifest carnality, produced many heirs by his two marriages. From his marriage to the

Bourbon princess Isabella, the daughter of Henry IV of France, only the *infanta* Maria Theresa had survived. The *infante* don Balthazar Charles had died while still a youth. By his second marriage to the archduchess Maria Anna, he had a daughter, the *infanta* Margarita Theresa who married her maternal uncle, Leopold I, and one son, the *infante* don Charles who was born after the Peace of the Pyrenees and came to the throne in 1665 at the age of four with his mother Maria Anna as regent. At Philip IV's death in September 1665, the future of the Spanish dynasty seemed bleak since the sole representative of the senior branch was a sickly, epileptic child. The courts of Europe expected this 'child-king' would die before his tenth birthday and that the question of the Spanish succession would soon be posed. The cadet branch of the Habsburg family was reduced to Leopold I who had a delicate constitution and at the age of twenty-five was still without an heir. It had long been envisaged that Leopold would marry his cousin, the *infanta* Maria Theresa, and so Vienna took the Franco-Spanish marriage of 1659 as an insult and a catastrophe for the dynasty. Leopold decided to ask for the hand of Maria Theresa's younger sister who had been born in 1650. The Spanish court replied that it was desirable to wait in such matters and did not make marriage arrangements for the *infanta* Margarita Theresa until 1666 and then insisted that Leopold settle at Madrid, a condition which the young emperor refused to fulfil. He received his wife at Vienna with joy and surrounded her with affection. Their marriage was a rare success among those of contemporary sovereigns. The empress had delicate health and found it hard to bear the chilling fogs of Vienna and the annual pregnancies which the interests of state imposed upon her. The archduke Ferdinand, born in November 1667, survived but a few months. Only the archduchess Maria Antonia lived to adulthood and in 1682 married the elector of Bavaria, Max Emanuel, and bore him a son, Ferdinand.

Leopold's second marriage to his cousin, Claudia Felicitas of the Tyrol, was without issue and it was only by his third marriage that the dynasty's future was finally assured. Unable to find an archduchess to marry, in 1676 he took as his wife Eleanora of the Palatinate-Neuburg who belonged to a collateral branch of the House of Wittelsbach. This empress was robust and gave birth to two sons, the archdukes Joseph and Charles, who in due course both succeeded as emperor. Always a firm believer in divine providence, Leopold decided to dedicate his first-born to Joseph, Christ's human father, and so introduced a new Christian name to the House of Austria. The birth of the archduke Charles in 1686 assured the dynasty's future. He was destined by his father for the Spanish throne should Charles II die without issue. His elder brother, the archduke Joseph, was elected king of the Romans in 1690 and was called upon to perpetuate the German line of the family and so make it the senior branch.

Charles II, however, lived on. He led a reasonably normal life and in 1679, to seal French–Spanish reconciliation following the Dutch war, he married Marie Louise d'Orleans, the eldest daughter of Louis XIV's brother. The young queen was made welcome and for a few years shook Charles II from his melancholy and made him lively and cheerful. She died in 1689, having reputedly been poisoned at the German party's instigation by countess Soissons, prince Eugene of Savoy's mother, who was knowledgeable on the subject of poisons and had quite wisely left the country. The German party then triumphed by marrying Charles II to one of the empress Eleanora's sisters, Maria Anna of Neuburg. The novennas, pilgrimages and devotions undertaken that the king might father an heir proved of no avail and Charles II remained impotent. The Spanish succession again became an issue during the War of the League of Augsburg. This eased the way for the Peace of Ryswick (1697) which was based on compromise. Louis XIV showed moderation and renounced the *réunions* in return for recognition of French sovereignty over Alsace and Strasbourg.*

THE FIRST PARTITION TREATY (1668)[2]

According to the dynastic principle of the House of Austria, if its senior branch became extinct, the whole inheritance would fall to the cadet branch. This meant that Leopold I stood to become sole heir, since at the time of their marriages Anne of Austria, wife of Louis XIII, and Maria Theresa, wife of Louis XIV, had renounced any claims to the Habsburg patrimony. Mazarin, however, at the time of the Peace of the Pyrenees in 1659, had made renunciation conditional upon receipt of 300 000 ducats as dowry and so had effectively made it null since in 1660 the Spanish treasury was incapable of handing over such a large sum of money. It is often overlooked that the most important consequence of the Peace of 1659 was not the annexation of Artois and Roussillon but the Spanish marriage and all the expectations it raised.

In 1666 the French government published *Le traité des droits de la reine Marie-Thérèse* and so showed that it had not renounced the inheritance and that a movement was already afoot to make good its claims. The War of Devolution (1667–68) enabled Louis XIV to reach a compromise with his brother-in-law Leopold I who had not been in a position to rush to the aid of the Spanish Netherlands, despite the urgent appeals of the regent, his sister Maria Anna, and the governor, the marquis Castel-Rodrigo. The Flanders campaign of 1667 under Louis XIV and Turenne's command was made all the more smooth by Spain's lacking the men and money necessary to resist the French army successfully.[3]** During the summer of 1667, the secret conference held many discussions but the imperial army for the most part had been demobilized at the end of the Turkish war to reduce the strain on the treasury. The head of the council, Wenceslas Lobkowitz, opposed attempts to send veteran regiments to Flanders and with respect to the future succession, persuaded the emperor to negotiate a secret treaty of partition. Louis XIV gave Gremonville, his resident at Vienna, full authority. After heated discussions, he managed to secure a compromise in exchange for the promise of a cardinal's hat for the prince of

---

* Translator's note: throughout volume two, the form Strasbourg rather than Strassburg will be used.

** Translator's note: Henri de la Tour d'Auvergne, viscount of Turenne (1611–75), marshal of France (1643), achieved lasting fame during the Dutch wars, 1672–75.

Auersperg, the former principal minister of Ferdinand III who had remained at the head of 'the Spanish party'. Leopold I recognized Maria Theresa's rights to her brother's patrimony and in return for this concession Louis XIV abandoned Spain and the Indies to the emperor while accepting compensation in Italy, the Netherlands and the Iberian peninsula. Louis XIV would receive the whole of Navarre and so recover its southern part which Ferdinand of Aragón had conquered in 1512. He would also receive Rosas in Catalonia, the Spanish presidios in north Africa, Naples and Sicily, which guaranteed France's preponderance in the western Mediterranean and eased commercial relations with the Levant. Finally, the treaty promised Louis XIV the Burgundian circle, the Spanish Netherlands and the Franche-Comté as well as the distant Philippines. The emperor Leopold would have Milan and the port of Finale in Liguria which guaranteed communications between Austria and Spain. Leopold would be free to give all or part of this inheritance to one of his children.

The promise of French military aid for the emperor when he eventually took possession of his patrimony was of vital importance. The two new allies undertook to persuade the Madrid government to agree to this settlement. Leopold sent the marquis of Grana to the regent Maria Anna to present her with the *fait accompli* while Condé invaded the Franche-Comté in early February 1668 and forced Spain to accept the idea of partition. The Bourbons and the Habsburgs of Vienna for the first time found themselves in the same camp against the Habsburgs of Madrid. The final clause, which was intended to ensure the operation's success, was kept a closely guarded secret. The Austrian monarchy's relative weakness meant that Leopold I would gain the most from the treaty. European politics resembled a family quarrel around a death-bed.

The Franco-Austrian rapprochement was short-lived since it was bitterly opposed by the emperor's council and prince Lobkowitz became increasingly isolated. For the moment, the partition treaty enabled Louis XIV to satisfy himself with some places in Flanders and in May 1668 to sign the Peace of Aix-la-Chapelle.

FRANCO-GERMAN RIVALRY[4]

The Rhineland princes, after the devastation of the Thirty Years War, valued peace above all else and feared a renewal of the conflict between France and the House of Austria. It was the elector of Mainz, Philip of Schönborn, who in 1665 proposed that the Spanish inheritance be divided. The War of Devolution provoked dismay and alarm at the rise of French imperialism. It was impossible to revitalize the League of the Rhine, the masterpiece of Mazarin's diplomacy. A fact which is often overlooked is that the occupation of the duchy of Lorraine by the French army in 1670 led to a deterioration in Franco-German relations. The duke of Lorraine, the elderly Charles IV, and his nephew, the future victor at Vienna and Buda, took refuge in Germany and passed into the emperor's service. The German party led by the chancellor Hocher and Montecuccoli, the president of the War Council, reduced Schwarzenberg and

Lobkowitz's influence and Leopold suspected the French of having fomented the Hungarian revolt. The Dutch war led to the end of good relations and Lobkowitz's disgrace. There were no other champions of a French alliance at the Viennese court until the eighteenth century when Kaunitz came to power under the empress Maria-Theresa. Relations deteriorated to such an extent that Leopold forbade the use of French as 'the language of his enemies'.

The Dutch war revealed the new system of continental alliances. It began as a small-scale operation carefully planned by Hugues de Lionne, but the French attack upon the United Provinces grew into a European conflict. Leopold I concluded an alliance with the United Provinces, former rebels against the House of Austria, and went to the help of the Spanish Netherlands. Louis XIV could count on active support only from the bishop of Münster and the elector of Cologne. Leopold I declared war on France in 1673 and the imperial troops under Montecuccoli's command forced Turenne to retreat into Franconia. The following year, the Empire declared war and decreed a boycott of French merchandise. The army of the circles with Bournonville's imperial troops and the Brandenburg army invaded Alsace in autumn 1674. A little earlier, the emperor had had Fürstenberg, the future cardinal and Louis XIV's agent in Germany, arrested and imprisoned at Wiener Neustadt.[5]

Turenne gave orders to burn the Palatinate as part of a plan to protect Alsace by depriving the enemy of all possible sources of food and so impeding the German advance. This prompted an indignant letter from the palatine, Charles Louis, whose restoration France had effected by the terms of the Treaty of Westphalia. This single incident signified a complete reversal of the situation a quarter-century earlier; it was now the Habsburgs who appeared to the German princes as the defenders of German liberties, of justice and of peace. Louis XIV's government did not completely grasp this change so prejudicial to French interests, but Leopold I had the wit to turn it to his advantage. Louvois put his faith in brute force and intimidation while the king underestimated the dignity and patriotism of those ministers and princes whom he hoped to turn into his clientele with gratuities and pensions.[6*] The situation deteriorated after the Peace of Nijmegen (1678) when Louis XIV went on the defensive and employed questionable, but according to his principles, justifiable means. Using selected historic documents and playing with the term 'dependencies', which was then current but ambiguous, he launched his policy of *réunions*. To guarantee the security of the north-east frontier, the Chambers of *Réunions* compelled numerous Rhineland princes to declare themselves vassals of the French crown; those who demurred saw their patrimonies 're-united' by force.[7] Leopold I undertook the defence of the Empire and also of Spain, which was able to hold on to Luxemburg until 1684. The Spanish party and Charles of Lorraine thought that the emperor's policies were too mild. In April 1682 they wanted the imperial army to be sent to the Rhine to attack France and so to retake Strasbourg and save Luxemburg.

---

* Translator's note: François Michel le Tellier, marquis of Louvois (1641–91), secretary of state for war under Louis XIV.

The League of Augsburg enabled Leopold I in 1686 to put together a coalition made up of dissatisfied elements and Louis XIV's enemies, namely the princes of the Empire including the elector of Brandenburg, the United Provinces, Spain and even Sweden whose king had suffered through Louis's policy of *réunions*. The burning of the Palatinate in 1689, which this time was not simply the result of a general's initiative but a concerted plan ordered from Versailles, led to a change in Louis XIV's image which had already lost much of its lustre in Protestant Germany following the revocation of the Edict of Nantes in 1685.

This was why Leopold I no longer found himself isolated when he again raised the issue of who would succeed Charles II in Spain. The birth of the archduke Charles also helped the emperor since it was his second son who would be brought up to become king of Spain, thus dispelling fears that Charles V's mighty empire might be reconstituted and ending any pretensions to universal monarchy. In addition, in 1689 William of Orange and the United Provinces had promised Leopold military and naval support to seize the whole Spanish inheritance.

The new element in European diplomacy was the emergence of the Maritime Powers: Britain and the United Provinces. After three Anglo-Dutch wars in twenty years (1654–74), the British and the Dutch, who had in common their religion, social structures, maritime and colonial economies and fears of continental hegemony, cast aside their commercial rivalries and were united in the face of Louis XIV's ambitions. The Glorious Revolution of 1688 brought William of Orange, stadhouder and captain-general of Holland, to the English throne after he had put to flight the Catholic Stuarts. Leopold would henceforth have a valuable partner in the struggle against France. William of Orange was a statesman of great stature and was moved by a deep-seated hatred of Louis XIV, which, even so, did not keep him from negotiating with the king of France over dividing Charles II's inheritance at the conclusion of the Peace of Ryswick.

THE SECOND PARTITION TREATY (1689)[8]

Louis XIV was fully aware of the promises which the Maritime Powers had made to the emperor and wanted to know whether William of Orange really felt under an obligation or if, at the right moment, he might be persuaded to accept one of his grandsons as a candidate for the Spanish throne. William had been established as a constitutional king and had to take account of parliament when conducting British foreign policy. The War of the League of Augsburg, which had been thought essential to prevent James II from returning to England, proved very costly and unpopular. Once peace had been established and France had recognized William as king, parliament wanted to reduce the army to the very minimum, to the great disappointment of the king. William was becoming increasingly bitter towards Louis and wrote to his principal Dutch

collaborator, Anthonius Heinsius, that 'his domestic enemies wanted his ruin'.*
This insecurity compelled him to follow the king of France's proposals.

The negotiations surrounding the treaty of partition were too complicated to
recount here, but the terms which William of Orange as stadhouder and king
exacted from Louis XIV in return for his recognition of the French candidate,
are too important to be overlooked. William made it clear that he would regard
the accession of one of Louis XIV's grandsons to the Spanish throne as tantamount to the union of France and Spain, even if a personal union between
the two monarchies was not effected. For this reason the Maritime Powers would
agree to the accession only if Louis XIV guaranteed their maritime commerce
and security. For the United Provinces, this was simply a question of enlarging
and strengthening the barrier created by the Spanish Netherlands. Documents
from this period show that the term *barrière élargie* was understood as extending to the Spanish Netherlands, which would reintegrate all the territories
acquired since the Peace of the Pyrenees. The idea of an extended barrier did
not simply disguise inadequacies in the United Provinces' security but also
their desire to extend their economic hold over the Netherlands to the south.
Louis XIV had learnt from experience and promised to give the United Provinces solid guarantees which would turn the Spanish Netherlands into a solid
rampart, but he refused to begin discussions over a *barrière élargie* which would
entail unthinkable sacrifices for France.

Negotiations with England were more complicated. Although William in
his discussions with Tallard pretended to know little about the proposed partition of the Spanish empire, it was clear that he was well-informed and that
the demands he made corresponded to what the English wanted and he needed
to win his subjects' support.

The negotiations marked a return to the terms of the Treaty of Dover of
1670: in return for military assistance to take the Spanish throne, Louis XIV
would help the English to capture Minorca, Ostende and certain places in
America. This second clause, though, was not formulated in the treaty. William
also asked, with little hope of success, for Cadiz and Seville and demanded
Gibraltar, Minorca and one or two islands in the Spanish Antilles as well as
three Spanish ports in north Africa – Ceuta, Oran and Mellila. Louis XIV was
taken aback. It would be impossible to put such demands to the Spanish since
neither of the Maritime Powers had the least right to the Spanish patrimony.
Louis asked William in vain to limit himself to one of the three north African
ports which, at least, he stood a reasonable chance of obtaining.

Once Louis XIV had decided that the price of William's support was too
high, the two parties searched for a candidate on whom they could both compromise since they wanted to maintain peace and the balance of power in Europe. In the second partition treaty, Joseph Ferdinand of Bavaria, the son of
Leopold's daughter, the archduchess Maria Antonia, was named as the residual
heir. Since he was still a minor, his father, the elector Max II Emanuel, would be

* Translator's note: Anthonius Heinsius (1641–1720) had been in charge in the Netherlands as
grand pensionary of Holland after William of Orange left for England in 1688.

appointed as his guardian. The *dauphin* would receive as compensation Naples, Sicily and the Tuscan presidios, as well as the small but important province of Guipuzcoa in north-west Spain, while the Austrian Habsburgs would receive the duchy of Milan. Leopold would gain the least since when Charles V gave Milan to his son, the future Philip II, he had expected that the imperial dignity would alternate between the German and Spanish branches of the House of Austria and remain within the limits of the Holy Roman Empire. It was, however, argued that since Leopold's grandson was to become the residual heir, Louis should have the right to more compensation. This was not a view Leopold, who did not know all the details of this partition plan, could be expected to share. He had opposed the 1668 partition being made public, but in 1698 it was William of Orange who forbade Louis XIV from making the treaty known. William wrote to Heinsius, 'How could I make it known to Leopold that I envisaged giving Spain to Maximilian of Bavaria?' When Joseph Ferdinand died in February 1699, William immediately embraced the idea that Max II Emanuel should become king.

THE THIRD PARTITION TREATY (1700)

The death of the electoral prince of Bavaria in February 1699 upset all plans. William of Orange suggested that the throne should be given to Max II Emanuel of Bavaria, but Louis XIV would not countenance this solution. News of the second partition treaty, but not all its details, had reached Spain where Charles II had responded by issuing a will in which he made Joseph Ferdinand heir to the whole inheritance. It was to be expected that he would choose a candidate without Spanish blood.

Negotiations between Louis XIV and William of Orange over the third partition treaty were swiftly concluded. Leopold's younger son, the archduke Charles, was designated the residual heir and France was granted Milan as compensation, with the possibility of exchanging it for the duchy of Lorraine since Leopold, it was generally understood, would not allow the French to hold Milan. The proposed exchange would safeguard France's eastern frontier. If the duke of Lorraine rejected this scheme, the duke of Savoy, Victor Amadeus II, would give up the valley of Barcelonette and so seal another possible invasion route. The Dutch did not sign immediately and took time to negotiate with the other powers, in particular the emperor.[9]

Although the treaties of partition did not decide the Spanish succession, they have an important place in European history. It was the first time that the great powers had attempted to solve a complicated problem through negotiation during peacetime. It laid the basis for further attempts to avoid general wars by convening congresses to lay the foundation for exchange, recompense and the establishment of secundogenitures which at the beginning of the eighteenth century weakened the rigid and outmoded dynastic principles.

Louis XIV and William of Orange were both shrewd statesmen and had practical objectives. The will designating Joseph Ferdinand as residual heir gave Louis XIV time to reflect.

At this point, Leopold I again became hostile to the idea of dividing the Spanish inheritance. This was not because he wanted to reconstitute the monarchy of Charles V. Since he had two sons, he hoped to give up his rights in favour of his younger son Charles who had been born in 1686, and to bring up his elder son Joseph, born in 1681, to be the future emperor. Joseph was given a German education under the direction of the learned Wagner von Wagenfels, who introduced a nationalist element into his studies which exalted the German past and emphasized the history of enmity towards France. The archduke Charles was taught Spanish and was prepared for the day when he would rule at Madrid. In the meantime, Charles II's second wife, with the support of the imperial ambassador count Harrach, assumed leadership of the German party. Relations between Madrid and Vienna were strained despite Leopold's regular intervention to defend the Spanish Netherlands against French imperialism.

Charles II and his ministers did not have any faith in Leopold's ability to defend the integrity of the Spanish inheritance. They remained unimpressed by the imperial forces' victories over the Turks and the reconquest of Hungary. For this reason, cardinal Portocarrero and the Castilian national party persuaded Charles to write his will of 2 October 1700 in favour of his great-nephew, the duke of Anjou, and to the detriment of the archduke Charles who was still of an age to marry and have children. The last of the Spanish Habsburgs and the Castilians believed that, as long as Louis XIV accepted the will, France alone was capable of saving the Spanish monarchy. The ailing king had been guided in his actions by national sentiment and the interests of Spain rather than the dynastic loyalty which should have counted above all else for a Habsburg. After a century and a half reigning at Madrid, the Spanish branch of the dynasty provided the only instance in the history of the House of Austria when the Habsburgs did not remain supranational princes, not showing partiality towards any one nation. The degree to which Charles II had been assimilated reflects well upon the Castilians who had shown that they could win over cosmopolitan princes who were convinced of the superiority of their House.

Charles II's will marked a turning-point in the history of the House of Austria. If France refused, the archduke Charles would be declared residual heir and receive the whole patrimony while the heirs of Maria Theresa would be without any territorial compensation. It was a solution radically different from the three previous treaties of partition put together by foreign courts. Louis XIV had to decide immediately whether to effect a reconciliation between France and Spain by sending a Bourbon to Madrid, or to practise a policy of 'backhanders' by annexing the duchy of Lorraine and Savoy.

The duke of Saint-Simon, using the papers of Colbert de Torcy, the secretary of state for foreign affairs, summoned the stormy meetings of the Supreme Council which had to decide whether the king should accept the will. Louis XIV has often been judged harshly for accepting, but, whatever his decision, unless he had forgone all compensation, the Spanish succession would have provoked a war, for Leopold I was determined to fight France for all or part of the Spanish crown lands. Leopold I defended the Italian possessions not simply as a matter of principle but because he had ambitions in the peninsula and did not want under any circumstances to give up Milan or Naples. Louis XIV was convinced, with good reason, that William of Orange would not join him in fighting to take possession of the territories granted to him by the treaty of partition. Finally, the French merchants realized that it was essential for the Atlantic ports and the French economy to gain a hold on the American market and that to accept the will would increase the likelihood of war. For these reasons, Louis XIV, to the Castilians' great joy, declared the duke of Anjou king of Spain on 15 November 1700. 'The Pyrenees', indeed, 'were no more' and all the conditions were in place for a great European war.

THE GRAND ALLIANCE OF THE HAGUE (1701)

Leopold I acted as a statesman and proved equal to the situation. He remained firm in his principles and prepared for the forthcoming fight to secure the succession for his son Charles. Although his entourage was made up of elderly advisers and ultra-conservatives, he was able to force upon 'the old Court' prince Eugene of Savoy who, in the most recent phase of the Austro-Turkish wars, had proved to have the skills of a great military leader.

German and Austrian historiography have turned Eugene of Savoy into a hero of the baroque age and of the German pantheon, but in fact he had a very complex personality. He was a younger son of the House of Savoy and proud of belonging to a sovereign dynasty. The son of count Soissons, a *prince étranger* at the French court, and Olympe Mancini, a niece of Mazarin, he grew up in Paris in an atmosphere hostile to Louis XIV. He had been destined for a career in the Church but did not have any vocation, and after a thorough and solid education he turned into a libertine. In 1683 he went with his lover, the prince of Conti, to take part in the defence of Vienna. The emperor presented him with a regiment of dragoons in autumn 1683 and he remained in Austria where his talents and birth enabled him to climb swiftly through the ranks of a military career. More honest than many of his colleagues, he was richly rewarded and became a great landowner with estates at Schlosshof in Lower Austria and Rackeve in Hungary. He was a notable patron and had built at Vienna a winter palace in Himmelpfortsgasse and a summer palace, the celebrated Belvedere. With the support of the archduke Joseph and Kaunitz, the imperial vice-chancellor, Eugene of Savoy persuaded Leopold to enter the war in spring 1701 to capture Milan, where the governor Vaudemont and the administration had rallied to Philip of Anjou, now Philip V of Spain. He was appointed generalissimo and amassed 30 000 men with whom he crossed the Alps, repeating, in his contempories' eyes, the exploits of Hannibal. This offensive seems all the more bold when it is understood that at this stage the Bourbons appeared in the stronger position.

All the lands of the crown of Spain had, like Castille and Milan, rallied to the new king. Max II Emanuel, now governor of the Spanish Netherlands, changed sides and with his brother, the elector of Cologne, suddenly became an ardent champion of the Bourbons, renewed the French alliance and provided

Louis XIV with Bavaria as a solid base from which to launch his armies. The king of France also secured the sure support of Savoy and excellent cooperation between France and Milan by marrying Philip V to a princess of the House of Savoy.

Two blunders by the French ended Leopold's isolation. The first mistake was when French troops entered the Spanish Netherlands and put to flight the Dutch garrisons on the barrier. With the complicity of the governor-general, the 'Anjou regime' became *de facto* a French protectorate, a development which could not but disquiet the Maritime Powers, England being as sensitive as Holland to a potentially hostile great power occupying Flanders. The second blunder was made by Philip V when he abided by the fundamental laws of the kingdom of France and, contrary to the terms of Charles II's will, refused to renounce his rights to the French crown. A Franco-Spanish monarchy would disturb the European equilibrium. In September 1701 William III, shortly before he died, concluded the Grand Alliance of the Hague with Leopold, who was forced to accept the principle of compensation for the archduke Charles: Philip V would retain the Spanish throne but would surrender the Netherlands and his Italian possessions to the Habsburgs, who would thus have the preponderance of power in Italy, in accordance with the new direction of their policy, while their hold over the Netherlands was intended to neutralize a region which was a sensitive issue for the Maritime Powers. The Castilians were the greatest losers under this arrangement, since the allies had intended to compensate themselves with Spanish colonies. The alliance anticipated their entrance into the field in the following spring.

In 1702 Great Britain was thrown into turmoil by the death of William of Orange, Louis XIV's fiercest opponent. France made the serious error of recognizing James Stuart, the 'Old Pretender', then in exile at Saint Germain-en-Laye, as king of England. Since James was Catholic, the whole country but especially queen Anne, who had succeeded William of Orange and her sister Mary in 1702, felt threatened. This pointless provocation convinced the parliament at Westminster that it should finance a war for which hitherto it had shown little interest.

All the conditions for a great European war were in place. Leopold I's obstinacy played an important part in precipitating the war when in 1701 he attacked Italy to seize the compensation he coveted. The image of Leopold I as pious, humble and pacific, a perpetual victim of French and Turkish aggression, needs to be modified. The elevated idea which he had of his House and of its imperial mission convinced him that he was defending a just cause. This short man dressed in black was incapable of directing an army in combat but was no less ready to embark upon war than his glorious cousin at Versailles. He knew that the monarchy had sufficient resources to fight in Italy and Germany and that the Maritime Powers could pin down the Franco-Spanish forces. Ever cautious, after the 1699 Peace of Karlowitz, he had not demobilized his army which still had more than 100 000 men, and, if needed, he had at his disposal a war budget equivalent to 40–50 million *'livres tournois'* since the Ottoman empire for the moment was no longer a threat. The Maritime Powers, contrary to a persistent myth, made hardly any contribution to the Austrian war effort, at the most 25 million '*livres tournois*'. Count Gundaker Starhemberg, the president of the *Hofkammer* and friend of prince Eugene, was able to mobilize credit in 1705 by creating the Wiener Stadtbank (Bank of Vienna).

THE FORCES FACE-TO-FACE

Despite the growth in the strength of the Habsburg monarchy, the Bourbons still held the trump cards and it was not until 1709 that Louis XIV could be forced to make a treaty. France was rich and could mobilize almost half a million men, militia and marines in a gigantic effort on a scale not repeated until the First World War. The greatest difficulty was the inadequacy of the generals in command. Villars, Vendôme and Max II Emanuel of Bavaria were not of the same class as Eugene of Savoy or Marlborough. The defensive strategy which had been followed since 1675 bore its fruits and Vauban's 'ring of iron' prevented the invasion of France after the fall of Lille and the defeat at Malplaquet in 1709.* The Spaniards, or more precisely the Castilians, fought loyally on the side of Philip V, sensing that a victory for the Bourbons would signify the end of the traditional liberties enjoyed by the provinces on the periphery and the beginning of a real period of centralization. For these very reasons, the Catalans rallied en masse to the archduke Charles who made Barcelona his capital.

The elector of Cologne, Joseph-Clement, and his brother Max II Emanuel remained loyal to Louis XIV even when their patrimonial states were occupied and subjected to heavy taxation by the imperial troops. The duke of Savoy, however, changed camp in the hope of acquiring Montferrat, which would make it much harder for the Franco-Spanish army to defend Milan.

The counter-alliance in Eastern Europe worked in an eccentric way. Charles XII of Sweden was in theory allied to France but the Northern War occupied all his forces, first in Poland where he expelled Augustus II, the elector of Saxony, and replaced him with Stanislas Leczinski, and then in Russia where he pursued Peter the Great. The Ottoman empire, exhausted by the long war with the Holy League, did not respond to the overtures made by French diplomats and withdrew into a benevolent neutrality with regard to Louis XIV and his allies. The Hungarians were antagonized by the policy of 'reconstruction' which Leopold and Kollonich wanted to impose on them and once again rose up and waged a war of independence under the leadership of Ferenc II Rákóczi, the grandson of György II Rákóczi, prince of Transylvania, and, on his mother's side, of Petar Zrinski, the rebel of 1670. He wanted Hungary to be an independent state, free of the Turks, and so to realize the national monarchy of which Hungarian patriots had dreamt since the Battle of Mohács.

The Bourbons supported the Catholic Stuart refugees in France and once again used their supporters, the Jacobite opposition remaining in Great Britain and the numerous Irish and their leaders, including the marshal of Berwick, who

---

* Translator's note: Sébastien le Prêtre de Vauban (1633–1707), created marshal of France in 1703.

had followed the Stuarts to the Continent. This lent an element of ideology to what would otherwise have been a straightforward conflict of interests and a war of succession. In the same way, the allies promised military aid to the Camisards, the Cevenol peasants who in 1703 had responded to the persecution of Protestants by organizing an armed insurrection. The landing of troops in Languedoc, however, remained only a plan and the Huguenots laid down their arms in 1704 after their defeat by Villars.

If the armed conflict between the English colonists in New England and the French in Canada is taken into account, it could be said that this was a world war.

The allies, though, also held some trump cards. The Maritime Powers still had great wealth and economic power, even though the combined French and Spanish war fleets equalled those of the English and Dutch. The most important factor, though, was that the emperor succeeded in involving the whole of the Empire in the conflict. After Bavaria had been neutralized, he was able to use the whole of Germany to his advantage, a scenario imagined with fear and trepidation half a century before by Mazarin. The elector of Brandenburg, Frederick, was won over to the Habsburg cause in 1701 when the emperor granted him the title of king of Prussia and so contributed to the rise of the House of Hohenzollern. The House of Habsburg would later pay dearly for this concession since it strengthened the position of Brandenburg within the Empire. The immediate result, though, was that the Prussian army, which was first-rate, joined the imperial troops and the army of the circles.

Hostility towards the Castilians led Portugal in 1703 to join the allied camp and through the Methuen treaty to become a satellite of Great Britain, a vital outlet for the wines of Oporto. This move gave the allies an operational base on the western border of Spain. The Catalans also rallied to the allies for much the same reasons and the archduke Charles became 'king of the Catalans'. As in 1640, the countries on the periphery took sides against Castile and the Madrid government.

THE HUNGARIAN WAR OF INDEPENDENCE (1702-11)

At the beginning of the eighteenth century the conditions were in place for a fresh Hungarian rebellion. This was not, however, as conservative Hungarian and Austrian historians affirm, the result of clever French intrigue. Bércsenyi's memorandum of 11 August 1711 to the French ambassador at Warsaw took account of the Hungarians' latest grievances. In the memorandum, Bércsenyi challenged the legality of the decisions imposed by the 1687 Diet and by the assembly of notables (concursus palatinalis) which had met at Vienna in 1696 and 1698. The points at issue were the introduction of a regular tax upon the nobility, the modification of judicial procedures, the obligations of noble proprieters to render a sum to the royal fiscus in order to repossess their domains liberated from the Ottomans, and restrictions upon religious liberties.

Bércsenyi proposed that Augustus the Strong of Poland should be crowned king of Hungary. He advocated a military alliance with France and asked Louis XIV to help Imre Thököly, then a fugitive in Turkey, to liberate Transylvania. The rebels returned to the traditional programme of the personal union of Poland and Hungary and to the idea of putting Polish mercenaries at Louis XIV's disposal, as at the time of the Dutch war. This programme, however, soon became obsolete when the king of Poland, in order to check Charles XII of Sweden, concluded an alliance with the emperor Leopold and so passed into the allied camp.

It was at this point that Ferenc II Rákóczi entered the scene after escaping from the prison at Wiener Neustadt.[10] He provided the Hungarian rebels with a charismatic leader who readily took the place of the elderly Thököly. Rákóczi was a Catholic magnate of enormous wealth, who had some 100 000 peasants on his estates, and came from a family which had always opposed the Habsburgs. Leopold I had treated him as a hostage, handing him over to the guardianship of cardinal Kollonich and arranging for him to be educated by Jesuits in Bohemia. Rákóczi had acquired a solid classical education and was fluent in Latin and French, alternating between the two languages in his numerous writings. He was a good Catholic who soon showed leanings towards Jansenism and was remarkably tolerant of other confessions. He was a man of great humanity, a characteristic stressed by all who knew him, and also quite hot-tempered. A francophile, he seemed eager to renew at the first opportunity the alliance between Louis XIV and the Malcontents.* Family tradition, French military power, his own intellectual formation and sympathies towards monarchical absolutism all urged him in that direction.

The French ambassadors at Warsaw, first Longueval then Bonnac, were well-disposed towards the Malcontents because the Hungarian rebels provided an unexpected diversion which kept a section of the imperial army immobilized in Hungary. Louis XIV never gave the Malcontents all the aid they desired because the Spanish alliance was a heavy burden upon French finance and, besides, he mistrusted popular uprisings.

Cooperation was much less direct than in Thököly's day. Ferenc II Rákóczi was officially recognized as prince of Transylvania. The legitimate heir of his grandfather György Rákóczi, he had been unjustly stripped of his patrimony by Leopold II and so was free to renew 'a good and fine alliance' in order to recover his rights. The Malcontents found the Versailles cabinet less generous than they had hoped and never received more than *de facto* recognition, even when in 1707 the Diet of Ónod declared the Habsburgs deposed.

French assistance took the form of subsidies which passed through Danzig and Poland: 200 000 '*livres tournois*' in 1703 and then 10 000 crowns a month. The king also sent engineers, notably the brigadier-general Le Maire and the marquis of Alleurs who exercised the functions of diplomatic representative and military advisor respectively. Alleurs's relations with the Hungarians

---

* Translator's note: The Malcontents were members of the Hungarian and Croatian nobilities who together hatched plots, tentatively intrigued with the French monarchy and with the Ottomans, and fermented rebellion with the alleged purpose of shaking off Habsburg rule. See volume 1, pp. 323ff.

deteriorated after 1705 because he did not understand the real difficulties that ensued from the recognition of Rákóczi. He was hampered by lack of money, the rudimentary nature of the administration, the self-interest of the orders, the troops' ill-discipline, the inability of the soldiers to fight in formation, the hostility of the Catholic clergy and geographical isolation.

A grandiose strategic plan based upon that of 1645 was put together which aimed at taking Vienna in a pincer movement and forcing the emperor to come to terms. To this end, combined French and Bavarian troops invaded Austria while the Hungarians marched on Vienna. In 1703, after Villars's victory at Hochstadt, Leopold I's position seemed desperate. Max II Emanuel, however, refused to march upon Vienna and instead took the Tyrol, which he coveted and where he encountered much resistance from the peasantry. Vendôme and the Italian army were too late with their offer of assistance and the opportunity for a decisive victory was lost once and for all. The following year, prince Eugene and Marlborough defeated the combined French and Bavarian forces at Blenheim. The Hungarians had to be content with raids on the outskirts of Vienna and on the emperor's zoological garden.

The political situation in Hungary was complicated by the fact that the noble party was incapable of bearing the sacrifices demanded by the war. After the reprisal operations encouraged by prince Eugene, the court at Vienna changed tactics and began to negotiate. The emperor offered to satisfy almost fully the Malcontents' requests by agreeing to restore their privileges, to withdraw the German troops and to abolish the taxes that had proved so contentious. The Protestants were willing to accept the offers of mediation made by the Maritime Powers which were unhappy about the lot of their co-religionists in Central Europe. Rákóczi recognized Leopold I as the legitimate ruler and acknowledged as valid the election and coronation of Joseph I. After Leopold's death in 1705, he had himself proclaimed *dux* (prince) by the Diet at Szécsen but he did not make a break until 1707 when he sought Peter the Great's support in his election as king of Poland. Louis XIV, however, refused to ratify the Treaty of Warsaw out of loyalty to his alliance with Sweden. The Malcontents had been condemned to military isolation by the defeat at Blenheim. The failure of the Treaty of Warsaw in 1707 now condemned them to diplomatic isolation since the military situation was not in the Bourbons' favour.

In 1708 a wide-scale offensive was launched against the Hungarians which was marked by their defeat at Trencin, not far from Pressburg. The following year, the French all but ceased giving subsidies which in 1705 had amounted to 50 000 livres a month. An outbreak of the plague also took a heavy toll upon the Hungarians who were already down on their knees. The plague came as usual from the east and attacked a population already tried by war and deprivation, carrying off more victims than the imperial troops and the Ottomans combined. The time to negotiate had come, especially since the Austrians were in a favourable position in 1711 after the unexpected death of Joseph I.

The war of Hungarian independence failed for several reasons. The economic weakness of the country, which was without the industries needed for war, combined with inflation, the age-old antagonism between the nobles and the peasants which Rákóczi's enlightened policies could not overcome, and the shortage of regular troops (in 1705 there were 4 000 regular troops and 40 000 irregulars), all contributed to the rebellion's failure. Another important factor was the diplomatic isolation in which the Hungarians found themselves, in particular when the French refused to play the Russian card after Charles XII's defeat at Poltava in 1709. The Hungarian nation resigned itself to compromise with the Habsburgs in order to survive and disappeared from the international stage until the revolution of 1848. Louis XIV, by withdrawing his support from the Malcontents, contributed to the rise of the House of Austria as a great continental power.

The Spanish succession revealed the clumsiness and lack of imagination of the state apparatus since the treaty was finally made on the basis of the terms existing at the beginning of the conflict: Leopold's propositions to the Hungarians in 1703 and the programme of the Grand Alliance of the Hague in 1701. Avoiding open war, the two adversaries from 1705 embarked upon a war of attrition in which most of the victories were tactical rather than decisive. When in 1709 Louis XIV, moved by the suffering of his subjects and the gravity of the military situation, proposed a compromise to the conference at Gertruydenberg, the obstinacy of the allies crippled the negotiations and relaunched the war.

JOSEPH I (1705–11)[11]

Leopold I died in 1705. In 1703 he had agreed to dismiss the 'old court' and had appointed prince Eugene as president of the *Hofkriegsrat*, Wratislaw as chancellor of Bohemia and Gundaker von Starhemberg as president of the *Hofkammer*.

After the Oppenheimer bank went bankrupt, Starhemberg organized the credit necessary to maintain an army of 105 000 men. Prince Eugene continued to hold effective command of operations and combined the functions of minister and commander-in-chief. He and Marlborough harried France in northern Italy as well as in the Netherlands. The Hungarian insurrection, though, also posed a serious threat to the security and integrity of the monarchy. Before contemplating reform it was necessary to fight.

The new sovereign was very different from his father in his morals and in his physique. A German nationalist, he was the first Habsburg to turn away from Latin culture. In the confessional domain, he was a less convinced Catholic than his predecessors and forbade preachers from attacking Protestants in their sermons. He vehemently condemned the electors of Cologne and Bavaria who were allied to the French king, and waged war on pope Clement XI who had sided with the Bourbons. In some ways he foreshadowed Joseph II but comparisons should not be taken too far. Joseph I had good advisors, among them Eugene of Savoy, and this makes it difficult to tell how much of his success should be directly attributed to him. While still the heir apparent, he had been severely critical of the delays and prevarications which characterized his father's policies and had decided to be vigorous in his own rule. Was this, though, possible? He lacked perseverance, the tenacity which makes great administrators, and that aptitude for work which was essential for anyone wishing to control the bureaucracy. In his youthful ardour, he preferred sport, music and dancing to the thankless tasks of 'the trade of king'. The Habsburgs, though, could only govern with the agreement of the aristocracy who, in Vienna as much as in the provinces, jealously safeguarded their political prerogatives.

His death at the age of thirty-three from smallpox posed a truly international problem. His brother Charles became the sole heir of the Habsburg monarchy and, it seemed, might reconstitute the empire of Charles V since Joseph I's only surviving children were daughters. The death of Joseph I made it possible to settle the conflict with the Hungarians through an acceptable compromise and contributed to the resolution of the War of the Spanish Succession, but the Habsburgs found themselves practically alone as they faced the Bourbons.

THE END OF THE HUNGARIAN CONFLICT: THE COMPROMISE OF SZATMÁR (1711)

The Hungarians negotiated the Szatmár settlement in early autumn 1711 while Ferenc II Rákóczi won over the Ottoman empire and then France. In France he was warmly received by Louis XIV and his followers formed the first French hussar regiments. The moderate elements of the nobility managed to safeguard Hungary's special status within the monarchy but failed to secure control of Transylvania and the Military Frontier in Slavonia. The empress, acting as regent, confirmed in the name of Charles VI the Hungarians' confessional privileges, administrative autonomy, the nobility's fiscal immunity and the existence of a small Hungarian army under Austrian command. The general Diet which was summoned the following year ratified these proposals. The cabinet at Vienna retained jurisdiction over diplomacy and general policy. After half a century of bitter conflict, the orders had saved what was essential and the task of reconstruction could now begin.

Hungary was worn out and would at last experience a long period of peace. The developments in Poland in the eighteenth century and the emergence of a powerful Russia bent on conquests in the west might suggest that Rákóczi's defeat was not such a great catastrophe for the Hungarians. To remain under the benign protection of the Habsburgs was better than to be absorbed afresh by a completely foreign power. The Hungarians had not waged their war of independence on the basis of a choice between absorption within a unitary Austria, which did not yet exist, and the type of Germanization advocated by Kollonich. Rather, they had faced the alternatives of complete independence for historic Hungary or Austrian protection on the terms established at the beginning of the seventeenth century. Even those Catholic magnates who favoured the Habsburgs, like the Esterházys, remained patriots. Kollonich was an exception but this may be excused by his being a foreigner. For the moderate magnates, the issue had been their fiscal privileges rather than the renunciation of their cultural identity and the politics of their fatherland.

The two most serious consequences of the Peace of Szatmár were economic and demographic. In order to promote the rapid reconstruction of the lands of the Great Plain, the Habsburgs encouraged German colonists, generally referred to as Swabians, and Serbian and Romanian peasants to settle in southern Hungary, with the result that the Great Plain, hitherto the centre of the Hungarian population, became a complex ethno-linguistic zone. The maintenance of the system of customs tended to accentuate the peripheral character of the lands of the crown of St Stephen and to make it a centre for agriculture, both a natural outlet and a bread basket for the Austro-Bohemian lands where manufacturing had become well established. This situation would become yet more pronounced during the age of the Enlightenment.

The immediate effect of the Szatmár agreement was that it left Charles VI free to turn all his forces against the Bourbons at the moment when the Maritime Powers were negotiating a separate peace with France, the Treaty of Utrecht.

UTRECHT (1713)

In 1710 Marlborough, even after the fall of Douai, was convinced that he would not be able to conquer France. The Tories, who were about to return to power, had never favoured the war. They thought that their real competitors were the Dutch, that the Habsburgs were not sufficiently important partners and that the expenses the war entailed were not justified by the ends pursued. The new secretary of state, Saint John, thought that the House of Austria was England's enemy and that faced with Charles VI's aspirations to rebuild the monarchy of Charles V, Philip V should retain the Spanish throne. As early as the summer of 1711, the French and the English had, in addition to their secret negotiations, established the basis for a separate peace: in exchange for a number of concessions from Louis XIV, Philip V could remain at Madrid.

This settlement was reasonable since only Catalonia was still under Habsburg control and the French victory at Denain (1712) had removed any risk of invasion. The diplomatic congress which met at Utrecht settled the points of contention between the Bourbons and the Maritime Powers. Philip Ludwig von Sinzendorf, who represented the emperor, however, refused to sign and the Austrian monarchy, as in 1700, found itself alone as it confronted the Bourbons. The chancellor Wratislaw was in favour of a compromise whereby, in return for recognition of the Austrian position in Italy, he would exchange Bavaria for the Netherlands, 'a province for which the emperor had no use but would rather find a burden'. Prince Eugene shared Wratislaw's view, but the balance within the conference changed when Wratislaw died on 21 December 1712. Trusted by both Eugene of Savoy and Charles VI, this Bohemian aristocrat had alone been able to counterbalance the Spanish faction which had surrounded the young emperor ever since his return from Barcelona.

After the chancellor of Bohemia's death, prince Eugene became Charles VI's principal minister and the Privy Conference was composed of his supporters: the chancellor Seilern, the ambitious Sinzendorf and Gundaker von Starhemberg. Even though coming to terms would mean that he would have to abandon the Catalans to Castilian centralizing policies, Charles VI was eventually persuaded by Eugene of the dangers the monarchy would face if he continued to pursue the war with Philip V without the Maritime Powers' support. The emperor hesitated for a long time but realized that without a navy he would be unable to protect the lines of communication between Italy and Barcelona. For the rest of his life he rued this step and continued to use the title of king of Spain, rather as the king of England kept the title king of France. He maintained a Spanish council at Vienna and harboured Catalan refugees. When Sinzendorf on 21 April 1713 signed the Treaty of Utrecht in the name of the Habsburgs, the dream of universal monarchy vanished for ever, as, indeed, has every dream of European hegemony. The English concept of the balance of power had triumphed and would dominate international relations until the First World War. The success of the Maritime Powers marked not only the birth of British preponderance but a new balance of power on the Continent guaranteed by Great Britain, which was now able to develop in peace its maritime, colonial and trading activities.

France was victorious in North America because of the military capabilities of its Canadian colonists, but even so it sought to repair relations with the English by granting them Arcadia (Nova Scotia) and the territories around Hudson Bay. The English also received concessions from Philip V, who surrendered to them the Spanish American slave trade *l'asiento* and allowed them to trade directly with the West Indies without passing through Cadiz. In return, the Bourbons in Spain received recognition from Louis XIV's opponents, and became the natural allies of the senior branch even though after 1715 there was some friction between Madrid and Paris. The Pyrenees were indeed 'no more' and the two nations, the French and the Spanish, buried the hatchet. The king of France, however, had to accept one further concession: he had to register solemnly with the Parlement of Paris Philip V's renunciation of his claims to the French throne even though such a clause was contrary to all the principles of French public law.

The real losers were the Castilians who in 1700 had wanted to preserve intact the Spanish monarchy as Charles V had realized it in 1555. Instead they had to resign themselves to partition, the Austrian monarchy, not France, receiving compensation in the form of the Netherlands and the possessions in Italy. Spain's vocation was modified. A European and a Mediterranean power, in the eighteenth century it became an Atlantic and colonial power and would recover its fortunes even though Philip V did not renounce Italy and so involved Spain in local conflicts in an effort to provide for the children of his second wife Elizabeth Farnese.

Charles VI was only partly satisfied with the compensation he had received. He knew that the Netherlands would be a grave responsibility, burdened as they were by the imposition of the barrier, the series of forts housing Dutch garrisons and paid for by the emperor, and by the closure of the port of Antwerp to maritime traffic. Austrian sovereignty might be a guarantee of security for the governments of London and the Hague, but for Vienna it was a troublesome burden. The Habsburgs, however, through the Maritime Powers, were able to complete the project begun in the last year of Leopold I's reign to take hold of Italy and so realize one of the dreams of Maximilian I. At Utrecht, Charles VI received Milan and Naples, while the fate of the kingdoms of Sardinia and Sicily remained in the balance. The emperor refused to sign the peace with Louis XIV and with no more than his forces and those of the Empire, decided to pursue a hopeless conflict with France which was considerably stronger than the hereditary lands then devastated by a serious plague epidemic.

The gains made by the Austrian monarchy at Utrecht, however, were considerable. Never before had the Viennese Habsburgs ruled over so vast a territory. It was now a great continental power extending from the North Sea to the Carpathians, from Bohemia to the Straits of Messina. It exercised its hegemony over Italy and remained the preponderant power in Germany. Ferdinand II would have found it hard to imagine such a revenge in October 1648, at the end of the Thirty Years War. Louis XIV's mistakes, the support of the Maritime Powers, Leopold's tenacious policy and that of his sons had combined to make Austria a vital element in the new European balance of power, despite the final abandonment of the dream of universal monarchy.

The serious problem of the Spanish succession was only resolved at the cost of heavy sacrifices by the belligerents and what amounted to a world war. No single power was capable of imposing a solution and it took twelve years of warfare for the parties to accept the reasonable terms put forward by the Grand Alliance of the Hague. The division of the Spanish inheritance, Philip V's installation at Madrid, the neutralization of the Southern Netherlands, the substantial compensations given to the Habsburgs in Italy, the recognition of the conquests made by the French during the seventeenth century, even the Hungarian question, were only settled through compromise. To impose the rational viewpoint of England and the United Provinces had taken much blood and tears. The continental powers had probably paid insufficient attention to the rise of England. Leopold I's obstinate insistence that the whole of the Habsburg patrimony should go to him had played an important part in resolving the conflict. The traditional thesis of Austrian historians that the emperor was the victim of aggression cannot be sustained. He was certainly justified in his claims but he had failed to take account of changes in the balance of forces. The policy of compensation helped to make the Austrian monarchy more than ever a mosaic of states and peoples without any other link than loyalty to their prince.

NOTES AND REFERENCES

1. A. Mignet, *Négociations relatives à la succession d'Espagne*, 4 vols, Paris, 1838–42.
2. J. Bérenger, 'Une tentative de rapprochement entre la France et la Maison d'Autriche:

le traité de partage secret de la Succession d'Espagne du 19 janvier 1668', *Revue d'histoire diplomatique*, 1965, pp. 291–314.

3. J. Bérenger, *Turenne*, Paris, 1987.
4. Ragnhild Hatton (ed.), *Louis XIV and Europe*, London, 1977.
5. John O'Connor, *Negotiator out of Season: the career of Wilhelm Egon von Fürstenberg 1629 to 1704*, Athens, Georgia, 1978.
6. Charles Boutant, *L'Europe au grand tournant des années 1680*, Paris, 1985.
7. O. Piquet-Marchal, *Les Chambres de réunion*, Paris, 1966.
8. Ernest Lavisse, *Louis XIV*, Paris, 1978.
9. The literature on this subject is abundant. To be recommended is Béla Köpeczi, *La France et la Hongrie au début du XVIIIe siècle*, Budapest, 1971.
10. Béla Köpeczi (ed.), *Autobiographie d'un prince rebele. Confessions et mémoires du prince François II Rákóczi*, Budapest, 1977.
11. Charles Ingrao, *Emperor Joseph I and the Habsburg Monarchy*, West Lafeyette, Indiana, 1979.

CHAPTER TWO

The Achievement of Charles VI (1711–40)

Charles VI was born in 1685 and was the last emperor to belong to the House of Austria, for the male line died out with him in 1740. The beginning and end of his reign were marked by dynastic wars, the War of the Spanish Succession at the time of his accession and the War of the Austrian Succession following his death. Eighteenth-century Europe did not succeed in freeing itself from dynastic politics. Historians have long shown how the question of the succession preoccupied Charles VI throughout the period of his rule and informed his actions. It would, however, be wrong to reduce the reign of this baroque sovereign simply to the matter of the Pragmatic Sanction, the act by which he hoped to secure the Austrian succession for his eldest daughter, the archduchess Maria-Theresa.

THE LAST BAROQUE SOVEREIGN[1]

Charles VI had much in common with his father and brother but he had been deeply affected by his experiences in Spain. The only members of his entourage whom he trusted were his *welsches* advisors, his Italian and Spanish counsellors and count Althann who had accompanied him to Barcelona. He always had reservations about, indeed was downright mistrustful of, those whom Joseph I had appointed, but he did not dare risk dismissing them. Like his father, he made it a point of honour to look after loyal servants regardless of whether or not they had given satisfactory service.

The 'Spanish faction' was organized into a permanent council with a secretariat which conducted all its business exclusively in Castilian. Its members administered Charles VI's Italian possessions and were paid for by the revenues from Milan and Naples. The most influential members of the faction were the archbishop of Valencia, who was the sworn enemy of prince Eugene, the Neapolitan officer count Rocco Stella, and the Catalan marquis de Rialp who became the emperor's confidant after Stella's death and who dominated the Spanish council, making all the appointments for Italy. They were feared by all the ministers and prince Eugene who overestimated their real influence.

The emperor guarded his authority closely and was much harder to influence than his father. He wanted to make all the decisions himself but without taking hold of the reins of government. Like Leopold, he allowed the ministers of the conference free discussion and then made a pronouncement based on the written report which they sent him. No minister of the conference, not even prince Eugene, could make a decision without having first referred it to the emperor. This procedure was all the more slow because the conference rarely met during the summer and because Charles VI was not particularly hard-working.

A great deal of his time passed in religious devotions and harmless pleasures, hunting and cards. The court spent the winter at Vienna, in the Hofburg, the comfortless palace which disappointed visitors, including Montesquieu and lady Mary Montagu Wortley, who were used to seeing rulers live amid some splendour. Strict Spanish etiquette prevailed. The emperor, like his father, rejected French fashions and imposed on his courtiers traditional Spanish black dress. While the festivals of Carnival were brilliant with theatre productions, sleigh-rides and grand receptions, the religious practices of Lent were markedly austere in character. The Spanish representatives in Vienna were obliged to observe the same customs, for Charles VI was as zealous as a cardinal at Rome. According to the duke of Richelieu, only a capuchin in good health could withstand such a regime. From April to June, the court moved to Laxenburg, a modest hunting lodge near the Hungarian border of which Leopold I had been especially fond. Falconry and card parties were the chief pastimes. The court would pass the summer at the chateau La Favorite in a suburb of Vienna. As at Laxenburg, the ceremonial was not so strict and 'German practices' were allowed. During the hot summer days at Vienna, billiards were the emperor's favourite pastime.

Charles VI was a man of culture, as had been his predecessors. Like all the Habsburgs, he knew many languages and he collected books and antique coins. By adding prince Eugene's library to his own he became the real founder of the Austrian National Library, comparable to the great libraries of Paris, Venice, London and Rome. Moreover he had constructed within the Hofburg a building which matched the splendour of his collections. Following his father's example, he assembled a pocket library made up of the works he was currently using and which accompanied him on all his travels.

A worthy son of Leopold I, he had a particular love of music and was accustomed to spending 200 000 florins a year in pursuit of this pleasure. In 1715 he appointed Johann Joseph Fux as Kapellmeister. Fux led an orchestra of sixty-three instrumentalists of whom twenty-six were violinists and thirteen trumpeters, and a choir of twenty-eight. As was the tradition at the Viennese court, these appointments at 3 100 florins a year were superior to those of a councillor of state. There was singing at the Hofburg opera and in the gardens of La Favorite. The emperor accompanied the singers on the harpsicord and the archduchess Maria-Theresa took part.

Charles VI was, like his father, very attached to his family with whom he spent his happiest hours. He showed great affection towards the empress Elizabeth of Brunswick-Wolfenbüttel, a Protestant princess who had converted to Catholicism at the time of her marriage.[2] Charles VI seems, like Leopold I, not to have taken a mistress. Of their children, only two daughters survived, the future empress Maria-Theresa born in 1717 and Maria Anna (1718–44).

CHARLES VI AND PRINCE EUGENE[3]

The emperor had great respect for the exceptional talents of Eugene of Savoy and, particularly at the beginning of his reign, supported him. His affection, however, cooled with time but never reached the icy reserve which Leopold I had reserved for the prince. Prince Eugene served as Charles VI's chief minister until 1718 and was the vital intermediary for all diplomats posted to Vienna. He owed his exceptional position to his great gifts as a captain rather than to his status as a younger son of a sovereign house. He wanted to remain outside factions and did not hide his contempt for the Austro-Bohemian aristocracy and for German culture. He turned his two palaces in Vienna into centres for French culture, although he never dropped his personal hostility towards the Bourbons. Eugene kept the presidency of the *Hofkriegsrat* and control over the imperial army right until his death and also directed the monarchy's foreign policy. He acted as president of the Privy Conference and was to all intents and purposes a prime minister. The Conference usually met at his home and brought together the chancellors Trautsohn, Seilern (until 1715) and Georg Ludwig von Sinzendorf and the president of the *Hofkammer*, Gundaker von Starhemberg, the last two being particular friends of the prince. The imperial vice-chancellor, Friedrich Karl Schönborn, who assiduously kept himself apart from the decision-making process until 1720, allied with prince Eugene who was happy to hand over to him the conduct of German affairs which he considered of secondary interest to the monarchy. Although he was solicitous of his reputation as a captain, prince Eugene was not an administrator and like his master preferred to devote less of his time to business than to spending whole days in conversation and playing cards with his friend the countess Batthyány. He was by vocation a soldier and was not inclined to play the first minister like Richelieu, imposing his point of view in every matter on his master who, in any case, would never have tolerated such an intrusion.

The monarchy continued to be governed as under Leopold I by a slow and negligent sovereign and a Privy Conference which managed affairs according to certain precepts and was very cautious about imposing real reforms. In the area in which his real genius lay, the army, prince Eugene proved to be especially conservative, refusing any innovation on principle. In this he was very similar to Charles VI, even though the prince appeared as active as his master was indolent. They both, like Leopold I, realized that it was better not to disrupt an aristocratic and multinational society.

THE PEACE WITH FRANCE[4]

The difficult German campaign of 1713 had been made yet harder for prince Eugene because the hereditary lands, like the imperial Estates, did not pay the financial contributions incumbent upon them. The hereditary lands were suffering from the plague and the circles of Swabia and Franconia were burdened by the enforced billeting and taxes in kind which the imperial troops had imposed over the past ten years. The German princes had much greater interest in pursuing the Great Northern War (1700–20) with Charles XII of Sweden. Despite Villars's successes in the Rhineland, Louis XIV was unhappy about pursuing a costly war without any real objective and prince Eugene put pressure on Charles VI to reach a settlement. The elector Palatine's mediation brought about a measure of understanding between Vienna and Versailles and prince Eugene opened negotiations at Rastadt in November 1713, in the palace built by the margrave, Louis of Baden.

The two generals respected each other but Villars, who was under constraint from Louis XIV's foreign minister, the marquis de Torcy, proved to be a mediocre diplomat when he confronted the prince. The preliminaries to the Treaty of Rastadt in February 1714 confirmed the general dispositions of the Treaty of Ryswick. France kept Alsace, Strasbourg and the three bishoprics (Metz, Toul and Verdun) as well as Landau and Fort Louis, two fortresses which were intended to guarantee the security of Alsace. The duchy of Lorraine remained independent and neutral. Charles VI, however, was no longer required to renounce formally his rights to the crown of Spain, and France granted him the kingdom of Sardinia even though at Utrecht this had been granted to Max II Emanuel of Bavaria.

After this diplomatic success, prince Eugene was celebrated in Vienna as a hero because another campaign threatened to be disastrous for the imperial troops. The treaty guaranteed the security of the north-eastern frontier of France in a way acceptable to the Germans, and confirmed Habsburg hegemony in the Italian peninsula. From now on, they would control Milan, Naples, Mantua, Mirandola, the Tuscan presidios and Sardinia. The duke of Savoy acquired Sicily and with it a royal title, and in 1718 was able to exchange it for Sardinia.

The emperor signed the peace at Baden without having gained anything and having lost the fortress of Landau which throughout the whole of the eighteenth century protected Lower Alsace. Charles VI was less convinced than his father of the importance of the emperor's role and acted more as a Habsburg than as head of the Holy Roman Empire, a direction approved by prince Eugene and his ministers.

The following year Louis XIV renewed diplomatic relations with the court at Vienna. He even established French diplomatic representation in an embassy there and, in his instructions to the count de Luc, raised the possibility of a Franco-Austrian alliance, a proposal which Eugene of Savoy opposed because he had based his system of alliances on friendship with England. The aged French king *in extremis* had wanted the reversal of alliances which eventually would be accomplished by Louis XV in 1756. Louis XIV realized that Europe needed peace, just as in 1659 at the time of his marriage to Maria Theresa, and that governments could now only expect to wage localized conflicts, a luxury which the Austrian monarchy enjoyed throughout Charles VI's long reign.

THE AUSTRO-TURKISH WAR (1716–18)

Eugene suspected the Ottomans of hostile intent, especially since they had drawn fresh strength from their victory in 1711 over Peter the Great. He was faced with considerable opposition from the rest of the privy conference and the Council of Spain which feared that Philip V would seize the occasion to launch an attack on Italy. But, strengthened by the renewed alliance with George I's England formalized in the Treaty of Westminster in 1716, he presented the Sublime Porte with an ultimatum and launched a pre-emptive attack. The monarchy enjoyed a measure of support from the imperial princes and the Republic of Venice whose troops the Turks quickly drove from the Morea; otherwise, it waged almost alone the war which prince Eugene directed with the support of his friend Starhemberg.

The grand vizier, Silahdar Ali pasha, assembled at Belgrade an army of 120 000 men, of which 30 000 were sipahis and 40 000 janissaries, and marched on Petrovaradin in Slavonia where on 5 August 1716 he was defeated by 70 000 imperial troops. This was one of the finest victories of prince Eugene's career and was due to his organizational skills and genius for strategy. The janissaries had mounted a strong resistance to the German infantry but the imperial cavalry achieved a decisive result. The Ottoman army was seized with panic. The grand vizier and 30 000 men were killed and the survivors fled as far as Belgrade. The imperial troops carried off 300 chariots full of booty. For the Turks, this defeat was a repetition of Kahlenberg.

Eugene wisely decided against an attack on Belgrade where the survivors of Ali pasha's army had taken refuge, and instead, from 26 August, laid siege to Temesvár (Timişoara) which, despite its impressive defensives, capitulated in mid-October 1716. Eugene entrusted its government and that of the Banat to one of his generals from Lorraine, the count Mercy, who achieved remarkable success on the human and economic level. The campaign of 1716 ended with a further personal triumph for the prince whose objective remained the recapture of Belgrade. As a good strategist, he fully realized the town's importance for the security of Hungary and peace along the monarchy's Balkan border.

For this reason, he demanded heavy financial sacrifices from the hereditary lands which were still recovering from the War of the Spanish Succession and from the plague. A new Turkish tax was levied as well as a special tax on the clergy and an extraordinary levy on the Jews. Meanwhile, the Vienna arsenal developed the Danube navy of galleys and frigates to combat the Turkish caïques and to prevent supplies from reaching Belgrade by water. The siege began on 15 June 1717 before the arrival of the fresh Ottoman army led by the grand vizier Halil pasha. The town was defended by 30 000 good combatants and at the beginning of August the imperial troops found themselves caught between the fortress and the Ottoman relief army. Prince Eugene was in almost an identical uncomfortable position to that in which Kara Mustapha had found himself outside Vienna in 1683. Reports were already being circulated that his army had been annihilated. He left, however, only a thin line of troops before Belgrade and with 60 000 men attacked and defeated the grand vizier's men who fled to Niš. The garrison at Belgrade lost heart and capitulated at the end of the month, after which 60 000 Muslims left the city. The campaign of 1717 had ended with a brilliant success.

The capture of Belgrade marked the peak of prince Eugene's military career. The soldiers immortalized his glory in the *Prinz Eugen Lied*. The prince was now considered the finest European general because by his decisiveness he had transformed certain defeat into a brilliant victory.

THE TREATY OF PASSAROWITZ (1718)

The Sublime Porte was forced to admit that it had lost Belgrade and the Banat of Temesvár. It would have been foolish for the prince to continue the war since the imperial troops' lines of communication were already dangerously stretched and Philip V was threatening Italy. Stella and the 'Spanish party' demanded immediate peace with the Turks so that Naples and Sardinia could be defended. The era of Leopold I, when an arrangement could be struck with the Porte to defend the interests of the House of Austria in the east, had passed. Prince Eugene, however, refused to send reinforcements to Italy because this would weaken the army in Hungary.

At the beginning of 1718, Charles VI was ready to agree to peace at any price, but Eugene preferred to make preparations for a campaign in Hungary and so to force the Porte to make a treaty. At Passarowitz, the Porte surrendered Belgrade, the greater part of Serbia and the Banat to Charles VI, which completed the Habsburg reconquest of Hungary begun in 1683. The Porte took back from Venice control of the Morea which had been ceded in 1699 but since reconquered by the sultan's troops. It granted the emperor's subjects substantial trading benefits within the Ottoman empire and so continued the trend begun by the Treaty of Vasvár.

The colonization of the Banat, was placed under the direct control of the *Hofkammer* which, in accordance with cardinal Kollonich's programme, retained the newly liberated land and did not restore it to the heirs of the Hungarian nobles who had owned it before 1552. Mercy was confirmed as governor of Temesvár and the Banat, while prince Alexander of Württemberg became governor of Belgrade.

THE AUSTRO-SPANISH CONFLICT (1717–19)

In the course of 1717, Philip V's troops invaded Sardinia. Charles VI and the Council of Spain took this act of aggression as an affront, as did the cabinets in Paris and London which for reasons of internal politics wanted to avoid a general European war. In Britain, George I's authority was no less precarious than that in France of Philip of Orleans, the regent since Louis XIV's death in 1715. Both powers had reached a remarkable understanding. In December, they demanded that the emperor make a formal renunciation of the Spanish crown and exchange Sardinia for Sicily, and that Spanish *infantes* be installed at Parma and in Tuscany, a move which would pose a serious threat to the House of Austria's new-found hegemony in Italy.

In 1718 the emperor agreed to enter into the Quadruple Alliance, despite the obvious indignation of prince Eugene and all the ministers, and gave his consent to the transaction proposed by the Engish and the French because he was convinced that he could not defend his Italian possessions without the aid of the British fleet, still less against a Franco-Spanish army. The French and English in fact had to turn their arms against Philip V in order to impose the terms of the mediation while the imperial troops landed in Sicily under the English fleet's protection. The marshal of Berwick invaded Spain at the head of a French army. This prompted Philip V to drive Alberoni from the ministry and to accept the Quadruple Alliance's conditions. He granted Sicily to Charles VI and Sardinia to Victor Amadeus, the duke of Savoy.

At the end of 1718, the Austrian monarchy had reached its greatest extent. Prince Eugene, however, fell into semi-disgrace and the privy conference lapsed into lethargy. Real power passed to the 'Spanish party' and this was the cause of the slow and irremediable decline which followed during the remaining twenty years of Charles VI's reign. The immediate future would show how fragile Austrian hegemony was in Italy.

CHARLES VI'S ECONOMIC POLICY[5]

During his stay in Catalonia, Charles VI had come to understand that large-scale overseas trade was an important source of income not only for those directly involved but also for rulers who had merchants as subjects. This led him to resume the projects which had been expounded by his father and the cameralists at the court in Vienna.

After the Peace of Passarowitz, he promoted trade with the Ottoman empire, which was in deficit, and Belgrade became the great market for Austro-Turkish commerce. In 1719 a second Oriental trading company was founded at Vienna but had difficulty competing with the Serb, Greek and Armenian merchants who were already firmly entrenched in Vienna, Buda and Belgrade. The Austrian authorities encouraged maritime trade and favoured the development of Fiume and Trieste, two fishing towns which Charles VI granted the status of free ports after the model of Livorno. The Oriental Company settled at Trieste and developed relations with Spain, Portugal, the Maghreb and, now that Venice was no longer in a position to prevent Trieste's expansion, the Neapolitan and Tuscan ports.

Charles VI wanted to create a navy to protect the merchant shipping. He gave the project to an English admiral, lord Forbes, and in 1726 two ships, the *Karl VI* and the *Trieste*, dropped anchor at Trieste. These were presently joined by two galleys which together employed 8 000 men under the command of vice-admiral Deigham who was replaced in 1733 by the Genoan, Giovanni Pallavicini.

The great commercial roads intended to link the hereditary lands with the

Adriatic ports and to reverse the traditional trade routes which had made Hamburg and Stettin the natural outlets for Bohemia, were of far longer-lasting significance. The track through the Semmering pass was transformed into a passable route joining Vienna and Trieste with labour supplied by the royal *robot*, a legal recourse previously only used to support and repair fortresses.

The Oriental Company attempted to expand the range of its activities and started industrial enterprises, but unfortunately it tied its fate to a lottery which failed, and it went bankrupt.

Sovereignty over the Netherlands gave the emperor the chance for colonial commerce and colonization but the Maritime Powers did not welcome interference in their quasi-monopoly. They refused to open up the Scheldt and opposed the Netherlands' entry into international trade. The successes of the Paris Mississippi Company and the London South Sea Company were admired by both the emperor and prince Eugene. Charles VI made no secret of his enthusiasm for a colonial venture but Eugene, who was formally governor of the Netherlands, a sinecure which brought him 150 000 florins, was more reserved. In 1720 the marquis of Prié was given permission to form the Ostend Company, which began operating in 1722 despite opposition from the Maritime Powers. It paid 6 per cent of its profits to the emperor in return for imperial protection. The enterprise was essentially a Dutch affair with most of the capital provided by Flemish nobles and some courtiers. It yielded dividends of 80 per cent and in 1730 distributed 6 million florins to its stockholders.

The official title of the Ostend Company was the Company of the Imperial and Royal Indies. The Company's activities were based on the lucrative trade with China and its first vessel, the *Stadt von Wien*, established posts at the mouth of the Ganges and elsewhere in India, and at Canton.

With the exception of the post at Banki Basar which continued to operate until 1744, Charles VI was obliged for diplomatic reasons to put a premature halt to the Ostend Company's activities. This was the price he had to pay for an agreement with the English government and its recognition of the Pragmatic Sanction. The provisional agreements of 1727 were confirmed in 1731 by the Second Treaty of Vienna.

THE PRAGMATIC SANCTION (1713)[6]

The House of Austria had wavered over the rules governing succession and, as has been seen, followed the German law by which princely houses could divide their patrimony according to the principal of primogeniture. Before the archduke Charles left for Spain in 1703, Leopold I imposed on his two sons a preliminary agreement in the form of a *pacta mutuae successionis*, which was to remain secret and which treated the two branches of the patrimony as one and assured the survivor the whole inheritance should one of the brothers die without a male heir. This was precisely what happened when, eight years later, Joseph I died leaving two daughters. Charles VI then claimed the whole patrimony of the House of Austria, despite the opposition from the Maritime Powers and the Bourbons, and did not recognize Philip V until 1718.

On 19 April 1713 the emperor, who still did not have a child, summoned his counsellors and read them the 1703 pact of mutual succession with the addition of one important clause: the lands of the monarchy 'indivisible and inseparable' could not be partitioned. He thus introduced the principle of primogeniture with the male line having precedence over the female, so that if he died without an heir, the monarchy would revert to Joseph I's daughters who otherwise would not have any claim to the succession. In fact he disinherited his nieces when his daughters were born in 1717 and 1718, the little archduke whom the empress bore in 1716 having died shortly after his birth. The emperor's declaration which was solemnly recorded by a notary is known to history as the Pragmatic Sanction.

It became one of Charles VI's principal concerns to secure recognition of the Pragmatic Sanction. The text of the Sanction established in law the unity of the Austrian monarchy and completed the work of Ferdinand II and Leopold I who had made the crowns of Bohemia and Hungary hereditary in 1627 and 1687 respectively. It was legitimate to have it adopted by the different lands of the monarchy, but to expect the concert of European powers to recognize it at any price was to expect too much.

In the course of the 1720 and 1721 sessions, the Pragmatic Sanction was presented to the different Diets, all of which adopted it without debate with the exception of the Tyrolean Diet which showed some doubts. The royal declarations which accompanied it emphasized the rights of Charles VI's daughters and the exclusion of the daughters of Joseph I. They did not make any reference to the unity of the monarchy.

The prestige of the House of Austria was very strong after the Peace of Passarowitz and the Diets of Transylvania and Croatia had already approved the Pragmatic Sanction (1721–22) when, in 1724, the Hungarian Diet was summoned at Pressburg. The two chambers of the Diet gave their unanimous approval and the Pragmatic Sanction became law within the kingdom and remained a cornerstone of Habsburg legitimacy in Hungary right until 1918. This vote was taken in the spirit of the Peace of Szatmár of 1711. The Hungarians preferred to work and to rebuild their country rather than to challenge the authority of the court at Vienna, as long as Vienna respected their liberties. For the first time since 1526, the kingdom of Hungary with Croatia and Transylvania was incorporated into the Habsburg patrimony.

As the emperor had anticipated, the exclusion of Joseph I's daughters provided the electors of Saxony and Bavaria with pretexts for intervening at the time of the succession. In 1719 the archduchess Maria Josepha had married Frederick Augustus, who was the son of Augustus the Strong and who in 1733, as Augustus III, became king of Poland. In 1722 Maria Amalia married Charles Albert of Bavaria, the future elector and the future emperor. Neither the king of Poland nor the elector of Bavaria took seriously the formal renunciations that had been made and when Max II Emanuel spent four million florins on celebrations for his son's wedding, he showed quite clearly that he saw him as the future emperor.

For this reason, in 1725 Charles VI, who no longer heeded prince Eugene, embarked on a foreign policy of no less complexity than the alliances of Italian city states in the fifteenth century. In 1725 he signed an alliance with his sworn enemy Philip V and promised the hand of Maria-Theresa in marriage to the *infante* don Charles, with the result that Spain was the first power to recognize the Pragmatic Sanction.

This potential marriage alliance was not a serious proposition for at the time the young duke Francis Stephen of Lorraine was being educated at Vienna as a future husband for Maria-Theresa. It did, though, almost provoke a European war which was only avoided through the cool-headedness of cardinal Fleury, the young Louis XV's minister of state. The crisis was finally resolved as a consequence of the reconciliation between Austria and England. In return for the suppression of the Ostend Company, Great Britain recognized the Pragmatic Sanction (1731). The Imperial Diet then followed suit, accepting the Sanction in 1732 despite the vehement opposition of the electors of Saxony and Bavaria.

Fleury and the French diplomats were less alarmed by the Pragmatic Sanction than by the prospect of a marriage between the House of Lorraine and the Habsburgs. If the marriage took place and if the duke of Lorraine was elected emperor then the security of the French frontier would come under threat. Austrian possessions would extend to Bar-le-Duc, just 250 km from Paris, and all that Louis XIV had achieved would be jeopardized. The duke Leopold of Lorraine was independent and neutral but a young prince educated at the Viennese court might reasonably be expected to be a less acceptable neighbour. Reports suggested that Francis Stephen was Germanized and ambitious. Fleury and his entourage feared that he would want to recover Alsace should a war provide the opportunity.

At this juncture the death of Augustus II and the difficulties arising over the Polish succession provided Louis XV's government with an excellent opportunity to intervene.

THE WAR OF THE POLISH SUCCESSION (1733–38)

The crown of the Republic of Poland remained elective and the candidacy of the elector of Saxony, Frederick Augustus, the husband of the archduchess Maria Josepha, was contested by a party of nobles who preferred to summon Stanislas Leczinski, Louis XV's father-in-law. If this magnate and long-time protégé of Charles XII of Sweden were installed at Warsaw, France would then turn Poland into its satellite in Eastern Europe and would revive its counter-alliance. Charles VI sensed the possible threat this might pose to his states and allied with Prussia and Russia to secure the election of Augustus III, trying at the same time to secure his recognition of the Pragmatic Sanction.

Foreign policy at Vienna in 1733 was increasingly under the emperor's direction. 'The Spanish party' had practically ceased to exist, prince Eugene was suffering from premature senility and Charles VI was proving more and more secretive. Every day he summoned the Privy Conference, which was now led by Bartenstein who acted as its secretary and advised the sovereign. Bartenstein was assured of a good future. He was a Lutheran from Strasbourg who had wanted to make his career at Paris under the Regency. He enjoyed the patronage of the Benedictines of Saint-Germain-des-Prés, was sent to Melk, and after a timely conversion to Catholicism, remained in Austria. Completely bilingual, he had been trained as a lawyer at Strasbourg and followed a typical career at Vienna. He was distinguished by his legal skills and his learning, rose through the ranks in political service and was rewarded and ennobled. Bartenstein, after Hocher, was the second Alsatian in less than a century to become Austrian chancellor. Even after the reconquest of Hungary and with the comparative preponderance of the hereditary lands, the Habsburgs continued to recruit their advisors in Western Europe and only Starhemberg and Sinzendorf were 'Austrians'.

The elderly Fleury manoeuvred skilfully because he saw the Polish succession as providing the pretext to settle the Lorraine question to France's advantage. It was also a means of reactivating the Franco-Spanish alliance by driving Charles VI from Naples and Sicily and giving these two kingdoms to don Charles, the son of Philip V and Elizabeth Farnese.

The cabinet at Vienna sensed the dangers that were threatening but did not act in time because Sinzendorf was convinced that Fleury would not involve France in a war. Fleury found his position strengthened by the support of Bavaria and Charles Emanuel, the new duke of Savoy, and in September 1733 declared war on the emperor in support of Stanislas Leczinski.

Marshal Belle-Isle, the grandson of superintendant Fouquet, led the French army in the invasion of the duchy of Lorraine. The regentess agreed on behalf of her son, Francis Stephen, to remain neutral. A French princess, the daughter of monsieur and the princess Palatine, she endeavoured to impress upon her subjects the horrors of war and through clever manoeuvring managed to ensure that the Rhineland bore the brunt of military operations.

Prince Eugene wanted to resume active service and presented the distressing spectacle of a once great captain reduced to senility. The imperial troops amassed one defeat after another, revealing the incapacity of their leader and the rapid decline into which the army, until recently one of the best in Europe, had sunk. The Austrian monarchy was almost without allies in Germany and Italy, and the Maritime Powers took refuge in a neutrality which favoured France, while Russia confined its field of operations to Poland. The sending of a French expeditionary force to Danzig ended in defeat and Stanislas, for the second time in his career, was defeated by his Saxon rival.

Prince Eugene saw the threat of French hegemony in Europe. Shortly before he died in 1736, he advised Charles VI to agree to peace at any price in order to save the hereditary lands. The first stage of the negotiations in Vienna in 1735 were not disastrous for the Habsburgs. Don Charles received Naples and Sicily and Charles Emanuel of Savoy annexed Piedmont to the western part of the duchy of Milan, but the emperor received as compensation the duchy of Parma. What was more important was that Francis Stephen exchanged the duchy of Lorraine for the duchy of Tuscany where the Medici family was verging on extinction. The House of Austria retained its outposts in Italy and the question of Lorraine, which had been unsettled since the beginning of the seventeenth century, was resolved to France's advantage. France no longer saw any obstacle to the marriage between Francis Stephen and Maria-Theresa and the royal wedding was celebrated at Vienna in 1736. The young duke took no account of his Lorraine subjects' loyalties and accepted the deal without hesitation. He never lived at Florence and never won the hearts of the Tuscans.

The people of Lorraine enjoyed a period of comparative independence as compensation. Stanislas Leczinski was installed at Nancy where he was happy to leave the government to French administrators and reigned until his death in 1766.[7] An additional compensation was that Fleury agreed to recognize the Pragmatic Sanction.

This settlement ended Charles VI's dreams of re-taking the Spanish monarchy. What was worse was that the loss of Lorraine marked the decline of the Habsburgs' influence in the Empire at the same time as Prussia and Hanover, which enjoyed British support, emerged as powerful Protestant states in the North. This decline of influence was also a consequence of the lack of interest shown by Charles VI who, unlike his father, was indifferent towards German affairs. During the War of the Polish Succession, the Imperial Diet voted only token support. At the same time, though, the Habsburgs' possessions in Italy became more homogenous and easier to defend.

After long negotiations with the French allies, the terms set out in 1735 were ratified by the Third Treaty of Vienna on 18 November 1738, while the monarchy was engaged in a disastrous war against the Ottoman empire.

THE AUSTRO-TURKISH WAR[8]

The Austrian monarchy found itself at war with the Ottoman empire as a consequence of its alliance with Russia. Since 1725 the monarchy had assiduously put itself at Russia's disposal in the event of Russia's becoming engaged in war with the Ottoman empire because of its wish to extend control over the north shores of the Black Sea. Bartenstein pushed for war. Vienna renewed its alliance with St Petersburg but the imperial troops were quite unprepared for the Turkish army which had been reorganized by a renegade of French origin, Bonneval pasha.

Duke Francis Stephen of Lorraine took command with the assistance of general Seckendorf, invaded Macedonia and in the course of summer 1737 seized Niš. A counter-attack by the Turks resulted in a serious reverse in Bosnia and the evacuation of Niš followed. Negotiations failed and the war was renewed with count Königsegg replacing the incompetent Seckendorf. After the victories at Krnya and Mehadia, the imperial troops in 1738 again faced reverses. Königsegg was replaced by Wallis who proved to be even more undistinguished and turned the 1739 campaign into a disaster. After the sudden rout at Grocka on 22 July, the remnants of the imperial army fled to Belgrade.

Negotiations were resumed through the mediation of the marquis of

Villeneuve, the French ambassador at Constantinople. The imperial diplomats led by Neipper proved as lamentably undistinguished as the military leadership. Indecisive and cowardly, they yielded practically all the territory gained in 1718. They handed Belgrade back to the Turks from fear of further disasters, although the Turks had not besieged the town. Serbia and Little Wallachia were both returned to the sultan. Only the Banat of Temesvár was unaffected by the great settlement. Austrian historiographers have naturally accused the French ambassador of the blackest designs for the monarchy but in fact during the 1730s Charles VI's government had shown little initiative. The loss of prestige was at least as damaging as the return of Belgrade and the chancelleries of Europe began to question the Habsburg monarchy's great power status. The loss of Belgrade was compensated for strategically by the consolidation of the Military Frontier which prince Eugene had entrusted to the prince of Saxe-Hildburghausen. The latter had built in Slavonia a border zone where the strongest elements were the colonies of Serbs who followed the hajduk tradition. Austrian expansion into the Balkans had been arrested and the 'sick man of Europe' seemed to be making a full recovery. Only the military genius of prince Eugene could create the illusion of a balance between the two forces. It was clear to the rest of Europe that the Austrian monarchy without effective support from Great Britain was a 'paper tiger', a fact which explains the resounding defeats of the War of the Polish Succession and the Turkish war (1737–39).

When Charles VI died in October 1740, he left his daughter a situation which was catastrophic compared to that of 1710–15 and the brilliant successes of the War of the Spanish Succession.

Was the effusive appearance of the imperial baroque and its most spectacular expression, the basilica of St Charles Borromeo, deceptive? The Karlskirche was built in fulfilment of a vow made in 1713 by the emperor during the plague. It is a copy of the basilica of St Peter in Rome, flanked by replicas of Trajan's column. It is a final witness to the deep Catholic faith of the sovereign and his dreams of universal monarchy which bore little correspondence to the real situation in Austria. Like Maximilian I, Charles VI did not have the resources that his policies required and the 'gifts' granted him by the Maritime Powers stirred in him dangerous illusions. Charles VI had embarked naively upon bold ventures – the Ostend Company, the Polish succession, the second Turkish war – for which he was ill-prepared and which proved futile. The obstinacy with which he insisted upon the Lorraine marriage rather than a Bavarian one and the yet greater obstinacy with which he excluded his nieces from the succession carried a heavy price for the monarchy which needed to examine its strengths and weaknesses.

NOTES AND REFERENCES

1. Oswald Redlich, 'Die Tagebücher Kaiser Karls VI', *Mélanges Srbik*, Munich, 1938, pp. 141–51.

2. See, Elisabeth Christine, 'Kaiserin', in Brigitte Hamann (ed.), *Die Habsburger, ein biographisches Lexikon*, Vienna, 1988.
3. Derek McKay, *Prince Eugene of Savoy*, London, 1977.
4. Heinrich Benedikt, *Das Königreich Neapel unter Kaiser Karl VI*, Vienna, 1927.
5. Heinrich von Srbik, *Der staatliche Exporthandel Österreichs von Leopold I, bis Maria-Theresia*, Vienna, 1913.
6. Gustav Turba, *Die Pragatische Sanktion. Authentische Textesamt Erläutterungen und Übersetzungen*, Vienna, 1913.
7. J.-P. Bled and R. Taveneaux (eds), *Les Habsbourg et la Lorraine*, Nancy, 1988.
8. Heinrich Benedikt, *Der Pascha-Graf Alexander von Bonneval*, Graz, 1959.

CHAPTER THREE

A Great Power on
a Fragile Basis

Superficial explanations are insufficient to explain the difficulties that Charles VI faced and the serious crisis to which the War of the Austrian Succession gave rise. The character of those who made the decisions at the Vienna court, the emperor's innate mediocrity, prince Eugene's senility, Bartenstein's lack of experience, the steps mistaken because of the Pragmatic Sanction and all the other reasons *histoire évènementielle* furnishes cannot of themselves account for the situation in which the monarchy found itself. In 1725 contemporaries sensed the fragility of the great continental power created by the Treaties of Utrecht (1713) and Rastatt (1714). The weakness of the structure is explained less by its demography than the poor state of the emperor's finances of which the Austrian historian Pribram wrote: 'In other states, the shortage of money came and went, in Austria it was permanent.' The reason for this shortage was the hereditary lands' weak economy. The monarchy did not have access to the resources of the Americas, nor the richness of the French soil, nor the Maritime Powers' trading empire.

The inadequacies of the public finances is further explained by the monarchy's political structure which Charles VI did nothing to remedy, despite the advice of prince Eugene. The territorial gains he had made at the beginning of his reign served to accentuate the varied character of his patrimony and prince Eugene recommended transforming his inheritance and its patchwork of peoples and states into *ein Totum*, one unit. The only political reform Charles VI made to this end was the Pragmatic Sanction, which was intended to exclude rival claimants as much as to bring his subjects together.

THE IMPERIAL ARMY

The imperial army which was such an effective force at the beginning of the eighteenth century was not prince Eugene's creation, indeed it might be said that the prince left the army in a worse state than he had found it in. The reconquest of Hungary had turned the imperial army into a formidable war machine which little by little had rid itself of its failings inherited from the time of the Thirty Years War.

In the event of war, the emperor raised the core of his army in the hereditary lands, even when he could count on the aid of the army of the circles which, circumstances permitting, was levied and paid by the imperial princes. The imperial army was a homogenous body staffed by officers appointed by the sovereign. The soldiers were recruited through voluntary enlistment in Austria and Bohemia. Although many were discharged after the Treaties of Vasvár (1664) and Nijmegen (1678) to lighten the burden of taxation, from the time of Wallenstein the army assumed the character of a standing army.

The true founder of the imperial army which came into being in 1649 was Montecuccoli. President of the *Hofkriegsrat* from 1668 onwards, he left a large corpus of writings in Italian on military theory.[1] On his death he bequeathed his theories of tactics to the imperial troops. He was cautious and methodical in the conduct of operations. He endeavoured to keep the enemy in check by clever manoeuvres, employing this tactic in 1673 when confronting Turenne in Franconia and again in 1675 in Baden. When circumstances conjoined favourably, he was swift to engage in battle. He was also a skilful diplomat and as such was well-suited to taking command of the coalition armies.

The imperial troops used the same weaponry as the other European armies but were much slower to develop artillery than the French. The arsenal at Vienna had an important stock of field-pieces of all calibres from field cannon of 4 lb to mighty siege cannon of 48 lb. Powder for cannon was the greatest expense. Bullets were made in the forges on the seigneurial estates.

Montecuccoli had attached great importance to the training of sappers and pioneers and he recruited military engineers. He introduced the battalion as the tactical unit for the infantry with four battalions to a regiment. An infantry regiment consisted of 2 000 men divided into twelve or sixteen companies. Staffing was low-level with one captain, one lieutenant and one ensign for each company or just three officers for a hundred men and as many non-commissioned officers. In 1680 Montecuccoli had secured the adoption of the rifle with bayonet which rendered pikes useless. In 1670 grenadiers were introduced and quickly became the elite among the infantry. As salvos from muskets struck fear into the hearts of the Ottoman soldiers, the fire-power of the infantry became decisive in Hungary.

The cavalry regiments had 800 to 1 000 horses divided into five squadrons. Montecuccoli established the practice of keeping two in reserve and only engaging three squadrons at any one time. The imperial army engaged many heavy cavalry regiments and developed dragoons, mounted foot-soldiers who dismounted to fight on the ground. In total there were as many cavalry as infantry regiments, between twenty and thirty after 1683, but the cavalry formed one stratum of combatants and the infantry two. The imperial cavalry's tactic was a combination of the caracole and sabre charges in the open which had been developed by Gustavus Adolphus. The knights advanced to 25 metres from the opposing line, fired their pistols and then instead of making a turn, attacked with cold steel, a manoeuvre which was very difficult in the face of Ottoman troops. In an effort to improve upon this, knights and foot-soldiers were mixed together. Field-artillery was used in conjunction with the infantry: 4 lb field-pieces were hidden behind a line of foot-soldiers who parted unexpectedly to reveal cannons at a range of 500 metres which could wipe out the enemy.

The position of commander-in-chief was in principle reserved for the emperor, though from Ferdinand III onwards the Styrian branch of the Habsburgs took little part in combat. The sovereign's powers were delegated to a *Generalleutnant*, a lieutenant-general who was *de facto* a generalissimo, and to the Virgin Mary who bore the title *Generalissima* of the imperial army in fulfilment of a special vow made in 1638 by Ferdinand III. All the flags and standards were embroidered with a picture of the Mother of Christ. The regiments constituted an administrative and basic tactical unit for which the colonel appointed by imperial patent was answerable. The colonel was a commissar in the French sense, perhaps uniquely so in the Austrian administration. When the emperor decided to reform the regiment, its commander fell into obscurity. Such was the fate of count Gaspard de Chavagnac, a supporter of Condé who had passed into the service first of Spain and then of Leopold I and fought against the French army in the Dutch war, was dismissed on the recommendation of Charles V of Lorraine and then asked for Louis XIV's pardon before returning in 1681 to France. The colonel was assisted by a headquarters *prima plana* and a lieutenant-colonel who was often a soldier of fortune since high military office was a privilege of the aristocracy. The higher nobility in the hereditary lands had little liking for military life and so generals were recruited in the Empire and in Italy. After the Thirty Years War, the great military commanders were Souches, Montecuccoli, Charles of Lorraine, Eugene of Savoy, Louis of Baden and Max II Emanuel of Bavaria.

The officer corps was also cosmopolitan in character and was made up of *Welschen* drawn from Spain, Italy, Lorraine, Savoy and from among the Walloons in Flanders. When the Irish, Scots, Poles and Croats are also taken into account it is clear that in 1699 the Germans were still in the minority. In the infantry 25 per cent and in the cavalry 40 per cent of officers were foreign and of the latter 6 per cent were Hungarian.

The officer corps in the Austrian monarchy was, contrary to what is generally supposed, dominated for the most part by commoners. In the infantry just 20 per cent and in the cavalry 25 per cent were drawn from the nobility. Commoners served as troop officers up to the rank of captain and all the generals but one and all the colonels were nobles. During the siege of Vienna in 1683, losses were so great that soldiers from the ranks were promoted. The army remained a means of social advance even though brilliant careers such as those achieved by Knigge and Melander in the Thirty Years War were no longer possible under Leopold I and Charles VI. An aristocrat could be almost certain of being a colonel by the age of twenty while a commoner would begin his apprenticeship in the rank and file and, as long as he had received a minimum of education, could climb step by step through the hierarchy.

Officers' pay was low and that of the ordinary soldiers even less, indeed they were lucky to receive anything since captains often pocketed their men's wages. Under Leopold I, pay was reduced by half while prices doubled. The army, though, presented some with the means for spectacular self-aggrandizement. Colonels and captains continued to be small-scale entrepreneurs who embezzled the money for expenses and themselves equipped their men. The looting of Ottoman camps as happened at Vienna, Zenta, Petravarazdin and Belgrade, provided commanders and their subordinates with some compensation. They also had recourse to exactions upon the civil population, especially in Hungary where the imperial troops treated the inhabitants as the enemy. The emperor was a generous master who rewarded his victorious generals with estates and large bonuses. After the siege of Vienna, Starhemberg received 100 000 florins at a time when a colonel's annual pay was 500 florins and that of a captain 150 florins a month when on campaign. Montecuccoli, an honest general and the penniless younger son of a good family in Modena, left in his will of 1675 a fortune valued at 3 million florins. Prince Eugene's assets in 1736 were almost the same according to McKay.[2]

Such generosity from the emperor had, since the reign of Ferdinand II, been part of imperial power strategy. The cosmopolitan army was the only supranational body entirely devoted to the emperor. Since Wallenstein's death, soldiers and officers had taken an oath to the emperor and the motto of the officer corps was 'Good German, faithful to the Emperor'. The oath of personal loyalty was more important than confessional or national loyalties. The regiment constituted a society within society where the colonel by the emperor's express delegation possessed absolute power of life and death over his men. Soldiers and officers escaped the tutelage of the orders and local governments and owed everything to the emperor, especially if they were foreigners. The ideology of the Holy Roman Empire could motivate equally the Walloons and those from Lorraine or northern Italy, for the same emperor was their sovereign. It was even more natural for a German from the Holy Roman Empire, especially a Catholic, to serve the emperor. Thiriet has shown that the prospect of making a fortune attracted many Italians into the army.

The size of the standing army continued to increase during the reign of Leopold I, rising from 40 000 to 60 000 during the Dutch war and reaching 100 000 during the War of the League of Augsburg and 129 000 at the beginning of the War of the Spanish Succession. At this point, the army attained its largest numbers and continued to oscillate around 110 000–120 000 throughout the eighteenth century because limited financial resources made it impossible to increase further the permanent manpower. In addition to these men, there were the 10 000–12 000 troops from the Military Frontier who, under Charles VI, provided marching regiments, the light cavalry of the pandours. The emperor, in common with all other contemporary European rulers, could really only rely on the professional army. That the champions of Hungarian independence were defeated is in part explained by their lack of professionalism. The soldiers of prince Rákóczi, despite their personal courage, were never able to conquer the imperial troops ranged in battle formation. Guerrilla tactics with all their attendant atrocities alone had enabled them to hold out for so long against their enemy.

THE WEAKNESSES OF THE IMPERIAL ARMY

Army administration has a bad reputation for slowness and inefficiency. The *Hofkriegsrat* at Vienna, which had been founded in 1556 to solve these problems, was the butt of many jokes. It had all the faults characteristic of collegiate administration and only energetic presidents of Montecuccoli's and prince Eugene's stamp could impress upon it any sense of urgency. Both had been torn between their desire to command an army and the necessity of remaining in Vienna to ensure that the imperial troops had the means to act efficiently. They could only present demands for loans and for recruits and had to negotiate with the chamber of accounts and the chancelleries of Bohemia and Austria. Ultimately, they were dependent on the goodwill of the orders and the Diets. Eugene was able to galvanize himself during wartime but during peacetime he proved a mediocre president of the War Council. Bored by paperwork, he abandoned all administrative tasks to his hard-working but easily corrupted secretaries, Öttel and Ignaz Koch.

Logistics – furnishing supplies for troops on campaign – remained the army's weak point. The pattern established during the Thirty Years War, whereby war nourished war, had not been improved upon. The army continued to requisition what it needed and quartered itself outside the hereditary lands. The victims of this system were usually the circles of Swabia and Franconia, the small Italian states and those regions of Hungary that were populated. Worse still, the soldiers were left to pillage and oppress the civilian population. There was a world of difference between their relatively civilized and humane mode of conduct in the hereditary lands and the barbarisms they perpetrated elsewhere with their officers' complicity. Montecuccoli was conscious of the threat such behaviour posed to the army's cohesion, but the remedies he tried to introduce were in vain since he lacked the funds to guarantee a steady supply of food for his men. This inherent weakness of the imperial army largely explains why the French twice razed the Palatinate, in 1674 and 1689. Turenne and Louvois knew that this action would prevent the imperial troops from invading Alsace since they would not be able to advance through devastated countryside.

The reconquest of Hungary forced the army command to consider seriously the provision of bread for the men and oats for the horses and to hand the business of supplies over to the House of Samuel Oppenheimer. In 1685 Oppenheimer extended his sphere of activity by buying from estate-owners in Bohemia and Hungary their surpluses and by then loaning to the imperial treasury the money it needed. As Montecuccoli had observed in his memorandum, *Dellaguerra col Turco*, the Danube was the vital communications route in a country where roads were all but non-existent. It was to protect the fleet of transport boats for troops, provisions, munitions and the sick and wounded, that the War Council developed the Danube navy. This was, in its early days, made up of *tchaïques*, small galleys armed with cannon and propelled by fifteen banks of rowers or under sail when conditions were favourable. These boats were invaluable as the Turks also had a river fleet which were able to attack the imperial convoys.

Prince Eugene applied sufficient pressure for the marine fleet to grow to the stage where it included real ships. The Austrian victory in the Turkish war of 1716–18 was mainly due to good organization because the prince saw to it that reinforcements and provisions were despatched on time. This was, however, exceptional and it was more usual for disorder to reign, as was the case during the Italian campaigns of 1718–79, when the Sicilian campaign against the troops of Philip V was, in McKay's words, 'an ignominious affair'.[3]

Prince Eugene was sometimes too confident of his own ability to take those swift decisions during battle which could reverse a situation, one of the many traits he and Napoleon, who admired him, both had. He did not delegate his powers and his generals were merely passive executors incapable of taking decisions themselves. Mercy, Seckendorf and Königsegg, the three assistants whose careers he promoted, proved to be incompetent army commanders, Mercy in Italy, the other two in the Turkish war of 1737–39. As for Francis Stephen of Lorraine, he did not take after his grandfather Charles V and this brought disastrous results.

Prince Eugene had abandoned the traditional practice of having a War Council with its corps of commanders but would not countenance the creation of a corps headquarters. The War Council at Vienna, in all its long history, had never had the character of a headquarters. Yet more serious, prince Eugene was opposed to the creation of a military academy for the education of young officers. Extremely conservative by nature, he put his trust in education in the field, as had been the practice in the seventeenth century. After one or two campaigns as a volunteer, a future commander was promoted to ensign and quickly rose to the rank of captain if he proved that he could lead men. This method was good only in times of continuous warfare but the period of peace which followed after the Treaty of Utrecht called for another method of training. He became aware of the need for a school of military engineers during the campaign in Hungary and agreed to the foundation of such an academy. He was quite unconcerned about training the rank and file.

In 1707 Leopold I's *Ordnung* regulating general discipline was slightly modified with the standardization of a pearl grey uniform for all the imperial troops. The uniforms were in fact made from an inexpensive off-white cloth which was produced in factories in Bohemia. Perfecting drill on the parade ground was the highest priority while target practice was neglected. Like Napoleon much later, prince Eugene thought that veterans made the best instructors for young recruits.

Another weakness of the imperial army was its all but non-existent medical provision. The losses in Hungary through wounds and sickness were appalling. It was not unusual for a company to lose half its men in the course of a campaign. Each company had a barber-surgeon and, after a ruling in 1718, a single doctor was provided for a whole regiment. An ensign was put in charge of health care. If one of his men was seriously wounded, he would give orders for him to be given the last rites and only then to be taken to the field hospital. Despite the considerable donations made by cardinal Kollonich, field hospitals remained unequal to their task. They were too few in number and were little more than places in which to die without doctors and medicine. There was a similar lack of provision for disabled veterans. In 1656 baron von Chaos founded a veterans' hospice which was revived by a donation from Kollonich, but no real provision was made for disabled veterans until Maria-Theresa's reign. Prince Eugene had refused to gather together veterans into 'veteran companies' to provide service for the forts at low cost, as was the practice in France.

Prince Eugene left Charles VI with an army which was badly commanded, badly officered and badly trained in infantry combat at the moment the firing-power of musketry made Prussian drill indispensable. But if these failings could be imputed to prince Eugene's pragmatic spirit and one-track mind, the faults in the organization of the health services and the quartermaster corps are explained above all by the monarchy's poor financial resources.

ATTEMPTS AT FINANCIAL REFORM: THE WORK OF GUNDAKER VON STARHEMBERG[4]

The gains made in 1713–18 brought little benefit to the Viennese financial administration since the Italian lands, Milan, Naples and Sicily, kept a large share of autonomy. They contributed to the common burden by providing garrisons for imperial regiments and guaranteeing their upkeep. In 1732 the Netherlands yielded 3.1 million florins and Italy 5 million florins. The contributions from the hereditary lands reached amost 15 million in 1732, including the 2.5 million voted by Hungary. The most spectacular development was that of the *cameralia*, the indirect taxation outside the orders' control and tied to the economic growth of the monarchy. It amounted to 14 million in 1732 but had been as high as 21 million in 1726 when it had been possible to reduce the sum total of contributions to 8 million and so to reduce the burden of direct taxation borne by the agricultural labourers. The taxation policy for which Leopold I and his cameralists had hoped, began to be implemented.

The architect of this great rectification was prince Eugene's friend, count Gundaker Starhemberg. He was not a brilliant economist but an intelligent man with a clear mind and sound good sense. He was a clever administrator and a conservative who shied away from innovation and structural reform, but he proved that he had the qualities necessary for the post which he occupied. He collaborated loyally with the *Hofkriegsrat* since he understood that his main task was to provide the funds necessary to conduct operations rather than to make general economies as had been the way of president Abele at the time of the siege of Vienna and cardinal Kollonich during the War of the League of Augsburg. His principal merit was that he inspired trust in state creditors at a particularly difficult time, at the beginning of the War of the Spanish Succession. In 1703 the public treasury lost the support of the House of Oppenheimer which had just gone bankrupt. On 3 October that year, prince Eugene had written to his friend, 'the whole monarchy is on a knife's edge and could really collapse. If 50 000 florins is not found in cash immediately, anything could happen and I do not know how to prevent it.' As in the years before 1690,

Starhemberg depended on the goodwill of those individuals who alone were capable of providing the services of a treasury. The Viennese bankers Gaun and Zankoni, the financier Bartholotti and count Przehorsowsky, president of the chamber of Bohemia, replied to his appeal and advanced 1.2 million florins.

Starhemberg became obsessed with the question of public credit and the treasury and finally imposed a workable solution by founding in 1706 the Wiener Stadtbank after the failure of the first fund for the extinction of the public debt, the short-lived Banco del giro.

The Wiener Stadtbank stood *in loco imperatoris* and from its foundation was responsible for all the emperor's financial obligations. A distinction was made between floating debt and consolidated debt. The bank undertook to pay interest on the oldest debts and acted on behalf of the treasury for the new debts. It received in return the proceeds from tolls and domains in Lower Austria.

The bank grew greatly between 1710 and 1715 but soon fell victim to a change of policy introduced by Charles VI, who did not hide his contempt for a private house which could drain off capital. He forced it to merge with the Bancalität and so transformed an autonomous credit institution into an administrative mechanism for indirect taxation. By guaranteeing 6 per cent to the *Hofkammer*, it became nothing more than an annex.

The Bancalität became the central cashier of the monarchy to which all the state revenues were returned, the *Hofkammer* losing the right to handle funds. The experiment which the emperor had wanted lasted from 1715 to 1723 and prompted Starhemberg's dismissal. The project was probably the inspiration of the Frenchman Mandat and was put into effect by a councillor of the chamber, the Czech baron Mikos. The general bank was controlled by a governor assisted by twelve councillors. Although it had been allotted all the revenues, it was prevented from rationalizing the situation by the resumption of the war with the Ottoman empire. The Wiener Stadtbank remained the basic source of credit and subsequently allowed the monarchy to find loans on honest conditions and to escape gradually the clutches of money lenders.

Gundaker von Starhemberg was probably too successful, for Charles VI tended to appeal constantly for credit. In common with the kings of France and of England, he left at his death an enormous public debt, whereas his father had managed to increase slowly and regularly the monarchy's resources.

EARLIER ATTEMPTS AT RECTIFYING THE MONARCHY'S FINANCES (1665–75)[5]

The emperor's budget continued to increase after the accession of Leopold I. During the 1660s, except at the time of the Turkish war, it was of the order of 5 million florins and remained less than 10 million until 1683 before rising to 20 million during the War of the League of Augsburg when the emperor had to conduct a war on two fronts. Expenses rose to 30 million during the War of the Spanish Succession but in February 1715 sank again to 20 million. Despite the reduction in the financial strain after the signing of the Treaties of

Utrecht and Rastatt, the monarchy's budget had quadrupled since the beginning of Leopold I's reign. Charles VI's resources were greatest in 1740, reaching a total of 22 million florins. Von Arneth's claim that Charles VI possessed revenue of 40 million during the second Turkish war seems wildly inaccurate.

Between 1660 and 1715 revenues grew continuously and there were four plateaux. Revenues remained very modest before the war with Holland except in 1664, a year marked by crisis when the emperor was forced to mobilize considerable resources in order to meet the Turkish threat. Leopold I wanted to 'husband' his subjects in the hereditary lands in order to ease economic reconstruction. His strategy of peace at any price was translated into a policy of cutting army manpower and reducing the level of contributions, and the repayment of creditors. From 1673 to 1690 revenues increased by half and the lull which followed the Peace of Nijmegen (1678) made it possible to repay the loans contracted by the *Hofkammer* in order to put right the financial situation all the sooner. This justified the orders' suspicions over the 'exceptional and provisional' taxes, such as the taxes on beverages, which the Diet of Bohemia had voted in 1664 and abrogated in 1701. The third plateau was reached after 1690 with the demands of the war on two fronts in Germany and Hungary. The receipts continued to grow, settling somewhere between 12 and 13 million to reach 16 million florins in 1699. This figure is explained by the doubling of the Hungarian contribution, effected in 1698 against the will of the orders and by the maintenance of wartime impositions in order to settle the debt swiftly. The burden of taxation had practically doubled since 1683 but continued to be sustained by economic growth in the hereditary lands.

The War of the Spanish Succession required a more moderate burden of taxation, the Austro-Bohemian lands paying no more than 4.5 million in contributions and in addition 3.5. million *cameralia* which provided the basic indirect taxation, the salt tax and the 'aides'. The direct contributions were reduced once more to the modest level of the first period when the economy was much more prosperous. It was only after 1712 that a tax on capital, *Vermögensteuer*, was again considered. New resources were provided by the war contributions levied on the Italian provinces and on Bavaria which was harshly exploited after 1704. When in 1705 the last of the French troops had been driven from the Italian peninsula, the imperial troops raised 4–5 million florins annually and lived off the land, including Tuscany and other 'neutral' territories. Hungary and Transylvania, however, were less than ever in a state to contribute to common expenses. Following the Peace of Szatmár in 1711, Starhemberg could still only count on a few requisitions and the country, worn out by forty years of civil and foreign wars, contributed only 1.8 million florins. As for the Maritime Powers, they only really aided the monarchy by maintaining the imperial troops campaigning in the Netherlands. For this reason in 1713 the budgetary shortfall was twice that of the previous year and prince Eugene found himself forced to negotiate at Rastatt. Britain did not finance the Habsburg war effort, as has often been claimed, and only offered the monarchy a small sum of money, as did the United Provinces which granted a loan guaranteed by the mercury mines in Idria.

The improvement in the monarchy's finances is explained by the economic progress made by the hereditary lands and not by dramatic administrative reforms and the emperor's increased power over the Diets in his patrimonial states. Moderate recourse to credit, the reduction in civil expenses and the budgetary deficit, limited in the worst years to 25 per cent and more generally to 12–15 per cent of the budget, made it possible rapidly to stabilize the situation.

THE MISTAKES OF CHARLES VI

Neither the emperor nor prince Eugene took advantage of the return to peace to implement far-reaching reforms. In 1726 marshal Richelieu, the French ambassador, drew a relatively positive picture of Charles VI's financial situation, observing that it depended on peace and that a war would upset the relative equilibrium.

His report, though, was made at the time of a peak in prosperity, when the emperor received 30 million florins a year. Later his revenues dropped to 20–22 million, the level they had been during his father's reign. This was why Charles VI relied on the support of the Wiener Stadtbank, and, in common with the rulers of the other great powers, had recourse to loans without having the means to finance them. In 1714 the public debt was only 52.1 million florins, which was nothing compared to the French debt, and grew to 70 million in 1718 and 99 million by the end of 1739. The public debt consequently doubled during the reign of Charles VI without taking into consideration the obligations undertaken by the administration in Brussels and Milan. The numerous loans contracted between 1732 and 1739, especially those with Jewish and foreign bankers, meant that the monarchy's credit in 1740 was almost nil. Eleven foreign loans were guaranteed by the contributions, which had the effect of reducing the army's resources, while a large part of the revenues of the *cameralia* were surrendered to the Wiener Stadtbank, more than 4 million in 1740 as opposed to 1.5 million in 1716. The policy of the last ten years of Charles VI's reign of taking out loans had mortgaged the revenues. Direct and indirect taxes were absorbed by servicing the debt. The revenues of the monarchy in real terms had dropped below the level at the beginning of the century.

Charles VI did not lack the will to carry out reforms but it is open to question as to whether he had the opportunity to break the power of the Diets, of bringing the aristocracy to heel and unifying his realms. Prince Eugene had swiftly abandoned the idea of making the monarchy *ein Totum*, a project which was more than any man could achieve.

THE NATIONALITIES

The Austrian monarchy in the baroque age was multinational, multiconfessional and, despite the Pragmatic Sanction, confederate. The juxtaposition of kingdoms did not result from the fantasies of lawyers or of heedless ministers but corresponded to the extraordinary national diversity which the Habsburgs had hitherto respected.

The American historian Robert Kann has written:

The question whether a national question existed in the Habsburg lands before the late eighteenth century is extremely complex. Certainly the concept of ethnic nationalism was not consciously formulated at that time; hence, political demands based upon it did not exist. Pan-Germanism, Pan-Slavism, the Southern Slav problem and Italian Irredentism were of course ideas alien to the Baroque period. A Rumanian, or in terms of Transylvania a *Vlach*, national entity was only slowly emerging and was not as yet a political factor of significance. The Poles and the bulk of the Ruthenians as well were not yet included in the Habsburg empire. Czech nationalism was, so to speak, 'frozen' after the battle at the White Mountain in 1620. Magyar national consciousness certainly was evident, though it was far more political than ethnic in character.... The religious problem, to a certain extent the language question, and definitely that of the historical-political entities already existed in the Baroque period. Whether or not these factors are to be called 'national problems' is an interesting sociological and psychological question; politically it is a moot one. The Habsburgs had to face the problem of more or less loosely organized groups of people whose interests to a very large extent coincided with those of the ethnic national groups of later days.[6]

In the Habsburg monarchy, excluding the Netherlands and the state of Milan, there were a dozen ethno-linguistic groups speaking and writing different languages, although they did not all have a very developed political consciousness and were content to be simply minorities, unlike the Hungarians, Bohemians and Croats who were convinced that they belonged to a 'historic nation'. There was already a marked difference apparent between the hereditary lands, i.e. the Austro-Bohemian complex, and the kingdom of Hungary.

The Austro-Bohemian complex was characterized by the relative preponderance of its German-speaking element which constituted the dominant population of the Alpine lands and an active minority in the kingdom of Bohemia. In the Austrian lands which had between 1.5 and 2 million inhabitants, the German element represented at least 90 per cent, and in the *Vorlande* (Further or Outer Austria including Breisach and Vorarlberg), 100 per cent of the total population. It included a large nobility which was uniformly devoted to the Habsburgs as their 'natural seigneurs' and constituted a potential source from which to draw the monarchy's higher officials.

The capital and the lands to the south had important minorities. Vienna was, like every modern city, home to many immigrants. This influx of settlers is not explained simply by Vienna's prestige as the imperial residence and by its being the centre for much economic activity, but by its chronic shortage of population. It had long been an outlet for the Moravian lands. It provided lodgings for an important Italian colony of artisans, musicians, singers, painters, bankers and officers in the imperial army and formed an autonomous parish, the church of the Minoritenkirche opposite the Balhausplatz. This Italian colony enjoyed a favoured place in the political and cultural life of the court, where Italian was the dominant language until 1720. In the southern provinces, the Latin element constituted the principal minority. There were the Italians in the bishopric of

Trente, the county of Gorizia (Görz) and Trieste, and the Ladin-speakers of Friuli who spoke romance dialects close to the Romansch spoken in the Swiss canton of Grisons. In Carniola there was an important Slav minority, especially around the capital Ljubljana (Laibach). The Slovenes were peasants, artisans and, in Idria, miners and were dominated by the completely Germanized nobility.

Relations between the Germans and the Slavs were very different in Bohemia where by 1725 the population had risen to 4 million inhabitants, its level in 1618. Most of the population in Moravia was Czech and in the eighteenth century constituted a complete sociological group, even though the elites were bilingual and somewhat condescending towards the Slav language to which the Catholic clergy nevertheless remained very attached because it did not want to be cut off from the peasantry. The German-speaking minority was made up of nobles who had been awarded lands by the different dynasties and of burghers and artisans as well as peasants in the peripheral regions of the Bohemian quadrilateral. Whole areas, much later called the Sudetenland, were colonized by Saxon miners and peasants coming from Rhineland Germany. The city of Prague had a German character.

Silesia was in theory a vassal duchy of the crown of Bohemia and consisted of neighbouring principalities. Upper Silesia, where the duchy of Brzeg belonged to the descendants of the Piast dynasty until 1675, kept its purely Slav character. Lower Silesia, around Breslau, was already deeply Germanized and the Hohenzollerns possessed fiefs there.

In Hungary, the position of German had been greatly reduced and its use was tolerated just among the German colonists. Hungary and Transylvania were dominated by the Hungarian element which made up 65 per cent of the population. The Magyars owed their cohesion to their language of Finno-Ugric origin which was marked also by Latin, the Slav languages and numerous other lexical elements but kept its original structure. It became a written language around 1530 and Hungarian was already in competition with Latin which remained the kingdom's official language. The nation, dominated by a rich and powerful nobility of 100 000–150 000 members, possessed a strong national consciousness which had gradually been forged in the face of the Ottoman invaders and German Austria, which was seen as an occupier rather than an ally. All witnesses, whether French, English, Venetian or Turk, and the grievances presented regularly by the Hungarian Diet to its Habsburg king, are in agreement: the union with the hereditary lands was a marriage of convenience, even a forced marriage since Hungary had been liberated from the Ottomans but was still under a foreign dynasty, the Habsburgs, whom the orders mistrusted.

The members of the German minority who lived in the royal towns were in a difficult position. They spoke an archaic form of German within the towns but the magistrate used Latin in his relations with the government at Pressburg. In Upper Hungary, the population assimilated out of fear of reprisals from the nobility. In fact the German burghers behaved like 'natives' when dealing with the Germans of Austria, even though they remained attached to their German culture.

The most significant minorities in Hungary spoke Slav languages but the Slovaks of Upper Hungary were distinct from the South Slavs of Croatia-Slavonia. The Slovaks were an example of an incomplete sociological group since the gentry had long been assimilated. They were peasants, miners at Banska Bystrica and Kremnica, and servants in the towns. The clergy, both Catholic and Lutheran, spoke Slovak and many were themselves Slovaks. They constituted a group conscious of their origin and attached to their traditions who, when confronted by the Germans of Austria, thought of themselves as Hungarians.

The question of the Serbs arose during Charles VI's reign. They were orthodox Slavs who had fled from the Ottoman empire in successive waves and were related to the Croats, speaking the same language but writing it differently. They served on the Military Frontier and made the best border guards, but these peasant soldiers expected Vienna to support them in evading the seigneurial regime and did not provide *robot*. The second wave of Serbs settled in Hungary in 1689 and hoped to defend the religious privileges which Leopold I ceded to their patriarch, Arsenije Crnojević. They wanted to remain free from any feudal lords and the Hungarian bishops and counted on the support of the War Council in Vienna.

In Transylvania, the Romanian question was not yet urgent. The country was governed by three privileged bodies: the Hungarian nobility; the Szeklers who were frontier guards; and Saxons, German colonists who had settled during the thirteenth century. They alone were represented in the Diet and most were Protestant, apart from the Szeklers who were Catholic. In 1689 power rested exclusively with the Hungarian nobles, who shared it with the Habsburgs and their representatives. The Romanian orthodox did not have any political rights, even though their religion had been tolerated since 1579 at the time of István Báthory. They were peasants who were supposed to be represented by their Hungarian lords. The Romanian literary language was already fixed. In the seventeenth century, a printer at Alba Julia (Gyulafehérvár) in Transylvania published the Bible in Romanian and the Orthodox clergy used the language of the peasantry. The fundamental problem was social rather than national and the Romanian peasants found it difficult to bear the burden of serfdom.

The clergy and local administration respected the peculiar cultures of all the various ethno-linguistic groups. In 1625 cardinal Pázmány, the primate of Hungary, supervised the publication of a liturgy in Latin, Hungarian, German and Slovak. Each group possessed a translation of the Bible in its mother tongue as well as psalters, catechisms, almanacs and alphabet primers. The parish priest and the pastor were assisted by the schoolmaster. There was no question of the German language being imposed. As the administration systematically used the local language, the judges received dispositions in the language of the defendant and the peasants did not feel threatened in their familiar universe.

Nationality was not yet an issue in the eighteenth century. The monarchy was a tower of Babel where the peculiar identity of each group was respected. The situation, though, was more complex because not only were there regional languages but the privileged and historic nations demanded that the central administration respect their tongues.

STATE-RIGHT AND LINGUISTIC PLURALISM

The orders in Hungary and Bohemia were both very attached to their own national languages. The lands of the crown of Bohemia raised the question of German–Czech relations. By the terms of the 'Renewed Constitution' of 1627, the state was bilingual, the first official language remaining Czech, the great victor of the Hussite revolution. This was not the case in Silesia where German was the only official language. The chancellery had two agencies, one German, the other Czech, and the articles of the Diet were promulgated in both languages. It is not clear whether this equilibrium was respected in the seventeenth century and whether the elites drawn from foreign cultures, the German, French and Italian nobles, neglected the national culture and reduced Czech to a provincial language. Nor is it known whether Leopold I's correspondence in Czech with his friend count Czernin was a marginal phenomenon.

In Hungary, Latin remained the official language. Hungarian was difficult and baffling for foreigners and yet further complicated relations with the Viennese court and the Croatian authorities. Latin, the neutral language par excellence, which all educated people knew to a greater or lesser degree, provided access to western culture and later in the eighteenth century Montesquieu and Rousseau were translated into Latin *ad usum Hungarorum*. On this point, the authorities in Pressburg would not be moved. Every act drafted in German was sent to the Viennese dicast who neglected to translate it. The official acts of the Diet were drafted in Latin even though the deliberations had generally taken place in Hungarian. This was also the case with the Croatian Diet.

The historic nations defended themselves zealously against every impulse to Germanization. Five languages had the status of official languages within the monarchy: Latin, German, Czech, Hungarian and Croat. The Habsburgs from Maximilian I onwards were polyglot and mastering languages was a fundamental part of the education received by the archdukes. The emperors generally knew enough Czech and Hungarian to appear courteous towards their subjects, and their knowledge of German was strongly marked by the Viennese dialect, which made them popular with the common people. It was, however, of the Latin languages – Latin, Italian and to a lesser extent French and Spanish – that their mastery was greatest. The Habsburgs of the baroque age were princes of Latin culture who had made Italian the customary language of the court. The first Viennese newspaper published in 1672 and the theatre were in Italian, and important discussions were conducted in Latin or Italian until the reign of Maria-Theresa when they were held in French. When the court gradually abandoned Italian after 1740, it was not to adopt German, which remained the language of the people and of the bourgeoisie, but rather French.

The Habsburgs did not seek to Germanize their subjects. Their policy of cultural and political unification was based on converting to Catholicism those who had joined the reformation churches and persuading the members of the Greek Orthodox Church, and among the Romanians and Ruthenians the Uniate bishops, to recognize the authority of the Holy See. Although this policy achieved greater success with the Greek Orthodox than the Hungarian

53

Protestants, Charles VI did not renounce it. In 1732, through a Jesuitical ruse, he drove the Calvinists and Lutherans from the state apparatus by imposing on all royal officers a form of oath which mentioned the Immaculate Conception of the Virgin Mary. A Protestant consequently could not take such an oath and the Calvinist nobility would have to wait until Joseph II to find official positions in their own country. The 'liberation' of the Hungarian plain in the long term favoured the advance of Germanization, even though Kollonich's programme, which envisaged the resettlement of the Great Plain with German and Catholic colonists, was never fully implemented. The cardinal preferred Germans to Hungarians because they were docile and loyal subjects of the Habsburgs. To keep the Hungarians in check, the plan was for the Viennese administration to introduce Greek Orthodox, Romanians and Serbs who were considered the natural enemies of the Hungarians, and to apply the old maxim of political science, *divide et impera* (divide and rule). German officials were appointed throughout the country and the towns were peopled with Catholic Germans.

The implementation of this project, which the Hungarians still judge diabolical, was slow and incomplete. It was chiefly concerned with the Military Frontier in Slavonia and the southern part of the Great Plain, the Banat of Temesvár, which had been reconquered in 1718. The Banat was parcelled out under Charles VI but its colonization suffered severe reversals because of the unhealthiness of its badly drained lands which were home to mosquitoes and full of malaria and dysentry. Despite count Mercy's worthy efforts and the incentives offered to immigrants, including the absence of feudal rights, a long period of tax exemption and the disposal of lands free of charge, the colonization of the Banat did not succeed until the time of Maria-Theresa. By creating a mosaic of German, Serb and Romanian villages, the imperial administration helped to create the nationality issue as it was raised at the time of the revolution in 1848. As ill-fated as they were, the projects of cardinal Kollonich and the chamber of accounts aimed at changing the internal balance within Hungarian society. It was not their goal to Germanize the Hungarians, which would have been impossible because of the vigour of Hungarian culture and the high level of political consciousness among the orders.

The Austrian monarchy, in the first half of the eighteenth century, was characterized by the existence of a dozen popular cultures, maintained by the different churches and respected by the seigneurial administration. In addition there were the six languages of culture, the five 'national' languages and that of the court and the sovereign, generally Italian. The orders resisted every attempt at Germanization and the Habsburgs respected national and cultural pluralism in so far as they did not have the authority necessary to impose the least change on local aristocracies.

The dyarchy on which the baroque state was founded served well and Charles VI by temperament and personal orientation was not one to threaten it. The achievements of his reign were far from brilliant. He left the imperial army and finances in a much worse state than he found them and he expended far greater effort in trying to reconstitute the empire of Charles V than consolidating the great continental power which had been created by the Treaties of Utrecht (1713) and Rastatt (1714). His daughter Maria-Theresa was the first to attempt to modernize the monarchy. The failings and errors of the last Habsburg in the male line meant that the process of reform would take place amid blood, tears and sorrow.

NOTES AND REFERENCES

1. The edition of Montecuccoli's work by Aloïs Veltze, *Ausgewählte Schriften*, 4 vols, Vienna, 1898, remains inadequate. Raimondo Luraghi has undertaken a complete edition of Montecuccoli's military writings.
2. Derek McKay, *Prince Eugene of Savoy*, London, 1977.
3. Ibid.
4. Brigitte Holl, 'Hofkammerpräsident Gundaker Thomas Graf Starhemberg und die österreichische Finanzpolitik der Barockzeit, 1703–1715', *Archiv für Österreichische Geschichte*, 132, Vienna, 1976.
5. Jean Bérenger, 'Á propos d'un ouvrage récent: les finances de l'Austriche à l'époque baroque (1650–1740)', *Histories, Économies, Societés*, 1982, pp. 221–45.
6. Robert Kann, *A Study in Austrian Intellectual History*, London, 1960, pp. 8–9.

CHAPTER FOUR

The Accession of Maria-Theresa and the Crisis of 1740

Maria-Theresa (1717–80) enjoyed the title empress only through her husband, Francis Stephen of Lorraine, who was elected emperor in 1745 and held the office until his death in 1765. She was born an archduchess of Austria in 1717 and in December 1740 on the death of her father, Charles VI, became queen of Hungary and, despite being challenged by the elector of Bavaria, queen of Bohemia. She was never empress of Austria because the Austrian empire did not exist.

The problems caused by her succession stemmed from Charles VI's having excluded from the throne Joseph I's two daughters who were married to Augustus III, the king of Poland and elector of Saxony, and Charles Albert, the elector of Bavaria and son of Max II Emanuel. The terms of the Pragmatic Sanction of 1713 overturned the arrangements which had been made by Leopold I and which his two sons, the archdukes and future emperors Joseph and Charles, had accepted in 1703. The balance of forces in Europe was not in the Habsburgs' favour and the death of Charles VI launched the War of the Austrian Succession, a European crisis which threatened to destroy the monarchy. The emperor had made his daughter, Maria-Theresa, his sole heir but he had not left her the means with which to defend this magnificent bequest and to discourage accusations of usurper. The young sovereign's first claim to glory was that she faced up to adversity and saved the Austrian monarchy when she could easily have witnessed the break up of her inheritance and found herself with only the crown of Hungary.

THE CRISIS OF 1740[1]

Charles VI died content in the knowledge that the European powers had guaranteed the Pragmatic Sanction. To gain their recognition had been his great goal but his assurance bespeaks a good measure of naivety, for an international agreement without the means to make it respected was no real safeguard. Spain in 1725, Russia in 1726, Prussia in 1728, then Britain, France and Piedmont-Sardinia had all guaranteed the Pragmatic Sanction. Some of the imperial princes immediately raised claims, some to give their support to Francis Stephen of

Lorraine on the occasion of the imperial election which could not fail to be called, but others on their own behalf because of their marriage alliances with the House of Austria. Frederick II, the new elector of Brandenburg and king of Prussia, promised his vote to Francis Stephen in exchange for Silesia. Charles Albert, though, was an implacable opponent and refused to recognize the Pragmatic Sanction, using Ferdinand I's will to support his claim to the Bohemian crown. In this there was a measure of revenge for the election of 1526.

These claims furnished the enemies of the House of Austria with the pretext for trying to deprive the Habsburgs of the imperial crown and reducing them to a second-rate power. In France, the anti-Habsburg party remained very strong under the leadership of Charles Fouquet, marshal Belle-Isle, a descendant of the superintendent Fouquet.* As secretary of state for war, Belle-Isle imposed his views on Louis XV and cardinal Fleury, who were quick to repudiate their earlier promises. Political circles in France saw an opportunity to support Spain against England which had been at war since the previous year. Those with interests in the colonies agitated in favour of conflict, and as the Habsburg monarchy and England were allies, France was resolved to wage war in the belief that it would be able to settle the question of the Netherlands in Louis XV's favour. It is questionable whether Austria was wise to campaign for the imperial crown regardless of the costs involved, but its determination demonstrates the enduring prestige of the imperial title and how little the monarchy had distanced itself from German affairs. The time for a Danubian monarchy separate from Germany had not yet come. Maria-Theresa considered that the imperial title was part of her patrimony no less than the crown of Bohemia or the duchy of Milan and it was only because she herself was ineligible that she supported the candidacy of her husband, Francis of Lorraine, grand duke of Tuscany.

To begin with, Fleury wanted to sign purely defensive agreements with his German allies, but he was very quickly outflanked and intervened after Prussia attacked Silesia in 1741. An army under Belle-Isle's command was sent to occupy Bohemia in the name of the elector of Bavaria and to ensure links with the Prussians. In the autumn of 1741, the marshal occupied Prague without any resistance and the notables readily rallied to the new king, Charles Albert, the *Afterkönig*. In July 1742, after many hours of hesitant and tortuous negotiations, Frederick of Prussia finally signed with Maria-Theresa the Treaty of Breslau which recognized his possession of the greater part of Silesia. Maria-Theresa's troops reoccupied Bohemia without difficulty after Belle-Isle's departure in the summer of 1742. A garrison of only 6 000 men held Prague for a few months. The Austrians invaded Bavaria and on the day of Charles Albert of Bavaria's election in Frankfurt as emperor under the title Charles VII, the Austrian army occupied his capital, Munich. Frederick II, worried by the turn of events, took up arms against Maria-Theresa in order to save his conquests in Silesia.

---

* Translator's note: Nicolas Fouquet (1615–80), the disgraced superintendent of finance under Mazarin, was convicted of embezzlement and sentenced in 1661 to life in prison.

It was Britain under the leadership of lord Carteret that saved the monarchy by raising an anti-French coalition and transforming the conflict into a European war in 1743. George II sent an Anglo-Hanoverian army to the Continent and Sardinia and Holland ranged themselves on the side of Austria while France allied closely with Spain. The affairs of Central Europe moved onto a wider plain with new theatres of war opening up in the Netherlands, Italy, the Mediterranean, the Atlantic and the colonies. The sudden death of the emperor Charles VII resolved the situation. His son made peace with Austria, promised to vote for Francis Stephen of Lorraine, and received back Bavaria. The elector of Saxony, Augustus III, who had earlier shown some inclination to come forward as a candidate for the imperial crown, passed into the Austrian camp. Francis Stephen of Lorraine was then elected without difficulty as the emperor Francis I. Maria-Theresa was resigned to making a treaty with Frederick II and confirmed him in possession of Silesia. The Austrian succession was settled and the last phase of the European war (1745–48) which ended with the Treaty of Aix-la-Chapelle was solely a conflict among the Maritime Powers.

The most serious result for the Austrian monarchy of these five years of war was the loss of the whole of Silesia apart from the Teschen region. This was a grave loss for Silesia was a very rich area with a large population. It was industrialized, with its cloth being exported as far afield as America, and it had always paid substantial contributions representing at least 20 per cent of the regular receipts of the government in Vienna. The Bohemian aristocracy held it as a grudge against the Habsburgs that they had abandoned one of the kingdom's finest provinces. The annexation of Silesia helped Prussia expand its economy and territory and to establish its preponderance in eastern Germany; Maria-Theresa was clearly aware of what was at stake when in 1741 she contemplated giving up the Netherlands and Milan in order to keep Silesia. The king of Prussia remained an elector no different from the other electors but was now the head of a state in direct competition with Austria. The change of ruler was welcomed by the people of Lower Silesia. The Counter-Reformation had left its mark and had caused much bitterness. The Protestant minority and recent converts saw Frederick II as a liberator rather than a conqueror. No popular movement arose in favour of resisting Prussia and returning to Austria. It was *a posteriori* a harsh indictment of the policy of unification by religion practised by Ferdinand III and Leopold I.

Maria-Theresa's subjects departed from their usual reaction, customary since the sixteenth century. The Hungarians proved to be the most sure supporters of their sovereign whereas the Czechs were passive to the point of complicity with the Franco-Bavarian forces. The Hungarians acted with due consideration of the consequences whereas the Czechs were subjected to the strictest rule of law. The events of 1741 were most revealing in this respect. Maria-Theresa, faced with the possibility of losing Bohemia and Silesia, turned to the Hungarian Diet despite the resistance of her Austrian advisors who viewed the Hungarian nation as nothing better than so many rebels in power. When, as ruler of Hungary, she convoked the Hungarian Diet in June 1741 in order to proceed with the coronation ceremony, the nobility demanded the renewal of its privileges and a guarantee of its autonomy within the monarchy. Maria-Theresa announced that a special council drawn from natives of the kingdom would be in charge of Hungarian affairs. She secured the election of the elderly count Pálffy and was able to win the goodwill of the ruling class. In September, she had no difficulty in obtaining a mass levy of troops such as had previously only been voted when Hungarian national territory was under threat. The Hungarian army was on a war-footing by the autumn and provided Maria-Theresa with 40 000 men in place of the 100 000 she had anticipated. Now that she had at her disposal six excellent cavalry regiments she could make a considerable psychological impact; the announcement of the *insurrectio* drove Frederick II in 1741 to sign the armistice of Klein-Schellendorf. The alliance between the Hungarian nobility and the sovereign was sealed for the whole of Maria-Theresa's reign. She was consequently solicitous to respect the privileges of the kingdom and of its ruling class, the nobility, who, assured of their exemption from taxation and administrative autonomy, in return became loyal subjects.

Bohemia presented a striking contrast. J.-F. Noël has recently shown that the whole population, the peasants as well as the bourgeoisie and the aristocrats, who had been showered with favours by the House of Austria, had no compunction about turning traitor. National pride more than concern over taxation led the nobility to hope for a more moderate ruler than the Habsburgs at Vienna, for a ruler who would restore Prague as the country's centre of gravity and put Bohemia on the margins of any large-scale European conflict. Most supported Charles Albert of Bavaria but some favoured the House of Saxony; the old nobility had not abandoned its centuries-old dream. Since 1650, the ruling class had rightly or wrongly developed the impression that Bohemia had been relegated to the second rank, to Austria's advantage, and was only good for financing ventures which had no bearing on its own security and prosperity. All the nobility hated the grand burgrave, count Schaffgotsch, the agent of Austrian authority. The burghers of Prague were rebellious in their attitude and for commercial reasons, namely the unification of the route along the Elbe, inclined towards Augustus III, elector of Saxony and king of Poland. The northern circles where the majority was German and reconversion to Catholicism only partial, went so far as to declare their unification with Saxony because of the elector's reputation for toleration. As for the peasants, they welcomed the French-Bavarian soldiers as liberators because the patent of 1738 had increased yet again the *robot* and fanned disturbances in the country. They used the change of regime to attack the *robot* while proclaiming their loyalty to the new king. As had been the case at the beginning of the century in Hungary in the days of Ferenc II Rákóczi, the social question had been raised but neither of the two parties was able to take a resolute stance. On 13 July 1742 Belle-Isle published a patent promising liberty to all serfs who took up arms against the Austrians, a promise which Maria-Theresa also made to all peasants enlisting for three years in her armies. These, though, were merely responses to the immediate situation, without real import, and confirmed the impression Bohemia had given since 1680: the country was unstable and the peasants were badly treated and ready to revolt. The Czechs' readiness to turn traitor, which was significant for the depth of feeling it revealed rather than its level of organization, did not end in disaster; some sentences of death were passed but not carried out, some were disgraced and Karel David, one of the peasant leaders, was imprisoned for life. Maria-Theresa was more lenient than Ferdinand II and the rebellion of 1741 was not comparable to the revolt of 1618. The supporters of the *Afterkönig*, Charles Albert, received far lighter treatment than had those of the *Winterkönig*, Frederick V.

The state apparatus was not equal to the task demanded of it. In Bohemia, the upper clergy with the archbishop of Prague, Manderscheid, and the aristocrats in the government had been disloyal. Frederick of Prussia had been able to occupy Silesia so easily in 1740 because the province's fortresses had been inadequately garrisoned. The level of indiscipline defied belief. The pandours, the formidable horsemen raised on the Military Frontier, were really only interested in booty. At the Battle of Soor, they transformed their initial success into defeat because they attacked the king of Prussia's baggage trains instead of carrying out the mission with which they had been charged. Each regiment remained under the absolute authority of its colonel. Negligence, indiscipline and favouritism were rife and Maria-Theresa's army needed reform if it were again to become an essential element of Austrian power.

What was most important was that the sovereign was able to test the weaknesses of her administration and the limits to her power. The orders and their agents would need to be deprived of their exorbitant powers in implementing royal decrees and an administration would need to be created which was solely dependent on royal authority. Until then, it would be all but impossible to realize any measure contrary to the will of the Bohemian chancellor, who was the ally of the Czech aristocracy. In wartime, such unwillingness to cooperate impeded army recruitment and provisioning. The country's finances were in much greater disorder than in the previous century. Maria-Theresa had only survived because of English subsidies and the cabinet in London twice forced her to ratify her surrender of Silesia. In 1740 most of the ordinary revenues were mortgaged, the Habsburgs' credit was almost nil and the collection of direct taxes still depended on the cooperation of the Diets. The extraordinary powers had to be limited to the aristocracy. The bureaucracy was overburdened and its functioning complicated by the complexity of the councils and tribunals. Maria-Theresa was forced to put into effect the reforms which had been proposed to her grandfather and father but which they had always shied away from, Leopold I through negligence, Charles VI through necessity. The question remains whether she should be thought of as truly a 'revolutionary Habsburg'.

THE CHARACTER OF MARIA-THERESA (1717–80)[2]

Maria-Theresa, 'the last true Habsburg', for her descendants belonged to the House of Habsburg-Lorraine or, as was said in the eighteenth century, of 'Lorraine-Austria', was one of the most fascinating personalities the dynasty produced.

Born in 1717, she was soon destined by her father's wishes to exercise the responsibilities of government. Although the constitution of the Holy Roman Empire forced her to step aside in favour of her son, Joseph II, she retained effective control of the government of the monarchy until her death in 1780, despite his impatience. She is remembered for her long reign of forty years during which she exercised the full and complete authority conferred on her by the monarchical constitution.

Her education as a future ruler had, however, been neglected. Her father had not cared to give her any practical instruction in addition to her study of the humanities. She received a good musical education and some of her compositions have great merit, but she lacked her grandfather Leopold I's talent. She learned dancing and drawing. Her Jesuit instructor taught her Latin and the romance languages. She had a perfect mastery of French and her style is not without a certain charm even though her aristocratic notion of spelling would have appalled a nineteenth-century teacher. So great was her preference for French that she imposed it on the court at Vienna and so broke the tradition of Italian as the court language. She also acquired a good knowledge of history.

She was unquestionably fond of her husband, duke Francis Stephen of Lorraine, who was chosen for her by her father and who was a distant cousin (both were great-grandchildren of Ferdinand III). Francis Stephen appealed to his father-in-law because his influence within the Empire was limited and the marriage would not rouse disquiet among the more powerful German princes. Charles VI calculated that this relative weakness would ease his son-in-law's election as emperor. After the preliminaries to their marriage at Vienna, he was adamant that Francis Stephen should renounce Lorraine, and Bartenstein, the Austrian chancellor who came from Strasbourg, told him 'no renunciation, no marriage'. The wedding took place in 1736, when Maria-Theresa was nineteen, and lasted twenty-nine years. Her husband's death left her an inconsolable widow and she wore mourning throughout the remaining fifteen years of her life.

Now bearing the official title the grand duke of Tuscany, Francis Stephen was admitted to the privy conference and promoted to generalissimo by Charles VI, but he proved to be a poor statesman and a yet more indifferent commander. His wife quickly limited his sphere of action to the administration of the economy and finances, an area in which he excelled. Partly through the indemnities which he had received from France for his duchy, he increased the Habsburg-Lorraine family's private fortune by speculation, creating industries and by managing the revenues skilfully. At his death in 1765, the Habsburgs found themselves for the first time rich. They were to remain so until 1918. The emperor Francis I lost all interest in the Holy Roman Empire and his Tuscan patrimony and busied himself with the education of his children. He went hunting and stayed away from the meetings of the privy conference. To the rest of Europe he was the emperor, but for the Austrians he remained the prince consort.[3]

The pomp of the baroque belonged to the past and the imperial couple led a rather simpler life than their predecessors, stripped of stiff Spanish etiquette and of an almost bourgeois tenor. The marriage was rich in progeny, not least because it was a departure from the practice of marriage between close relatives. Maria-Theresa enjoyed good health, took regular exercise in the fresh air and was of a robust constitution, unlike the empress Margarita Theresa* who died of consumption at the age of twenty-one. She was good-looking and grew stout with age and the many pregnancies which helped to develop her image as the *Landesmutter* of her people, which is how she is remembered in Austria today. She liked to be portrayed in her family circle where she spent most of her time.

From 1738 to 1756 she gave birth to five sons and seven daughters. Four of her children did not take any political role: the archduke Charles-Joseph died young and three daughters remained unmarried; all the others, as in the past, served the political plans of the illustrious house and of a mother who wanted the best possible matches for her daughters. She truly believed that she would ensure happiness for the archduchess Marie Antoinette, whom she particularly loved, by securing for her the throne of France. She was convinced that she should save the best possible marriage for her and at the same time strengthen the Franco-Austrian alliance. When the young woman was settled at Versailles, she had her watched closely by her ambassador Mercy-Argenteau and showered her with maternal advice, but also gave her precise instructions to defend Austria's interests which amounted to direct interference in the affairs of an ally.

Maria-Theresa believed in strengthening the monarchy's new system of alliances by concluding more marriages with the Bourbons. Maria Carolina married Ferdinand, king of Naples, and was soon able to take hold of the reins of government. Maria Amelia became duchess of Parma and Maria Christina, the wife of duke Albert of Saxe-Teschen, was, according to long tradition, entrusted with the government of the Netherlands. Archduke Ferdinand, by his marriage to the heiress of the house of Este, founded a secondary line at Modena and helped to strengthen Austrian hegemony in northern Italy, while the younger son, Maximilian Francis, renewed an old Habsburg tradition by becoming archbishop-elector of Cologne and directed from Bonn an enlightened policy which his brothers Joseph and Leopold would not have disowned. Joseph II and Leopold II were great rulers, worthy successors to their mother, and both illustrate how ill-founded are the clichés depicting the House of Austria as obscurantist and reactionary.

Maria-Theresa was pragmatic and had no time for theories. She adopted as her device the motto *Justitia et clementia*, and took a firm position on matters of religion. The last representative of the Styrian branch, she was too fervent a Catholic to proclaim religious toleration in her hereditary lands. Conscious of her duties and anxious to ensure respect for the authority of the state she was creating, she proved opposed to tyranny and despotism in any form. Her humanity and kindness won her the love of her subjects, including the Hungarians.

---

* Translator's note: Margarita Theresa, daughter of Philip IV of Spain and wife of emperor Leopold I. See vol. I, pp. 306, 350.

Her most conspicuous virtue during a particularly difficult decade was her courage in adversity and, like her grandfather Leopold, her tenacity. She impressed those around her by her vigour and great decisiveness, a trait of character which her predecessors had lacked. By her personal qualities, she saved the monarchy in 1741 when there was the risk that her patrimony might be reduced to Hungary alone. For a second time she revealed her aptitude as a statesman, imposing the fundamental reforms proposed by Haugwitz before the signing of the Peace of Aix-la-Chapelle. It was vital that she profit from circumstances and put an end to the omnipotence of the orders which had nearly been the Habsburgs' ruin. This reform was essential for the Austrian monarchy to survive and to be straightened out. Without it, the honourable settlement of the War of the Austrian Succession risked being a postponement of its inevitable demise.

HAUGWITZ'S REFORMS (1749)[4]

Count Friedrich Haugwitz, the son of a Saxon general of humble birth, tried to apply to Austria the methods which had been tried and tested in the Prussian state. A convert to Catholicism, he was distinguished by his assiduousness and his cameralist education. He withdrew the Estates' right to collect taxes but left them the privilege of debating the total sum. This was a major reform which he had already implemented in Silesia amid the general disorder and in Carinthia where he was appointed extraordinary commissioner in 1747. He was convinced that leaving the orders to administer the finances was defective as a system and that the lands returned only a fraction of what they were capable. He ensured that the empress and other privy councillors were brought round to his point of view.

Haugwitz presented his plan at the beginning of 1748. Maria-Theresa needed to maintain 108 000 men on a peace-footing and to have an annual budget of 15 million florins to put the finances in order and to support the army. He managed to wrest financial administration from the orders and to put it in the hands of the central government. The project met violent opposition from the aristocracy, especially the Bohemian chancellor, count Friedrich Harrach, who wanted to restore the financial autonomy of the individual states. The great confrontation took place at the cabinet meeting of 29 January 1748. For the first time a councillor in office proposed a plan in accordance with the proposals made by reformers during the reign of Leopold I. It was the empress who took the decision to follow Haugwitz's advice against the unanimous opposition of the other councillors, Harrach, Kinsky, Colloredo and Khevenhüller. The Diets listened to Haugwitz and agreed to pay a quota of 14 million florins over ten years.

After this initial success, Haugwitz turned his attention to institutional reform by separating administrative affairs from the exercise of justice, according to the modern principle. This went against the supremacy which the judiciary had preserved in the governments of the *ancien régime*. The reform created two new institutions, the Directory of Administration and Finance and a Supreme Judiciary. The former, the *Directorium in publicis et cameralibus*, was divided into seven sections directed by two privy councillors (Bohemia and Moravia) and presided over by Haugwitz. The Privy Conference remained but its advice was purely formal. In this way, the Czech and the German-speaking hereditary lands were united; the Cisleithania of 1867 was already on the horizon since Hungary kept its own institutions and Lombardy and the Netherlands remained autonomous. The Supreme Judiciary (*Oberste Justizstelle*), presided over by the chancellor of Austria, Seilern, acted as the court of appeal for all the hereditary lands.

The chancelleries of Austria and Bohemia were thus stripped of their financial and judicial roles and the office of chancellor of Bohemia became purely honorary. Bohemia was reduced to the status of a province within a federal state. The role of the Estates was reduced and they had nothing more to do than vote the contributions proposed. After 1750, it is possible to speak of an Austrian bureaucracy. The reform was badly received by the Viennese public who regretted the reduction in the Austrian chancellery's authority and came to detest Haugwitz, whose initiatives threatened the status quo.

Reform in the army proceeded in the same spirit. Contributions were handed over entirely to the central government and taxpayers had to provide nothing but lodging for the military. The practice of giving contributions in kind, which had been so valued by the orders and peasants but which had provoked so much abuse, was abandoned. The different lands no longer had to provide contingents of recruits since this task now devolved upon the authorities in Vienna. In 1749 Bohemia requested the stationing of permanent garrisons since the regiments now promised to be a source of profit rather than a drain on resources. The money paid in contributions would be recovered through provisions, forage, horses and material for soldiers' uniforms.

To transform the officer corps and to assure the homogeneity of the army as well as the competence of its regulars, Maria-Theresa installed at Wiener Neustadt a military school on the Prussian or French model which until 1918 was to provide regulars for the imperial army. In the same spirit, she gave the Jesuits the palace La Favorite and so founded the famous Theresianum where economics, mathematics, mechanics and architecture were studied in Vienna. Here the future recruits to the army and bureaucracy were educated in the new disciplines rather than the humanist programme of traditional colleges. The creation of a Hungarian guard forced the young nobles to leave their lands for city life and in this way the Hungarian aristocracy encountered the Enlightenment and the French philosophes. In every case, the ruler established the principle that birth alone was insufficient and that without education the nobility was unfit to serve the state.

THE BIRTH OF THE MODERN STATE[5]

The reforms of 1749 were nothing short of a revolution within the Austrian monarchy since they marked the birth of the Austrian state and confirmed the existence of the kingdom of Hungary as entirely autonomous, distinct from the Austro-Bohemian complex.

The union of the chancelleries of Bohemia and Austria ended, not so much Bohemia's independence, as its complete autonomy, and the kingdom was truly integrated into the hereditary lands. It was the end of a long process of change, for Ferdinand II in 1627 had not dared take so bold a step. The monarchy now had a solid core which would provide the Habsburgs with the means for their great schemes. This integration was made much easier because Bohemia was cut off from one of its essential parts, Silesia, and because its weight relative to Austria was somewhat diminished.

By taking away the collection of contributions from the orders, Haugwitz deprived them of a fundamental element of their real power. Small executive commissions, of which the members were appointed and paid by the crown, replaced officers elected and paid by the orders. The task of these *Deputationen* was to control the apportionment and raising of contributions and to make sure that what was collected was handed over efficiently to the army. They also took care of payment for winter quarters and the provisioning of troops. The execution of these tasks in the Bohemian crown lands was delegated to 'the captains of the circle' who were appointed by the crown and the institution was extended to all the hereditary lands. The *Statthalterei* (government) of Bohemia was abolished on 2 May 1749 and turned into a simple court of appeal. Similar measures were taken in the hereditary lands where the councils within Austria were dissolved. The Privy Council at Graz was transformed into a court of appeal, the council of war was suppressed and the chamber of accounts became a simple Deputation. The Tyrol, which was fiercely jealous of its autonomy, lost its privy council and chamber of accounts, survivals from a previous age.

The number of officials doubled between 1740 and 1763, rising from 5 000 to 10 000 and reaching 20 000 at the end of Maria-Theresa's reign. The Austrian bureaucracy, so celebrated in the nineteenth century, came into being. The officials' main role was the surveillance of seigneurial and municipal officers, who were as numerous as the royal officers, of whom there were at least 10 000. The bureaucracy remained concentrated at Vienna where 1 000 were employed at the court, and in the various capitals. Bureaucrats received regular salaries, an average salary being 400 florins a year, and in most cases on retirement a pension, although this was a favour rather than a right. There was no definite criterion for recruitment but a minimum of education was necessary and the lower positions were open to educated commoners. Administration became a path to social advance, especially as the sovereign readily granted ennoblement. These new nobles were not welcomed by the old aristocratic families and little by little formed the 'second society'.

There was another revolutionary aspect to Haugwitz's reform: peasants could appeal to the king now that they were no longer subject to seigneurial justice. The seigneur ceased to be sovereign in his domain, even though for practical and financial reasons the Austrian peasant, like the French peasant in the eighteenth century, was content with the sentence pronounced by the seigneurial court and did not launch an appeal. The sovereign, nevertheless, became the supreme justice.

These arrangements did not apply in Hungary which kept its particular status. 'King' Maria-Theresa remained mindful of the aid which the Hungarian nobility had brought her in 1741, and many years later, in 1774, told the archduke Maximilian that it was the Hungarians to whom she was indebted for being on the throne of her forefathers. In 1763 the kingdom was required to pay 4 million florins when the direct contributions from Austria-Bohemia amounted to 9.9 million florins and the total revenue of the monarchy, including Lombardy and the Netherlands, was 48 million florins. Hungary paid but a small part of the tax Maria-Theresa raised from her subjects. The session of the Diet which met in 1764–65 ended in a government defeat because the government had tried to abrogate the fiscal privileges of the nobility.

The royal bureaucracy in Hungary was limited to the services of the government of Pressburg and Buda, to the mines and customs. Maria-Theresa strengthened the prerogatives of the administration elected by the counties and guaranteed the nobility's power. All the officers were elected for three years from among the wealthy nobility living in the county. In 1780 the orders employed in total 4 400 persons and the crown 2 500. Although Maria-Theresa entrusted the orders with the administration of the counties, she rarely summoned the Diet and elected only two palatines, leaving the office vacant after 1765.

The succession crisis had been a serious warning for the Austrian monarchy, revealing to the world the weaknesses of a state apparatus which previous rulers had failed to modernize. The fortunes of the House of Austria became identical with those of the sovereign herself who showed courage and a rare presence of mind. She owed her survival to the unconditional support given her by the Hungarians, but also to the divisions among the rival claimants and the support of Britain which did not want to see France use Charles VII to exercise its hegemony over the whole continent.

The crisis led to a good programme of reform but it also left a gaping wound. Silesia had been lost and the balance of power had shifted in the German world where the monarchy's preponderance would henceforth be challenged by Frederick II's Prussia.

NOTES AND REFERENCES

1. Victor Tapié, *L'Europe de Marie-Thérèse*, Paris, 1973, pp. 43–80.
2. Alfred von Arneth, *Geschichte Maria-Theresias*, Vienna, 1863–79. Peter Reinhold, *Maria-Theresia*, Frankfurt, 1979.
3. Friedrich Walter, *Männer um Maria-Theresia*, Vienna, 1951.
4. Friedrich Walter, *Die österreichische Zentralverwaltung in der Zeit Maria-Theresias*, Vienna, 1938 and *Die theresianische Staatsreform von 1749*, Vienna, 1958.
5. P. G. M. Dickson, *Finance and Government under Maria-Theresa, 1740–1780*, 2 vols, Oxford, 1987. See 'Government', vol. I, pp. 205–486.

CHAPTER FIVE

The Age of the Enlightenment and Austrian Society

Changes in the intellectual life of the Danubian lands were already apparent in 1750, but the age of the Enlightenment was relatively brief in the region, lasting from 1770 to 1790, from the last decade of Maria-Theresa's reign to the end of that of her son, Joseph II.

The Enlightenment, the intellectual or philosophical movement known in German as *die Aufklärung*, questioned the very foundations of established society. In politics, the emphasis was upon strengthening the state and developing economic programmes. In religion, it challenged the orthodoxy of the different Christian confessions and gave importance to the role of heterodox currents, Pietism among Lutherans, Jansenism among Catholics and Methodism among Anglicans. The idea of 'happiness' emerged in ethics and combined with knowledge and love of humanity. Epistemology and natural philosophy replaced metaphysics in the sciences. In literature, fantasy was less valued and poetry was in decline. Ideas became more important than fiction and the concept of literature expanded. All these developments reflected the determining role of critical thought which stole a march upon tradition and respect for authority.

The ideas of the Enlightenment appeared in philosophy, the sciences and literature and were slow to be adopted. Winter has claimed that in the German world, the tendencies which prepared the ground for the Enlightenment were already noticeable from 1650 onwards.[1] The struggle against 'confessionalism', official churches linked to monarchical absolutism, should be understood as a manifestation of the Enlightenment. This was especially the case with Pietism in Prussia and Jansenism in Austria. Winter also emphasizes the influence of Leibniz, Samuel Pufendorf and Christian Wolf, and also Eugene of Savoy, who was a champion of modern science and set an example for others to follow.

A distinction should be made between attempts in Danubian Europe to modernize old ideology, of which Jansenism is a conspicuous example, and attempts, fraught with difficulty, to introduce truly new concepts. German, French and English influences all played a part, but the philosophical movement in Italy, especially in Milan, left a particularly profound mark upon the development of ideas in Austria. The Habsburgs' acquisition of part of Italy brought them particular benefits because it strengthened cultural links between the Italian peninsula and the Danubian lands which increasingly ceased to be a simple province in the German world subservient to the Protestant traditions of Prussia and Hanover.

The Enlightenment affected only a very narrow elite. There was no bourgeoisie to assist the Habsburgs in their reform programmes; instead support came from the emergent bureaucracy being created by Maria-Theresa and from the supranational army. The creation of a corps of educated officers played an important part, as did individuals within the traditional elites, the clergy and nobility, which explains the prime importance of freemasonry. Every far-reaching reform ultimately depended on the goodwill of the sovereign.

Problems of religion, education and national culture occupied the 'enlightened' rather more than political and economic theories. To a certain extent, this was what gave the Austrian monarchy its originality.

JANSENISM[2]

Jansenism in eighteenth-century Austria had two main characteristics: the moral rigour which distinguished the anti-molinists who challenged the real, or supposed, laxist views of the Jesuits, and the serious study of the Bible and Church fathers, a trend which was in keeping with the rejection of medieval and modern scholasticism. The Aristotelianism of the Jesuits was cast aside in favour of Cartesianism, which had at last been recognized. The history of the Church underwent revision. The Middle Ages were no longer held to have been Christianity's heyday but rather an era of barbarism. The Austrian Jansenists did not admire the austere Augustinianism and doctrine of grace of Cornelius Jansen, the bishop of Ypres. The appeal lay not on the theological but the intellectual and moral plain as a way of breaking the Jesuits' monopoly.

The Jansenists of the Habsburg monarchy, no less than their French brethren, placed central importance upon the sacrament of penance and would often refuse absolution to those who had made their confession. They were strongly opposed to the practice, introduced by the Jesuits, of frequent communion and also to private masses and the many little acts of devotion which were the mainstay of popular piety. They wanted to restrict the cults of saints and exaggerated devotions to the Virgin Mary. They rejected the rosary and the devotion to the Sacred Heart of Jesus so favoured by the Jesuits. In short, they were opposed to the *pietas austriaca* which the Styrian branch of the House of Habsburg had developed. The Jansenists criticized baroque bombast, wanted to strip the churches of all baroque ornamentation, and after 1780 favoured neoclassicism as a style. Strict in the extreme in the practice of their daily lives, they condemned on principle plays, balls and festivals as well as pilgrimages. They might have seemed at one with the Puritans but, unlike the latter, they did not show any interest in public life and wordly success achieved through hard work.

Jansenism, in all these respects, was completely contrary to the prevailing currents in Vienna, among both the clergy and the laity, who were deeply influenced by the Society of Jesus and by baroque devotional practice. The confraternities which the Jesuits promoted were still flourishing at the end of the eighteenth century in the smallest rural parishes as much as in Vienna where, in 1780, there were 103 such sodalities. The members, who were drawn from all sections of society, paid dues which, with donations, provided confraternities with a modest income to pay for priests outside the parish to say mass and also for the preachers who gave the sermons on the feasts of Epiphany, Corpus Christi and St Michael. The confraternity Remembrance, active from 1690 to 1783, for example, embraced Italians of all social origins, bankers, artisans and aristocrats, who venerated a little statue of the Immaculate Conception in the church of St Leopold. It was rich. Its members gave 15 000 florins in 1783, and it paid for a preacher for each sermon.

The Jansenists found support among conservatives who suffered from the Jesuits' monopoly, built gradually in the previous century with the dynasty's complicity. Early in the eighteenth century, count Sporck introduced and distributed Jansenist literature from the printing press which he had had installed at Kuks, his castle in Bohemia. During Charles VI's reign, he had had serious disagreements with the civil and religious authorities and was only pardoned because of his status as a noble descended from a general who had served on the Habsburg side in the Thirty Years War. It was while staying in France on his *Kavaliertour* that Sporck had first encountered this new vision of Christian spirituality. The prince of Salm, tutor and later chief minister of Joseph I, did not hide his Jansenist sympathies. Prince Eugene and chancellor Bartenstein were similarly well-disposed. All these nobles were influenced by the time they had spent in France or at Louvain. The empress Elizabeth Christina, a princess of Brunswick-Wolfenbüttel and the mother of the empress Maria-Theresa, had been raised within the traditions of the Augsburg Confession and only converted to Catholicism at the time of her marriage. A Catholic from convenience rather than conviction, she always distanced herself from the excesses of *pietas austriaca*. Jansenism offered all these grand figures a religiosity which could replace the effusions of baroque piety. The basis of their devotion was the *Catéchisme de Montpellier* of Colbert de Croissy, the bishop of Montpellier, and of M. Pouget, a work which was circulated widely in France.

Paradoxically, it was Rome and the Collegium Germanicum which had contributed most to the evolution of the Austrian episcopate and to the success of Jansenism.

REFORMKATHOLIZISMUS

Reform Catholicism (*Reformkatholizismus*) first appeared around 1720 in circles at Rome where there was a reaction against the domination of the Jesuits who had become the scapegoats for all recent errors. The movement favoured *sana dottrina* (holy doctrine) and was hostile to the small acts of devotion, exaggerations of baroque piety and superstitions which were all rolled together in manifestations of popular piety.

The War of the Spanish Succession had promoted good relations between Austria and the Italian peninsula, where a neo-Ghibelline party had emerged recalling the Ghibellines of the Middle Ages who had supported the emperor and opposed the pope. The War of Comacchio in 1708, during which imperial troops invaded the papal states, showed that the emperor Joseph I, as good a Catholic as he was, was prepared to defend his interests against a papacy which readily muddled spiritual concerns with partisan alliances. Some Italians saw the emperor as the only serious counterweight to the Curia's ambitions.

At this stage, Muratori, librarian to the duke of Modena, had a decisive effect upon *Reformkatholizismus*. His treatise *Della carità cristiana* (On Christian Charity) was slow to become known but became widely circulated and was translated into Czech and Hungarian. *Delle regolate devozione delli cristiani*, his work on devotion published in 1747 in Venice, had an enormous impact after 1760 in Austria. A Latin translation was published in Vienna in 1759, and German and Czech translations were printed in 1776 and 1778 in Augsburg and Prague respectively. Creator of a spiritual revival related to Jansenism, Muratori contributed to Josephinism's success but he was not its creator.

The *sana dottrina* was a moderate current which from 1720 onwards exerted a gentle but profound influence in Italy. Like seventeenth-century Jansenism, it advocated a return to the true sources of Christianity, scripture and the Church fathers, and it too rejected scholasticism. The current infiltrated the Collegium Germanicum at Rome where priests from the Habsburg lands were prepared for prestigious careers; all the Austrian bishops at that time had studied there. In this way, the *sana dottrina* influenced the 'reforming bishops', the counts Thun, Firmian, Waldstein, Schaffgotsch and the Hallweils. It played an important part in the education of two archbishops of Vienna, count Trautson (1751–57) and count Migazzi (1757–99) who retained his position of eminence under four succesive rulers and was able to have a considerable effect upon the evolution of the Church in Austria.

Migazzi encouraged openness by breaking the Jesuits' intellectual monopoly. He founded diocesan seminaries which trained a generation of Jansenist prelates who quickly secured prominent positions as canons of St Stephen's cathedral in Vienna, chairs in theology at the university and places on the commission for censorship. When, in 1765, the archbishop realized that he had gone too far and wanted to retract, it was too late. Maria-Theresa and the other members of the imperial family had Jansenist spiritual directors. The spirit of reform was sweeping through Vienna. Migazzi, openly disquieted, after 1780 adopted a purely reactionary stance.

THE REFORM OF THE CENSORSHIP[3]

It was Maria-Theresa who reformed the censorship commission and took from the Jesuits the monopoly with which Ferdinand I and Ferdinand II, to hasten the triumph of the Counter-Reformation, had entrusted them. Since the sixteenth century, the magistracy of Vienna had been deprived of its authority to police the book trade. In 1620 a reform made censorship habitual by instituting the *Bücherkommission* under the presidency of the bishop or his vicar-general and with many posts occupied by Jesuits. The commission had authority to inspect bookshops and to search private houses for any 'bad books', books on the Index. Civil legislation was harsh. During the sixteenth century, possession of a book on the Index was a capital offence. The decision to found the commission resulted in the total submission of the individual to the authorities. This, at least, was the case in Lower Austria, but research by Élisabeth Ducreux has shown that in Bavaria in the first half of the eighteenth century there were numerous legal actions against individuals who had kept Protestant devotional works.

By 1750, the Jesuits were being vigorously threatened. They were criticized for their stranglehold on intellectual life, their prejudice and incompetence, and as teachers they were no longer excellent. Some faithful Catholics thought that the *ratio studiorum*, no less than the Jesuits' attachment to neo-Aristotelianism, was unsuited to the needs of the time. The Society of Jesus was seen as having exorbitant powers on the book commission since they censored works on medicine as well as theology. After the turmoil which had all but brought about the dissolution of the monarchy, society needed to be opened up to currents in western thought.

Gerard van Swieten, doctor and advisor to Maria-Theresa, did not have great difficulty convincing her that the commission should be modified. Originally from the Netherlands and a convert to Catholicism, he exercised considerable influence over the sovereign. He played a role similar to that taken by Becher with Leopold I, had the title of special advisor, but held no other official position than that of the empress's personal physician. In 1759 Maria-Theresa exercised her authority, deprived the Jesuits of their control over the censorship and placed the commission under her direct control. She appointed van Swieten as president, and reserved the right to decide in cases of litigation. Belles-lettres were no longer subject to censorship. Van Swieten was responsible for censoring philosophical and medical works and Fr. Debiel and Fr. Franz, two Jesuits who favoured openness, censored theological publications. The commission was limited to censoring works from abroad and allowed Jansenist literature to circulate.

Maria-Theresa, probably through her mother's influence during her youth, looked benignly on the Jansenists. As Klingenstein has shown, this reform amounted to the secularization and liberalization of the censorship. After 1765, almost any book could be bought at Vienna, although visitors still had their luggage carefully searched. Censorship was not abolished during this phase of the monarchy's openness to foreign influences (1765–90) and Joseph II used it to promote his own interests. Maria-Theresa had subtly resumed, as was her way, control of intellectual life. The authorities had wide-reaching powers to direct opinion and, when desired, to ward off supposedly corrupting foreign influences.

JANSENIST CIRCLES

The small but influential circle which lay behind *Reformkatholizismus* was made up, as Peter Hersche has shown, of a few strong characters. They came, as was so often the case, from a variety of backgrounds and not one was Viennese. The canon von Stock, the Swiss Blarer, the abbot of Terme and the Silesian Wittola who translated Bossuet, Arnauld and Nicole into German, and Ramaggini from Rome gathered at the home of canon Ignaz Müller, the provost of the College of St Dorothea, near the Hofburg. Müller acted as confessor to Maria-Theresa from 1765 to 1780 and was thoroughly disliked by Joseph II, who thought of him as 'the head of the Jansenist sect'. The canon did, however, enjoy the support of De Haen, the Dutch doctor who succeeded van Swieten as the empress's and later Joseph II's personal physician. Eschewing strident proselytizing, he acted by exercising a discreet influence upon individuals, in particular recommending the reading of 'good books', in other words books from Port Royal.* He did not publish any writings and, lacking the temperament of a leader, did not draw disciples in the strict sense, but even so the circle of St Dorothea exerted a decisive influence in Viennese cultural milieux. Reserved and dispassionate, Müller never held an official position and was content to play the role of personal advisor to the sovereign. His influence declined sharply after his death, as did that of Austrian Jansenism which was very different from the state Catholicism which Joseph II wished to impose. Even though both currents were in common opposition to baroque piety and the ultramontane party, and espoused simplified practices, moral rigour and recourse to reason, their sensibilites diverged. Not the least incompatibility was the Jansenists' hostility to state control of religion.

'The sect' divided in two directions in the face of Joseph II's reforms. Some clergy accepted a subordinate position, and indeed the excesses and stupidities to which the emperor subjected them in the mistaken belief that the two movements were closely allied. Many other clergy understood that their own moderate reformism had led to the extremes of Josephism and so, like cardinal Migazzi, took refuge in conservatism.

After 1784, Joseph II no longer had a Jansenist spiritual director and the following year he appointed an ex-Jesuit, father Diesbach, as confessor to the archduke Francis, the future emperor Francis II. The leading members of 'the sect' returned to Italy and the *Nouvelles ecclésiastiques*, the Jansenist periodical published at Utrecht, no longer had any readers. The elite turned towards the philosophy of the Enlightenment while the people continued to demonstrate their devotion to baroque piety. The Jesuits and the clergy of the Counter-Reformation, despite the difficulties they had faced, had made a deep and lasting impression on popular sensibilities.

---

* Translator's note: the convent at Port Royal, near Paris, was founded in 1637 by du Vergier, an intimate friend of Jansen, and was the most important centre for Jansenism in France until 1665 when the community was dispersed.

BOOKS AND PERIODICALS

Jansenist literature was initially smuggled into the country, but before long the great Viennese bookdealer Trattner took charge of its distribution. A Jansenist sympathizer, he took part in the reform of the book-dealing commission from which he greatly benefited. This journeyman printer who rose to become the leading publisher of Maria-Theresa's reign, was a strict observant Catholic. He opposed the Jesuits because they published in their own houses and so were competitors. He combined finer feelings with a good business sense and, according to Hersche, was responsible for publishing at least a quarter of all Jansenist literature. Of the Jansenist writers, all except Trassler at Brno in Moravia were based in Vienna. It was Hörling who in 1785 took charge of the *Wiener Kirchenzeitungen* (Vienna Church News), the Austrian version of the *Nouvelles ecclésiastiques* published at Utrecht by count Dupac de Bellegarde.

Trattner published large numbers of German translations of French devotional literature with a Jansenist character. He printed as diverse works as the *Catéchisme de Montpellier*, the writings of the abbé Duguet, and Pierre Nicole's *Essais moraux*, as well as books in Latin of a similar character, including the works of Opstraet, and in French, Nicolas de Fontaine's *L'Histoire du Vieux et du Nouveau Testament*.

Hersche has not investigated the spread of *Reformkatholicizmus* among the lower clergy. It appears, however, that the dichotomy between court life, between a polyglot, cosmopolitan elite and the literate commoners, the petite bourgeoisie of purely German culture, was greater than ever. The members of the court could read the new philosophical works in the original language and so more or less escaped the constraints imposed by the censorship. The Viennese outside the court, however, depended on translations and it was they who benefited most in the Josephinist era from the opening up of frontiers and the liberalization of censorship. Works of philosophy were, though, rarely translated and only reached a wider audience through the theatre, for which the Viennese were especially enthusiastic. Sermons rather than reading the Bible were the mainstay of theology for the Viennese, while their philosophy came through the intermediary of plays adapted from the French theatre of obscure authors expounding a philosophical theme. Wangermann[4] found artisans touched by the ideas of the Enlightenment but Wernick's catalogue makes it quite clear that the ideas of the Enlightenment reached at the most only a limited circle outside the court.[5]

The Hungarian aristocrats who appeared at Vienna after 1760 could read the writings of the French philosophers in the original and were strongly influenced by French culture. The inventories of large private libraries reveal a high proportion of works in French: count Csáky had 5 000 French books, while 5 000 of the 8 500 volumes in count Sztaráy's library, and 6 000 of the 15 000 in the Hedérvary library, were in French. There were twenty-seven Hungarian magnates at Vienna, who represented twenty of the 108 aristocratic lineages of Hungarian origin, as distinct from the *indigenae*, the 205 landed aristocratic families of non-Hungarian extraction. Conspicuous among these enlightened magnates were Ferenc Esterházy, Petár Baloch, the two Orczy brothers, the Almassys, the Forgachs, the Batthyánys, the Váys and the Festetichs. The two most celebrated were Samuel Teleki from Transylvania who assembled a remarkable library in his castle at Márosvásarhely, and count Fekete who corresponded with Voltaire. In 1780 it was the height of fashion among Hungarian magnates to be Voltairean, while the influence of Goethe and Lessing was growing.

The first serious periodicals were published and a little later started to appear in Hungary, adapted to the country's needs. After 1780, the *Hungarian Courier* was published twice weekly at Poszony with a run of 500. Of the subscribers, 275 have been positively identified and of these 145 were aristocrats and members of the middle gentry (*bene possessionati*) and 130 were gentry practising an intellectual profession. The newspaper's editor, Mátyás Rát, did not hide his intention of dragging Hungary out of its backwardness and stimulating the educated public's interest in reading. From 1786, the *Hungarian Messenger*, a journal in Hungarian, was published at Vienna. In 1789 the *Hungarian Mercury*, the Buda newspaper, ceased publication and for the next twenty years the Austrian capital was the centre for Hungarian publishing. Szacsvay, the editor of the *Hungarian Messenger*, was a confirmed supporter of the Enlightenment and had close links with a secretary in Joseph II's cabinet and with members of the Hungarian guard who were all leaders in the movement for a Hungarian national literary revival. His journal was well-informed and had a high intellectual tenor. In 1787 it had 370 subscribers. It enjoyed the emperor's support and had no qualms about attacking the Catholic Church in Hungary or about taking issue with a capuchin in Vienna who had preached against it. In 1789 it kept its readers informed about events in Paris and as early as 9 May saw the summoning of the Estates General at Versailles as the logical consequence of the American Revolution.

What is striking is the small number of subscribers, less than 500, to each of the two leading journals, the *Hungarian Courier* and the *Hungarian Messenger*. These, with the *Pressburg Gazette* which appeared in German from 1764 and which was less informed, made up the sum of the press in Hungary during the Enlightenment. Through coffee-houses and reading-rooms, these papers reached a slightly wider public, but even so their impact was limited to an elite of nobles and intellectuals.

THE SPREAD OF THE ENLIGHTENMENT

Masonic lodges probably played a greater part in the Habsburg monarchy in propagating the new ideas than they did anywhere else in Europe. The masons in this most Catholic of countries enjoyed protection from leading figures in the state. Prince Eugene had almost certainly been initiated, as had count Sporck, the protector of the Jansenists, and by 1735 there was a masonic lodge in Prague. Francis Stephen of Lorraine had been initiated in 1731 during his visit to the Netherlands. Strong conviction and a reasoned decision made him the protector of freemasonry in the Empire. He refused to apply the papal bull of condemnation issued by Clement XIV and it was probably he who first interested Joseph II in philosophy. Until 1790, the freemasons were able to find protectors to ward off any impulses towards persecution which the pious Maria-Theresa, who was sensitive to the Holy See's repeated condemnations of freemasonry, might have. Her husband was simply following the precepts of his grandfather, Charles V of Lorraine, the liberator of Buda who in his political testimony of 1687 recommended resisting the pope, no longer tolerating excommunications in temporal matters, defying the Jesuits and excluding all *religieux* from the Privy Council, since 'they were a type of man which never did a sovereign any good and was destined only to do him harm'.

The first lodge in Vienna, The Three Cannons, was founded in 1742 as a daughter lodge of The Three Skeletons in Breslau. It was closed the following year on the orders of the empress who, despite Francis Stephen's involvement, applied strictly the bull *In eminenti*. Austrian freemasonry was divided into many currents: The Brethren of Saint John, The Filiation of High Grades, The Asian Brethren, The Enlightened. It spread disquiet because of its secretive character and its strange rites. Freemasonry attracted more aristocrats than members of the bourgeoisie and despite its egalitarian principles it was not in the least revolutionary. Concerned with fraternity and human happiness, it played a part in disseminating philosophical ideas among the elites of the Habsburg monarchy. Joseph II was initiated and was surrounded by freemasons who collaborated with his reform policies and supported him against conservative opposition. It was during his ten-year reign that freemasonry reached its apogee.

The emperor's sympathies did not prevent him mistrusting freemasonry. In 1785, probably under the influence of prince Dietrichstein, who became the grand master of official freemasonry, and Ignaz von Born, an eminent mineralogist from Prague who was promoted to the Aulic Council, he promulgated a decree regulating masonic lodges. The decree obliged the masons to regroup within a single lodge in each provincial capital and to have no more than 180 members, less than 3 000 in total. Every meeting was to be announced in advance through the civil authorities and the public was encouraged to denounce secret meetings. These restrictions did not prevent the decree from representing a marked advance upon the interdictions formulated by Maria-Theresa. Joseph II feared that the freemasons constituted a state within the state and that, because of their international character, they could be transformed into the agents of a foreign power. He had supported The Enlightened, who were a force in Bavaria, at the time when he sought to annex the principality, but later turned to persecute them in particular.

The emperor knew about the activities of the Viennese lodge True Harmony (*Zur wahren Eintract*) which kept archives and published them in the *Journal of Freemasons*. Ignaz von Born was master of the lodge which had several eminent men among its members, including Joseph von Sonnenfels. An eminent lawyer of Jewish extraction, Sonnenfels secured the abolition of torture as part of the penal system and participated in compiling the Josephine code which found its definitive expression in the civil code of 1811. Doctors, writers and composers, most notably Haydn and Mozart, were members of the lodge. It was for the festivals of True Harmony that Mozart composed his masonic music, including a cantata in honour of Ignaz von Born and a funeral ode commissioned on the occasion of the death of two brethren, the duke of Mecklenburg-Schwerin and prince Esterházy.

THE PRINCIPAL THEMES OF REFLECTION

Enlightened absolutism was the basis of the political philosophy of Sonnenfels, Gerard van Swieten and Karl von Zinzendorf.[6] Their position was bred of pragmatism, although they were well-acquainted with the works of Rousseau and the great theorists before him, Hobbes, Locke and Montesquieu. Constitutional government for the latter three signified government by law without any reference to democracy or the principle of the separation of powers. For Sonnenfels, the prime responsibility of the state was to guarantee the correct distribution of wealth among the social groups. He expounded the idea of the 'vital minimum' for a poor peasant after paying property and state tax. For this reason, he criticized the abuses of traditional society, of the feudal system, of appointments being made on the basis of birth rather than ability. The abuses stemming from social inequality undermined the cardinal virtue, patriotism. An enlightened monarchy, as the guarantor of social progress, was the only conceivable form of government in Austria. For Sonnenfels, this was more than a matter of imitating the English monarchy in a system where the state assemblies were bulwarks of conservatism. There was a paradox in following Montesquieu's theory of intermediary powers since Montesquieu had been inspired by the Hungarian model which he had encountered during his long sojourn in Central Europe. All the leading men of Maria-Theresa's reign were convinced that it was the weakness of the state that had marginalized the Habsburgs in Europe in the face of competition from Great Britain and France.

Maria-Theresa remained very devout. She did not, however, in marked contrast to her grandfather Leopold I, consider the spiritual welfare of her subjects the supreme goal of government. The material well-being of her subjects concerned her even though she did not confuse the truth, as taught by the Church, and error, as propagated by the churches of the Reformation and the freemasons. The education of the masses and the elites would have to be improved in order to assure the happiness of her subjects. The nobles would need to be inculcated with philosophical principles to fit them for state service and to transform young bloods into conscientious bureaucrats. Most of the high officials of the period 1770–80 were disciples of Sonnenfels who held a chair in political science and taught at the Theresianum. Robert Kann, however, was right when he remarked that the results were mediocre.[7] It created executives devoid of critical faculties and imagination.

Sonnenfels and Karl von Zinzendorf were chiefly concerned with the economy as the guarantor of progress and social advance. In the west, thinkers were preoccupied with the development of political rights, but in Austria and Germany the main desire was for economic prosperity. Neo-mercantilism, the theories of the physiocrats and of Adam Smith were seen as the means to create the middle class which was so critically absent in Austrian society. The inspiration to curtail or overturn feudal society came from the French physiocrats Quesnay and Turgot, and from Adam Smith.

Sonnenfels placed great importance upon demography. Inspired less by the theories of Smith than the populationist theories of Heinrich von Justi, he thought that a large population was the precondition for power, security and wealth. Providence would never create more human beings than it could nourish. The advance of the economy should not be abandoned to the caprices of the market but controlled by the state, which should assure growth while avoiding uncontrollable inflation. Sonnenfels drew attention as early as 1769 to the exodus from the countryside. He wanted to prevent it by creating industries the length and breadth of the country and by establishing colleges in the small towns. He glorified the peasant's life as the most ancient and useful but rejected the physiocrats' cardinal idea that agriculture was the essential sector of economic life. He insisted, instead, upon the importance of industry. When conditions were favourable, the state should encourage births, repress abortions and illegitimate births and forbid religious celibacy. The citizen for his part should abstain from idleness and dishonesty and eschew emigration. In 1767 he clashed with cardinal Migazzi because he wanted to reduce the number of days off work because of religious festivals, a programme supported by Maria-Theresa. He waged an incessant war against serfdom. He wrote: 'The despotism of tyrannical princes over the people is shocking. The most damaging and most intolerable of despotisms is that exercised by citizens over their compatriots. Serfdom, that shameful blot on the constitution, that blot on a sham jurisprudence reduces man to nothing but an object and fabricates false justifications.'

Sonnenfels delivered this harsh condemnation the day after Joseph II had declared the abolition of personal servitude. In his attitude to serfdom, he shared the preoccupations of the enlightened spirits in Hungary who were more concerned with agriculture than industry. Hungarian agriculture by 1790 had reached the limits of its productivity under the traditional system of farming. This posed a serious problem for a country where agriculture was the main occupation and where only reform of the feudal mode of working the land could yield a substantial remedy. Farming was, with a few exceptions, so backward than any change brought immediate benefit. It was not simply a question of technical advance at a time when the *robot* had been raised to 150 days a year and the principle behind it remained unquestioned except by Gergely Berzeviczy (1763–1822), a Protestant noble, and Samuel Tessedik, a pastor.[8]

Practical measures were taken through private initiative. A number of nobles used hydraulic engineering and by draining marshlands and building protective dykes brought waterlogged regions into cultivation. They introduced into Hungary new crops (tobacco, potatoes and forage plants), tried to improve breeding-stock and through brewing and distilling laid the foundations of the agro-alimentary industry. Although they did not abolish the *robot*, they limited its harmful effects, obtained an improved yield and appointed competent and honest intendants on their estates. These innovations brought them vast profits. Baron Lilien, during the fifteen years of his management, invested half a million florins in his lands and became one of the richest men in Hungary. Count Amade in 1788 derived 10 000 florins net profit from his estates and by 1809 his revenues had risen to 800 000.

The true enlightened agronomists did not restrict themselves to technical innovations. Pastor Tessedik was a pioneer in his parish of Szarvas in Transdanubia which he transformed by planting acacias and vegetable gardens so that a deserted region became a real oasis. He introduced fodder crops and so offered a serious alternative to the classic cycle of leaving a field fallow every third year. In 1780 he started the first practical agricultural school open to commoners. The teachers came from Vienna, Poszony, Sopron and Buda and gave the students lessons in agronomy and the sciences, including the natural sciences, hygiene and meteorology, a syllabus which represented a complete departure from traditional classical studies. In 1790 the school had about a thousand students, despite the hostility of the county authorities who were disturbed by the sight of young peasants making such rapid progress. Tessedik did receive support from the Habsburgs. Joseph II decorated him in 1787 and Leopold II accorded him many audiences. The school, however, later fell victim to reaction. It was closed by an administrative decision in 1796 but was reopened in 1799 exclusively for the sons of intendants on the estates. Two years later, count Festetich, an enlightened aristocrat, opened at Keszthely an agricultural college to educate intendants who had been admitted to the lesser nobility.

Tessedik published his writings on agronomy in Germany and Hungary, his most important work probably being *The Peasant in Hungary; what he is and what he ought to be.* He recommended that the system of three-year rotation should be abandoned and that new crops be introduced together with intensive farming. Root vegetables and forage plants made it possible to raise stock away from the field and animal manure increased the yield from cereal crops. Marc Bloch in *Les Caractères originaux de l'histoire rurale française* referred to this as the agrarian revolution. Tessedik extended his proposals to include demands for social reform. He thought the peasant should be free and own his own holding.

Gergely Berzeviczy also developed new ideas which, without going so far as to abolish feudal society, would have profoundly modified it. Such ideas were quite alien to most of the Hungarian nobility who were still attached to the archaic system of the *robot*. The debate continued until 1848.

The Enlightenment in the Austrian monarchy was distinct in many ways from that in Western Europe. In a society dominated by Counter-Reformation Catholicism and the nobility, the Enlightenment took the form of Reform Catholicism with Jansenist overtones, and the strengthening of the state and monarchical authority. Parliamentary control in the English manner did not seem desirable and philosophers put their faith in the Habsburgs to modernize the state and society. Government by the orders was seen as backward and as posing a threat to the security of the monarchy at a time when it was confronted by a modernized Prussia.

The Habsburg lands' 'backwardness' and 'marginalization' when compared with France and Britain was most apparent in economics. Progress in agriculture, the development of industry and demographic growth were the fundamental concerns of the enlightened, who were probably closer to the Neapolitan and Milan philosophes than either Montesquieu or Rousseau. The inventiveness of van Swieten, Martini, Sonnenfels and Berzeviczy brought about useful and effective changes within the monarchy without slavishly copying what was said and done in the west.

The reform period included the reign of Maria-Theresa and those of her immediate successors, Joseph II and Leopold II. Censorship reappeared in 1792 with the accession of Francis II at the point when the Habsburgs became directly involved in the counter-revolution and war with revolutionary France. Joseph II's reforms were certainly more radical than those of his mother but it is wrong to contrast mother and son as the conservative empress and the reforming emperor. The brief reign of Leopold II bears undeniable traces of reaction but Maria-Theresa's younger son tried to save his predecessors' reform programme by modifying it.

NOTES AND REFERENCES

1. Eduard Winter, *Der Josephinismus und seinne Geschichte. Beiträge zur Geistesgeschiche Osterreichs 1740 bis 1848*, Munich and Vienna, 1943.
2. Peter Hersche, *Der Spätjansenismus in Österreich*, Vienna, 1977.
3. Grete Klingenstein, *Staatsverwaltung und kirchlilche Autorität im 18. Jahrhundert. Das Problem der Zensur in der theresianischen Reform*, Vienna, 1970.
4. Ferdinand Wernick, *Bibliographie der österreichischen Drucke während der erweiterten Pressefreiheit 1781–1791*, Vienna, 1973.
5. E. Wangermann, 'Joseph II-Fortschritt und Reaktion', in *Österreich in Europe der Aufklärung Kontinuität und Zäsur in Europa zur Zeit Maria-Theresias und Joseph II*, vol. 1, pp. 37–44, Vienna, 1980.
6. Hans Wagner (ed.), *Aus dem Tagebuch des Grafen Karl von Zinzendorf*, Vienna, 1973.
7. Robert A. Kann, *A Study in Austrian Intellectual History, from Late Baroque to Romanticism*, New York, 1985.
8. Eva H. Balazs, *Berzeviczy Gergely*, Budapest, 1969. J. Bérenger, 'La philosophie des Lumières en Hongrie à la fin du xviiie siècle', *Journal des savants*, 1974, pp. 171–89.

CHAPTER SIX

The Reforms of Maria-Theresa and the Consolidation of the State

Haugwitz's reforms, as essential as they were, were not an end in themselves. Behind them lay the need to provide Austria with an army capable of defeating Prussia. Maria-Theresa had not accepted the loss of Silesia and she viewed the 1748 Treaty of Aix-la-Chapelle as a temporary truce until the right moment for renewing the war presented itself. She plotted her revenge on the diplomatic as much as the military level. Frederick II of Prussia alone was satisfied with the 1748 settlement. Britain was dissatisfied because it did not derive from it any decisive success overseas and because the Anglo-American colonies felt threatened more than ever by French penetration into the Ohio valley. France was dissatisfied because it had gained nothing from the conquest of the Netherlands and Austria was disappointed with the English alliance. The London cabinet had forced Austria to sign the Treaty of Dresden in 1745 ratifying the loss of Silesia and to continue the war in Italy which ended with the loss of Parma and Piacenza and the strengthening of Bourbon power in the peninsula. The Seven Years War took no-one in official circles by surprise.

THE SEVEN YEARS WAR

For Maria-Theresa, this second and final great conflict of her reign was a just war since its aim was to recover Silesia, an integral part of the kingdom of Bohemia and therefore, since 1526, an integral part of the Habsburgs' patrimony. The alliance with the empress Elizabeth of Russia and Augustus III, elector of Saxony and king of Poland, and the dramatic reversal of alliances, brought Maria-Theresa a solid continental coalition, capable, at least in theory, of defeating Frederick the Great's Prussia.

Bartenstein, the sovereign's mentor, and count, later prince, Kaunitz-Rietberg forged the rapprochement with France. In 1749 Königsegg, the grand master of the court, chancellor Uhlfeld, Colloredo, Khevenhüller the grand chamberlain, Bartenstein and Kaunitz gathered in a 'secret conference'. Kaunitz, who had negotiated the peace treaty, did not hide from the Bourbons the benefits they might accrue from such a rapprochement even though Fleury in 1741 had behaved scandalously by breaking his word. The promise of compensations in

Italy for the Spanish Bourbons would be sufficient to secure French neutrality in the event of an Austro-Prussian war.

To win over Louis XV, Kaunitz was appointed ambassador at Versailles where he remained for three years (1750–53). He won over Madame de Pompadour and fended off at the same time the hostility of the French ministers. Recalled to Vienna, he became chancellor of state, a position which he held for forty years under Maria-Theresa, Joseph II, Leopold II and Francis II.

Diplomacy and government were now under the direction of an aristocrat imbued with the spirit of the Enlightenment and with little respect for religion or for German or local traditions. Kaunitz was a European, with a perfect mastery of French, knowledgeable about other countries, well-informed about contemporary ideas and capable of great schemes. He was also a pompous aristocrat for whom it was a point of honour to serve the state and the dynasty without undermining the privileges of his order. He believed it was incumbent upon the higher nobility to occupy important posts in government and to ignore public opinion. He was a man of great refinement but he could also be rude and was panic-stricken when confronted by illness and death, a surprising characteristic in one otherwise so courageous. He was deeply mistrustful of others and insolent in a way which was ill-received by the good-natured Viennese and the affable royal family. He inspired in Maria-Theresa neither friendship nor esteem but won her admiration for his intellectual capacities, his experience and imagination, qualities which she herself lacked. She valued his sense of state and of grandeur. She trusted him and even in the final years supported him against her son.

In summer 1755, Franco-British hostilities resumed in North America. Louis XV sent 5 000 foot-soldiers as reinforcements to Canada and the British admiral Boscawen had captured two French men-of-war off Newfoundland and had then turned to inspecting French merchantmen. Maria-Theresa refused to dispatch troops to the Netherlands because she did not want to withdraw soldiers from Bohemia. Frederick II, by the Treaty of Westminster (1755), reached an agreement with the British government which continued to refuse Austria help in reconquering Silesia. Maria-Theresa sent Starhemberg to Paris with precise instructions to negotiate an agreement with France. He held secret discussions with abbot Bernis which resulted in the Treaty of Versailles of 1 May 1756. It was a true reversal of alliances. The agreement consisted of three conventions guaranteeing the possessions of both parties and the neutrality of the Netherlands, as well as the mutual promise of 24 000 men or a subsidy of the same value in the event of either of the two powers being attacked.

Maria-Theresa ratified the treaty on 25 May 1756, remarking that it gave her no pleasure to put her signature to such an agreement. Ten years earlier, she had had three redoubtable enemies, France, Prussia and the Ottoman empire, now she had two. Kaunitz had explained to her that it was her only chance to recover Silesia. The accord was fragile since it clashed with French public opinion and found no favour with Louis XV's ministers. Choiseul was sent as ambassador to Vienna and did not hesitate to draw attention to the inconveniences of the new alliance. The Houses of Habsburg and Bourbon were able to bury the hatchet in order to make common cause against the further advance of Frederick II into Germany and to halt English colonial expansion. It brought a half-century of peace to the Rhineland electorates which had long been the traditional theatre for clashes between imperial and French troops. During the Seven Years War, the French went on campaign in north Germany to occupy Hanover, the personal possession of the king of England. Life, meanwhile, continued peacefully in Mannheim, Mainz and Bonn, and Alsace was spared a visitation from the imperial troops.

Contemporaries and some historians have blamed this treaty for the disasters of the Seven Years War and the loss of the French colonial empire because Louis XV was obliged to engage important contingents of troops in Germany and to give Maria-Theresa subsidies to the order of 25–30 million pounds a year, without which the imperial troops would not have been able to support the great war effort in Bohemia and Silesia.

A further treaty considerably strengthened the 1756 settlement. By the Second Treaty of Versailles (1 May 1757), Louis XV promised to supply 130 000 men and 12 million florins a year to Austria, to pay subsidies to Sweden and Saxony, and to direct the war on the Continent until Prussia could be forced to abandon Silesia and the county of Glatz. The House of Austria would cede to France some towns in the Netherlands. These would be given to don Philip of Bourbon who would give his Italian duchies to Maria-Theresa. In this way, the Austrian position in Italy would be reinforced and the government at Vienna would be relieved of its responsibilities for the Austrian Netherlands. For Starhemberg and Kaunitz, it was a triumph made possible by the changes within the Paris ministeries, since Argenson and Machault d'Arnouville, the minister for foreign affairs and the controller general of finance, were opposed to the alliance with Austria whereas Bernis, Belle-Isle and the controller general Silhouette supported it. The whole project rested on the illusion that Frederick II would not be able to withstand for long a vast continental coalition of Russia, Saxony, Poland, Sweden, Austria, the Empire and France. Louis XV believed that France could easily be disentangled from the war on the Continent, could occupy the Netherlands and devote itself entirely to waging war on Britain. 'This, though, was precisely what did not happen', wrote Tapié.[1] 'Two wars, one on the Continent where France assisted Austria, the other on the sea between England and France and, in the final months, Spain, unrolled in parallel and constituted one of the first world wars of modern times.'

It was the coalition's great misfortune that it was confronted by a military genius. Frederick II knew very well that at stake was his life's work, the status of Prussia as a great power. He mobilized all his resources. He had at his disposal an exceptionally well-trained army, quite out of proportion to the size of his kingdom's population. He took his central position in the face of a coalition which made the error of not concentrating its forces and coordinating its action. Providence smiled on the House of Brandenburg to a near miraculous degree. One of the most remarkable events of the war was when tsar Peter III who had just acceded to the throne, out of admiration for Frederick the Great, immediately recalled his troops who were marching on Berlin.

Once the incompetent Charles of Lorraine, whose chief distinction was being the emperor's brother, had been replaced, the Austrian generals Daun, Lacy and Laudon demonstrated their undisputed skills as tacticians. Their soldiers proved their endurance and courage and the Hungarian and Croat light cavalry achieved some remarkable feats. General Hadik and his hussars managed a raid on Berlin in 1757 and Frederick II was defeated several times, on 8 June 1757 at Kolin outside Prague, on 14 October 1758 at Hochkirch in Saxony, on 12 August 1759 at Kunersdorf in Brandenburg, and in June 1760 at Landshut near Glatz. Austrian and Russian forces occupied Berlin for several days in August 1760. Frederick II, though, enjoyed a decisive victory over Daun and Lacy at Torgau in Saxony on 3 November 1760. After 1761, operations lost their vigour. Kaunitz had overestimated the resources of the Habsburg monarchy. No battle, however bloody and humiliating, brought any nearer the prospect of an end to the war. At Rossbach in 1757, Soubise's French troops and the army of the imperial circles were pulverized by Frederick's men. A victory, however, could not be secured in 1757 and so the conflict continued and the number of engagements which were not exploited, the number of sieges and levées of recruits, and the number of occupied regions milked of their resources, grew ever greater. It was a difficult war which took place principally in Saxony and Silesia, but also in Bohemia, northern Moravia and Brandenburg. It marked a return to the situation in the Thirty Years War when the heart of the monarchy had been the battlefield and only Vienna and the countries on the periphery, Hungary, Milan and the Netherlands, were spared.

Maria-Theresa despaired of ever achieving a total victory after her armies were defeated at Torgau on 3 November 1760. Want of resources forced her to cut back manpower. France had reduced its subsidies by 50 per cent, its navy had been destroyed and its Canadian and Indian factories lost. As early as 1761, Kaunitz thought that a diplomatic congress would be the best way of re-establishing peace since changes in the British government made it possible to consider a compromise. George III had come to the throne in 1760 and, although elector of Hanover, he was indifferent towards Germany. Public opinion in Britain longed for peace. The intransigent Pitt the Elder had resigned and his place was taken by the more moderate earl of Bute. In the end, the war was settled by two separate negotiations. Britain was the great beneficiary of the peace. At Versailles, it restored the Antilles to its old adversary, France, the very minimum possible to ensure that it could keep the snow fields of Canada. At Hubertsburg castle in Saxony, the Prussians and Austrians, who did not want to undertake another campaign, felt that a return to the status quo was the least unsatisfactory solution and so signed the peace agreement on 13 February 1763, three days after the Treaty of Paris. The imperial troops evacuated the county of Glatz and the Prussian territories which they had occupied. Silesia remained in the hands of Prussia without hope of recovery. Augustus III received back Saxony and Frederick II promised to vote for the archduke Joseph in the election for king of the Romans. That he abided by his promise shows the importance which he still attached to the imperial crown at Vienna.

A new balance of power in the German world and in continental Europe had been consecrated as a result of this war which Kaunitz had willed and to which Maria-Theresa had given her assent. Prussia entered the ranks of the great powers on a par with Russia and the Austrian monarchy. The latter had held onto the imperial crown and with it, its preponderance in the German world. Despite some disappointments, it had ended up in a position of greater strength. Freed from British tutelage, the monarchy had strengthened its alliance with France. The House of Habsburg-Lorraine was allied, through a family pact, to all the Bourbons, in Madrid, Parma and Naples, and no longer faced a challenge from them to its position in Italy. Maria-Theresa had learnt another lesson. She set her mind against any further military operations and devoted all her efforts to domestic reforms.

KAUNITZ'S REFORMS[2]

The defeat at Torgau convinced Kaunitz that Haugwitz's reforms had not brought the hoped-for results. The directory created in 1749 was blamed for the financial difficulties which had become apparent after the war had started, at a time when even Britain and France had had to have recourse to loans and were massively indebted. Kaunitz estimated the shortfall on the budget at 6 million florins, the same as the peacetime revenue. The state's debts had risen to 100 million in 1756 and there was a risk that it would not be able to meet interest payments and was heading for bankruptcy. He also thought that the army should be reduced to 60 000 men with a peacetime standing army of 50 000, hardly half the number thought essential in 1748 to guarantee security in the face of Prussia and the Ottoman empire.

In his memorandum of 9 December 1760, Kaunitz proposed to Maria-Theresa the creation of the *Staatsrat*, a council of state responsible for the direction of all the internal affairs of the hereditary lands (Austria and Bohemia but not Hungary), the Netherlands and Italy. Three ministers of state drawn from the *Herrenstand* and three from the *Ritterstand* would sit in it. The council would be assisted by a permanent secretary and by the chancellor of state who would take part in important meetings. No member of the council was to direct a ministerial department or to carry out Aulic duties. Such an institution, which closely resembled Louis XIV's Supreme Council, would take the place of a prime minister, a post which Kaunitz did not want established. Each councillor would receive an annual salary of 10 000 florins. 'For my part', Kaunitz concluded, 'I am deeply convinced that only such an institution can furnish Your Majesty with the means of saving the state, of bringing its domestic government from the state of disorder and decadence in which it finds itself, to a degree of perfection enjoyed, perhaps, by no other government in Europe, and thus earn God's blessing and the happiness of its subjects and posterity and it is this alone that urges me to make this proposal.'

Maria-Theresa approved this project without delay in order to counter those led by Khevenhüller who longed to return to the situation prevailing in 1740.

In 1761 she created a council of state as proposed by Kaunitz and chose to reduce its members' salaries from 10 000 to 8 000 florins. It was a tradition of the Habsburgs that they did not pay their staff regularly, even though this meant that they had constantly to complain about corruption. Appointed as ministers of state were: Kaunitz, who kept his position as chancellor and exercised, without saying so, that of prime minister; Haugwitz and the field-marshal Daun, who thus received a measure of consolation after having been deprived of their offices; count Blümegen, baron Borié and Anton Stupan, three talented officials, who were made 'state councillors'; and the refendary König, a protégé of Kaunitz, who was made secretary. Count Rudolf, whose name was raised several times, was not retained by Maria-Theresa. The *Staatsrat* was made up of Germans from the hereditary lands and this strengthened the pre-eminence of Austro-Bohemians in the state apparatus. During the Seven Years War, the hereditary lands had contributed greatly to military expenses and their political weight was in proportion to their financial sacrifices.

Maria-Theresa in the same year, without waiting for the war to end, proceeded with other reforms intended to correct the errors made in 1749. The fundamental principle of modern government, the separation of justice and administration, was maintained but the weighty financial mechanism installed by Haugwitz on the Prussian model proved to be inefficient during wartime. The directory was replaced in 1762 by six ministerial departments which, as was customary at Vienna, had the character of colleges. Only their presidents, who had the rank of ministers, became intermediaries for the *Staatsrat*. These colleges (or dicasteries) were assisted by a bureaucracy of clerks (or, in the terminology of Vienna, chancelleries). In this way a new system of government was put in place which continued until the revolution of 1848.

The *Hofkammer* was refounded in 1762 with increased powers and under the presidency of count Herberstein. It was a ministry of finances and controlled all the revenues from the monarchy, the *cameralia*, as in the past, and the contributions. Count Hatzfeld, Herberstein's successor, showed the efficiency of this structure. The management of the public debt was entrusted to the *Creditsdeputation*, a central chest for the hereditary lands which was responsible for collecting the revenues and regulating expenses.

A *Hofrechenskammer* (exchequer) was responsible for handing all financial accounts and paying out money. The head of this new dicastery was Ludwig von Zinzendorf, an intelligent, imaginative and dilligent young man who, like Kaunitz and the emperor Francis, was in contact with Parisian financial circles and was committed to the modern management of the economy and public finances. The general council of commerce responsible for manufacture and economic development had the status of an executive commission (*Hofstelle*).

The Supreme Judiciary created in 1749 was maintained to act as the court of final appeal for the hereditary lands. A chancellery was established for the hereditary lands which was a prototype for the ministry of the interior for Austria and Bohemia. It was released from the judicial tasks it had formerly exercised and was common to all the hereditary lands. The creation of this council set the seal on the Czech lands' loss of autonomy as the chancellery of

Bohemia was subsumed with the chancellery of Austria. In each of the Austro-Bohemian lands, a government, that is a council, was established under the presidency of an aristocrat who exercised administrative tasks in the sovereign's name. In Hungary, Maria-Theresa followed a cautious policy, ever mindful of the moral obligations she had towards the nobility after 1741. She had sworn to respect the privileges of the kingdom, in particular the nobility's immunity from taxation. The Diet of 1763–64 only voted a contractual contribution of 4 million florins whereas the Austro-Bohemian lands at that time payed 14.2 million florins. If the various 'extraordinary' revenues paid by those liable to contribute are added on, Hungary's share of the total contributions did not exceed 5 million (out of a total of 38.2 million florins in 1763) or 12 per cent, which did not reflect the demographic and economic situation of a country which, unlike Bohemia, had been spared the Austro-Prussian wars. Hungary had become the monarchy's wheat granary and supplier to the imperial army.

Kaunitz wanted, as the Hungarian historian Ember has shown, to change the Hungarian constitution because the nobility alone benefited from the country's economic advance. Maria-Theresa proposed to the 1764 Diet that the orders should contribute to public expenses, but the nobility stood firmly by the terms set out under Leopold I and, every inch as stubborn as the privileged nobility in France, refused to countenance any compromise. She insisted that Hungary's particular legislation should be respected and also that Hungarian councillors should be present in the government at Vienna which was not the case in the *Staatsrat*. Blümegen, Stupan and Kaunitz were hostile towards the Hungarian nobility and, so long as noble fiscal privileges remained untouched, refused, in 1762 and 1766, to found factories in Hungary. Borié alone wanted Hungary to lose its status as a 'colony', rich only in primary materials. In 1766 the *Staatsrat* wanted to apply a policy analogous to that imposed by Britain on its North American colonies. The crisis was avoided through the wisdom of Maria-Theresa. In 1780 Hungary's bureaucracy was limited to a hundred persons employed by a council of lieutenancy (*consilium locumtenentiale*) which had been created in 1723 with the Diet's assent. Composed originally of twenty-eight representatives of the orders, it was gradually abandoned and its responsibilities were entrusted to officials recruited from among the educated and poor nobility and appointed and paid by the monarch. Although they were *regnicolae*, their economic position made them dependent upon central power and in the long term they formed that part of the court which continued to exist in the nineteenth century. Despite the increased control which had accrued to the royal towns, the presence of customs officers and the officers belonging to the five military commands, political life in Hungary took refuge in the county assemblies. The departmental administration was elected for three years from among the members of the middling nobility (*bene possessionati*) and continued to exercise its administrative and judicial functions. Even the recruitment, lodging and upkeep of the Hungarian regiments created in 1715 devolved upon them.

In 1771 conscription was introduced in the hereditary lands but was not applied in Hungary because Maria-Theresa did not want to touch the military privileges which her father had granted in the 1715 Diet. Joseph II and marshal count Lacy, president of the War Council, thought that the counties were deliberately sending as recruits n'er-do-wells and vagabonds.

Maria-Theresa agreed with Kaunitz and Borié that the monarchy would at last be a great power if Hungary were to be integrated within it and to share in the fortunes and responsibilities of the hereditary lands. She decided, like her great ancestors, to follow a long-term policy which was subtle and discreet. She 'froze' constitutional life. After 1765 she no longer summoned the Diet, from 1767 she left the office of palatine vacant, in which condition it was to remain until 1790, and governed in consultation with the *Staatsrat*, where Borié sat with his knowledge gained from detailed study of the files and of Hungarian public law.

Maria-Theresa, through her shrewd political instincts and through recognizing the existing situation, maintained the traditional Austro-Hungarian dualism which was deeply rooted in the political traditions and realities of Danubian Europe.

ECONOMIC POLICY

In the field of economics, members of the government were eclectic and not wedded to any one particular doctrine. Faithful to some aspects of cameralism, of traditional mercantilism, they were also open to the teachings of the physiocrats. Sonnenfels was, as has been seen, a populationist and was open to the ideas of Adam Smith.

Maria-Theresa took some measures towards limiting the privileges of corporations and continued to attract entrepreneurs from Western Europe. The loss of Silesia, where there were many factories, prompted the creation of industries in other countries.

The emperor Francis I, and some aristocrats, founded factories on their personal domains and Maria-Theresa favoured them by lowering the import tax on raw materials to 0.25 per cent and by allowing Saxon artisans to practise as Lutherans. Artisan cloth makers from Verviers provided the workforce for a factory founded in 1749 at Kladruby which was supplied with staples of wool from the royal estate at Pardubice, also in Bohemia. The factory founded at Brno in 1764 was bought, after the sovereign's death, by a member of the bourgeoisie, Johann Leopold Koffiler. In 1755 the emperor Francis I founded at Potstejn in the north-east of Bohemia a mill for bleaching and finishing unbleached cloth, two stages of the cloth production which up to then had been carried out in Silesia. Part of the cloth manufactured was exported through Trieste to New York and Philadelphia. The director, Chamaré, calculated that the annual turnover was 2–3 million florins, a figure which could be doubled. In 1780 spinning wool and linen occupied around 133 000 and 34 000 workers respectively. This was still a hand, not a mechanized, industry spread throughout the country and operated by merchant-manufacturers.

Manufacturers in Austria also experienced a measure of prosperity. Cloth production at Linz passed into state control in 1754 and continued expanding until 1780, at which date it employed 40 000 persons, most of whom were home-workers spread throughout the whole of Upper Austria. Vienna was also a centre for industrial growth. The long-established mill for cotton cloth at Schwechat was joined by others at Friedau in 1752, Neukettenhof in 1765 and Ebreichsdorf in 1773. In 1754 Johann Fries, a merchant of Alsatian origin and founder of the mill at Schwechat, opened a factory for velvet in Döbling, a suburb of Vienna, and was soon cutting a figure as one of the wealthiest men in the capital. Silk production began to develop in another Viennese suburb, Schottenfeld, and in the country, on the north bank of the Danube. These entrepreneurs, however, faced fierce competition from Lyons until the French Revolution.

In 1750 Maria-Theresa founded in the free port of Fiume the first sugar-cane refinery in her lands. Sugar-refining developed in Lower Austria after 1780, with new refineries opening at Klosterneuburg and Wiener Neustadt. Markov has shown that the government still remained very circumspect with respect to colonial trade, even after the break with Britain. In 1775 a Dutch adventurer received a charter to establish an Imperial-Asian Society for five years. He fitted out an English indiaman of 650 nautical tonnes, renamed it *Giuseppe e Teresa*, and founded a series of short-lived trading posts on the coast of Malabar. In 1792 the company was shut down. Joseph II never had any faith in Zin-zendorf's colonial projects nor in those of Kaunitz and his mother, for the simple reason that he was without a navy.

The Habsburgs' real colonial adventure unfolded 500 km from Vienna in the Banat of Temesvár and began in 1718 when the Sublime Porte ceded the territory to Charles VI by the terms of the Treaty of Passarowitz. Prince Eugene had advocated adhering to the policy outlined by cardinal Kollonich whereby estates within the newly liberated territories were not returned to their former masters and supreme ownership of the land was credited to the emperor who would manage it through the chamber of accounts. As the Banat had been freed by imperial rather than Hungarian troops, it was possible to invoke the law of conquest and so to give it special status. Prince Eugene did not trust the Hungarians, not least because prince Rákóczi had settled at Rodosto on the sea of Marmara with the express purpose of resuming the war, and preferred to repopulate the Banat with German rather than Hungarian colonists. The Banat was administered from Vienna by the chamber of accounts. It had been devastated by war and was all but completely depopulated. To bring it under production became priority. An appeal was made to the Germans for reasons of security since they were assumed to be loyal to the dynasty, and to the Serbs and Romanians who wanted to escape from Ottoman rule. The terms of settlement were particularly generous. Every family received a house comprising two rooms, a kitchen, a stable, ploughing tools, seeds and a plot of land consisting of 24 acres of arable land, 6 of grassland and 1 of garden. The main elements of the infrastructure were built from scratch by military engineers at the imperial treasury's expense. The magnificent plans are preserved in the archives of the chamber of accounts in Vienna and show the outlines for the church, school, presbytery, mill, fountain, inn and slaughter-house. The layout was that of a linear village on the lines of those in the Hungarian plain or in Lorraine. These colonists were free from all ties of serfdom and enjoyed three years of tax exemption, a dispensation which was first made in 1721 and which Maria-Theresa extended by the patent of February 1763 to six years and ten years for artisans.

During Charles VI's reign, recruiting agents settled at Trier, Kehl, Alt-Breisach and the search for settlers still continued under Joseph II. Colonists came from western Germany, from Lorraine and from Alsace. They were generally known as Swabians but some inhabitants of the alpine provinces came to try their luck despite the poor sanitation and malaria which in the beginning were prevalent. The Rhinelanders assembled at Kehl, went to Ulm and went down the Danube as far as Pest, each couple receiving 12 kreuzers a day while travelling.

The Lorraine and French authorities tried to prevent emigration as much under Charles VI as under Maria-Theresa. After the Peace of Hubertusburg in 1763, Borié resumed the colonization of the Banat to assure that the land was put under cultivation according to physiocratic principles. Some 50 000 persons settled in the Banat between 1764 and 1772 and were followed by another wave of 25 000 colonists under Joseph II. Among these were at least 3 550 families from Lorraine who were aggrieved by the impositions made by the intendant La Galaizière, taxation and the billeting of troops. For the Alsatians the incentive to move was poverty. They preferred the virgin lands of old Europe to those of North America. The Banat was devoted to the production of cereals and had the right geographical conditions with warm summers, and fertile soil once it had been drained.

In 1778 the Banat was incorporated into the kingdom of Hungary and placed under the authority of the Hungarian chamber. Three counties were created and a share of the domain lands was sold to the highest bidders, rich Serbian or Armenian merchants. Serfdom was introduced and the condition of the peasantry swiftly deteriorated. The colonists found themselves reduced to the lot common to the mass of peasants.

MARIA-THERESA AND THE CONDITION OF THE PEASANTRY

Tapié wrote in *L'Europe de Marie-Thérèse* that after the Seven Years War, the major question for the monarchy was the agrarian question. The old forms of the domain-based economy and seigneurial authority persisted. The *robot* was especially resented by the peasants as an unjust tax and an intolerable burden. The gentry, though, as much from reluctance to countenance change as from a belief that they were not sufficiently wealthy to pay wages to labourers, remained wedded to the *robot* even though it hampered growth in productivity. The agrarian problem greatly concerned Maria-Theresa during the fifteen years of her co-regency with Joseph II, all the more so because her son's advice combined with Kaunitz's caution thwarted her impulses to abolish the *robot*, even though this measure would have been welcomed by the peasantry. In the past, Maria-Theresa had always been mindful not to upset the nobility and her conservatism had counterpoised the revolutionary spirit of her son who was waiting in the wings for the day when he could be sole master and liberate the peasants. Joseph II's attitude to the issue was, right until 1780, ambiguous. In 1775 he in fact dissuaded his mother from abolishing the *robot* in Bohemia and in 1778 put the peasants of the Banat under the seigneurial yoke on the pretext that the officers of the chamber of accounts were inefficient and the domain lands needed to be 'privatized' to produce better returns.

In Hungary, Maria-Theresa forced the seigneurs to accept a clear definition of the *robot* and feudal dues, and of peasant property. The *Urbarialregulation*, the decree of 1767 regulating the peasants' services and lords' rights, had been prepared with the help of the court librarian, Adam Kollár, a Slovak and vehement opponent of the orders and their privileges. The decree set the extent of peasant holdings at 15–30 acres at a time when growth in population was leading to the multiplication and reduction in size of such plots. If the holding was less than 4 acres of arable land, the peasant was classed as a labourer and was exempt from taxation. The right to use the woods and common pastures was confirmed. The *robot* was limited to fifty-two days a year on a manse and was scaled down in proportion to its surface area. A florin a year tax on every hearth was owed to the state as well as the tithe and a ninth of the harvest, or a fifth of the total yield in kind. These charges were heavy but at least a limit had been set upon them. Implementation of the decree was entrusted to a prefect and an elected commissioner in each county. The results corresponded to the sovereign's intentions of putting seigneurial affairs in order. Some aristocrats, including the palatine Lajos Batthyány, the primate Barkoczi and Antun Grassalkovich, the president of the royal chamber, resented this legislation which, incidently, did not stop the peasants from revolting.

In Bohemia, it was the great peasant revolt of 1775 that forced Maria-Theresa to act. After twelve years, the ideas of the physiocrats had had their day. A thriving agriculture was the primary condition for the well-being of the people and wealth could only be gained once the peasant had recovered his entire liberty. In 1768 an Aulic commission was constituted and put in charge of examining the peasants' obligations in response to the first peasant revolt, which had taken place in 1766 in Upper Silesia. The commission's work was influenced by Franz von Blanc, the defender of natural law and enemy of custom, and led to a patent in the peasant's favour.

A series of natural disasters recalling the worst years of the seventeenth century hit Bohemia and in 1768 and 1769 resulted in two bad harvests and, in turn, a steep rise in prices and a shortage of food made worse by the export of grain to Saxony and Bavaria. The most difficult year was 1771. Frosts and rains in spring had prevented sowing and the authorities faced a real shortage. The beggars as always flocked towards the towns. Nobles and some merchants took charge of distributing wheat and flour as acts of private charity and the government had to arrange for grain to be brought from Hungary and through Trieste. Maria-Theresa granted a million florins in aid. A population already weakened by poor nutrition was then assailed in the summer of 1771 by a plague epidemic of similar proportions to those in 1680 and 1713. At least 160 000 died overall and a decade's population growth was wiped out in Prague. Public opinion expected some gesture and raised the question of the *robot*. The administration exerted all its powers and the *Staatsrat* prevented Maria-Theresa from making a decision. It was hoped in 1774 that the situation could be resolved by publishing, through the intermediary of the chancellery of Austria-Bohemia, the *maxima* (the limits) of the *robot*. The seigneurial chancelleries were slow to change the rules while the peasants continued to hope that the *robot* would soon be abolished. In 1775, tired of waiting, they revolted.

The revolt, as in 1680, was a general movement and accusations were again made that enemy powers, this time Prussia, had fomented agitation. The condition of the peasants, though, was so bad that it was hardly necessary to posit the existence of foreign *agents provocateurs*. The revolt began among the village elites during the winter, the traditional time for agitation in the country when labourers were relatively unemployed. The movement broke out in the circle of Hradec Králové (Königgratz) and spread throughout the whole kingdom. The village notables protested in favour of the abolition of the *robot*. Their movement took the form of a march by the delegations which had met on 16 March for the feast of St Jan Nepomuck, and was rapidly taken over by the masses. Banners proclaimed '*Svoboda nego smrt!*' ('Freedom or death'), a slogan which was assured a good future. The rebels marched in disorderly fashion and arrived at Prague earlier than planned on 25 March. For two years, the grand burgrave and leader of the *Gubernium* had been a young enlightened aristocrat, Karl Egon von Fürstenberg. He went to meet the insurgents and demanded, in vain, peace envoys. The peasants merely hurled abuse and made threats and the grand burgrave was forced to resort to cold steel. There were no deaths but some prisoners were taken who later benefited from the amnesty decreed at the beginning of April.

The revolt of 1775 had a positive result. On 13 August, Maria-Theresa promulgated by her own authority, without preliminary agreement with the Diet, the *robot* patent which was immediately published in all the circles of Bohemia by commissioners accompanied by soldiers. This text was written in the tradition of the charters which followed the great peasant revolts. Those liable to the *robot* were now divided into eleven classes defined according to the area of the land under cultivation: the brassier/landless labourer who had no land and did not pay any tax to the state was only obliged to serve thirteen days of manual *robot* a year; the peasant belonging to class 7 who paid 9.5 florins, provided three days labour a week; the rich peasants, the members of class 11 who contributed more than 42 florins tax, were to provide two teams of two draft animals thrice a week.

The patent was formulated by the conservative elements in the *Staatsrat* and was welcomed by the peasant notables who secured its acceptance by the masses. It was equally well-received by the nobility of Bohemia who in the session of 1776 made it a law of the kingdom. A similar patent was published for Moravia.

Maria-Theresa was probably the least satisfied with this settlement. She saw the patent of 13 August 1775 as a temporary measure. Eighteen months later, she expressed her innermost thoughts in a letter to the archduke Ferdinand. During the thirty-six years of her reign, successive rulings had failed to end the oppression of the poor and the tyranny of the seigneurs. Maria-Theresa was probably advised by Franz von Blanc. She had shown her ministers how determined she was and if Joseph II had remained neutral, she would have succeeded in suppressing the *robot* and abolishing serfdom. The emperor, Kaunitz and the ministers thought such a step premature and prevented it. Von Blanc resigned over the issue.

The crisis shows clearly how the government functioned during the *Mitregenschaft*, the co-regency which from 1765 to 1780 was a 'troika' with Kaunitz exerting his influence alongside Maria-Theresa and Joseph. After the emperor Francis's death, Joseph, who had been elected king of the Romans in 1764, succeeded his father as ruler of the Holy Roman Empire. The empress was grief-stricken and wanted to retire but shared with her eldest son the government of the lands of the Austrian monarchy.

It was in the field of public education that Maria-Theresa, supported by her son and by enlightened opinion, was able to make real progress.

THE ADVANCE OF PUBLIC EDUCATION

The issue of education had been raised by the first government reforms after the War of the Austrian Succession, since the creation of a real bureaucracy implied the education of competent officials. The Theresianum and the Military Academy at Wiener Neustadt were inadequate to cope with the increased numbers. After 1750, Maria-Theresa had questioned the Jesuits' predominance and their universal monopoly in education. This need for intellectual openness combined with the increase in the recruitment of 'men of talent' led to a remarkable series of reforms.

Maria-Theresa's personal doctor, the Dutchman Gerard van Swieten, was appointed life-long president of the faculty of medicine at Vienna in 1749. Robert Kann has shown the discreet but influential role this convert from Protestantism played as advisor to the empress who, in a sign of the times, had replaced a man of God with a man of science.

Van Swieten revitalized the faculty of medicine and established a chair in surgery with Ferdinand Leher as the first professor at what was to become this prestigious school of surgery, sometimes called 'the first school of Vienna'. Leher took up his post at the *Bürgerspital*, arranged for renowned surgeons from abroad to come and obliged students to assist at operations. Van Swieten also organized the study of pharmacy and botany and brought to Vienna Jaquin, the botanist from Lorraine, who with the emperor's support created the botanic garden at Schönbrunn on the model of the Jardin du roi in Paris. In twenty years, Jaquin trained enough students to supply the provincial universities at Prague, Pest and Freiburg-in-Breisach with good teachers and so to assure the monarchy a place in its own right within the world of European science.

A commission for public education was formed within the directory established by Haugwitz's reforms. Placed in 1760 under the presidency of cardinal Migazzi and subordinated to the chancery, it became a *Studienhofkommission*, an Aulic commission, and played the role of a ministry for public education. It took steps to improve studies in the various faculties, to standardize syllabuses and teaching methods in schools throughout the monarchy and to restore Vienna university's reputation which had lapsed under the control of the Jesuits. They had gradually turned this once prestigious institution into a 'seminary' where students from poor families destined for the priesthood were instructed in scholasticism and theology. Young men from wealthy families attended German or Italian universities and on their return paid to have their diplomas accredited, a process known as 'nostrification'.

Migazzi, in conjunction with the reform of censorship, replaced the Jesuit professors of theology with Augustinians and Benedictines. In 1759 the Jesuit heads of the faculties of philosophy and theology were removed and the Jansenist Simen and canon von Stock appointed.

In 1761 the director of studies at the faculty of theology at Prague was also dismissed and secular priests, Augustinians and Dominicans replaced the Jesuits who lost their intellectual monopoly. New chairs in patristics, ecclesiastical history and oriental languages were created and the abbot Rautenstrauch, a confirmed supporter of *Reformkatholicizismus,* was appointed director of studies while the position of dean became that of a mere figurehead.

The imperial government paid special attention to the advance of legal studies at a time when public law and the political sciences were developing in important directions. The professors of law were often high officials such as Martini who worked for twenty years editing the *Codex theresianum* (the Theresian code) promulgated in 1768. The code is often criticized for its conservatism, especially with respect to penal procedure. Torture at this stage, despite the advance of natural law and the ideas of Beccaria, was retained and only totally abolished by the decree of 1776 issued by Maria-Theresa under the influence of Sonnenfels. Those found guilty of homosexual practices were still liable to death at the stake but trials for witchcraft were ended.

The empress was greatly troubled at having to comply with the suppression of the Society of Jesus, decreed in 1773 by the Holy See. The Jesuits provided most of the teachers in secondary schools and secondary education depended on their dedication and competence. Their departure forced the government to assume responsibility for the education of the young.

The commission of public education, presided over by the chancellor of state Kressel, proposed the total secularization of secondary education regardless of the merits of some individual clergymen and the difficulty of recruiting good teachers from outside their ranks. The *Staatsrat* was more concerned with efficiency than education and adopted the proposal of father Gratien Marx who became rector of the Theresianum and was a member of the Piarist teaching order which had settled in Hungary and Poland. Secondary education was modernized as it had been in the Rhineland electorates. Latin lost its position of prime importance and students could choose to study German, mathematics, history and geography. The programme of studies lasted five years. These reforms were promulgated in December 1774 by an imperial patent.

These changes did not apply to Hungary. A former Jesuit, Joszef Urményi, editor at the Hungarian chancery, was put in charge of organizing another programme of reform in schools. Sanctioned by Maria-Theresa, in 1777, this text became the *Ratio educationis*. In secondary schools, as at university, the monopoly on the study of Latin was broken and German was taught. Nine districts were created and placed under the authority of a royal inspector of schools. The revenue from property formerly belonging to the Society of Jesus served, as throughout the whole of the monarchy, to pay the salaries of teachers.

Maria-Theresa had found a compromise which would long endure. The state controlled education but involved the Church by employing priests as teachers and by making religious education obligatory.

The spirit of the Enlightenment also affected primary education. Maria-Theresa admitted into the Aulic commission a priest from Silesia, Ignaz Felbiger, who was inspired by the Prussian model for education. Only the advance of education could promote the Enlightenment and a good Christian needed to receive a minimum of educational instruction. Primary schools were created in the country with the help of the large estate-owners. In Hungary as in the hereditary lands, the vernacular was used for instruction, a step which the churches had taken long ago. The patent of 1774 entrusted schooling to provincial commissions which appointed inspectors and, what was most important, it instituted in every provincial capital a teacher-training college on the Prussian model intended to train schoolmasters or youths destined to practise a trade. Pedagogy, one of the key words of the *Aufklärung*, found its place.

The programme of 1774 and in Hungary that of 1777 gradually produced results. Progress was uneven but literacy made great strides. It is wrong to contrast an educated Prussia with an ignorant Austria, a Protestant and enlightened north Germany with a Catholic and obscurantist south Germany. Maria-Theresa has her place among the 'enlightened sovereigns' of her age. She prepared the way for the great reforms of Joseph II but she acted in a different spirit. She advocated cooperation with the Church, respect for social order, real compassion for her poorest subjects and concern for political balance.

THE FOREIGN POLICY OF THE CO-REGENCY (1765–80)

In theory Joseph II had sole control of the army and foreign policy with the assistance of the chancellor Kaunitz, but Maria-Theresa sometimes used her authority to temper the emperor's war-mongering. Although mother and son shared the same objective of recovering Silesia, or at least gaining some compensation, they worked in very different ways since the empress wanted to avoid war at all costs.

After the Peace at Hubertusburg in 1763, Austrian foreign policy continued to be based on the alliance with France which was tied to the sovereign's mistrust of Prussia, although Joseph II for his part greatly admired Frederick II. Despite some wavering and crises, the alliance endured until 1792. The Ottoman empire had ceased to be an enemy to be feared and instead was a partner offering outlets for goods manufactured in the hereditary lands. Catherine the Great, who was allied to Prussia for opportunistic reasons, proved to be a cumbersome ally who wanted to expand Russia at the expense of the Polish Republic and the Sublime Porte.

The election of Stanislaus Augustus Poniatowski in 1763 as successor to the Saxon Augustus III had done nothing to improve the situation. A client of Catherine the Great, he was an enlightened patriot well aware of the need to reform the state if the Polish Republic was to survive. Two confederations were formed. The conservatives in 1766 constituted the confederation of Radom and demanded assistance from Russia, while the 'patriots' in 1768 created the confederation of Bar. Urged on by Choiseul and Vergennes, the ambassador to Constantinople, the Porte declared war on Catherine the Great in order 'to save' Poland. The result was a disaster for France's allies. The Ottoman fleet was destroyed at Çesme on the Aegean coast and while the Russian army was installed in Moravia and Wallachia in 1770, it was only the vigilance of baron von Tott, a Frenchman of Hungarian origin, that saved Constantinople from invasion. In 1771 the chancelleries of Europe began to contemplate the partition of Poland. Maria-Theresa did not want Russia to annex any part of the Balkans. In 1771 she signed a treaty with the sultan in which she promised him part of Moldavia in return for making peace with Russia. A clumsy initiative by Joseph II to occupy militarily the towns in the Zips region, since 1412 the subject of legal wrangling between Hungary and Poland, led to negotiations over partition and the Treaty of Warsaw, concluded on 25 July 1772.

Poland was still isolated. Turkey was defeated and the duc d'Aiguillon, who had replaced Choiseul in the French foreign ministry, did not want to take any action. Maria-Theresa found her good Christian sensibilities upset at taking part in this unprecedented division of a state, but she gave in to pressure from Kaunitz and Joseph II. After much pleading, she received the largest share, the whole of Galicia except Kraków and its 2 million inhabitants which she turned into an autonomous province. Russia received White Russia with Vitebsk and Mohilev and a population of 1.5 million. Prussia annexed only 'Polish Prussia' with 600 000 inhabitants. Gdansk and Torum remained within the Republic. Although Frederick the Great received the smallest share, he received the greatest benefit since Prussia and Brandenburg were finally joined together. It was possible to travel from Berlin to Königsberg without leaving Hohenzollern territory and to prevent access to Poland from the Baltic. The Russian ambassador Repnine worked on the proconsuls at Warsaw.

The Habsburgs had not acquitted themselves well on the legal and moral level. For the first time they had extended their lands through conquest and not through marriage or by election. Maria-Theresa was right and her son wrong, although Joseph II nurtured plans to exchange Galicia for Silesia. The balance within the composition of the population of the monarchy was altered as the annexation of so many Slavs decreased the proportion of Germans at a time when education policy spread the German language and promoted the Germanization of the elites. The Poles, who were Catholic, never posed any serious problem for the Habsburgs and proved loyal subjects right until 1918.

The first division of Poland was a violation of the rights of nations and opened a new era in international relations. Since the beginning of the eighteenth century, diplomats contrived to exchange provinces like sacks of corn for the sake of the balance of power in Europe. For the sake of the same balance, the great powers dismembered a nation-state without arousing any protest, least of all from the philosophes who had been captivated by Catherine the Great. Maria-Theresa showed great perception when she observed,

Prussia has always been and will always be our most formidable enemy. . . . Its further expansion is consequently the greatest real evil which can present itself to us and which we must endeavour to forestall and prevent at any price. . . . If we had stood by this principle and instead of fishing in troubled waters for the sake of acquiring a few wretched districts of Poland and if, instead of uselessly assembling at great expense a considerable army in Hungary, we had been content to maintain an army ready to enter Silesia in the event of the king of Prussia making a move upon Poland, and had limited ourselves to the simple office of impartial mediator between Russia and the Porte, there is no doubt that by this straightforward, decisive and honest action, the war could have been ended last year, the dismemberment of Poland could have been prevented, the interests of the two parties recognized and our reputation in Europe increased.

After signing the Russo-Turkish peace at Kutchuk Kainardji (1774), Joseph II received, on the pretext of straightening the frontier, the Bukovina, which brought him strategic advantages and made easier communications between Transylvania and Galicia. Populated by Romanian peasants, the northern cantons of Moldavia were soon subject to the same policy of German colonization as had been carried out in the Banat. Maria-Theresa disapproved of this annexation. She wrote to her daughter Marie-Antoinette that 'the whole business of Poland and Moravia' was quite contrary to her way of thinking.

In the final years of the empress's reign, differences again appeared within the 'troika' of Prussia, Russia and Austria, this time over the Bavarian succession, and between 1778 and 1779 this prompted a serious crisis.

The elector Maximilian Joseph, son of the emperor Charles VII, died without an heir and his inheritance should have passed to his relative in Mannheim, the elector Palatine Karl Theodor who did not have any heirs. The succession passed instead to the duke of Deux-Ponts, colonel of Royal Germany, and a client of France. Joseph II, to begin with, declared that he demanded only a few fiefs, then changed his position at the end of 1777 after Maximilian Joseph's death. In exchange for allowing the enfeoffment of Bavaria to Karl Theodor, in 1778 he annexed part of Lower Bavaria, Landshut and Straubing against the will of his mother and Frederick II. By occupying the ceded lands with imperial troops, he launched a diplomatic crisis. In July 1778 the Prussian army invaded Bohemia and the imperial troops fell back before them. This campaign of intimidation was dubbed the 'Potato War'. The Czech peasants were harassed by the occupying forces and yet again bore the cost of conflict between Vienna and Berlin.

France, which had just become involved in the American War of Independence, had a good reason not to intervene. Vergennes was hostile to the Austrian alliance and there still existed, at the court and in France at large, a party which favoured Prussia. The French foreign minister skilfully withdrew from the alliance, leaving Britain on its own, and so avoided repeating the mistakes made during the Seven Years War.

The proposal that France should act as mediator won support from Catherine II and Maria-Theresa, who put all her energies into finding a compromise and putting an honourable end to her son's follies. A diplomatic congress met at Teschen during the winter of 1779 and by the spring had reached a compromise. The Habsburgs kept the Innviertel, a small part of Bavaria. Frederick II was given the prospect of acquiring the margraviate of Ansbach. There was no further discussion of exchanging Bavaria for the Netherlands, an exchange which would have strengthened considerably the weight of the hereditary lands within the Empire. France maintained its influence in the Empire through Bavaria. Finally, Russia strengthened its prestige by acting as mediator. Everyone could be reasonably satisfied except Joseph II who had suffered a humiliation and made no secret of his impatience to be finally freed from his mother's protection.

A comparison of the state of the monarchy in 1740 and in 1780 shows that the forty years of Maria-Theresa's reign brought great credit to the last sovereign of the House of Habsburg. Despite the loss of Silesia, the population within the boundaries of the monarchy had increased by 28 per cent. In 1740 the hereditary lands had had approximately 7.4 million inhabitants and Hungary 3.6 million. In 1780, with Galicia, the monarchy had almost 20 million subjects, a figure which had been surpassed by the time the census of 1787 was taken.[3] Even after the wars and the economic crisis of 1771, the monarchy had enjoyed a period of glory under Maria-Theresa.

There had been a growth in state resources from 22 million florins in 1740 to over 50 million in 1778. Haugwitz's reforms had straightened out the monarchy's finances. Maria-Theresa's state was less indebted than France or Britain. The Austrian public debt only rose from 250 million florins in 1775 to 300 million florins because of the War of the Bavarian Succession.[4] The army which in 1740 had had 38 000 men, in 1775 reached 175 000 men stationed throughout the Danubian lands as well as Italy and the Netherlands. In addition there were 35 000 *Grenzer*, the soldiers on the Austro-Turkish frontier.

Grete Klingenstein's conclusions seem correct: that Maria-Theresa should not be set as a conservative ruler in opposition to Joseph II, the 'revolutionary Habsburg'.[5] The empress was a woman of deep convictions but she was also wise enough to take into account the spirit of the age, the enormous changes which the *Aufklärung* represented for the elites of Central Europe and the models which Britain, France and Prussia provided. In the first five years of her reign, she showed her mettle and proved her political genius by practising 'the art of the possible'. Her successor did not have the same wisdom and was forced by reality to think again.

NOTES AND REFERENCES

1. V. L. Tapié, *L'Europe de Marie-Thérèse*, Paris, 1973.
2. P. G. M. Dickson, *Finance and Government under Maria-Theresa 1740–1780*, Oxford, 1987.
3. Derek Beales, *Joseph II: In the Shadow of Maria-Theresa, 1741–1780*, Cambridge, 1987.
4. Béla Kiraly, *Hungary in the Late Eighteenth Century*, London, 1969.
5. P. G. M. Dickson, *Finance and Government.*
6. Grete Klingenstein, 'Österreich und Europa 1780', in Klingenstein (ed.) *Österreich in Europa der Aufklärung, Kontinuität und Zäsur in Europa zur Zeit Maria-Theresias und Joseph II*, Vienna, 1980.

CHAPTER SEVEN

Joseph II, Enlightened Despot

Following Maria-Theresa's death on 24 October 1780, Joseph II was left sole master of Austrian politics. As fond as he was of his mother, during the last years of her reign, he had found it difficult to hide his impatience. The change of ruler marked a break in the style of government, for although Maria-Theresa had supported reform in some areas, especially education, the young emperor wanted to impose what amounted to 'a revolution from above', to realize the ideal of an 'enlightened despot' whose role it was to assure the happiness of his people without their being consulted.

Joseph II was not an intellectual but he was immersed in rationalism and the Enlightenment, the great ideas of his age. He had an elevated conception of his mission and thought of himself as the first servant of the state. He combined indomitable energy with great imagination but lacked psychological insight and political acumen, the two qualities which had been his mother's great strength. His natural reserve made it difficult for him to develop a rapport with those around him. He could sometimes appear quite abrupt and by his crushing remarks did nothing to foster goodwill. He lacked the Habsburgs' character-istic affability, so prized by the Viennese, and had few admirers outside the narrow circle of his followers who formed a restricted elite, loyal to his reform programme.

Joseph was incapable of seeing beyond his own vision of the world. He disregarded those traditions which were still so important to the popular im-agination, and discounted national sentiment, among the Hungarians no less than the Belgians. Authoritarian and convinced that his reforms were funda-mentally right, he thought that the people should simply obey without criti-cizing or passing judgement. He wanted to be, not just the sovereign, but also the great educator of his peoples. An ardent patriot, like his role-model Frederick the Great, he devoted himself entirely to the state. He passionately wanted to create an Austrian state which transcended traditional particularisms, an idea which in itself was a revolution in the Habsburg monarchy.

THE CENTRALIZED AND UNIFIED STATE[1]

For the first time, a member of the Habsburg family wanted to unify and to centralize the states which made up the monarchy. Even though Joseph II had sought to be better informed by travelling widely, he still dismissed national cultures and particularisms as being of no account. The word liberty had a special meaning for him, it was synonymous with order. He took an interest in everything and supervised in minute detail the execution of his orders. The state took on the aspect of a dictatorship in which the ruler governed without regard for intermediary institutions. Even the Church was to yield to the state and enter its service. Joseph II's real model was Hobbes's *Leviathan*. Hostile to the society of orders, he rejected all the ceremonial, etiquette and luxury which were visible manifestations of differences in hierarchy. He was also critical of the prevailing extravagance of the Viennese, the bourgeoisie no less than the aristocracy.

The conviction that he was right very quickly turned into intolerance. Joseph II, the idealist who valued so highly humanity and tolerance, would upbraid all those who contradicted him. An ardent Catholic, he had no qualms about clamping down on all forms of baroque religiosity. In short, Joseph II was an iconoclast in a deeply conservative society.

He resumed the task, begun in his mother's reign, of refashioning institutions and counted on the bureaucracy to enforce his will. He adopted Haugwitz's idea of concentrating all the civil affairs of the Austro-Bohemian complex within a single chancery which united the chancery with the chamber of accounts and the state bank. He entrusted this whole body to count Kolowrat. The provinces were placed under the authority of six 'governments' based in Vienna, Innsbruck, Graz (Styria, Carinthia, Carniola), Prague, Brno and Trieste. The Estates' administration was suppressed and two deputies from the *Herrenstand* were admitted into each government. The Estates lost their financial autonomy. It was a total victory for absolutism.

Paradoxically, Joseph II strengthened the autonomy of Hungary. The royal chancery at Pressburg was given full authority in financial matters and the chamber of accounts of Transylvania was incorporated into the chamber at Pressburg. Hungary now enjoyed political, financial and judicial autonomy. Joseph II at the same time crushed the counties, the basis of Hungarian liberty, suppressing their administration in 1785 and replacing them with ten districts of equal weighting. The royal commissars appointed by the emperor replaced the elected prefects. Joseph II refused to be crowned because he wanted to avoid being bound by the coronation oath, and he had the crown of St Stephen brought to Vienna.

The loyalty of its officials alone was insufficient to ensure the smooth-running of the bureaucracy; a common language of administration was needed. This was a technical and political rather than a national matter, but the choice of German as the common language of administration had serious cultural repercussions. The emperor himself was bilingual in French and German and had been subject to strong Italian influences. German was the language most widely used by the educated in the monarchy and Maria-Theresa had imposed instruction in German in all the schools. The advance German had made in Bohemia and Hungary seemed to promise well for the future since the existing national cultures had not been suppressed, indeed Joseph II thought of giving them a new lease of life. After 1784, German became the sole language of administration. All officials would have to learn it and schools in Bohemia, Hungary and Galicia would have teachers of German. The emperor referred to the example set by France, England and Russia.

Joseph II soon had to revise his policies. He had discounted the significance of his ruling over a multinational state and not a homogenous nation using simply variations of dialect. He had confused the idea of a province with that of a historic nation. The decree was well received where the government had already acquired a solid position, as in Bohemia and Moravia where the reception was favourable even among those using Czech. Hungary and Galicia, which had been recently annexed, reacted violently. There were disturbances and the decree roused the national consciousness of the different peoples. This was certainly one of Joseph II's most ill-conceived reforms.

After wounding national sentiment by limiting the political privileges of the nobility, he then offended the religious sentiments of most of his subjects by re-aligning relations between the Church and the state, a task which he entrusted to an ecclesiastical commission dominated by Jansenists. He was inspired by the ideas of Febronius (J. H. von Hontheim) who argued that the Church's principal function was to dispense the sacraments and to take charge of the moral formation of the faithful. As 'supreme defender of the Church in Austria', Joseph II expected complete obedience.

The influence of the papacy came under attack. The decrees of the Holy See could only be made public with the sovereign's permission. Bishops were forbidden to address the pope directly. More than 400 monasteries were suppressed and their property, which came from ancient donations, was given to 'the religious fund', a state organization which used its revenues to subsidize the Church's other expenses. In many cases the precious contents of the monasteries' libraries were scattered in a way tantamount to vandalism. The spirit of the age was unsympathetic towards patristics, scholasticism and canon law. The buildings were sold off cheaply or else put to secular use. Many monasteries were all but empty and their supression not unjustifiable, but what the Catholics reproached Joseph II for was the manner in which these secularizations were carried out. Officials hostile to the cultural traditions which the monastic orders represented did not hide their contempt for those in religious life and in so doing caused deep offence to popular feeling. Where the work of the Counter-Reformation was unfinished, however, new parishes were created and others formally abandoned. Joseph II created new dioceses to ensure that the population was better organized, notably at Linz, Saint-Pölten, Ljubljana, Hradec Králové and Budejovice. These new bishops were far less well provided for than their fellow bishops of Passau, Vienna and Prague, and saw themselves as officials in the service of the government that paid them.

The government founded 263 new parishes in Lower Austria, 180 in Moravia and more than 1 000 in Hungary. The negative side of this was the level of state interference in parish life. Confraternities were harassed and the processions and pilgrimages which were so important a part of the lives of the mass of Catholics, were suppressed. Imperial decrees regulated preaching, liturgy and decoration. Civil officials would listen to sermons to hear whether the priests criticized the authorities. Denunciations became more frequent and led to penalties and transfers for recalcitrant clergy. The Church was to become an instrument of the state, or more precisely an instrument for the instruction of the people. The state did not need saintly priests but rather 'enlightened' clerics, dispensing a morality which appealed to reason rather than the hearts of the faithful. The end result was the bureaucratization of pastoral life and the standardization of divine service. Pastoral care was no longer so esteemed among the clergy. The new Catholicism which was much closer to reason than faith was intelligible only to the educated.

In order to assure the success of his programme, Joseph II suppressed the diocesan seminaries and conventual colleges where he could not be certain of obedience. He replaced them with state foundations for teaching theology, the 'general seminaries' which were subject to the bishops' authority and run by instructors who were converted to the new ideas. An almost military discipline was introduced, together with hatred of Rome. Future priests were convinced that they would be the pillars of the Josephist state.

The emperor might have been more moderate if he had not encountered such intransigent prelates as cardinal Migazzi, the archbishop of Vienna. Count Colloredo, the archbishop of Salzburg, and the bishops of Hradec Králové and Ljubljana wanted to acquire the reputation of being 'philosopher prelates' and on their own initiative introduced reforms. Vacancies in sees were filled one after the other with members of the ecclesiastical commission. These prelates were men of moral and intellectual strength, who allowed the growth of anti-clerical propaganda which lampooned traditional forms of piety and employed biting irony against the opponents of the Josephist Church.

To make it yet clearer that the age of the Counter-Reformation and of the 'Church triumphant' was at a close, Joseph II promulgated on 13 October 1781 an edict of toleration which granted Protestants and Orthodox the freedom to worship and restored to them all their civil rights. Catholicism still remained the 'dominant' state religion. Places of worship which were not Catholic still could not be built with a steeple or square in front and the registers of the civil state were still held by Catholic clergy who collected 'casual offerings' from all subjects, regardless of faith.

In Carinthia about fifty Protestant communities re-formed and the edict was welcomed in Hungary where almost 5 million inhabitants were not Catholic. According to Benda, in 1790 25 per cent of Hungarians were Calvinists, 20 per cent Greek Orthodox and 5 per cent of the Augsburg confession. Since 1732, Protestants had been *de facto* excluded from all official posts and for this reason the edict caused a section of the Protestant nobility, including such men as Gergely Berzeviczy, to rally enthusiastically to Joseph II, notwithstanding his measures favouring the German language and the centralization of the administration. As for the Jews, although they did not receive full civil rights, their lot was improved. They were given permission to practise manual trades, to found industrial enterprises and to attend university. Discrimination in dress was also abolished. These decisions were well received by the communities in

Bohemia and Austria but the Orthodox Jews of Galicia showed much less enthusiasm. Anti-Semitism broke out in some sections of the Christian population and many Catholics thought that toleration had gone too far.

In 1783 the sphere of action of the commission of education and censorship was extended to the whole monarchy. The commission was charged with continuing the work begun in 1774. Although in 1780 there were 200 000 pupils divided among fifteen training colleges, eighty-three secondary schools, forty-seven girls' schools and 3 848 primary schools, Joseph II wanted to complete the task undertaken. Education would be exclusively the task of the state but in a confessional framework since, according to the emperor, religion provided the best moral education. Teachers would be subject to close scrutiny by inspectors, both with respect to their conduct as well as the knowledge they dispensed. This system was effective at the level of primary education and made it possible to deliver the peasant masses from ignorance, but it yielded indifferent results in the colleges and proved catastrophic for higher education. The emperor had no interest in scientific research or research in general. To his way of thinking, it seemed the state needed officials and so only public law and economics were useful. The universities lost their autonomy. The director, who was appointed by the state, saw to it that the emperor's instructions were obeyed by poorly paid professors. The universities in Austria found it difficult to submit to Josephist legislation.

The imperial education policy naturally gave rise to conflict with the Curia, conflict which chancellor Kaunitz, 'a true philosophe', accepted with a touch of irony. In 1782 Pius VI, anxious to preserve the unity of the Church, decided to travel to Vienna. He was received triumphantly by the people and the court showed him polite deference while Kaunitz 'gritted his teeth'. The discussions which were held did not lead to any dramatic conclusions and both sides remained firm in their positions. Pius VI did not press for the reforms to be abolished but managed to secure the retention of the bull *Unigenitus* which had condemned Jansenism. The pope was reassured on essential issues and kept his primacy in doctrinal matters. He may even have looked with favour upon Joseph II's reorganization of the dioceses and parishes.

A 'philosophe in a crown', Joseph II was not so naive as to believe that political reforms alone would suffice. His travels in France in 1776 under the name Falkenstein* had made him aware of the importance of economics and had given him the chance to learn about the theories prevailing there: mercantilism, which gave priority to industry and balancing accounts, and the physiocracy of Quesnay and Turgot** who both emphasized agriculture. He created a synthesis with the Austrian cameralist doctrines of the previous century and resolutely aligned himself with the protectionists to favour industry

---

* Translator's note: Falkenstein was a small county on the French border which was administered as part of the monarchy.

** Translator's note: Anne Robert Jacques, baron de Turgot and François Quesnay, with the elder Mirabeau, formed the first circle of Physiocrats who took up their pens against mercantilism. Turgot was appointed controller general of finance by Louis XVI in 1774 and wrote the highly influential *Réflexions sur la formation et la distribution des richesses* (1766).

and eliminate foreign competition. He restricted imports, which he thought were motivated principally by social rivalry among the wealthy, and favoured exports, which would increase profits and improve the prosperity of the Austrians. The result was a rapid rise in productivity which opened the way for the industrial revolution.

The emperor understood that agriculture would only advance if the peasants were free and serfdom suppressed in those lands where it was still practised. His model was the regime in Lower Austria where the peasant did not suffer personal servitude and could choose to pay an indemnity instead of the *robot*. The peasant was a free man who paid dues to his lord. The patent of 1 November 1781 abolished personal servitude in Bohemia, Moravia and Silesia. A peasant no longer had to obtain his lord's permission to get married, to leave the domain, to send his children to school or to apprentice them. Children were no longer tied to personal service in the lord's castle. Peasants could build on their plots, sell or mortgage them. The patent allowed country-dwellers to move and made easier the rural exodus. A second patent issued on 10 February 1789 planned to suppress the *robot* from All Saints' Day the following year. The *robot*, which had been obligatory and perpetual, would be superseded by a contract between the peasant and his lord which would last three years and could be revoked. The implementation of this most radical measure was forestalled by Joseph II's death and it was not until the revolution of 1848 that the *robot*, the chief obstacle to the modernization of Austrian agriculture, was abolished.

Joseph II's 'enlightened policy', for all his good intentions, was a failure. It was in his foreign policy that his failure was greatest. He encountered opposition from Prussia and Russia and the alliance with France became increasingly insecure. Perpetually dissatisfied, he felt the need to act on the grand scale but his initiatives threatened the security of Europe on a number of occasions. In 1775, three years after the first division of Poland which had brought his mother Galicia, Joseph II annexed the Bukovina which had previously been part of the Ottoman empire and inhabited by Slavs and Romanians. Catherine the Great of Russia allowed the annexation and the Porte was obliged to cede. Bukovina remained an Austrian province until 1918.

Joseph II was firmly wedded to the status quo in Italy, where he exerted direct control as duke of Milan, and indirect control through his brother Peter Leopold the grand duke of Tuscany, and his brothers-in-law at Modena and Naples.

He did not, however, hide his ambitions in the German world and the Bavarian succession crisis provided him with the pretext for intervention. Vergennes*, the French foreign minister, refused to support him, even in return for compensation in the Netherlands, and Frederick II would not allow the Austrian state to expand and destroy the equilibrium that had resulted from his conquests. The Prussian army intervened after Joseph II occupied Bavaria. The campaign was brief, without a battle, and known as the 'Potato War'

---

* Translator's note: Charles Gravier, comte de Vergennes (1717–87), Louis XVI's foreign minister, wanted to keep France free to concentrate on the struggle with the British in North America.

because it took place during the potato harvest. The Peace of Teschen in May 1779 left Austria with only a district of Bavaria and the bitterness of defeat.

Joseph II tried to raise the emperor's prestige by re-activating the Aulic Council and by exercising his rights as supreme justice for the small principalities of the Empire.

In 1785 he approached Karl Theodor, the elector Palatine and of Bavaria, with the suggestion that he exchange Bavaria for the Austrian Netherlands. Karl Theodor would have happily swapped Munich for Brussels but Vergennes would not countenance such an arrangement and sought a preliminary agreement from Prussia and the German states. It was a brief affair. Joseph II was intimidated by Frederick II's fulminations. The Franco-Austrian alliance was over. It was a serious defeat for the Habsburgs in the long term because they were never able to establish preponderance in the central and southern regions of the Reich and so to assemble a state with a German majority. The annexation of Bavaria would have compensated for the loss of Silesia. Joseph II wanted to open the Scheldt for navigation in breach of the Treaty of Westphalia but the Dutch, with the support of France and Prussia, forced him to retire. After his last defeat in the west, the best option before Joseph II was to turn towards the Balkans. In February 1788 Austria joined Russia in the war against the Ottoman empire which had begun the previous year. Catherine the Great, in her famous 'Greek project' of 1786, envisaged sharing out the Ottoman lands in Europe. The 1788 campaign went badly for Joseph II who rode at the head of his army in Serbia, but the following year marshal Laudon took Belgrade and Cobourg occupied Bucharest. Austria made peace in 1791 and returned its conquests.

In his domestic policies, Joseph II's mistakes were yet more serious and provoked revolts in Belgium and Hungary. In 1789 the Belgians presented their demands. Gradually a consensus was reached among the different groups of discontented led by the lawyer Vonck. Their aim was the emancipation of Belgium without recourse to French aid. An army of patriots opened fire against the imperial troops and gradually insurrection took hold of the whole country. The Austrian authorities evacuated Brussels and the principal towns, finally leaving Antwerp in March 1790. At the death of the emperor, the Netherlands were lost to the Habsburgs. Hungary was on the verge of open rebellion, aristocratic reaction was at large and the nobles burnt the cadastres. Shortly before he died, Joseph II promised to summon the Diet.

He thought it wisest to abrogate most of his reforms with the exception of the patents of 1781, the edicts of tolerance concerning the emancipation of the serfs and the statute of the Church. He composed his own epitaph, 'Here lies a prince whose intentions were pure but who had the misfortune to see his plans all fail.'

JOSEPH II: *PATER PATRIAE* OR PHILANTHROPIST?[2]

Joseph II's disappointment and the final days of this ailing and unpopular prince should not obscure the importance of his work which is still admired in many different quarters. A distinction should be made between the short and the long term. In the short term, the defeat, the evident muddle and withdrawal of almost all his reform edicts at the end of his reign amounted to self-criticism on Joseph II's part, a reappraisal of his own methods which were quite alien to the Habsburgs. Only by establishing a brutal dictatorship, which was not Joseph II's intention, could the course of history be changed without support from the powerful elites and the people. Joseph II the idealist ran up against the harsh laws of reality, the vested interests, the forces of habit and of inertia, and incomprehension. He proved that the happiness of the people cannot be achieved against their will.

The last two years of his reign turned into a disaster. The defeats in the Turkish war were the moment of revelation. After the defeats in Serbia, the Banat of Temesvár in southern Hungary, land which had been colonized and was the great pride of his mother's reign, was invaded by the age-old enemy, the Turks. Villages were set ablaze by the Ottoman troops ahead of the imperial forces who were quite powerless. It was a return to the darkest years of the baroque age and the patient efforts of half a century were reduced to nothing because the emperor had committed a series of errors.

Joseph II was not wise enough to abandon his imperialist policy which led to a series of resounding defeats in Germany. He believed Austria needed to expand, to increase its land area and population to compensate for the loss of Silesia, the effects of which were felt for half a century. He dreaded Russian expansion into the Balkans, a fear which Kaunitz and Cobenzl shared and which continued to haunt them throughout the revolutionary period.

A fervent admirer of Frederick the Great, the emperor thought that by donning a uniform and busying himself with military matters he could become the strategist of genius which he was so far from being. The campaign in Serbia was the moment of truth for an army which lacked good men. The aged marshal Laudon, hero of the Seven Years War, had had to come to the rescue.

In common with all the other 'enlightened minds' of his day, Joseph II was convinced that the Grand Turk was the 'sick man of Europe'. Some European military advisors and the natural qualities of the Turkish soldier had sufficed to shatter such illusions which had arisen during the last Russo-Turkish war. The dream of Balkan conquest and sharing out the Ottoman empire with Russia evaporated. This defeat served as a lesson for Austria which in the future would modify its Balkan ambitions. The conflict left the imperial army weakened and disorganized at the moment when it was most needed in Western Europe by the cabinet in Vienna.

Much more serious were the revolts in Belgium and Hungary since they revealed the weakness of the philosopher-in-a-crown's domestic policies. The disturbances in the Austrian Netherlands had been provoked by Joseph II's blundering religious policy. The clergy refused to establish general seminaries where future priests would be recruited for state-service. The emperor had overlooked the fact that the peace-loving inhabitants of the Netherlands remained attached to their Catholic religion above all else and for two centuries had made sacrifices in favour of the House of Austria out of devotion to the faith of their fathers. The orders, the noble and municipal oligarchies, were equally attached to their traditional liberties: the political privileges symbolized by the 'joyous entry' of the duchy of Brabant which dated from 1384 and which, in common with all the particular constitutions of the different Estates of the monarchy, Joseph II had refused to recognize. He had turned conservative notables into revolutionaries. As for the peasant masses who should have been his allies against the nobility, he was unable to win them over, as much because of his hesitancy in his social policy as his blunders and insensitivities in religious matters.

Joseph II, out of caution, did not extend to Transylvania the legislation abolishing personal servitude. This discrimination provoked one of the most serious peasant revolts in the country's history. The insurrection which was led by Horia, a peasant, broke out in 1786 and developed into full-scale assaults on castles and the nobles living in them. It was brutally suppressed. The emperor became aware of the gravity of the problem, placed a limit on feudal dues and in the end abolished the *robot*.

The peasants of Bohemia and Austria welcomed the decrees which would progressively free them from feudal oppression but were deeply upset by the measures concerning religion. Profoundly marked for a century and a half by the efforts of the Counter-Reformation clergy, they were attached to the processions, pilgrimages and local saints and their exuberant cults as well as the ornate church decoration, the pomp and elaborate ceremonies. The manifestations of baroque piety regulated their daily lives and offered diversion. They saw nothing wrong with the havoc accompanying pilgrimages nor in the ever-increasing number of festivals. Their sensibilities were untouched by a cold and rational religion inspired by Jansenism, based on morals and the zeal for work. The old clergy attached to the traditional values and gestures of piety still remained in place. The process of transforming or replacing them was slow and would not occur until there were new promotions in the general seminaries. Rural society was remarkably resistant to Josephism.

The people of Vienna, especially the poorest elements, fared little better. In the baroque tradition, the drunks and beggars who thronged in the capital were treated with indulgence, but Joseph II wanted to purge the city and to impose measures which verged on the purely despotic. Harsh sentences of imprisonment and forced labour in Hungary were meted out for minor crimes such as bilking, brawls and breaches of the peace. Few of those condemned to hauling boats along the Danube in the Russian manner survived their sentence.[3] What was yet worse, Joseph II exercised his royal right as supreme justice to interrupt trials and to condemn a defendant without further judgement to several years' deportation for a minor misdemeanour. His was a strange conception of the rule of law.

Joseph II did have some supporters, not any one social class but individuals such as certain freemasons who constituted a political elite within the social elite. The bureaucracy was still only partially developed, the nobility was very divided, the clergy for the most part hostile. As a group, the non-Catholics, the beneficiaries of the patent of 1781, lent their support out of gratitude. The support of Protestant nobles in Hungary gave the emperor some hope of imposing his reforms there.[4] Among the Hungarian Catholic hierarchy, however, the patent of toleration had only excited a hatred which could not be propitiated.

The two patents issued in the autumn of 1781 which instituted civil tolerance and abolished personal servitude nonetheless had considerable impact since they marked a clear break with the most controversial aspects of the policy hitherto followed by the House of Austria, namely the enslavement of the free peasantry and unification by Catholicism. The speed with which the patents were promulgated, a year after Joseph II's accession, demonstrates the importance which the emperor accorded them. It also showed that he would maintain Catholicism as the state religion and that he did not intend a direct confrontation with the nobility, the principal political force within the Austrian monarchy. He granted freedom of worship to Protestants in 'Cisleithania' and by giving political rights to the Protestants in Hungary he put an end to a policy which had been understandable in 1650 but which had been thwarted by the determination of certain bold subjects. It marked the obsolescence of the theories of Justus Lipsius and Fr. Lamormain. The ideal of the good ruler had changed. It was no longer a question of ensuring the eternal salvation of his subjects by obliging them to embrace 'the only true faith', but of procuring for them happiness in this world.

The secularization of numerous monasteries and convents had led in some instances to acts of vandalism and iconoclastic outbursts by minor officials of limited vision. It was, however, fundamentally commendable and demonstrated a concern to ensure better pastoral work from the clergy and a better level of staff in rural parishes, a problem which Leopold I, as devout as he was, had been incapable of solving in the face of the self-interested resistance of the orders.

Joseph II, by continuing the work his mother had begun after 1749, was the true creator of the Austrian state as it existed until 1918, where officers and officials accepted that they would leave the narrow framework of their national state, be it Bohemia, Hungary, Galicia or Milan, and put themselves at the service of a much larger entity. This development coincided with the prodigious rise of German culture in the Protestant states of the *Reich*. The emperor, a contemporary of Goethe and Schiller, gave permission for the young and gifted to study at the university of Göttingen which, in time, was rivalled by the university of Bonn founded in 1784 by Joseph II's brother, Maximilian Francis, the elector of Cologne. The emperor imposed German as the sole language of administration but at the same time supported the rebirth of Czech national culture and helped other national cultures. He created the German national theatre at the court, the celebrated Hofburg theatre which was assured of a glorious future, and finally broke the monopoly of Italian culture at Vienna.

He relaxed censorship and by directing it to the advantage of his own policies, for ten years he opened Austria to foreign intellectual influences. The theatres played as important a part as translations of works by western writers in disseminating the new ideas which were adapted in plays accessible to the vast Viennese public. Schikaneder, installed in a suburban theatre just outside the capital, staged operas by Mozart, including his masonic opera *The Magic Flute*, as well as a wide variety of plays for the petite bourgeoisie who hitherto had been excluded from all cosmopolitan currents. Joseph II's reign was marked by the opening up of the country which until then had of its own accord kept itself protected from foreign influences or more precisely those foreign ideas judged subversive by the Church and government. For the first time since the sixteenth century, the Germanophone bourgeoisie could read something other than the narrow range of works approved by the ecclesiastical censors.

For this reason, the nineteenth-century liberal bourgeoisie was Josephist. The Catholic conservatives did not forgive him for the secularization of the monasteries and for calling to account the clergy. This was why Hungarian historians, leaving aside Joseph II's policy of Germanization, see him as a courageous reformer who for once and for all ended the Counter-Reformation and guaranteed their country's cultural advance. But could the emperor achieve anything more than a cultural revolution in a monarchy where the nobility still retained economic power, social prestige and, to a great extent, political power? The rise of the bourgeoisie only became possible when manufacturing industry developed as a consequence of the abolition of serfdom. The diversification of the elites was a slow process and in the end it was Francis Joseph who in the era of neo-absolutism reaped the dividends of Joseph II's policies. The process of Germanization, however, came too late and would probably never have been possible in Hungary and Lombardy. Joseph II roused strong feelings in all his subjects and only when everything is taken into consideration can his achievements be judged.

NOTES AND REFERENCES

1. Paul von Mitrofanov, *Josef II, seine politische und kulturelle Tätigkeit*, 2 vols, Vienna, 1910.
   Eduard Winter, *Der Josefinismus. Geschichte des österreichischen Reformkatholizismus*, Berlin, 1962.
   Oszkar Sashegyi, *Zensur und Geistesfreiheit under Josef II*, Budapest, 1958.
   R. Rosolsky, *Die grosse Steuerund Agrarreform Josefs II*, Warsaw, 1961.
   Ernst Wangermann, *Aufklärung und Staatsbürgerliche Erziehung Gottfried van Swieten als Reformator des österreichischen Unterrichtswesens, 1781–1791*, Vienna, 1978.
   Catalogue for the exhibition shown at Melk, *Österreich zur Zeit Kaiser Josefs II*, 1980.
   Derek Beales, *Joseph II: In the Shadow of Maria-Theresa, 1740–1780*, Cambridge, 1987.
   François Fejtö, *Joseph II: un Habsbourg révolutionnaire*, Paris, 1949.
   Alfred von Arneth (ed.), *Maria Theresia und Joseph II. Ihre Korrespondenz samt Briefe Josephs an seinen Bruder Leopold*, 3 vols, Vienna, 1867–68.
2. Kalman Benda, *Jozsef II: eberbarat vagy hazafi*, Budapest, 1980.
3. Pierre Paul Bernard, *The Limits of Enlightenment. Joseph II and the Law*, Chicago, 1979.
4. Eva H. Balazs, *Berzeviczy Gergely*, Budapest, 1969.

CHAPTER EIGHT

Leopold II and the End of the Enlightenment (1790–92)

Joseph II died on 20 February 1790. Peter Leopold, his brother, left Florence and arrived at Vienna on 6 March. The Hungarians, meanwhile, celebrated at Buda the return of the Holy Crown, the symbol of the unity and independence of the kingdom of St Stephen. The grand duke of Tuscany, presently emperor Leopold II, was not a political novice. For a quarter of a century, he had ruled Tuscany after succeeding his father, the emperor Francis I, in 1765. The experience he had gained and the close contact he had maintained with his elder brother helped him to overcome the serious difficulties he faced at the time of his accession. There were revolts in Hungry and Belgium, the Turkish war was yet to be resolved and revolutionary propaganda was spreading from France.

PETER LEOPOLD, AN ENLIGHTENED DESPOT[1]

The Florentines have not forgotten the archduke's achievements in his 'second homeland'. Visitors to the basilica of Santa Croce in Florence, the former Franciscan church which has been transformed into an Italian national pantheon, can see the monument to *Pietro-Leopoldo* beside the tomb of Galileo.

The archduke was born at Schönbrunn in 1747 and received his first name in honour of his godmother, Elizabeth Petrovna, the empress of Russia. Intended for the throne of Tuscany from 1761, he married the Spanish *infanta* Maria Luisa in 1765 and had twelve children. Leopold II, by his fruitful marriage, assured the continuation of the House of Habsburg-Lorraine which was vital for stability within the monarchy and good foreign relations. The secundogenitures enabled the government in Vienna to maintain its preponderance in Italy. Leopold's sister Maria Carolina ruled at Naples; another sister, Maria Amalia, married Ferdinand of Bourbon, the duke of Parma; and his younger brother, the archduke Ferdinand, married Maria Beatrix, the heiress of the House of Este, and ruled at Modena.

Leopold had received a good cultural education. Maria-Theresa had entrusted him to count Thurn and, more significantly, to the jurist Martini who taught natural law at the university of Vienna. By the time he was fifteen, Leopold knew Latin, French and German and later adopted Italian as his 'mother tongue' and so resumed the Habsburgs' tradition of mastering the languages of those over whom they ruled. He had an enquiring mind, was alert and intelligent and was interested in science and technology. He applied himself to his studies, had a melancholy temperament like his father and disappointed his mother by his indifference to the niceties of appearance and behaviour and his liking for the company of 'small people'. Much later, he would, like his brother, win the hearts of his subjects and take as his motto *Opes regum corda subditorum* ('the riches of kings are the hearts of their subjects').

In 1764 and 1765 he accompanied his brother Joseph on his travels to Frankfurt, Hungary and Bohemia. He was at Innsbruck with the whole court at the time of the emperor Francis I's sudden death. Well supplied with precise instructions from his mother, he went straight to Florence with his young bride. At eighteen, he was ruler of Tuscany, an illustrious Italian principality which his elder brother, however, treated almost as a protectorate.

Nobody found Joseph II easy to deal with, but the strained relations between the two brothers were made worse when the emperor confiscated part of the inheritance, about 18 million florins, which the late emperor had accumulated by his own frugality and able management. Joseph II's demands for the return of funds from the Tuscan 'reserve treasury' antagonized Leopold. Later, in 1784, the young ruler was prevented by his 'despotic brother' from promulgating the constitution which he had prepared for Tuscany.

After count Thurn's death, the government in Florence was directed by count Franz Xaver Ursini-Rosenberg. From 1767 onwards, Leopold worked closely with a team of Tuscan reformers – Pompeo Neri, Angelo Tavanti, Francesco Gianni – and began to put his plan into action, practising the principles of physiocracy, in particular free trade in grain. Diligently pursuing his reforms, in a quarter of a century Leopold made Tuscany a model country, a real trial-ground for the philosophy of the Enlightenment. He stopped the general farming of taxes, transferred ecclesiastical property into the hands of the secular clergy, instituted perpetual tenancies for farms to improve the lot of the peasants and suppressed the right of criminals to refuge in churches.

In 1770 count Ursini-Rosenberg returned to Vienna and Leopold began his period of personal rule. He suppressed the guilds and created a chamber of commerce, of arts and of industry. He introduced municipal reforms so that Tuscany gradually acquired a modern administration. He reformed the police and the health administration and replaced the army with an 'urban' militia. It was typical of his scientific method that he began by introducing changes on an experimental basis in some municipalities before presenting them to the whole grand duchy as obligatory.

In 1778 Leopold was recalled to Vienna by Maria-Theresa during the 'Potato War' and noted the position in which the illustrious house and the monarchy found itself. He left a very critical memorandum in which he showed his profound dislike for his brother's despotic ways. He condemned the co-regency from its beginning and the centralization of the bureaucracy. Instead of developing a costly state apparatus, he advocated decentralization, the renewal of the Diet's administrative apparatus and the liberation of the peasantry. He extolled absolute toleration in the confessional field, the suppression of censorship and the participation of the governed in government.

Confident of the rightness of his convictions, on his return to Tuscany he prepared a constitution which was obstructed when Joseph II visited Florence. The emperor, certain that he himself would not produce an heir, was preoccupied with the succession. In 1784 he proposed that the principle of secundogeniture should be abolished and that the young archduke Francis should be sent to Vienna to receive an education appropriate for the heir to the throne. Leopold complied but in 1790 he re-established secundogeniture and entrusted the government of Tuscany to his younger son Ferdinand. The House of Habsburg-Lorraine ruled Florence until 1859 when Tuscany was annexed by the kingdom of Italy.

Joseph II wanted Tuscany to be re-incorporated within the Habsburg family's patrimony and it is for this reason that he, with Kaunitz's support, prevented the promulgation of the constitution which would have given the duchy's subjects a representative assembly. Peter Leopold, it should be noted, was the only 'enlightened despot' who had really bestowed a constitution upon his people. He ruled, however, over a small country, an Austrian protectorate, and could not override his elder brother's wishes. This episode shows the limits of Joseph II's openness to reform.

Leopold embarked upon a bold religious policy because, even more than his brother Joseph, he supported Reform Catholicism. The Church in Tuscany was more tyrannical and backward than in the monarchy. In 1786 the sovereign, greatly influenced by the Jansenist Scipione de' Ricci, proposed to the bishops fifty-seven 'ecclesiastical points' which would serve as the basis of discussion for reforms in the 'national' council which met at Pistoia. In the course of preliminary discussions, Peter Leopold and de' Ricci were repudiated by the conservative bishops who constituted the majority. The grand duke did not want to break with the Holy See and made minor reforms. This defeat served as a lesson and made him cautious in dealing with relations between the Church and state after 1790.

In 1786 Leopold published a code of criminal procedure which was very novel and not only abolished torture but also the death penalty and imprisonment for debts. He planned to reform the education system but was prevented by his urgent recall to Vienna in February 1790 when he faced the difficult task of rectifying his brother's follies.

Faced with the catastrophic situation in the monarchy and his mortally ill brother, Leopold had time to work out a system of government which he entrusted to his sisters Maria Christina, governor of the Netherlands, and Maria Carolina, queen of Naples, his younger brother Maximilian Francis, elector of Cologne, and his son the archduke Francis, heir to the throne, then aged twenty-three.

He dealt with the most urgent issues in a few months. On 27 July 1790 he broke the international deadlock by signing the Convention of Reichenbach with Frederick William II of Prussia who had succeeded his uncle Frederick II in 1787. Prussia stopped supporting the Hungarian rebels and the Belgian separatists and smoothed the way for the imperial election in which Joseph II had never shown any interest. The revolt of the Netherlands collapsed and Austrian troops entered Brussels without firing and were shortly followed by the governor and her husband, Albert of Saxe-Teschen. Leopold II also concluded an armistice with the Turks and the following year signed the Peace of Sistowa which re-established the status quo. In September 1790 he reached a compromise with the Hungarian nobility and appeased the discontented nobles of the hereditary lands by suppressing the 'reglementation urbariale' imposed by Joseph II and the accompanying fiscal reforms. He was even able to pacify the clergy by closing the general seminaries which had been the reason for the revolt in the Netherlands. This gesture cost him very little as he had thought it fundamentally ill-advised since the restrictions only served to promote hypocrisy.

The coronations at Frankfurt on 9 October 1790, at Pressburg on 15 November and at Prague the following year demonstrated to the world at large that Leopold II had renewed tradition, that the Habsburgs held the imperial crown and that the monarchy continued to respect particularisms, in particular the autonomy of the kingdom of Hungary. The three ceremonies enhanced the prestige of the sovereign who was hailed as 'the prince of peace' and 'Leopold the Wise'. It was no coincidence that he commissioned from Mozart a grand opera entitled La Clemenza di Tito for the coronation at Prague in September 1791. It was intended to reassure the elites who for ten years had been buffeted by reforms and contempt for the identity of the kingdom of Bohemia, and who were now shocked by the events in Paris which held out no promises for the protection of noble privilege.

Leopold II welcomed the beginnings of the French Revolution and the Polish Revolution of 1791 which, in appearance at least, was led by an 'enlightened king', Stanislaus Augustus Poniatowski. He saw in both revolutions the triumph of his own ideas in the field of the constitution and a curb on 'monarchical despotism' in Paris as in Warsaw. He did not cease to advise his sister Marie-Antoinette and Louis XVI to reach an accommodation with their subjects, but he underestimated the power of the revolutionary movement. Alarmed at the consequences of the Flight to Varenne, he feared for the safety of the royal family. Under pressure from the French refugees who came to him and whom he mistrusted, he agreed to sign the declaration of Pillnitz by which he threatened with Prussia to intervene in France to re-establish order. It was only at the end of his life, on 7 February 1792, that he agreed to sign with Prussia the defensive alliance of which Frederick William had been dreaming as the means to crush the Parisian revolutionaries. Leopold II, despite the worrying turn taken in French politics, did not yield to the war party at Vienna which wanted to invade France to save Louis XVI and Marie-Antoinette.

His sudden death was a great misfortune. He was not poisoned, as has often been claimed, but died within forty-eight hours of contracting pleurisy. One of the most brilliant rulers of the House of Austria, he was snatched away from his people's affection after only two years of rule at Vienna, where he had proved a worthy son of Maria-Theresa.

LEOPOLD II AND HUNGARY[2]

In March 1790, Hungary was yet again on the point of revolt. Apart from the small number of enlightened, and often Protestant, nobles who had rallied to Joseph II and the German-speaking bourgeoisie, every social class had serious grievances against the government at Vienna and was ready to defend its interests with violence.

The new revolt by the orders was an attempt to re-establish the autonomy of the kingdom. Coming at the same time as the revolt in the Netherlands, diplomatic pressure from Prussia, the effects of the French Revolution and the difficult consequences of the Turkish war, the revolt was extremely serious. Leopold II proved his skills as a politician. The revolt had taken on the character of a national struggle with anti-German but also anti-fiscal overtones, as all the documents which could assist the imposition of tax on the nobility were carefully collected and destroyed. The movement was led by the gentry, the *bene possessionati*, who had been deprived of their political power by Joseph II's reforms. They put forward their own candidates in the elections for the county deputies and terrorized those who had cooperated with Joseph II. The movement was supported by the lesser nobility in the county assemblies and held sway in the lower chamber of the Diet. The clergy and great aristocrats in response formed a solid block of support behind the dynasty. The political gamble made by the Diet when it met in June 1790 at Buda, was not thwarted.

There was a great public debate. A great outpouring of pamphlets, at least 500 in 1790, and newspapers expressed the views of diverse political and religious currents. Some 5 000 copies of *Oratio ad nobiles regni Hungariae*, a pamphlet by Ignác Martinovics, were printed, but the most significant text was the forty-page tract entitled *Pia desideria cordis Hungarici* (The Pious Desires of a Hungarian Heart Longing for the Good of its Fatherland), which had a profound influence on the Diet of 1790. Its goal was to limit royal power and to extend the privileges of the 'nation', i.e. the orders, and it issued the first demand for a written constitution which would be integrated within public law. The tract was influenced by the Polish model and called for the creation of a Senate elected by the Diet and which would sit permanently while the Diet was in recess. The Diet would control the finances and the army.

Other pamphlets were yet more reactionary and, inspired by the Catholic hierarchy, contained demands for the complete abrogation of religious toleration and the re-establishment of the dominant position of the Church within the state. *Hungarus pro rege* defended royal absolutism and denied the sovereignty of the nation.

This literature, published in Latin, Hungarian and German, revealed the existence of an intense political life among the elite. It was soon joined by an impressive number of constitutional projects which show a level of real political maturity.

The gentry had managed to form a party which drew its support from among the Protestants and the freemasons and their lodges and which was led by Petár Balogh, the deputy for the county of Nograd. In June and July 1790, the party drew up plans for a constitution which, if adopted, would have put into question not only the reforms enacted in the eighteenth century but also the 1711 Peace of Szatmár. The following demands were set out in this document: the Diet should meet annually at Pest and vote on any taxation; the crown should no longer enjoy the power of veto; a senate should control the acts of the executive power; the Hungarian chancellery should return from Vienna to Buda and the chancellor should be answerable before the Diet; the prefects appointed by the king should be chosen from among four candidates elected by the county; all officeholders should be appointed by the king from a list of four candidates presented by the senate; Hungary should have its own national army independent of the War Council in Vienna and commanded by a headquarters recruited from among the middle nobility; the palatine, as head of the Hungarian army, should receive his instructions from the Senate; the right of insurrection, the *jus resistendi* abolished in 1687, should be reinstated. In common with the Polish constitution of 3 May 1791, the proposed Hungarian constitution did not entail the nobility according any rights to the peasants who were kept in their state of servitude. The most enlightened of deputies justified their attitude on the grounds that the peasant masses lacked education and political consciousness, but in truth the nobility saw the *robot* and servitude as the only guarantee of their economic power. They imagined that the introduction of waged labour would ruin them outright.

The whole of the formal political debate was focused on the oath which Leopold swore on the day of his coronation, the *diploma regis*. This was a fundamental element of the old Hungarian public law because the text had the force of law throughout the whole of the monarch's reign.

The nobles did not hesitate to support their claims with armed force and raised a militia or *banderia* in each county. These troops were raised to begin with to accompany the crown of St Stephen during its return to Buda in March 1790. The poor nobles ruined themselves to buy weapons and uniforms, and soldiers deserted the Hungarian regiments of the imperial army.

At the same time the peasants began once again to stir in support of Leopold II. During the age of the Enlightenment, there had been peasant revolts directed against the magnates in Hungary as in Bohemia, but these movements had been local, focused in a particular county: Bihár in 1751, Hodmezövásárhely in 1753, Slavonia in 1755, the Székelys in 1763 and in Somogy in 1765. Horia's revolt* in Transylvania under Joseph II had spread concern among the authorities in Vienna. The revolt was brutally suppressed but it led Joseph II to reflect on the condition of the peasantry and, at least in principle, to abolish serfdom. In March 1790 the disturbances began to affect the north-east of the country. Although the meetings which took place and the pamphlets which were distributed supported the crown and were hostile towards the orders, Leopold gave orders for the army to intervene to maintain peace and public safety but expressly forbade it from acting like a police force to collect taxes.

---

* Translator's note: Nicolae Horia (1730–85) led a peasants' revolt in the spring of 1784 in the region of Hunedoara and Alba Julia.

Leopold appealed to the urban bourgeoisie to help excite feelings against the nobility and used the services of Gotthardi, the former head of the secret police in Hungary, and Hoffmann, a German professor at the university of Pest. A 'civil guard' was organized in the royal towns to put a check on the nobles' *banderia*.*

The campaign of petitions collapsed because the bourgeoisie did not dare challenge the national party led by the middle nobility. Leopold also started a policy which would be used again in 1848: he played on the national minorities, in particular the Serbs in the south of the country, who were alarmed by the eruption of Hungarian nationalism.

Although Kaunitz and the *Staatsrat* disapproved of this straightforward application of the principle *divide et impera*, the king found himself placed on the defensive with regard to the nobles who were undertaking negotiations with the Prussian government. Even after the opening of the Diet, a delegation of nobles again went to Berlin to offer the crown of St Stephen to Karl Augustus, the duke of Saxe-Weimar and a patron of Goethe. The Hungarian nobles did not intend to put themselves in the position of being guilty of high treason but they found themselves mere pawns on the international chess-board and were not taken altogether seriously by the cabinet in Berlin. The Reichenbach accord signed by the emperor on 27 July 1790 made any collaboration between Hungary and Prussia ineffective. It broke the deadlock in internal affairs and eased the way for a fresh agreement between the Habsburgs and the Hungarian nobility.

At the end of August 1790, the court at Berlin's volte-face and the concentration of imperial troops in Hungary left the Diet very disenchanted. The leading politicians hoped that the essentials at least could be saved and renounced the elective monarchy. Leopold II was by temperament inclined towards compromise. During the autumn, negotiations took place through the influence of Károly Zichy who, in the absence of a palatine, presided over the upper chamber, and József Urményi, the man behind the *Ratio educationis* and the president of the lower chamber. Petár Balogh lost his ascendancy over the nobility and then, in 1794, passed over to the court party. The agreement was gradually adapted to the programme of the *diploma regis*. Kaunitz and the *Staatsrat* refused to waver from the diploma's conservative character which could do no more than simply resume the programmes of the diplomas of Charles VI (Charles III of Hungary) and Maria-Theresa. The orders were no longer in a strong position, but through the skill of Zichy and Urményi, their principal demands were mentioned in a decree promulgated after the coronation which took place on 15 November. The Diet, having been foiled, elected as palatine the king's son, the archduke Leopold, and so began a new tradition: until the revolution in 1848, the office of palatine was always given to an archduke.

The compromise of 21 September 1790 showed that Leopold was prepared

---

* Translator's note: in medieval Hungary, prelates and barons were obliged to command troops under their own banner, hence the term applied to such units.

to go against Kaunitz's advice and make peace with the orders. He behaved as a true successor to Maria-Theresa in his dealings with the Hungarian nobility. In the end it was the peasantry who paid the price of the compromise. The orders recognized the prerogatives of the crown while the Habsburgs confirmed the orders' privileges. In practice, the serfs remained without legal protection in the face of the whims of their feudal lords and the prelates. The accord sounded the death-knell for enlightened despotism which was buried once and for all in 1795 with the execution of the Hungarian Jacobins.

THE STATE OF THE MONARCHY IN 1792

Leopold II's sudden death put an abrupt end to half a century of 'enlightened' government during which Austria was not only a great power but also a model for progress with respect to local liberties and national traditions.

Maria-Theresa had enacted reforms without endangering cooperation between the orders and the dynasty. The ruler still depended on the aristocrats' goodwill, their money and their credit, especially during wartime, even after Haugwitz's reforms. Joint commissions continued to administer the country and to promote changes in education. Joseph II's administrative reforms did not take account of social and national realities but Leopold II saved the essentials by returning to the situation in 1780. This was especially so in the case of Hungary which could only be kept within the monarchy through guarantees of its special position and the sometimes exorbitant privileges of the nobility. In 1792 the different countries were not always unified, even though the Austro-Bohemian lands had, since 1749, represented a solid core around which the Danubian lands and the 'European dominions' organized themselves.

Did an Austrian national sentiment come into being at this time? The Austrian historian Rautenstrauch detected the first signs of a sentiment distinct from the local patriotism which had existed since the Middle Ages. With Sonnenfels, the elite became conscious of belonging to a state, the Austrian monarchy, which was defined for the first time by the Pragmatic Sanction and prince Eugene's wish to make the Habsburg domains *ein Totum*. Maria-Theresa's educational reforms and, above all, Joseph II's moves towards a unified administration could have helped to promote this Austrian national consciousness by imposing German as the language of communication. This is what the sentiment most resembles in the light of the violent reactions in favour of Latin from the Hungarian nobility at a time when a number of noblemen were quite ignorant of the language of Cicero. On the eve of the French Revolution, the Habsburg monarchy appeared very fragile. Joseph II had not succeeded in creating a centralized and unified state and, with death approaching, had had to cancel most of his reforms.

The Habsburgs' financial position and the condition of the army, by contrast, were a great improvement upon the situation in 1740. After 1765, Joseph II had continued the skilful policy of his father who, though a mediocre general, was a good financier. He had reduced expenditure, imposed an equal basis of taxation which included the nobility and the clergy and, contrary to physiocratic theory, taken advantage of economic growth to increase the share of indirect taxation. At the beginning of his reign, the net revenues of the monarchy varied between 65 and 75 million florins. In 1785 the state budget showed receipts of over 3 million florins and the public debt rose during the same fiscal year to 300 million florins. Under Leopold II, the net revenues of the state in 1790 reached 86 million and in 1791, 89 million florins with an annual deficit to the order of 22 per cent, approximately 25 million florins.

The revenues in 1740 had been 22 million florins and so had quadrupled in half a century during a period of great financial stability. Wars, however, in particular the Austro-Russian war, could only be financed through massive recourse to credit. The public debt rose from 300 million florins in 1785 to 400 million in 1792. In 1790 military expenditure represented 65 per cent of the state's total expenses. The rapid swelling of the public debt during the period from 1788 to 1792 meant that the monarchy was in a difficult position at the time it had to go to war against revolutionary France. The issuing of paper money by the Wiener Stadtbank, some 28 million florins in 1790, marked recourse to an expedient subsequently resorted to frequently.[3]

Reforms in the method of recruitment led in half a century to the doubling of the army's manpower from 150 000 in 1740 to around 300 000 in 1790. Joseph II had established throughout his lands, with the exception of Hungary, the principle of military service for all men between the ages of seventeen and forty. Priests and nobles were exempt, otherwise every man had to serve for life, which in practice meant for several weeks a year. In Hungary, it was agreed in 1785 that the counties would supply directly the recruits for the Hungarian regiments. The army had been thrown into some confusion by the defeats in the Balkan campaigns and in 1790 by desertions, but it quickly recovered its military capacity which enabled it to confront with some measure of success the French revolutionary army and the army of Napoleon's empire.

Demographic growth in the eighteenth century meant that the monarchy nearly equalled France in terms of its population, the monarchy having 22 million and France 26 million inhabitants. The real problem remained the masses, who were still peasants. Industrial growth had only come about in Bohemia as a result of the abolition of serfdom, a measure which gave a much stronger impulse to proto-industry than had mercantilist manufacturing policy. Koci has argued that Joseph II's reforms marked a major change in the history of the Czech people.

Life in the countryside changed very little during the Enlightenment. The physiocratic leanings of Maria-Theresa and her sons had made some changes to the structure of agriculture in Lower Austria, a region where the seigneurial reserve was already reduced, the large landowners abandoning *Gutsherrschaft* (direct farming by the owner) in favour of systematic exploitation of the forests and *Grundherrschaft* (rent from the land). Large-scale cultivation continued to dominate the rural landscape in Hungary, Bohemia and Galicia. For Hungary, a vital element of the monarchy representing 52 per cent of its total land area and 41 per cent of its total population, the reign of Joseph II represented, according to Wellmann, a brief and happy interlude in the pattern of Hungarian life – the particularly onerous and very inefficient feudal system which lasted until 1848. After the Diet of 1790–91, the Hungarian peasant remained a second-class subject. Maria-Theresa had estimated that 90 per cent of the population of Hungary was subject to seigneurial rule and her reforms of 1767, which in theory put limits on the taxation of the serfs, had done little to change the situation if it is taken into account that in 1780 two-thirds of the peasantry were owners of a plot. Population pressure tended to cause the reverse situation since the serfs' manus were parcelled out and agricultural workers who until lately had represented only a third of the rural population became its major element. The 5.5 million hectares under cultivation in the census was no longer enough. The Hungarian peasant had little reason to regret the passing of the 'beau XVIII century'. Only the landowners and a small number of rich labourers had benefited from the century's prosperity.

Although the Catholic Church had lost its monopoly over cultural life, the clergy and nobility remained the dominant elements in a society which was rural and conservative and which only the revolution could disturb. The 'enlightened' elite was recruited from these milieux and surprised itself with its own daring. It would be much easier for reaction to triumph in a state where the East European party represented by Hungary and Galicia carried increasingly more weight in the face of the Austro-Bohemian complex.

The capital city alone had benefited from this half-century to rise to the level of a great European metropolis.

VIENNA, A EUROPEAN CITY[4]

Even though Vienna had more than 200 000 inhabitants, 213 000 in the 1785 census, its relative importance in the monarchy was less than the influence Paris exercised over the whole of French territory. A particular characteristic of the monarchy becomes clear when the degree of centralization is measured in relation to the concentration of population.[5]

Since the sixteenth century, the Austrian capital's importance in the Danubian region had steadily grown. Buda had not been replaced in importance after it had fallen to the Turks and after 1620 the decline of Prague was irreversible. The Habsburgs hoped that Vienna with its good geographical position would combine the functions of regional capital and imperial residence. Once the threat from the Turks had gone, Vienna occupied a central position in the monarchy and continued to expand at the expense of the smaller towns in Lower Austria which were still represented in the Diet. After 1740, it became a model town because of its large population and economic importance, the reciprocal relationship which developed between the state and the town, and its brilliant culture. The social position of the Viennese had been defined during the reign of Leopold I by the police ordinance of 1671. The inhabitants were ranked beneath the three 'superior' orders of the diet. The burghers, notably the artisans, were *déclassé* and ranked with the domestic staff at the court. The creators of the new culture – the printers, engravers, painters, sculptors and musicians – found themselves in the same class as those engaged in commerce, the merchant-bankers and the officers of the treasury who constituted an intermediate category.

The development of a court aristocracy divided Viennese society into two worlds: the court whose personnel enjoyed a privileged status, and the burgers of the town who depended on the municipal magistrate. The aristocracy was cosmopolitan, polyglot and in the age of the Enlightenment spoke French as did the Habsburgs from Maria-Theresa onwards. At the end of the eighteenth century, as a result of the formation of the Hungarian Guard, the Hungarian aristocracy was finally brought to heel, took the path to Vienna, spoke French and German and forgot its mother tongue.

This outward-looking elite should not be confused with the Viennese petite bourgeoisie which only spoke a German dialect sprinkled with French and Italian vocabulary. These burghers had their own particular culture based in the theatre and on music. Profoundly marked by the Catholic Reformation, they thoroughly enjoyed the displays of baroque piety, processions and great choral masses. They belonged to fraternities and some perhaps were freemasons and touched by atheism. The Viennese received pope Pius VI with great fervour during his official visit in 1782, while Kaunitz was openly discourteous and Joseph II somewhat capricious.

At Vienna, the different social classes were closely intermingled, as in all old towns, and this was true not only in the fortified part of the city around the Hofburg where in 1776 the noble palaces and burgher houses were freed from the obligation to give lodging to the court personnel, but also in the neighbouring districts where the summer palaces, the theatres and promenades were growing in number. In 1766 the public was admitted to the Prater, which hitherto had been the Habsburgs' special hunting ground but became a public park where Joseph II was happy to visit. In 1775 the emperor opened the gardens at La Favorite where his father, Francis I, had established a porcelain factory, and at Schönbrunn a zoo open to the public completed the facilities offered within the palace park.

The era of building palaces was, in general, almost at an end in the eighteenth century. Even at Schönbrunn, work in progress was limited to decoration and completing the interior under the direction of Nicòlo Pacassi. There were no more grand projects of urban planning. In the old city, the labyrinth of *Gasse*, the alleys which were so important for maintaining a through-draft, was retained and each suburb was built around a large road linking it with the city gates. The system of now obsolete fortifications inherited from the baroque age was carefully preserved. The emphasis was on constructing functional buildings in the spirit of Enlightenment thought. The architect from Lorraine, Nicolas Jadot, a protégé of the emperor Francis, built the palace for the newly invigorated university, which today is the seat of the Academy of Sciences, and in 1775 a training college was installed in the former convent of St Anne. Vienna had sixty-five primary schools of which six were in the old city. There were only three traditional parishes in the old city and the religious orders dedicated themselves to pastoral care. The Protestants were granted an oratory in the former convent of St Dorothea where a pawn shop was opened to save the poor and improvident from the usurers' clutches.

Poverty in Vienna was, as in all eighteenth-century cities, the cause of great and widespread misery. It was possible to live decently for 500 florins a year and the city offered a plentiful and varied supply of food. The average annual per capita consumption of meat was 100 kg. Joseph II sent the police after the vagabonds and beggars. In 1750 it was estimated that there were 5 000 poor receiving help, living at home and as pensioners in hospices. A vast orphanage had been built in 1742 at Rennweg, not far from the Belvedere, but it was not until 1784 that the *Allgemeines Krankenhaus* (the general hospital) was opened in the district of Alserstadt, following the conversion of an already existing poorhouse. This great complex of buildings left its mark on the landscape and intellectual life of Vienna since it became the seat of the faculty of medicine, one of the glories of the Austrian capital. A psychiatric clinic was built alongside in the form of a tower.

Additional proof that the age of the Enlightenment was not an age of irreligion is that fifty parish churches were built in the suburbs. The Viennese were equally passionate about the theatre and there was a growing number of halls for popular entertainment such as the theatre at the Kärnthnertor. Typical of such establishments was the theatre in the Wieden district which was run by Mozart's friend Emanuel Schikaneder who deployed his considerable talents as a director and increased the repertoire of traditional burlesque comedy.

There was still little difference between opera and drama, between sung and spoken plays. Neither the official court theatre nor that at the Kärnthnertor distinguished between the genres. Maria-Theresa founded the Hofburgtheater, now the Burgtheater, in 1741, handing the redundant salon of the Ballhaus to Karl Sellier, 'entrepreneur of opera, comedies, serenades and oratorios' whose preference was for plays offering grand spectacle. Until 1765, the repertoire was dominated by French tragedies and ballets. These extravaganzas were enjoyed by high society but ran at an enormous financial loss. German theatre continued at the Kärnthnertor. Sonnenfels condemned the farces featuring Hanswurst, the Viennese Punchinello, and spoke forcefully in support of morally improving drama. In 1772 a troupe of German actors was installed at the Burgtheater and extended its repertoire with Italian opera.

In 1776 Joseph II gave the Burgtheater the character of a German national theatre and promoted German-language drama as pre-eminent. Translations of English and French plays, and the classic German drama which was flourishing at Weimar, provided it with an excellent repertoire and it quickly established itself as a theatre comparable to the Comédie Française.

It was at this period that Vienna became the international capital of music. None of the great masters who gave the city its glory were, with the exception of Schubert, Viennese. Haydn was from Moravia, Beethoven and Gluck were German as, technically, was Mozart for the archbishopric of Salzburg was a principality of the Empire and yet to be incorporated within the monarchy.

Maria-Theresa chose the young Christoph Willibald Gluck as her children's music master and so presented him with the chance to reform the opera. Gluck's father was originally from the Palatinate and was a domestic servant of prince Eugene. He himself enjoyed the patronage of prince Lobkowitz in the palace of the prince of Saxe-Hildburghausen, prince Eugene's heir, where there was a fine orchestra and theatre. He married a wealthy wife, Marianne Perg, the daughter of a Viennese merchant. The first evidence of the opera revival was *Don Juan ou le festin du Pierre*, a ballet on the theme of Don Juan which Gluck staged in 1761 at the Burgtheater. The following year *Orfeo ed Euridice* was performed for the first time on the same stage and in the presence of the imperial couple. Opera now expressed feelings and passions and the librettist became a poet. Musical drama was born. In 1767 Gluck composed *Alceste* in which he drew on the logical consequences of his theories and won warm praise from Sonnenfels. Marie-Antoinette appointed him as her music teacher in Paris so that he could impose his ideas on the French public. He composed a French version of *Orfeo* which was staged in Paris in 1774 and in the same year staged a performance of *Iphigénie en Aulide*. His final opera *Iphigénie en Tauride*, which he composed in 1779 and which is still on the stage at the Royal Academy of Music, created great controversy and roused the famous quarrel between the 'Gluckistes' and the 'Piccinistes', between the champions of Italian traditional opera and of 'bel canto'. On his return to Vienna, the chevalier von Gluck was appointed court composer and died in 1787.

Gluck had supported the early career of Mozart who had been born in 1756 and was celebrated by Maria-Theresa as a child prodigy. In 1768 Joseph II commissioned from Mozart an opera and received *La finta semplice* (The Feigned Innocent) which was performed by a troupe of Italian players. It was a Viennese doctor who commissioned *Bastien und Bastienne*, which was performed in his private theatre in the Landstrasse.

When the young Mozart returned from his European tours, he wanted to return to his post at the court of the archbishop of Salzburg, his father Leopold Mozart's patron. This proved a disaster. Hieronymus Colloredo, the archbishop, was an enlightened prelate who supported Joseph II and was hostile to the Curia, but he was also malicious and insisted on a rigid hierarchy at his court where musicians and secretaries ranked almost as equals and had to conduct themselves according to their rank. Mozart seems to have transgressed the rules of conduct and to have been an independent spirit. He welcomed his dismissal since this guaranteed him his freedom. In advance of his time, he wanted to live as an independent artist without making concessions to the customs of the capital. A musician could expect to enjoy a reasonably comfortable way of life if he gave private music lessons, but Mozart was bored by this and preferred to devote his time to composition. It might be asked whether the Viennese, who adored the thoroughly honourable composer Salieri, really appreciated Mozart.

Joseph II prided himself on being a music lover. He commissioned Mozart to write the first opera in German, *Die Entfurhung aus dem Serail*, which was performed in 1782 at the court theatre and enjoyed modest success before making a triumphal entry onto the German stage and prompting Goethe to hail

Mozart as a genius of the theatre. It was a musical comedy and *Singspiel* rather than opera free of dialogue. A century after the siege of Vienna, orientalism was in fashion and the opera features Turks, some brutal and hateful like Osmin, and others like the Pasha who has been touched by the Enlightenment and the ideals of freemasonry. This masonic element is not surprising since Mozart himself was a brother. The music itself is very pleasing but Mozart subsequently turned his back on musical comedy and it was not until shortly before his death in 1791 that he presented another German opera, *The Magic Flute*, to his friend Schikaneder who wrote the libretto. The masonic element in this opera is very pronounced and the model for Sarastro is thought to have been Ignaz von Born.

The Marriage of Figaro, which was sung in Italian, could only be performed in 1786 with the express permission of the censor and the emperor, who was too clever not to notice the opera's subversive character. In Lorenzo da Ponte, Mozart had found a first-class librettist and *Le Nozze di Figaro* was a triumph in the court theatre. On the first night, all the arias were repeated and Joseph II admitted to being well-pleased but added the comment, 'too beautiful for our ears and, dear Mozart, truly too many notes'.*

Mozart's life was not one continuously marked by success since he refused to yield to the whims of fashion. He was fortunate in having some patrons such as the Russian ambassador to whom he dedicated a series of string quartets, a genre which he developed. The Estates of Bohemia commissioned *Don Giovanni*, which was first performed on 27 October 1787 in Prague where he later staged *La Clemenza di Tito*, a work commissioned for the coronation of Leopold II and based on a text by Metastasio, the aged Italian poet at the Vienna court.

Mozart succeeded Gluck as court composer and received a salary of 800 florins. *Così fan tutte* was performed at the court theatre in 1790. This fine comedy with its libretto by da Ponte is a little melancholy. It did not appeal greatly to the Viennese and was a partial failure. Mozart did not live for long after the resounding success which *The Magic Flute* brought him.

Mozart died on 5 December 1791, an exhausted genius. Leopold II, a great Habsburg, died on 1 March 1792. Like his mother Maria-Theresa, he had devoted all his strength to the service of his subjects in order to advance as harmoniously as possible the conservative society over which he presided and to correct the excesses of the revolution imposed both from on high and from outside. He had endeavoured for two years to preserve peace in Europe. He had never shown himself to be indifferent to the fate of his brother-in-law Louis XVI and his sister Marie-Antoinette, and had preserved the essential part of his mother's reform programme.

The declaration of war on 20 April 1792 was a turning-point in the history of the monarchy. The forces of progress would lose ground, never to recover it, and the old demons of reaction and intolerance would seize power as in the

---

* Translator's note: Beales argues that this comment is one of the many spurious observations foisted upon Joseph II.

heyday of Ferdinand II and the Jesuits. Fortunately, music escaped censorship and the Viennese could forget their troubles in the inns of the Prater and at Grinzing while 'good papa' Haydn continued to compose until 1809.

NOTES AND REFERENCES

1. Adam Wandruszka, *Leopold II, Erherzog von Österreich, Grossherzog von Toskana, König von Ungarn und Böhmen, Römischer Kaiser*, vol. 2, Vienna, 1963–65, remains fundamental. See also, Helga Peham, *Leopold II, Herrscher mit weiser Hand*, Graz, 1987.
2. Béla K. Kíraly, *Hungary in the Late 18th Century*, London, 1969.
   Charles Kecskeméti, *La Hongrie et le réformisme libéral (1790–1848)*, Rome, 1989, pp. 35–64.
3. P. G. M. Dickson, *Finances and Government under Maria-Theresa, 1740–1780*, vol. 2, Oxford, 1987.
4. Marcel Brion, *La Vie quotidienne á Vienne au temps de Mozart et de Schubert*, Paris, 1957.
5. György Granasztoi, 'L'urbanisation de l'espace danubien', *Annales E.S.C.*, 2, 1989, pp. 379–99.

CHAPTER NINE

Austria Confronts the French Revolution (1792–1815)

The French Revolution was, in the beginning, greeted with more enthusiasm than might be expected. The grand duke of Tuscany, the future emperor Leopold II, declared, 'The rebirth of France will be a model which all the sovereigns and governments of Europe will imitate, whether or not they wish to do so, since it will be forced upon them by their peoples. It will result in unbounded happiness and the end of injustice, war, disputes and anarchy and it will be the most useful fashion that France has introduced to Europe.' The young prince was not the only disciple of Montesquieu in the Habsburg lands and the censors allowed French journals to reach Vienna where the new ideas excited genuine enthusiasm among some sections of the bourgeoisie.

The ruling class in Bohemia soon turned from enthusiasm to hostility and became familiar with the opinions of Burke and his German translator, Friedrich von Gentz. The political writer Kramerius explained to the peasants that they had no reason to revolt since, in comparison to the French peasantry, they lived like lords. A series of pamphlets was directed at them, reflecting the degree of disquiet among the authorities. Mika, a professor at the university of Prague, justified the need for inequality and demonstrated to the peasantry that life in the country was the life most to be desired. Vavak defended the *robot* and described the wretchedness awaiting the peasants if the French arrived. Böhm, a priest, condemned democracy and the spirit of enquiry as the antithesis of that vital social virtue, obedience. The peasant masses were well-disposed towards the French. Vavak himself wrote that the peasants hoped that the burden of taxation would be lightened and that they would enjoy freedom from the economic protection of the Jews. The village assemblies discussed the Revolution and expected that the *robot* would soon be abandoned. Leopold II had suspended the application of Joseph II's measures affecting the *robot* and had made worse the conditions for the redemption of feudal dues. Leopold had to restore everything to the state it was in before reform. Conditions were ripe for agitation. The effects of Joseph II's reforms, however, reduced the impact of revolutionary propaganda.

The changes ordered by the late emperor had generally satisfied the champions of reform but their relative defeat had proved that society was not prepared for so radical a transformation. In Austria, reform could only be enacted from above and with the nobility's support. The liberal portion of the nobility was severely alarmed by the excesses of the Constituent Assembly of 1789 which had abolished the seigneurial regime, the basis of the whole social system in Danubian Europe. The members of the bourgeoisie were less inclined to long for change because their careers in the administration held out the prospect of ennoblement. Joseph II had abolished the most pressing abuses of the *ancien régime,* and the state apparatus, strengthened by the support of the ruling classes, was more powerful than ever and seemed capable of crushing any subversion. Finally, the masses, who had remained Catholic, were alienated by the revolutionaries' anti-religious excesses.

In Hungary, the situation was different. Its literate population amounted to about 10 000, both nobles and commoners, who formed a homogenous group of support for Joseph II's reforms. Of these, a few were magnates but most were Protestant, burghers, members of the lesser nobility and the sons of peasants who had received some education. Hajnóczy, the son of a Lutheran pastor, led the movement, demanding fresh reforms and an independent state.* He wanted the whole population to become one nation and demanded freedom of expression and the right for everyone to possess land outright, for peasants still only had the right to work land on payment of the rent due to the owner of the fief. In 1790 the Hungarian nobility still supported the French Revolution in so far as it weakened the authority of the king and clergy.

The political class also hoped for Hungarian independence. Only when Leopold II made a treaty with Frederick William of Prussia did the Prussians abandon the Hungarians in favour of their ally in Vienna. The nobility began to realize that the revolution did not favour their interests. In 1791 the nobility of the county of Szábolcs, a region traditionally little inclined to support the Habsburgs, declared that there would be 'no nobility without the king and no king without the nobility'.

THE DOMESTIC RESPONSE

The change of ruler was decisive. Leopold II died in 1792 and left the throne to his son Francis who reigned until 1835.[1] The young emperor, born in Florence in 1768, was by temperament and education a man motivated by reason of state alone. Horrified at the thought of innovation, he took after neither his uncle, Joseph II, nor his father, whose intelligence and generosity he had not inherited. In private, though, he was courteous and genial and he was quite popular with the Viennese. He succeeded his father at a difficult time, for Leopold II had just undone the harm caused by Joseph II's reforming zeal, Europe was seized by revolutionary ideas, and relations with Paris had become openly hostile. After the first moments of euphoria, the Austrian aristocracy quickly realized that the French Revolution represented for them a mortal

---

* Translator's note: József Hajnóczy (1750–95), a former secretary and protégé of Ferenc Széchenyi, had begun as a supporter of Joseph II but was inspired by English, American and, most importantly, French political thought.

danger. Some feared for the seigneurial regime and the maintenance of their privileges, others were stricken by the old Francophobia which for half a century had more or less been laid to rest. In Paris, the Girondists, despite the army's lack of organization, considered war a political necessity. Louis XVI and Marie-Antoinette were conducting a desperate policy in the hope that defeat by a foreign power would lead to the restoration of their authority. Francis II allied with Prussia on 7 February 1792, and was determined to fight revolutionary France which was preparing to overthrow social order and the balance of power in Europe. He would not make any concessions and left the French Legislative Assembly the pleasure of declaring war on 20 April 1792 on 'the king of Bohemia and Hungary'. Thus began a confrontation which lasted for almost a quarter of a century and only ended with the Treaties of Vienna in 1815.

Although he was not surprised by the declaration of war, Francis II was not in a position to undertake operations immediately because of the parlous financial situation and the *Hofkriegsrat* could not mobilize an army of 50 000 men. Count Chotek* had left behind a deficit of more than 2 million florins, the treasury was financially embarrassed and the rise in prices made it impossible to reduce current expenses. The contributions from the hereditary lands were uncertain and the only possible solution was to borrow from a bank, whatever the rate of interest. From 1794 to 1797 England provided money, £6 220 000, and granted more in subsidies. Austria issued paper money which did not cease to depreciate and provoked serious inflation. In 1797 this paper money had an artificial rate of exchange and in 1800 currency with backing had all but disappeared from circulation. In 1797 anyone hoarding coinage was forced to bring it to the Mint. In 1811 the state declared itself bankrupt, despite having introduced the previous year a tax intended gradually to pay off the state debts. All the bills in the bank were exchanged at a fifth of their nominal value against new paper money, or 'Viennese money', which was practically without any bullion backing. In 1815 the financial situation was the same as in 1809. The following year, 'a national Austrian bank' succeeded in cleaning up the financial situation and the monarchy was able to sustain the war-effort for more than twenty years.

The new man in charge of foreign policy was baron Thugut, a protégé of Kaunitz.[2] Of bourgeois origin, he dreamt only of annexation and territorial expansion. He detested Prussia and revolutionary France and hoped to recover Alsace from the French. He wanted to exchange Bavaria for the Netherlands and negotiate a fresh partition of Poland. The Viennese ministry saw the Jacobins simply as a band of troublemakers who could be dealt with by reason. This was why it was in favour of fighting to the bitter end. After the treason of the French general Dumouriez** who passed to the enemy in March 1793, it

---

* Translator's note: Chotek, the Austro-Bohemian chancellor, replaced Karl von Zinzendorf as president of the tax regulation court commission.
** Translator's note: Charles François du Périer Dumouriez (1739–1823), when accused of monarchist sympathies by the revolutionaries, went over to Austria to save his head.

preferred to lose the royal family rather than sign an armistice with the Convention, for the Convention would have agreed to free the prisoners in the Temple if the Austrians signed an armistice and agreed to release the four representatives of the mission whom they had taken prisoner after Dumouriez's treachery. Vienna wanted to restore strong monarchical power in Paris and Thugut's classic imperialism was contrary to the revolutionary spirit favoured by count Colloredo Waldsee, a childhood tutor of Francis II and his principal minister. For Colloredo, it was not simply a matter of fighting the Jacobins but of rooting out all manifestations of the spirit of the Enlightenment. The execution of Louis XVI made it possible to organize noble reaction. The Diet of Lower Austria presented its grievances which were polite but firm and served as the programme for the new sovereign. Francis II did not hesitate to declare himself the nobility's protector and the resolute enemy of the philosophy of the Enlightenment and to throw himself into the arms of the reactionaries from fear of the Revolution. Any project for the complete liberation of the peasants was postponed indefinitely.

The archduke Francis, while heir apparent, had supported the forces of counter-revolution. Censorship was re-established by imperial decree on 11 September 1790 and count Pergen, the minister of police, was granted extensive powers. Any article from a foreign journal deemed 'to spread dangerous new ideas' was excluded from the newspapers. In 1791 the archduke Francis re-organized the police-force which was as lazy and corrupt as ever. The police were to keep an eye on 'clubs and subversive assemblies' as well as the freemasons. After his accession, Francis strengthened the bureaucracy, the censorship and the police, the instruments of power which Joseph II had put in place for a quite different purpose. The police pursued those who supported the Revolution. In the course of summer 1794, there came to light in Vienna a Jacobin plot to kill the sovereign and overthrow the monarchy under cover of a great fire. Some notables including count Hohenwart, the seventeen-year-old nephew of the archbishop of Vienna, were arrested. The Jacobin trial led to rumours that political prisoners were being executed under cover of darkness. Many of those arrested were freemasons and the government tried to prove freemasonry's subversive character, inspiring many pamphlets demonstrating that their goal was revolution. The lodges were subject to police surveillance and kept a low profile. The emperor also made use of secret agents such as Feldhofer, a retired official who flooded the cabinet with trivial reports in return for an annual gratuity of 600 florins. A suspicious regime was established, grounded in *raison d'état* and incapable of profiting from the genuine popularity which the dynasty enjoyed. The system lasted until the revolution of 1848 and was one of the causes of Metternich's downfall.

At the end of the eighteenth century, the emperor, the court and the administration had the support of pubic opinion which condemned the excesses of the Paris revolution. The execution of Louis XVI, but particularly that of Marie-Antoinette, an Austrian princess, stirred real hatred towards France, and in addition there were the émigrés who had taken refuge in Austria and were the most confirmed opponents of the Republicans. Those who until late had been well-disposed towards the Revolution rallied spontaneously to the government viewpoint. The police regime did the rest.

Hungary, once again, went its own way. A section of the nobility did not welcome the reactionary measures taken by the new sovereign. In 1793 radical intellectuals and patriot nobles met in the county assemblies, but the following year Ignác Martinovics organized the 'Hungarian Jacobin conspiracy', a movement with Girondist tendencies and more symbolic than political importance.[3] Martinovics was a questionable character. Born into the petite bourgeoisie, he took holy orders, became an army chaplain and then professor of science at the university of Lemberg in Galicia. In 1788 he published his *Mémoires philosophiques* which were a profession of democratic and materialist beliefs. In 1791 he entered into the service of Leopold II's secret police and was in charge of keeping Hungary under surveillance. Following the accession of Francis II, he turned towards the Hungarian intellectuals and entered into contact with Hajnóczy. He established two revolutionary organizations, one for the nobility in favour of reform, whose goal was Hungary's rise to independence, the other for democrats, whose ideal was social revolution and agrarian reform. During four months of activity, the movement drew 300 or so to Buda and Buda province. The police made inquiries without finding anything, but Martinovics revealed all after 'the Viennese Jacobins' had been arrested. The government took advantage of the occasion to make an example: fifty-one nobles, intellectuals and moderate patriots and democrats were accused of high treason and tried by a Hungarian tribunal. Of these, seventeen were acquitted, sixteen sentenced to imprisonment and eighteen to death, although only seven, including Martinovics and Hajnóczy, were executed and the rest were pardoned. The executions of 20 May 1795 left a deep impression. Hungary henceforth remained calm because the nobility understood that it was being threatened by a bourgeois revolution, a prospect which held no attraction for them. The nobility, despite its feelings towards the Habsburgs, remained loyal throughout the Revolutionary and Napoleonic Wars.

THE WAR WITH FRANCE (1792–1815)

For the Austrian monarchy, the French Revolution no longer represented the risk of internal subversion but was an enemy to defeat on the battlefield. A bastion of conservatism, Francis II's Austria proved to be a tenacious opponent of the Convention, the Directory and Napoleon. After the first successes of 1792, the conflict quickly became indecisive, increasingly so after the Polish insurrection led by Kosciuczko when it no longer had its hands free in Eastern Europe but also had to keep its eyes on Prussia and Russia. Following the Battle of Fleurus, in the summer of 1794, the army of the Convention occupied Belgium. Next year the Austrians on their own held the line along the Rhine after Prussia had concluded peace with the French Republic and was occupied with the final partition of Poland. Austria had as allies only Britain and Russia. In 1796 the archduke Charles confronted Jourdan victoriously in south

Germany, but Napoleon's brilliant campaign in Italy, in which he took Lombardy and Mantua, put an end to the emperor's hopes.[4] The French army threatened Vienna, and on 18 April 1797 the archduke Charles signed the armistice of Leoben which was confirmed in October by the Peace of Campo-Formio. Austria had to surrender Belgium, Lombardy and Breisach and recognized the French annexation of the left bank of the Rhine. As compensation, it received Venice, Istria and Dalmatia.

The monarchy did not admit defeat. It was ready to resume combat at the first opportunity as long as it found allies to support its war effort. In 1799 the Directory's blunders in Italy supplied the monarchy, which now had the support of Paul I of Russia and Pitt in England, with the pretext to intervene. Napoleon was detained in Egypt, the Directory's regime was decried in France, revolutionary imperialism was hated throughout Europe. The occasion seemed favourable, a conjunction of events which was to be repeated in 1805 and 1808. Austria, however, did not re-enter the war and achieve any success until 1813.

After the initial victories in Italy and Switzerland, 1799 and 1800 were two years of futile war which set the seal on the loss of Lombardy and the Austrian Netherlands and confirmed the annexation by the Republic of the whole left bank of the Rhine. Moreover, the Peace of Lunéville in February 1801 reduced the role of the emperor in Germany. To compensate the princes whose possessions were on the left bank of the Rhine, the Diet proceeded with secularizations and by the recess* of 1803 distributed the ecclesiastical lands as compensation. The Habsburgs accordingly received the bishoprics of Trento and Brixen in the south Tyrol as compensation for the Lorraine county of Falkenstein which the 1738 treaty had awarded to the future emperor Francis I when he became grand duke of Tuscany. The defeat led to changes in the ministry. Colloredo remained in place but Thugut was replaced by count Cobenzl and the archduke Charles was appointed president of the *Hofkriegsrat* and undertook reform of the army. The emperor created a ministry charged with coordinating government action. The new ministry, convinced of French superiority, conducted a cautious policy. But this was not for long since in August 1805 the war party finally triumphed. It formed a new alliance with England and Russia, despite the reservations of the archduke Charles.

Napoleon's response was sudden. Although French troops were stationed at Boulogne, ready to invade England, the Grande Armée immediately turned towards Swabia. After the fall of Ulm, the route to Vienna was open to the French and on 13 November 1805 the Austrian capital was occupied for the first time while Francis II went to meet his ally, the tsar Alexander. The Austro-Russian defeat at Austerlitz put an almost immediate end to the campaign in Moravia and Francis II preferred to limit damage by signing the Peace of Pressburg which marked the dissolution of the Holy Roman Empire and the birth of the Austrian empire. Francis renounced the title of Holy Roman emperor and contented himself with the title of hereditary emperor of Austria

---

* Translator's note: recess, from the Latin *recessus*, were the acts by which the Diets of the Holy Roman Empire recorded their deliberations before retiring.

which he had taken in 1804 at the time of Napoleon's coronation as emperor of the French. As Holy Roman emperor he had been Francis II, as emperor of Austria he was Francis I. The Habsburgs had been completely driven from Germany, as from Italy following the loss of Venice and Dalmatia. Napoleon gave them as compensation Salzburg, which up to then had been an independent prince-bishopric. Bavaria, a vassal of France, annexed the Tyrol, a move which was bitterly resented by the Tyroleans who were enemies of their Bavarian neighbours and loyal subjects of the House of Austria. For the first time, Austria was exclusively a Danubian power. The loss of prestige was much greater than after the Treaties of Campo-Formio in 1797 and Lunéville in 1801. Thugut's policy had failed. Austria had failed to defeat the Revolution and had gained nothing. The foreign minister Cobenzl was dismissed and replaced by a new team directed by count Johann Philip Stadion, whose goal was revenge since the emperor, being tenacious, did not admit defeat. For him and for his army, the Peace of Pressburg was only a truce.

The chain of events forced Francis I to adhere to the Continental Blockade; the French victory at Friedland and the Treaties of Tilsitt with Russia and Prussia (1807), Napoleon's alliance with tsar Alexander and the break-up of the Prussian state after Jena and Auerstädt (1806) left Francis I obliged to accept the Blockade which proved beneficial to Austrian industry, temporarily freeing it from English competition. For the first time, the cabinet at Vienna was willing to appeal to public opinion and promote an Austrian national sentiment. Friedrich von Gentz urged the Austrians on towards revenge, archduke Charles reorganized the army and raised battalions of militia, while the archduke John, who wanted to create a real national army, supported the Tyrolean patriots.[5] Spanish resistance to the French invaders was encouraging but the Austrian ambassador to Paris, Metternich, advised against an immediate break with France. He thought that Napoleon, even when entangled in Spain, could still defeat the Austrian army in six weeks. Like the archduke Charles, he wanted to gain time so that Austria could strengthen its economic and military position. The resounding defeat of 1809 justified his position.

In February 1809, the emperor and Stadion decided to resume hostilities. Austria soon realized that it was isolated apart from the moral and financial support of Britain. Prussia maintained cautious neutrality and the Franco-Russian alliance remained solid. Austria had to rely on the imperial army alone and on an uprising in the Tyrol against the occupying Bavarian forces. Once again Napoleon reacted swiftly. On 13 May 1809 the French occupied Vienna and Napoleon installed himself at Schönbrunn. The Grande Armée, intent on crossing the Danube, suffered a serious defeat at Aspern. The archduke Charles, though, did not exploit this undeniable success and was defeated six weeks later at Wagram and on 12 July was forced to conclude an armistice at Znaïm. An attempt by the English to disembark at Walcheren in Holland failed. Only the rebellion in the Tyrol succeeded. Long prepared by baron Hormayer and the archduke John, the insurrection was led by Andreas Hofer, an innkeeper and a former captain in the militia who was confirmed in his hatred of the Bavarians. With his partisans, he defeated the Bavarian troops and allowed the

Austrians to reoccupy Innsbruck. The emperor Francis assured him in a letter that whatever happened, he would not abandon the Tyrol. Austria without an army and without allies found itself forced to sign a disastrous peace which confirmed Napoleon's victory. The monarchy lost all access to the sea in Italy and did not receive any compensation. The Treaty of Schönbrunn, signed on 14 October 1809, confirmed the monarchy's loss of Upper Austria and Salzburg to the Bavarians, who also kept the north Tyrol, while the south Tyrol went to the kingdom of Italy, a vassal of France. Part of Carinthia, Carniola and south Croatia were yielded to France and with Dalmatia and Istria constituted the Illyrian provinces which were intended to thwart the smuggling of English contraband and to prevent British merchandise from reaching Central Europe. Austria also had to pay a war indemnity, reduce its army to 150 000 men and abandon the Tyrolean insurgents who in August had forced marshal Lefebvre and his 40 000 men to evacuate the lands which they had just occupied. For two months, Andreas Hofer had become master of the Tyrol, but in October a combined Franco-Bavarian action won over his men by promising them an amnesty. Hofer, however, continued guerrilla actions which succeeded locally. Betrayed, abandoned by the government at Vienna, he was tried by a French council of war and shot at Mantua on 20 February 1810. Thus ended the only popular uprising in the Habsburgs' favour.

Francis I used the occasion of the defeat to abandon Stadion's policies. He stopped trying to draw the masses into political life and returned to conservative government supported by the notables. Stadion, like his predecessors Thugut and Cobenzl, was dismissed, as was the archduke Charles. The emperor turned to the two representatives of the aristocracy, Metternich and Schwarzenberg, who would eventually lead Austria to success in 1814. Prince Karl Philipp Schwarzenberg, a soldier by vocation, had worked in the War Council with the archduke Charles. In 1809 he replaced Metternich in Paris and negotiated Napoleon's marriage with the archduchess Maria Louisa. Like Metternich, he did everything he could to gain time. In 1812 he was entrusted with the command of the Austrian expeditionary corps sent to Russia with Napoleon's Grande Armée and was able to restore order, to both his master and Napoleon's satisfaction. Appointed marshal, he was again Austrian ambassador at Paris where he tried to avoid a new conflict. As for Metternich, he began in 1809 a career as a statesman which lasted until March 1848. From 1809 to 1817 as chancellor of Austria he was essentially put in charge of foreign affairs. For the next thirty years he increasingly became master of Austria.[6]

METTERNICH

Metternich, so often condemned by liberal historiography, was not an uncouth champion of a police-state but a cosmopolitan aristocrat and an ardent admirer of the Enlightenment. He was, however, closed to revolutionary and romantic ideas which he did not understand. He belonged to a Rhineland family, some of whom had served in the cathedral chapters of Mainz, Trier, Spire and Worms, while others had fought with the imperial troops and received lands in Bohemia. His father, who had served Joseph II as a diplomat, had sent him to study at Strasbourg and then at Mainz. All his life, Metternich read scientific works and mistrusted fiction and fantasy. Besides Latin and German, he knew Italian, English and French, which he handled with vigour. Educated, he was neither an atheist nor a mystic. Religion was for him a matter of convenience, but most importantly it was vital for government. His only real passion was the exercise of power. In 1809 he became one of Napoleon's most determined opponents. He was not anti-French but he thought that the French emperor was the embodiment of the revolutionary ideal and posed a lasting threat to the European equilibrium. He would, however, avow in his *Mémoires* that his fundamental characteristic was his refusal to be swayed. He was able to ally a conservatism based on principle with great tactical skill and in 1809 was considered one of the best European diplomats. This was how he managed the Austro-French alliance from 1809 to 1813. After the campaign in Russia, he even proposed Austrian mediation to conclude a peace based on compromise which would give France her 'natural frontiers', i.e. Belgium and the left bank of the Rhine. Napoleon's rejection of these moderate proposals enabled him in August 1813 to abandon his mask and rejoin the Russian and Prussian coalition. For the last time, Austria found itself on the side of England and its allies. Through Metternich's diplomatic skills, Austria derived great benefit from the campaigns of 1813 and 1814. Schwarzenberg was appointed marshal and commander-in-chief of the Russian, Prussian and Austrian troops, who were divided among the armies of Bohemia, Silesia and Saxony. He was in command at Leipzig, at the Battle of the Nations on 15–18 October 1813, and it was he who conquered the French. In January 1814, his troops reached the Marne and Schwarzenberg continued as Napoleon's principal opponent during the campaign in France.

After Napoleon's abdication at Fontainebleau on 6 April 1814, and Maria Louisa's departure for Vienna with the king of Rome, Metternich's policy triumphed. His master invited his allies to Vienna to decide the fate of Europe now freed from Napoleon's control. Metternich was able to turn the occasion into a brilliant victory for Austrian diplomacy.

THE CONGRESS OF VIENNA (1814-15)

The Congress of Vienna was a celebration by newly liberated Europe. Monarchs and aristocrats who for a quarter century had lived in fear, were invited to Vienna by the House of Austria which was re-established in its former glory. Balls, dinners and plays followed one after another and during them the activities of the emperor's intelligence service defied belief, leaving him free to entertain potentates of secondary importance while the representatives of the great powers worked. A strong supporter of the European equilibrium, Metternich did not exclude Bourbon France, which was represented by

Talleyrand and was violently opposed to Prussia which longed, in the spirit of vengeance, to dismember the ancient kingdom. He was content to surround France with strong buffer states, the kingdom of the Netherlands and Piedmont-Sardinia. In a general way, he was careful not to give any one of the victors an advantage over the rest. This was why he confirmed the partition of Poland to prevent Russia from expanding too far to the west. The grand duchy of Warsaw became Congress Poland and obtained a status similar to that of Hungary in the Austrian empire.

Metternich thought that the Austrian empire had reached its optimum extent and so denied it any territorial gains. He was prepared to surrender the Austrian Netherlands, the future Belgium, to Holland, and to forego Bavaria, so coveted by Joseph II. Austria's only compensation was not in Germany but in Italy, the Veneto, which recovered none of the independence it had lost in 1797. Annexed to Lombardy, it formed the kingdom Lombardy-Venetia, the Austrian version of the Napoleonic kingdom of Italy and the basis of Austrian domination of the Italian peninsula. Apart from Piedmont, which annexed Genoa, all the other states which were reinstated passed into the protection of Austria, most notably the Bourbons of Naples who, after Murat's betrayal during the Hundred Days, were not restored until 1815.

The tendency apparent at Rastatt a century earlier was confirmed: Austria wanted to be an Italian power, a position which it retained until 1866. It was, however, a bad decision. The laborious and partly Germanized administration of the kingdom of Lombardy-Venetia came to be universally hated by Italian patriots. In Germany, Austria renounced its old Rhineland possessions but had already entered into conflict with Prussia, which wanted to annex Saxony but above all to achieve German unity in some form or other. The emperor did not want to revive the Holy Roman Empire which he himself had solemnly dissolved in August 1806, and was content to create and accept the presidency of a German Confederation with very loose links and which grouped together the sovereign states, Prussia, Saxony, Bavaria, Hesse and Baden. The Diet which met at Frankfurt was a diplomatic congress of princes and their representatives whereas the statute did not envisage either a federal army, single diplomatic representation or a common economic policy. Austria kept a measure of influence in Germany but the legal framework imposed by Metternich deeply disappointed the German patriots who in 1813 had taken arms against Napoleon in order to effect the unification of their country. The great omission at the congress was the people and the nations, but this was entirely logical as Metternich totally ignored the question of the nationalities. For him there existed only princes and states.

Metternich was as hostile to the romantic ideas of the Catholic right as he was to Jacobin principles. He was indifferent to the traditional Holy Roman Empire which was still defended in the eighteenth century by the great writer on legal matters Johann Jacob Moser. He did not conceive of the union of the emperor and the Empire, of the *Kaiser* and the *Reich*, as it had been defined by the Treaties of Westphalia and the perpetual Diet of Ratisbon. The disappearance of the Holy Roman Empire was not received with indifference in

Germany, especially by the smaller states which did not want to be subject to either Austria, France or Prussia. In the course of the struggle against Napoleon, Austria had become conscious of its mission as a Catholic power. The Schlegel brothers went to Vienna at the time of the Congress to defend the thesis of the European aristocracy and to re-establish the old order in the face of the 'revolutionary hydra'. They were disappointed when Francis I refused to restore the Holy Roman Empire to the benefit of his own House in order not to arouse among his allies suspicions of Habsburg pretensions to European hegemony. Moreover, Metternich was hostile to any sign of religion in politics and was exasperated by medieval tradition.

He was equally hostile towards the Austrian patriotism which was growing around the archduke John and his advisor, baron Hormayr, who, by publishing his *Austrian Plutarch,* had tried to bring into being a consciousness transcending membership of diverse historic nations. The movement also provoked great mistrust in the emperor who had never had any sympathy for the political activities of his two brothers, the archdukes Charles and John. Thus the last opportunity was lost for creating an Austrian national consciousness in response to the national ideology stemming from the French Revolution.

Metternich wanted to establish Austrian power on a secular and rational basis in the tradition of Kaunitz. He was influenced by Friedrich von Gentz who was a disciple of Edmund Burke and in the name of liberty and tradition was fiercely opposed to the Revolution. He was also marked by his brief sojourn at Strasbourg and his studies at the diplomatic academy of professor Koch. He did not wish for hegemony but for a measure of balance. He thought that nationalism sought only to destroy states and he had faith only in the historic states which would prove their solidarity. This was why he wanted to rebuild Europe on a federal system, the 'European concert' of the five great powers, the allies Austria, Prussia, Russia and Great Britain, and Bourbon France. Habsburg Austria's only mission was to watch over Central Europe, i.e. the German Confederation, the Swiss cantons and the Italian peninsula. He wanted to curb the Italians and had no qualms over re-establishing the old states since he believed, much to the theorists' displeasure, that Italy was a geographical concept without any reality.

He had the same disillusioned vision of the German nation which in his eyes was only an abstract concept. The Germans needed union, not unification, which meant a confederation of states *(Staatenbund)* and not a federal state *(Bundesstaat).* Austria would be the guarantor of this arrangement as it did not nourish hostile sentiment towards Prussia. The two conservative monarchies united within the Confederation would be a formidible barrier against any French, or indeed Russian, impulse towards expansion.

The German Confederation created in 1815 under the presidency of Austria greatly disappointed the German patriots who had risen in 1813 against the French occupiers. It was a response to moderate views but had the disadvantage of breaking historic continuity. It could satisfy neither romantic conservatives, those nostalgic for the glory of the Holy Roman Empire, nor the liberals who were inspired by the French model. The problem was provisionally resolved but, with the advance of liberalism, the awakening was a rude one and the solution imposed by Bismarck was far from satisfactory for Germany or Europe as a whole.

Metternich had created a Central Europe of 65 million inhabitants under the authority of the Habsburgs, to whom he gave a defensive mission. He wanted to prevent the monarchy from becoming embroiled in the eastern question. The Danube and the North Sea did not concern him. Hungary was for him nothing but a bridge to the East, an 'asiatic' state which could at most serve as a bulwark. Moreover he thought it necessary to preserve the integrity of the Ottoman empire to maintain the balance in Europe. He was totally indifferent to the aspirations of the Christians in the Balkans whom he mistrusted no less than he did the Hungarians.

Metternich saw himself as a servant of the Habsburgs invested with a European and counter-revolutionary mission. He was devoted to political power and to Johannesburg, the Rhineland estate given to him by the emperor Francis. Neither he nor the treaties of 1815 should be judged too severely.

Although the terms of the treaties set the seal on the French defeat, confirmed by the disaster at Waterloo on 18 June 1815, they were well received by a Europe still largely rural, aristocratic and conservative where the bourgeois elites were still without political influence. The Rhineland and plain of Padua were exceptional in their dissatisfaction.

Metternich's mistake was not that he restored Europe in 1815 as it had been conceived in 1790 but that after 1830 he did not sense a profound change of mood. In 1815 the nations, tired of war, longed for order and peace. A generation later, the same nations no longer accepted the norms of aristocratic society re-established by Leopold II. By refusing this change, he provoked the very reaction he feared.

The arrangements made by diplomats and experts insensible to the aspirations of the most enlightened portion of public opinion but anxious to maintain the European equilibrium, stood the test of time better than the brilliant constructions elaborated a century later at the Paris Peace Conference in 1919. Metternich had been a good student of professor Koch.

The Congress of Vienna set the seal on Austria's new role as the great power guaranteeing the new European order. Finally driven from Western Europe by the loss of Breisach and Belgium, it nevertheless received some recompense for its tireless efforts after March 1792. It had won the ideological war, the Revolution was provisionally conquered. In the long term, Francis I's policy paid. The legendary tenacity of the Habsburgs got the better of revolutionary enthusiasm. With the support of Prussia and Russia, Austria became champion of the European order. *La Marseillaise* gave way to the imperial hymn composed by Haydn, *Gott erhalte den Kaiser* (God protect the emperor).

The long period of sustained warfare had demonstrated the solidity of the state reformed by Maria-Theresa and her sons. The imperial army, although often defeated, never experienced total defeat as had the Prussians at Jena, and the Hungarians in 1809 did not respond to the approaches made by Napoleon. The only difficulty was financing the expenses of the army.

Recourse to bank notes had led to the first enormous rise in the national debt in the monarchy's history. In 1811 paper money had lost 90 per cent of its nominal value and the government decided in March to organize an operation of 'easement' which was nothing but a disguised bankruptcy; notes were exchanged against five paper-florins. Only the payment of a war indemnity by France and the creation of an Austrian national bank in 1816 made it possible to stabilize the currency of a state which had not been seriously ravaged by war; the French invasions, as dramatic as they were, had been very brief. After the Peace of Lunéville, Austria ceased to be a mercenary in the service of Britain and became a real partner as eager as the English cabinet to conquer Napoleon and revolutionary France. And, like England, it paid a heavy price for this obstinacy which led it to triumph in 1815.

Was the victory an illusion? Napoleon was conquered but the principle of nationality and the ideas of liberty remained very much alive. This was why Metternich would fight tirelessly for the victory of his ideas, right to his death in 1859, and with the assistance of the Habsburgs, would conduct a long campaign to keep these forces at bay.

NOTES AND REFERENCES

1. Hermann Maynert, *Kaiser Franz I*, Vienna, 1872.
   Viktor Bibl, *Kaiser Franz, der Letzte römisch-deutsche Kaiser*, Leipzig and Vienna, 1938.
2. A. von Vivenot, 'Thugut und sein politisches System', *Archiv für Österreichische Geschichte*, 42, Vienna, 1870.
3. Denis Silagi, *Jakobiner in der Habsburger Monarchie*, Vienna and Munich, 1962.
   Ernest Wangermann, *From Joseph II to the Jacobin Trials*, Oxford, 1959.
4. Oskar Crise, *Erzherzog Karl von Österreich. Ein Lebensbild*, 3 vols, Vienna, 1912.
   Helmut Hertenberger and Franz Wiltschek, *Erzherzog Karl, der Sieger von Aspern*, Graz, 1983.
5. Grete Klingenstein (ed.), *Erzherzog Johann von Österreich. Beiträge zur Geschichte seiner Zeit*, Graz, 1982.
   Othmar Pickl (ed.), *Erzherzog Johann von Österreich. Sein wirken in seiner Zeit*, Graz, 1982.
   A. Veltze (ed.), *Erzherzog Johann, Feldzugerzählung 1809*, Vienna, 1909.
6. Guillaume de Bertier de Sauvigny, *Metternich*, Paris, 1984.

CHAPTER TEN

The Age of Metternich (1815–48)

The period from 1815 to 1848 was dominated by the character of the chancellor of Austria, and in Austrian historiography is referred to as the age of Metternich. Klemens Wenzel Nepomuk Lothar, count, later prince, Metternich was the true successor to Kaunitz, whose granddaughter he took as his first wife. In 1809, after his recall from the embassy in Paris, he was in charge of foreign affairs and from 1817 was the emperor Francis I's chief minister. After Francis I's death in 1835 and until the revolution of 1848, he was the true ruler of Austria since, with count Kollowrath, he controlled the Regency Council which until 1848 assisted Ferdinand I 'the Benign' (1793–1875) who had succeeded Francis I as emperor but was incapable of managing affairs on his own, even with the assistance of a prime minister.

Metternich belonged to a family of aristocrats which had always served the House of Austria, as canons in the cathedral chapters of the Rhineland or in the diplomatic service and army; since 1648 there had been a Metternich heavy cavalry regiment. The chancellor loved society, especially that of beautiful women. He was intelligent and lively, not especially inclined to hard work, and found administration boring in the extreme. He left a copious private correspondence which reveals his intellectual qualities as well as his limitations and obsessions.

METTERNICH AND EUROPE: THE HOLY ALLIANCE

Metternich devoted all his effort to maintaining the system put in place in 1815 and to countering the ideas of the French Revolution. He remained unshaken in his resolve and did not cease to parade his self-confidence before the emperor, despite the fleeting differences of opinion between them over the modernization of institutions.

In 1832 he wrote to count Apponyi, 'in Europe, there is only one matter of import and that is revolution'. He had a mission to join Prussia and Russia in guaranteeing the order restored by the treaties of 1815. This was one of the reasons he imposed Austrian preponderance in Germany and Italy and distanced himself as far as possible from any ventures in the Balkans. It is also the reason he used every means at his disposal to render permanent the Europe of ruling elites and princes which he had created. He agreed to join the Holy Alliance although, as a confirmed rationalist, he had serious reservations about tsar Alexander I's mysticism. The Congress system was based on frequent diplomatic congresses which brought together the great powers, Austria, Russia, Prussia, Great Britain and, after 1818, France. On three occasions, at Troppau in December 1820, at Ljubljana in January 1821 and Verona in summer 1822, the powers, despite British reservations, followed the course advocated by tsar Alexander. In the name of European order, Spain was restored to Ferdinand VII through French military action and Austria received the mandate to intervene with arms against the liberal regime in Naples and, at the request of the king of Piedmont-Sardinia, crushed the liberal uprising in Piedmont in April 1821, and so safeguarded Austrian preponderance in Italy. The prospect of Greek independence raised fears that the status quo in the Balkans would be overturned, with potentially serious consequences for Austria since there was the risk that Russia would gain the advantage. True to his beliefs, Metternich refused to intervene in support of the Greek insurgents. He saw no need for an independent Greek state. The intervention of France, Britain and then tsar Nicholas I caused him serious disquiet. The long crisis from 1821 to 1832 was finally resolved by a compromise, the Treaty of Adrianople (1829), which was instigated by British diplomacy. Greece became autonomous and in 1832 independent. Russia gained some advantages, in particular the autonomy of the principalities of Moldavia and Wallachia, but the principle of the integrity of the Ottoman empire was maintained and the Russian thrust into the Balkans was contained.

The July Revolution of 1830* cast doubts upon the Congress system. The revolution in Paris was the first breach in the European status quo established in 1815. Unwise actions by Louis-Philippe encouraged revolutionary movements which combined liberal and nationalist aspirations. During the Belgian crisis, Metternich was in favour of intervention but refused to engage Austrian forces alongside those of Russia and Prussia since armed intervention would provoke a response from France which no-one wanted. The powers abandoned William I, king of the Netherlands, and recognized Belgian independence under the guarantee of neutrality.

During the Polish uprising against Russia, Austria joined Prussia in closing its frontiers at the beginning of 1831 to prevent the Galicians supplying the Russian Poles with arms and volunteers. Austria had Polish provinces of its own and so could not hope for success for a movement which was challenging the political balance in Eastern Europe. *Les Trois Glorieuses*** roused liberal movements scattered throughout Saxony, Brunswick, Hesse and Rhineland Prussia. The spectacle of the national insurrection in Congress Poland stirred

---

* Translator's note: the July Revolution forced Charles X (1757–1836), the grandson of Louis XV and the last Bourbon king of France, to abdicate. His successor Louis-Philippe (1773–1850) of the House of Orléans ruled as king of the French until 1848.
** Translator's note: *Les Trois Glorieuses* were the 27, 28 and 29 July 1830.

in intellectual circles the desire to prepare for German unification. The historian Ranke proclaimed in a series of articles the necessity of realizing union. Metternich was unsettled by the movement, as weak as it was, and managed to stifle it with the cooperation of Frederick William III, the king of Prussia, who was greatly alarmed by the growth of liberalism. Against this background, in June 1832, the Austrian chancellor was able to secure the vote in favour of 'the protocol of six articles' aimed against the liberals and the nationalist movement; the German governments would neither tolerate the legislative assemblies' attempting to take away effective power from the executive power nor would they allow the confederative system of 1815 to be publicly criticized. In August 1833 a commission of the Frankfurt Diet received investigative powers to thwart revolutionary activities with the aid of the secret police. In 1834 a conference meeting at Vienna agreed to the strengthening of censorship in the German states and to the establishment of new newspapers.

Metternich had broken the resistance which the liberals had been able to mount against Austrian hegemony in the Confederation. It was, however, a Pyrrhic victory, for Prussia at the same time realized the *Zollverein* (customs union) among the numerous German states. The small states of north Germany had been integrated before 1830 and Prussia then secured the accord of Hesse in 1831 and of Bavaria and Württemberg in 1834. The Austrian empire was excluded and Metternich understood that the German states henceforth would be 'a compact body under the direction of Prussia'. Austria would be 'a foreign body' and this physical exclusion would have political consequences. Metternich did not respond and so put Austria's position in Germany in the balance, because he needed to secure Prussian support against the liberals.

Metternich gradually saw his field of action limited to Italy, where he intervened in 1831 to crush the revolutionary movement which had broken out in the Romagna, within the Papal state, and had then spread to Parma, where Napoleon's widow Maria Louisa was duchess, and to Modena. He believed that a neo-absolutist system was essential in the Italian states to maintain the Habsburgs' preponderance. The government of Louis-Philippe wanted to put a stop to Austrian influence in the Papal state and sent an expeditionary force to Ancona but it was wary of becoming involved in a movement for Italian independence which would entail great risks. The king of Sardinia, Charles Albert, sided with the Austrians because he was afraid of France and the liberals, the *carbonari*, who were members of secret revolutionary associations. With the complicity of Charles Albert and Ferdinand II, king of Naples, Metternich was still master in Italy, which remained the only place still guarded by Austria after 1848.

The challenge facing Metternich was to maintain the solidarity of the conservative powers, Russia, Prussia and Austria. Tsar Nicholas I proved ever more determined to resist the forces of upheaval for fear that their success would threaten the autocratic regime in Russia and provoke an insurrection in Russian Poland. In 1847 he told Metternich that he would not become involved in military action if a state was threatened with dissolution and remarked, 'the [Austrian] Empire will live as long as you do but what will follow?'. The contradiction in Nicholas I's policies is explained by his hope that the Ottoman empire would be divided and he saw Austria as a potential rival in the Balkans even though Metternich was in fact very loathed to become involved in the region. In Germany, Austria had, since 1840, clashed with Prussia, where Frederick William IV, the new king, was mistaken for a liberal. Metternich was worried that institutional reform in Berlin would furnish a dangerous example. He was equally afraid of any initiatives Prussia might take with respect to the German question. In 1845 he refused to strengthen the military organization of the German Confederation, a project which conformed to the act of 1815.

Austria's international position was made yet weaker by Britain's attitude after 1846 when lord Palmerston and the liberals came to power. The liberals were convinced that every state on the Continent should adopt constitutional regimes in the interests of the nations as well as of the British economy. The Franco-Austrian rapprochement of 1847 was intended to form a front of great continental states which would paralyse Palmerston's policy. That Austria could not rely on effective support from France in its opposition to Britain became clear during the Swiss crisis of the *Sonderbund*, the separatist league formed in 1845 by the Catholic cantons in order to oppose the radicals' anticlerical measures. France was content merely to be associated with the 'collective memorandum' of January 1848 in which the conservative powers tried to intimidate the Swiss radicals and so stop them from turning the Swiss Confederation into a federal state. At the end of 1847, when the Swiss civil war was coming to an end, Metternich's system was severely threatened. In Germany, Italy and Hungary, the liberal political leaders demanded that political institutions be transformed and that measures be taken in support of nationalist claims. Liberalism was becoming a force that could not be discounted and its triumph in Berlin, Turin, Naples and Pest risked opening the way to forces which threatened the territorial status quo and the preponderance of Austria and the forces of conservatism.

METTERNICH'S DOMESTIC POLICIES

To devote himself better to the task of being Europe's policeman, Metternich conducted a firm conservative policy within the monarchy, using police surveillance, censorship and the arbitrary imprisonment of members of the liberal opposition. In 1817 a French dipomat noted 'This country is sustained by its own mass but the government does nothing and nowhere is it visible . . . There is here neither will nor authority and everyone does practically whatever he wants and the lower orders are master. Prince Metternich does not exercise any influence beyond his jurisdiction.' The government of Vienna respected traditional constitutions because they left power with the nobility and the chancellor was convinced that intermediary bodies were necessary. For this reason the Diets, which Leopold II had restored, were summoned regularly. The assemblies of the Estates, however, had their traditional privileges curtailed for fear that they would mount too violent an opposition. The administration of the Estates was progressively stripped of its prerogatives to the benefit of the royal and imperial officials. The Estates' functionaries were no longer appointed by the Diets but by the emperor. The nobility still preferred to transfer power to the monarchy rather than see its privileges suppressed by a liberal constitution. The legislative power of the Diets was reduced. In 1811 the government took the initiative and distributed new taxes leaving ordinary tax collection to the Diets as their one prerogative. The Austrian civil code was also introduced without the Diets having been consulted.

The limits of their power can be measured in the constitutions bestowed on Carniola and the Tyrol after the two provinces were returned to Austria. These texts, 'a grace' of the sovereign, granted the orders the distribution and raising of property contributions according to local custom, but the emperor reserved the right to levy tax as a whole and the orders could only present 'requests and representations' on this subject. The Tyrolean Diet consisted of a grand commission of fifty-two members, thirteen from each of the four orders. The president was appointed by the emperor who alone authorized the admission of new members. The assembly of the kingdom of Lombardy-Venetia was made up of representatives of the landowners, nobles and commoners, as well as delegates from the towns. It obtained certain powers of deliberation and the right of petition. In this way the nobility was associated with the administration and the system of Diets made it possible to maintain a large measure of decentralization.

The Hungarian Diet was, once again, the only assembly to cause the Austrian government difficulties, even though the Hungarian constitution had not been changed. The Hungarian political class tried, quite simply, to use the Diet to obtain reforms.[1] During the Napoleonic Wars the Diet had been summoned every three years to grant subsidies and military quotas. After the 1811 Diet refused to devalue by 20 per cent the bank notes issued for the duration of the war, Metternich did not summon the national assembly for thirteen years and approached the county assemblies for recruits and subsidies. In 1825 he was forced by the resistance mounted by the counties to summon a new Diet which reminded the king of his obligation to summon the Diet every three years. The government at Vienna later respected Hungarian state-right but relations became increasingly strained after the formation of the reform party which demanded a liberal constitution and was supported by the *Dietal Reports*,* the journal run by Lajos Kossuth, the young deputy. The Diet of 1832 announced that Hungarian had replaced Latin as the official language of state. In 1836 Kossuth took up his position as the parliamentary leader of the reform party. The court at Vienna, however, soon reneged on its concessions of 1836 and

---

* Translator's note: *Országgyülési tudósitások* (Dietal Reports) were edited by Kossuth who represented two absent magnates in the Diet. They were widely read and perhaps had greater effect on forging public opinion than any other publication in Hungary at that time. When the Diet closed, Kossuth continued to stimulate interest in progress and reform by publishing the *Törvényhatósági Tudósitások* (Municipal Reports) which were based on the proceedings of the county assemblies.

had Miklós Wesselényi* and Kossuth arrested. After his release in 1840 at the Diet's insistence, Kossuth took over the editorship of the liberal *Pesti Hirlap*** and emerged as leader of the left wing of the liberal party. He attacked Austria vehemently and broke with István Szechényi,*** a magnate who favoured reform but whom Kossuth dismissed as being too moderate. Kossuth now made no secret of his wish to secure political and economic independence for his country. In 1847 he was elected to the Diet as the deputy for Pest and immediately became leader of the radicals, increasing his influence by his passionate eloquence. The political importance of the Hungarian Diet is explained by its consisting of the elected representatives of the political class. It was not simply an assembly of notables content to be associated with the administration of their country. Metternich did not like the Hungarian nobility but he could grant its members some concessions since the police, the Church and the bureaucracy guaranteed the cohesion of the system. The organs of government were no more than administrative bodies responsible for carrying out the sovereign's wishes. The emperor, as king of Hungary, reached his decisions on his own and relayed them to the council of state, to the chancelleries and the financial administration for implementation.

Under Metternich, there did not exist a real cabinet in Austria, despite his efforts to persuade the *Staatsrat* to play this role in the spirit of Kaunitz's reforms. In 1817 the emperor refused to unify the government and never accorded Metternich the prerogatives of a prime minister even though abroad the chancellor was assumed to be the master of Austrian politics.[2] It was not long before the chancellor clashed with count Kollowrath, a Bohemian aristocrat in charge of financial matters. Paradoxically, Metternich was the master of continental Europe but not of Austria.

After 1835, the trio of Francis I, Metternich and Kollowrath was reduced to a duo of Metternich–Kollowrath because Ferdinand I, Francis I's successor as emperor of Austria,[3] lacked the intellectual powers to govern and only performed ceremonial duties. The eldest son of Francis I and Maria-Theresa of Bourbon Sicily, Ferdinand was born at Vienna in 1793 and when young suffered from epilepsy. He was musical, interested in botany and soon showed those qualities which earned him great popularity with the Viennese and the epithet *gütig*, 'the Benign'. He was, though, thought of as an invalid and posed a serious problem for his father who would have liked to have excluded him from the succession. Metternich, however, insisted on respecting the principle of legitimacy which was fundamental in the Austrian monarchy. Ferdinand I refused to abdicate and after 1830 was admitted to the *Staatsrat*. In 1831 he married Maria Pia of Piedmont-Sardinia but the union was without issue. His father, when mortally ill, left him only the appearance of authority while real

---

* Translator's note: baron Miklós Wesselényi was leader of the Transylvanian liberal opposition.
** Translator's note: *Pesti Hirlap* was first published in January 1841 and issued twice a week. It was read by a quarter of literate Hungarians who read newspapers.
*** Translator's note: István Szechényi, author of *Hitel* (On Credit), argued for the superiority of a money-based, rather than subsistence, economy. He travelled extensively in Western Europe and the Balkans and greatly admired Benjamin Franklin.

power devolved upon a state conference presided over by the archduke Louis and made up of the archduke Francis Charles, Metternich and Kollowrath.

This arrangement suited the archduke Francis Charles who was no more gifted than his elder brother Ferdinand, but it was deeply disappointing to his wife, the archduchess Sophie, an ambitious and energetic Wittelsbach princess who had hoped through her marriage one day to be empress. For this reason she vested all her hopes in her son, the archduke Francis Joseph, who was born in 1830 and who she brought up as heir presumptive to the Austrian empire. In 1839 the state conference promulgated a statute for the House of Habsburg establishing precise rules for succession. These rules were closely based on the strict principles of primogeniture and the exclusion of illegitimate offspring which the French monarchy had followed under the *ancien régime*.

Relations between the Church and state continued in the Josephist tradition. The administration of ecclesiastical property remained the prerogative of the state; direct correspondence between the Holy See and the bishops was still forbidden. Monasteries were secularized in Galicia and Venetia once the provinces passed to Austria. Although the government did not dare to authorize divorce, which was contrary to the prescriptions of canon law, it allowed separation. The government in Vienna, however, like all conservative governments after 1815, proved rather more inclined to favour the Church out of concern for maintaining order and countering revolution. The Jesuits were allowed to return and the clergy obtained the right to inspect primary and secondary schools where the catechism was obligatory. The state, though, kept control over education, the syllabus and textbooks. In fact, the Church became an instrument of government and of keeping watch over the population.

From 1808 to 1848, higher education was also closely surveyed by directors of study appointed by the authority in each faculty. Deans and rectors acted as officials so that professors were spared administrative responsibilities. Those professors who, like Bolzano, discarded the official programmes were suspended. The university of Vienna was seen as an 'honourable retirement home' since professors from the provinces were sent there towards the end of their careers. The model provided by the north German universities which had been set out in the reforms of the Prussian Alexander von Humboldt, was abandoned and education was deliberately separated from research to create, as the emperor Francis remarked in 1821, brave citizens and docile subjects who would carefully reject any innovation. The faculty of letters and all instruction in philosophy remained dormant until 1848, although the humanities had constituted a compulsory preliminary course after six years at the gymnasium. The reform of 1810 had stripped courses at the faculty of law of any historical content. It was thought sufficient to combine positive law with some courses in natural law. Technical education at the higher level was favoured. In 1815 a polytechnic was opened at Vienna and directed for thirty-five years by Johann-Joseph von Prechtl who paid close attention to the advance of science and technology. It was only in 1847 that the Austrian Academy of Sciences was founded, although proposals for such an institution had been made in the seventeenth century by Leibniz to Leopold I and later in 1749 revived in discussion by Gottsched. It was finally the orientalist Hammer-Purgstall[4] who from 1837 put pressure on Metternich. Ferdinand I gave his assent to the scheme on 14 May 1847 and the first forty members were appointed from among the monarchy's different nationalities. Hungary had had an Academy of Sciences since 1825.

The universities experienced an influx of students. The number of students in the faculty of law in 1848 was five times that in 1810 and the faculty, by training officials for the bureaucracy, contributed to the rise of the bourgeoisie. These students were recruited from among the sons of officials and especially among the young poor who paid for their studies by giving lessons. Although German literature was not taught, Goethe and Schiller were studied, as well as prohibited authors such as Kant and Hegel.[5] After 1801, the censors shared the powers of the ministry of police and all publications were closely surveyed.

THE AWAKENING OF THE NATIONALITIES: THE SLAVS

Precautionary measures did not prevent national movements from developing after 1820 among the Slavs, Hungarians and Italians. The Italians seriously troubled Metternich because, from the *carbonari*, patriots and liberals to the various tendencies of the Risorgimento, they posed a great challenge to Austrian domination of the peninsula. They also provided a model for the Slav nations, the Czechs and Croats, who, under the influence of Herder, the German philosopher, placed great emphasis upon their national languages which had been neglected during the eighteenth century.

The Slav languages were undergoing a revival. Until the end of the seventeenth century, they had remained the languages of culture and administration. It was only during the eighteenth century that they were reduced to the status of popular languages while the elites spoke and wrote in German, French or Latin. In 1809 the Czech philologist Josef Dobrovský published *A Scientific Czech Grammar* and Josef Jungmann published *A History of the Czech Language*. In 1824 Kollár's poems, which recalled how the Slavs had suffered at the hands of the Germans, enjoyed considerable success with young Czech intellectuals. Šafarík, a Protestant Slovak who had settled in Bohemia, reminded the Czechs that they belonged to a large family of peoples who should establish solidarity amongst themselves. A former student at the university of Jena, he was greatly influenced by the German liberal movement and the Polish insurrection of 1831, but he was a scholar who devoted himself to studying the origin of the Slavs and did not seek to draw political conclusions. František Palacký, the historian of the Diet of Bohemia, engaged firmly in the struggle for state-right. In 1836, in the first volume of his *History of Bohemia*, the first edition of which was published, paradoxically, in German, he showed that Bohemia's history was dominated by the conflict between the Germans and Czechs.* Palacký, as leader of an intellectual movement, invited the nobility

---

* Translator's note: Palacký's *Die Geschichte von Böhmen*, published 1836–67, was followed by a Czech edition, *Dějiny národu Českého*, 1848–76.

and bourgeoisie to claim political liberty. Karel Havlícek, a journalist who had spent much time in Russia, was more oriented towards practical action and wanted to free the Bohemian Slavs from their dependence on the Germans. They all demanded for the Czech people the place they were rightfully owed in Bohemia and in the Austrian empire. They welcomed reforms but never demanded independence.

In 1822 the National Museum of Bohemia was opened on the initiative of count Sternberg and the grand burgrave. In 1827 the *Journal of the National Museum*,* which was edited by Palacký, helped the growth of Czech literature. The aristocracy, with count Leo Thun-Hohenstein, took part in the struggle in favour of a bilingual national culture in which Czech would be favoured. The work of Slav linguistics played an important part in the national revival. In 1816 a decree abolished any discrimination against Czech and authorized its being taught in schools, but this arrangement was abolished in 1821 after the conference at Carlsbad.

The Czech national movement was weakened after 1830 by a schism between those who admired Russia, and so were conservative in character and ready to collaborate with Metternich, and a radical wing which was democratic in orientation and did not hide its sympathy for the Polish insurgents. They gathered in the Matica Česka** and in 1848 numbered some 3 500 militants. Noble conservatives and bourgeois democrats were strongly disposed in favour of 'Austro-Slavism' which foresaw the eight Slav nationalities of the Empire transforming the monarchy into a great Slav power. They feared the initiative taken by the German liberals and their tendency towards hegemony.[6]

Among the South Slavs, the Croats showed the most acutely developed national consciousness as a consequence of their constantly taking refuge in Croatian state-right during their continuous enmity with the Hungarians. German had become the language of education and of the press. Ljudevit Gaj, a Croatian lawyer and the son of a doctor, studied at Graz and Vienna universities and chose one of the Croatian dialects, *stokavski*, to create a modern literary language. He founded a publishing society, a lecture society and a library in Zagreb. Inspired by the French annexation of the Illyrian provinces (1809–14), he tried to create an Illyrian movement which would gather together the South Slavs: the Croats, Serbs and Bosnians. Their cultural awakening helped the Croats to defend their political autonomy within the Austrian empire.

A new and significant development came when the 'non-historical' nations, those that did not have the advantage of state-right, most notably the Slovaks, began to manifest national consciousness. The Slovak pastor L'udovít Štúr codified the Slovak language on the basis of a dialect from the centre of the country, rejecting the Czech translation of the Bible and resuming the work of the Counter-Reformation clergy. Two other Protestant Slovaks, Ján Kollár and Pavel Šafařík were followers of pan-Slavism. In 1826 Safarík published in

---

* Translator's note: *Časopis Narodního Musea*.
** Translator's note: Matica Česka, 'the Czech beehive'. Other Slav groups also called their cultural associations 'beehives', e.g. *Maticahrvatska*, the Croat cultural centre and publishing house.

German *A History of the Languages and Literature of the Slavs in their Different Dialects* and in 1837 in Slovak *The Slav Antiquities*.* Kollar's fame rested on an epic poem, *The Daughter of Slava*, in which he celebrated the glory of the Slav past and predicted a brilliant future for the Slavs.** For the Poles, the most important part of their cultural life was focused in the area of their homeland annexed by the Russians. Theirs was a problem of particular complexity.

The nations awoke during the 'age of Metternich' and the labours of poets and scholars gradually bore fruits.

THE HUNGARIANS

In Hungary, the period 1810–40 was most important for the 'awakening' of national consciousness. Political opposition in the Diet is explained by the reformist movement. Count István Széchenyi, an enlightened magnate who was representative of this current, was more inspired by the English model than the French Revolution. His travels in Great Britain enabled him to draw analogies between the English 'constitution' and his own country's Diet system. In both cases, he saw the whole nobility, both the aristocracy and the gentry, as being of prime importance, and throughout the nineteenth century liberal Hungarians were characterized by their anglomania. Széchenyi believed that the oppressed should be provided for by improving agriculture and developing transport and it was to this end that he introduced horse-racing and selective horse-breeding. The road system in Hungary was very poor and as the Danube was the only route by which the country could be entered, he promoted the advance of steam navigation. He had the first bridge built to link Buda with Pest, the famous Chain Bridge*** which is still a feature of the capital. In 1844 Hungarian replaced Latin as the official language of administration.

In 1825 Széchenyi founded the Hungarian Academy of Sciences and after 1840 a quality press came into existence in imitation of the English press. The journals in Hungarian like the *Pest Gazette* through their high intellectual content contributed to the renewal of political life and literature among the ruling clases, gentry, intellectuals and a bourgeoisie which was still in the earliest stages of development and often German-speaking. The intelligentsia, many of whom were lawyers, were generally the educated younger sons of noble families. On the eve of the revolution of 1848, there were more than 500 000 nobles

---

* Translator's note: Safarík's works were published as *Geschichte der Slavischen Sprache und Literatur nach allen Mundarten* (1826) and *Slovanské starozitnosti* (1837) published in German as *Slawische Altertümer*.

** Translator's note: Kollar's great verse was published as *Slávy dcera*.

*** Translator's note: known today to Hungarians as the Széchenyi Lánchíd, plans for the bridge were drafted by William Tierney Clark, an English engineer. Its construction was supervised by Adam Clark, a Scot who took a Hungarian wife and whose descendants long played an important part in Budapest's economic and social life. In the winter of 1944–45, Hitler's army blew up the bridge but it was rebuilt according to the original design and re-opened in 1949, on the hundredth anniversary of its first opening.

out of a total population of 12 million in Hungary and the nobility remained the only political class.

After 1830, count Széchenyi's reform party was supported by the youngest radicals, gathered around Kossuth. They were inspired by the traditions of the French Revolution and demanded total independence as well as the abolition of the seigneurial regime. The liberals, however, remained a minority in the face of the conservative Hungarians who were allied to the court at Vienna and feared the emancipation of the peasants.

The national movement was accompanied by a romantic literary movement which raised the Hungarians to the same level as the Italians. That it was the Hungarians and the Italians who in 1848 demanded secession, whereas the Slavs developed Austro-Slavism, is not coincidental. Of all the peoples who revolted in 1848, only the Hungarians possessed a legal base. Their old constitution provided them with a springboard. Engels in the *Neue Rheinische Zeitung* expressed his opinion that Hungarian political life had made great progress between 1831 and 1848 and that the feudal forms of the old constitution had contributed as much to democratic advance as the liberal constitutions of the south German states. Historians agree that the revolution of 1848 derived from changes in mood at the end of Metternich's era which in its last phase, 1840–48, is often referred to as the *Vormärz*.

ECONOMIC PROGRESS IN THE EMPIRE

The contrast between the industrializing hereditary lands and rural Hungary, a trend already apparent during Maria-Theresa's reign, became increasingly marked in the first half of the nineteenth century. Hungary was almost without any industry and exchanged its agricultural surplus for manufactured goods from the Austro-Bohemia complex for which it provided a natural outlet. From the work of David Good, it seems that by 1790 the industries of the Czech lands were capable of satisfying the internal market and replacing foreign merchandise.

The industrial revolution affected metallurgy much later than in Germany because the owners of great estates were content to take wood from their own vast forests and had no need to use coke. It was only in 1836 that the first blast-furnace fed by coke was opened at Vitkovice in an engineering works owned by the archduke Rudolph, the archbishop of Olomouc and, incidentally, a pupil and patron of Beethoven. Not until the railways developed in Austria after 1848 did the iron and steel industry expand in response to the sudden increased market for iron and casting.

The textile industry was well established and was encouraged by the government to absorb the excess of rural manual labour created by the growth in population. The number of factories increased rapidly after 1790 but protection did nothing to promote technical advance. In 1799 some 40 000 were still engaged in spinning cotton by hand. The Napoleonic Wars did, however, favour a measure of industrial growth. The Continental Blockade combined with the mobilization of part of the manual labour force obliged industrialists to mechanize. The first factory for spinning cotton was founded in 1797 and in just a year some 10 000 workers abandoned the distaff. In 1825 only 5 000 or so in Bohemia were still spinning with a spindle and by 1840 spinning by hand had completely died out in the Czech lands. The cotton industry, as in many other lands, was the pioneer of mechanization.

In the early stages of industrialization, hydraulic power was sufficient and it was not until 1816 that the first steam-engine was put into service in Moravia, and in Bohemia, some seven years later. By 1841 there were seventy-nine steam-engines working in Bohemia and seventy-seven in Moravia with a total force of 2 000 horsepower. These beginnings, as modest as they were, still led to the growth of capital and an increase in the number of industrial enterprises. In Bohemia the manufacture of printed cotton developed at Prague, Litoměřice and Boleslav. The industrial revolution did not affect weaving until after 1848.

The textile industry was concentrated around Brno in Moravia and exported six times its domestic demand to Hungary, Italy and North America, as well as providing for the Viennese market. By 1835, mechanized wool-spinning had overcome all competition and had reduced the numbers employed in the industry. In 1840 the textile industry was using thirty-one steam-engines. The mills in Brno led to the ruin of the remaining handcraftsmen. Machine-weaving was introduced in Liberec in north Bohemia in 1830. The mechanization of cloth manufacture came much later. Mechanized spinning expanded around 1848 but machine-weaving only became widespread after 1848.

Sugar-beet had been introduced because of the Continental Blockade but its production expanded noticeably after 1830. Its importance equalled that of beer in Bohemia, where there were a thousand breweries in 1840, and it provided a valuable outlet for the great estates which achieved their 'industrial revolution' on the rich soils of central Bohemia.

A revolution in transport accompanied the development of industry. In 1831 a railway line was opened between Linz and České Budějovice with locomotives replacing the draught animals which had operated along the track since 1825. It was financed by a consortium of Viennese bankers and was the first railway in Central Europe, making easier the connections between Bohemia and the Danube. In 1837 a private company began building a line from Vienna to Bohumin which was completed in 1847, but it was public money in 1842 that paid for the line from Vienna to Olomouc which was opened in 1845 by the Company of the Railways of the North, the *Nordbahn*. The construction of a line linking Vienna, Prague and Dresden was undertaken in 1841 and in the same year the Company of the South, the *Sudbahn*, started a project to provide a rail link for Vienna and the Adriatic ports, Trieste and Venice. However, only sections of the Vienna–Graz line were in operation by 1844 and it was not until 1848 that the obstacle of the Semmering pass was overcome. Salomon Rothschild's bank in Vienna contributed to the collection of the necessary capital.

In 1829 navigation on the Danube was modernized with the creation of the

Danube Steam Navigation Company (DDSG*), which used a fleet of paddle-steamers ideally suited to river traffic. As early as 1834, it was possible to travel from Vienna to the Black Sea by boat. The Elbe was also used after 1841 when the steam-boat *Bohemia* maintained a regular service between Prague and Dresden.

The state of agriculture in Hungary was a much greater cause for concern. Land under cultivation was divided into seven categories: the allodial lands which were farmed directly and owned by the nobility and were exempt from taxation; allodial lands rented out to peasants; lands on the census which were occupied by peasants, subject to state taxation and the feudal dues, the *robot* and tithe, and amounted to 10 million acres or 6 million hectares; the vacant lands; the 'reclaimed' lands; the communal lands; and the vineyards amounting to 170 000 hectares. The resumption of direct farming of the allodial lands by the nobility is noticeable in the years around 1800 because Hungary supplied the imperial army during the Revolutionary and Napoleonic Wars. It was one of the wheat granaries of Europe but the nobles were incapable of increasing productivity on their estates in the face of an ever-increasing demand. For this reason, they tried to drive out those occupying the allodial lands, but who had only a precarious claim, at the very time when the population growth meant that the peasants had ever more need of these lands. There were numerous trials after 1820 between estate-owners and peasant tenants and by 1848 there were only 100 000 hectares of allodial land still rented to peasants. As in eighteenth-century France, the peasants turned to viticulture as an additional resource and in 1848 the produce from vineyards represented a quarter of their revenues.

The estate-owners wanted to divide the communal lands in the woods and plains in order to extend the reserve. Hungary was short of pasture and only some sections of the Great Plain, at the most 10 per cent of cultivable land, could be classified as such. The patent of 1767 had envisaged a ratio of pasture to arable of just 3 acres of grassland to 22 acres under the plough. The practice of leaving land fallow was abandoned, peasants were banned from grazing their animals in the undergrowth and the nobles refused to rent out pastureland on the reserve. The Diet of 1832–36 proposed to share out the communal lands but this only increased the suffering since, in the past, nobles who did not farm the reserve allowed open access to the pastures, but with the distribution of the communal lands they demanded that they be allotted the best grasslands.

During the reign of Francis I, there was an increase in the number of agricultural workers who possessed, at most, a house and less than 3 acres, while the number of proprietors with tenure remained stable at around 500 000, although their holdings diminished in relative value. In 1780 the ratio of *coloni* (peasant proprietors) to *inquilini* (agricultural labourers) was two-thirds to one-third, but by 1850 this had been reversed and three-fifths were agricultural labourers for whom the abolition of the *robot* had made little difference, and two-fifths were peasant proprietors who were the real beneficiaries of the 1848 revolution.[7]

* Translator's note: Donau Dampfschiffahrts Gesellschaft.

This change in the rural world is explained by the growth in population which was only checked by the famine of 1810 and the cholera epidemic which came from the Near East and in 1832 afflicted France as well as Prussia and the Austrian empire. Hungary experienced an annual growth of 7–8 per cent, an average rise in the number of people of 45 000–50 000 in Hungary proper. Land reclamation reached a plateau. Those already farming objected to new lands being brought into cultivation. Productivity remained poor in the manner characteristic of extensive farming with cereal yields of 1–4 for small undertakings and 1–6 for the large well-managed estates. English travellers were struck by the archaic character of Hungarian agriculture and were as astonished as Arthur Young travelling in France on the eve of the Revolution. In Hungary, industry did not offer the same outlet as in the hereditary lands.

In general, the economic situation during the first half of the nineteenth century was good, with the exception of the crises of 1816 and 1846 which affected the whole of Europe. The 1816 crisis is explained by the end of the Napoleonic Wars, the reopening of markets to English manufactured goods and Russian wheat, and the imperial army no longer being a privileged client. A slump in Hungarian wheat followed and some aristocrats tried, unsuccessfully, to make up the loss by breeding sheep. English industrial products were, despite the customs duty, relatively inexpensive and competed with goods manufactured in the hereditary lands, which in the end had the effect of concentrating industrial enterprises and modernizing modes of production. In the United States, the output of cotton cloth grew by 16 per cent per annum and in the hereditary lands by 11 per cent per annum. Expansion continued at such a rate that by the 1840s, coal, cast iron and textile production equalled, or indeed surpassed, that of the *Zollverein* from which the Austrian empire had been excluded at Prussia's behest. Bohemian industrialists who were excluded from the German market strengthened their hold on the domestic market and increasingly turned towards outlets in the Balkans, Near East and Ottoman empire.

The general crisis of 1846 was caused by the unfortunate conjunction of bad weather and bad harvests and led, as in the past, to peasant disturbances in Galicia and Bohemia. It was the last crisis of the old economy before the crises, no less severe, of the capitalist era.

Final proof of the deep changes in the Austrian economy is provided by the pattern of taxation. Taxes on consumption had been introduced in 1829 as well as duties on alcohol, customs and official papers requiring authorization, so that by 1848 two-thirds of the imperial budget's revenue came from indirect taxation, and no more than a third from direct taxation, tax on private fortunes and property. The state continued to be in debt and found in the Rothschild bank a ready purchaser of government bonds. In 1848 the public debt had grown to 1 250 million florins.

The growth in population and the economy during the Metternich era was reflected in urban development, most of all in Vienna which was, more than ever, the capital of Central Europe with a population in 1828 of more than 300 000, an increase of 87 000 since 1785 when, during Joseph II's reign, the city's dominance had been somewhat less. The middle-sized towns showed the greatest increase in population. Brno doubled in size as a consequence of industrial growth, by 1845 Pest had tripled its population to reach 100 000 and was larger than Prague which in 1828 had just 89 000 inhabitants. The changes of the years 1785–1830 were at least as rapid as in the previous three centuries. In Hungary, the towns continued to grow in size. The rural exodus towards small and middle-sized towns, of which, according to Granasztoi, there were thirteen in 1828, increased and gave Danubian Europe its distinctive pattern of urbanization.[8]

VIENNA IN THE AGE OF BIEDERMEIER*

The term Biedermeier is used of the period from the Congress of Vienna in 1815 to the revolution of 1848 and for the educated Austrian has many more resonances than the cold and technical term 'the age of Metternich'. It symbolizes the arrival of the bourgeoisie and is epitomized in a style of furniture less cold than that of the French empire and more elegant than the ephemeral style of Napoleon III. It is a light, comfortable, functional and graceful style which still imparts charm to many Viennese interiors. The Viennese mentality is further encapsulated in 'the Congress dance'. This vast diplomatic gathering was a great fête at which the activities of Metternich's secret police never ceased to amaze and the Viennese, happy that peace was restored, set the tone, wittily commenting on the Congress which cost the emperor and the taxpayers so dear.

No traveller failed to be charmed by the capital of the Empire. In 1840 Gérard de Nerval eulogized it thus: one passes the long suburbs of uniform houses, then, in the middle of a ring of streets, behind an enclosure of banks and walls, is the town, as grand as any quarter of Paris. Imagine that a district of the Palais-Royal were set on its own and given the walls of a fortified town and boulevards of a quarter of a league and that around it were extensive suburbs then you will have a thorough idea of Vienna's situation, its wealth and its activity.

The districts and villages on the periphery housed those who worked at home, in particular weavers, especially silk weavers, who earned 2 florins a week and set women and children to work thirteen hours a day. Children from the age of nine were 'authorized' to work in contravention of the Theresian rulings on schooling. Poorly fed and poorly housed, this proleteriat was also badly organized. The crisis of 1846 led to a series of bankruptcies in 1847 and provoked discontent and unrest. These artisans and workers became the footsoldiers among the revolutionary troops of 1848. Besides its textiles, Vienna

---

* Translator's note: the name used to refer to this style is taken from a fictional character in satirical literature of the time, Gottlieb Biedermeier, who personified bourgeois philistinism and whose very stolidity seems reflected in Austrian and German furniture and architecture of the period.

was also distinguished for its luxury industries, porcelain from Augarten, furniture, and especially musical instruments. The first Bösendorfer pianos were made during the Biedermeier era and for some virtuosos are still the best pianos in the world.

Music remained one of the central activities at Vienna. Beethoven had taken the place of Mozart and of Haydn, who had died in 1809, shortly after Napoleon's troops arrived in the capital. Haydn lived long enough to have a second career after the tremendous reception he had enjoyed in London. During the Enlightenment, while he was *Kapelmeister* to prince Esterházy at Eisenstadt, he invented the string quartet and the classical symphony. In his last years, he composed choral works of great perfection, the *Theresienmesse* and other masses, and two oratorios in the English fashion, *The Seasons* and the magnificent *Creation* of 1798 in which he gave extraordinary resonance to the German version of the text from Genesis.

Beethoven came from the Rhineland but was of Flemish origin. His grandfather had been *Kapelmeister* to the elector of Cologne and it was there that the archduke Maximilian Francis, the town's last archbishop-elector, gave his patronage to the young composer. Beethoven sympathized with the ideas of the Revolution and with Napoleon, to whom he dedicated his third symphony, 'the Eroica'. In the end, however, he fitted himself into the Viennese system far better than Mozart had done, and ended up living as an independent artist, receiving royalties from his editor, the Saxon Breitkopf, and giving lessons. Besides his beautiful female students who have given rise to much romantic and ill-founded literature surrounding his work, Beethoven was music master to the archduke Rudolph, the younger brother of the emperor Francis. It was to him that he dedicated his celebrated Trio and his Mass in D on the occasion of the archduke's installation as archbishop of Olomouc. He knew how to use to the full the possibilities presented by the pianoforte and perfected the instrumental forms, the symphony and string quartet, developed by Haydn. A tormented hypochondriac, deaf for the latter half of his life, he was a true romantic figure. The message he projected, while it did not fall foul of the censors, failed to amuse the Viennese public. *Fidelio*, his only opera, was a hymn to liberty and conjugal love, but he handled the vocal parts badly and the various versions were badly received. The first night was held in November 1805 in front of an audience of French officers in the Theater an der Wien. The Viennese had a marked preference for Italian opera. Salieri and then, after 1815, the young Rossini pleased audiences in Vienna as much as in Italy and Paris.

Franz Schubert, who was from Vienna, was more characteristic of the Biedermeier age and, unlike Beethoven, never established himself in the salons of the aristocracy. He had become a teacher in order to escape conscription and in the course of his brief career earned his reputation as a dreamer who excelled at the romantic art of *Lieder* and composing for the pianoforte and also chamber music, notably the string quartet *Death and the Maiden*. A shy and melancholy man, he lived surrounded by a circle of bourgeois friends and artists. He was much less at ease with the large-scale musical genres, but nevertheless composed symphonies and masses, for he had received an excellent musical education at the imperial chapel. After Beethoven died in 1827 and Schubert in 1828, no other great composer settled in Vienna. Liszt, Chopin, Schumann and Wagner only visited.

Cultural life at Vienna was thereafter dominated by the waltz and by the popular theatre. The city remained one of the great capitals of European music and the Burgtheater enjoyed a period of brilliance under the artistic direction of Leher. Between 1814 and 1832, Leher introduced to the Viennese the great German classics, although Schiller's *William Tell* was stripped of its anti-Habsburg passages, as well as the foreign repertoire and the work of the young poet and dramatist Franz Grillparzer who worked as an official in the chamber of accounts. The official theatres, the Burgtheater and the Theater an der Wien, competed with numerous stages in the suburbs, of which the Leopoldstadt theatre was the leader, situated in the avenue leading from the old town to the Prater. The plays performed there were in the Viennese dialect. Ferdinand Raimund, a comic actor, grew tired of the feeble dramas in which he was called upon to act and after 1820 wrote some plays of his own. Johann Nestroy, an actor and writer, put the Viennese themselves on stage in his works and went beyond comedy of mere manners, mocking love, friendship and everything else besides to make egotism the motive behind every action.

The plays of Nestroy and Raimund are still acted but the real purveyors of popular comedy are now forgotten. Bäuerlé, Gleich and Meisl were prolific writers who endeavoured to supply a public eager for new plays. Working 'on a production line' like the writers for B films much later, they applied formulas to turn out ten plays a year. This was the character of the genre. A drama from the previous season could not be revived since the public demanded new plays and a theatre director could not allow a series of failures without risking bankruptcy. This torrent of scripts provided an enormous amount of work for the offices of baron Sedlnitský, the unbending minister of police who examined all the texts.

When the Viennese were not going to the theatre, they danced to forget their worries or simply to amuse themselves. The waltz, the symbol of Viennese culture, appeared around 1815 and was developed from the Tyrolean Ländler. For the first time, the couples danced entwined, to the great scandal of the moralists. Two orchestras shared between them the public's favour, that of Joseph Lanner with his pleasing style, and Johann Strauss the elder who was more imperious and authoritarian. Their charming compositions, the essence of amusement and a reflection of Viennese frivolity, troubled neither the censors not Metternich.

Austria from 1815 to 1848 was characterized by the police regime, the growth of liberalism and nationalism, the transformation of the economy and a refined culture. The image of Metternich as the policeman of Europe and Austria as the prisonhouse of the people corresponded to a certain extent with reality, but first and foremost it was an image of how French and Italian liberals perceived Austria. Intellectual life was not completely dead. Music and theatre kept their prominence, particularly in Vienna. Metternich's system was in the long term, however, under threat from the rise of capitalism in Bohemia and in Austria, developments in Hungarian agriculture, the appearance of a bourgeoisie, a working class, a prosperous peasantry and a liberal nobility, to say nothing of the formidable national opposition in Italy.

NOTES AND REFERENCES

1. Charles Kecskemeti, *La Hongrie et le réformisme libéral*, Rome, 1989.
2. Guillaume de Bertier de Sauvigny, *Metternich*, Paris, 1984.
3. Hans-Leo Mikoletzky, 'Bild und Gegenbild Kaiser Ferdinands I. Ein Versuch', *Archiv für Österreichische Geschichte*, 125, Vienna, 1966.
   Gerd Holler, *Gerechtigkeit für Ferdinand*, Vienna and Munich, 1986.
4. J. von Hammer-Purgstall, *Histoire de l'Empire ottoman*, 18 vols, Paris, 1835–41.
5. Waltraud Heindl, 'Universitäten und Eliten im österreichischen Vormärz', *Études danubiennes*, 2, 1987, pp. 117–31.
6. Jean-Paul Bled, *Les Fondements du conservatisme autrichien, 1859–1879*, Paris, 1988.
7. János Várga, 'Typen und Probleme des baüerlichen Grundbesitzes in Ungarn 1767–1849', *Studia Historica*, 56, Budapest, 1965.
8. G. Granasztoi, 'L'urbanisation de l'espace danubien', *Annales E.S.C*, 2, 1989, pp. 379–99.

CHAPTER ELEVEN

The Revolution of 1848

The revolution erupted violently in March 1848. The deep underlying forces which had been contained for so long during Metternich's government, suddenly rose to the surface and radically challenged the political as much as the social basis of the established order. The revolution of 1848 was liberal and national. It was critical for the future development of Danubian Europe and posed more problems than it could solve. A society which was still predominantly rural, dominated by the nobility and divided into numerous ethnolinguistic groups, was ill-prepared for a rapid transition to nation-states under the leadership of an unevenly developed bourgeoisie. The revolution also provoked a formidable reaction.

THE IDEOLOGICAL FOUNDATIONS OF THE REVOLUTION[1]

The ideas of the French Revolution had slowly infiltrated the Austrian monarchy, despite censorship and police vigilance, and had been adapted to the particular problems of individual nations.

The German bourgeoisie had national and liberal aspirations. Its members, though, were a minority within the population and relied on the discontent roused by the government's practices. Growing hatred for the police-state and its arbitrary methods was unquestionably one of the causes of the revolution. The bourgeoisie had lost patience with the obstinacy of the bureaucracy as well as the close surveillance of intellectual life. Artisans and intellectuals were most affected by these measures and formed the two most active groups at the heart of the movement.

If those in power had renounced these oppressive practices, their subjects would probably have been satisfied with progressive reforms. Only a very few envisaged the nation participating actively in government and then only in terms of power being shared between the monarch and the elected assemblies. The doctrine of popular sovereignty had few supporters. Ministerial accountability before the *Kammern* was understood, not as the cornerstone of a regime, but as judicial accountability, the right of parliament to bring ministers before a tribunal in cases where they had violated the law. The German nation, which lived in Austria and the other states of the German Confederation, did not want to break with the world of dynasties and monarchical institutions, but rather wanted the establishment of a *Rechtsstaat*, a state where law would be fully respected, an end put to all arbitrariness and the individual protected. It was, in fact, a continuation of the policies of the *Aufklärung*, which had been cut short after 1792.

The national aspirations of the German bourgeoisie, though, conflicted with those of the other nations living within the Austrian monarchy. Although Metternich might be held to be the first partisan of the idea of *Mitteleuropa* because of his support for the union of Austria and Germany within the German Confederation, it was the economists who longed, by uniting the *Zollverein*, to constitute a vast block which would be capable of resisting Nicholas I's Russia. The German economist Friedrich List foresaw around 1840 the threat that Russian power represented for Central Europe and wanted the Germans and Hungarians to collaborate, a proposition which to Metternich the Rhinelander was utterly unthinkable. List wanted to integrate Hungary within an enlarged *Zollverein* and to establish a *Mitteleuropa* which was unified in its economies, maintained the particularism of individual states and extended from the Baltic to Trieste and from Hamburg to the Black Sea. He found numerous supporters among the south German press, for example the *Augsburger Allgemeine Zeitung*, which was attracted by his economic programme, and among Austrian politicians such as Schuselka and Moering who feared Russian imperialism.

A section of the German bourgeoisie in Austria longed for a vast Austro-German ensemble. The parliament at Frankfurt, however, was not slow to pose the problem in different terms and to force the Austrian Germans to choose between the Danubian monarchy and German national unity. Even in June 1848, the German nation, despite its preponderance within the monarchy, did not have particular national claims. In Bohemia, the German bourgeoisie, who enjoyed the leading position in the economic life of the country, did not appear hostile to the Czechs' national claims because they were in one mind with the liberal bourgeoisie in wanting to bring down the absolutist state and seigneurial society. On 20 March 1848 the German poet Ebert and the Czech historian Palacký signed a *Declaration of Men of Letters* which supported the autonomy of the peoples of the crown of Bohemia within the framework of the monarchy. It was Ebert who had written, 'If there exists a nation which has fought for liberty, it is the Slavs. The spirit of liberty is in the blood of the Czechs.'

The Czechs, Hungarians and Italians had a programme of claims which brought into question the very existence of the monarchy. The Habsburgs' subjects in Lombardy-Venetia wanted to make Italy a nation-state and so clashed with both Austria and the principalities of Tuscany, Parma and Modena.* The

---

* Translator's note: Austria ruled Lombardy-Venetia directly. Tuscany and Parma were ruled by members of the House of Habsburg and the duke of Modena was also an Austrian. Maria Luisa, the daughter of emperor Francis I and second wife of Napoleon, ruled Parma.

subjects of the pope in the Papal states and the Neapolitans shared their ambition. Antagonism between Austria and Italy after 1815 played an important part in the 1848 revolution even though the Transalpine provinces were not essential for the monarchy's survival. A much more dangerous threat in the long term was posed by the Czech and Hungarian irredentists.

In the first half of the nineteenth century, the Czechs became a leading nation in European culture, if indeed they had ever ceased to be such. Czech intellectuals who were influenced by German idealism and culture devoted their talents to the idea of the nation. The seeds of the national revival had been sown during the Enlightenment. Josef Dobrovský, a linguist and a founding father of Slavistics, and Dobner, the historian, published their work in Latin or in German. The great Austrian patriotic movement which developed after 1805 had the unexpected consequence of fostering 'provincial patriotism' and reached the public mainly through publications. The public also discovered the different national cultures among the peoples making up Austria. The Bohemian Royal Scientific Society, the state theatre in Prague, which dated from the reign of Joseph II, the Prague Conservatoire founded in 1810, and the National Museum created in 1818 were Bohemian institutes in which the nobility were particularly involved. Although they had not been established by the Czech bourgeoisie, they gradually became centres for the transmission of Slav culture. The political tendencies they later expressed reflected the rise of the middle classes who considered the preponderance enjoyed by the country's German speakers as an unjustified domination and organized themselves for political protest. In 1830 a Committee for the Scientific Deployment of the Czech Language and Literature was founded as an adjunct to the National Museum. Palacký became Bohemia's official historiographer and wrote its history in terms of a perpetual conflict between the Slavs and the Germans. The first volume of his *History of Bohemia* was published in 1838 in German. His writings had a profound effect on the political conceptions of the Czech bourgeoisie and Palacký soon acquired the status of master among the Czechs, a position he maintained right until 1867. The Bohemian aristocracy, who were the real masters of the country, joined the movement because of their mistrust of the bureaucracy and centralism, and did not forget the role that the orders and the Diet had in the past played in the life of the nation. The nobles were in alliance with the new strata who did not aspire to restoring the decrepit seigneurial system, but rather longed to give the country a constitution corresponding to their liberal and national aspirations. It was an equivocal alliance which would last a quarter century and give a solid basis to Austrian conservatism, as Bled has shown.

In Hungary the nobility played a yet greater role in the evolution of the national idea. The movement for renewal was led by a noble, count István Széchenyi, who was supported by a party of aristocrats and gentry who saw their sole political mission as the fight against Viennese absolutism and the defence of the orders' privileges. The Hungarian nobility was once more the champion of liberty and the country's independence. Széchenyi, though, did not fight solely for the maintenance of state-right since he also wanted to develop the national economy and to assure the prosperity of the governing classes. He thought that the poor could be provided for by improvements in agriculture and transport. Political life, meanwhile, continued to function at the county level. Financial difficulties forced Metternich to summon the national assembly in 1825 and 1832, then regularly after 1840. True to its tradition, the Hungarian Diet proved to be a permanent institution for debate.

After 1840, a good quality press developed in Hungary. Most newspapers were published in Pest and tried to imitate the English press, for Hungary was in the grip of anglophilia. *Pesti Hírlap* and other similar newspapers had a high intellectual content and contributed to political renewal among the ruling classes.

Széchenyi founded at Pest in 1825 the National Club, which he based in style and manner on an English club, and gathered together nobles open to liberal ideas and eager to support reforms. In the same year in the company of some other aristocrats, he founded the Academy of Sciences, which was intended to promote the advance of the national language and culture. The years prior to the revolution of 1848 witnessed the blossoming of a great literary movement which drew its inspiration from the French Revolution and the Romantic movement. János Arany with Petőfi and Vörösmarty played a role which exceeded that of being simply writers. Arany (1817–82) came from a ruined family of nobles and after studying at a college in Debrecen, he joined a group of travelling actors. At the age of nineteen, in 1836, he returned to his birthplace and enjoyed his first success as a writer in 1845 with *The Lost Constitution*, a satire on regional elections. In 1846 he achieved fame with his epic poem *Toldi*, in which he recounted the heroic exploits of a Hungarian hero from the Middle Ages. He became friends with Petőfi, with whom he established a common programme of which the main features were the introduction of an element of realism into poetry and the raising of folk poetry to the level of national poetry. Mihály Vörösmarty (1800–55), who was the standard bearer of the Romantic school, also belonged to the impoverished nobility. After studying law at the university of Pest, he became a tutor. At twenty-five, he published an important work *Zalán futása* (Zalán's Flight), an epic about the arrival in the country of the Hungarians, which brought him immediate and resounding success. His work was well received amid the atmosphere of triumphant nationalism. Vörösmarty applied himself to satisfying the nobility's demands for national history, recreating a Hungarian mythology long lost or which perhaps had never existed. From 1830 onwards, he made some remarkable translations of Shakespeare and produced historical dramas inspired by Victor Hugo. After 1836, he edited the journal the *Athenaeum*. He became the leading figure in Hungarian literary life and did not hesitate to join Kossuth.

The poet who played the greatest political role was Sándor Petőfi (1823–59). The son of a village inn-keeper, he managed to receive an education, became a travelling actor, joined the army and was discharged in 1841. In 1844 Vörösmarty helped him to publish his first collection of poetry which made an immediate impression. He immersed himself in Latin, German, French and English poetry and translated Shakespeare into Hungarian. He soon involved himself in public life, hailed the revolution with gusto and read passionately about the events of 1789. Petöfi was far more radical than the reformers gathered around Széchenyi.

Lajos Kossuth, the son of a gentry family in Upper Hungary, first gained experience in regional political conflicts before sitting in the 1832 Diet as deputy for a magnate. In 1833 he had the idea of editing a 'parliamentary gazette' in manuscript, the *Dietal Reports*, and so established political journalism in Hungary. From 1841 to 1843, he worked on the *Pesti Hírlap*, then directed his attention towards industry. Elected to the Diet in 1847 as a representative for the county of Pest, he became one of the leaders of the opposition, advocating the emancipation of the peasantry and the political separation of Hungary from Austria.

Among the 'historic nations', the many liberal elements demanded a return to the more flexible structures of a confederation as it had existed at the beginning of the monarchy.* Many reformers had also raised social issues and questioned the seigneurial system in the form in which it survived after the reforms of the Enlightenment. The problems confronting workers were for the moment a marginal concern.

In Hungary in 1848, 60 per cent of the peasantry worked as agricultural labourers and 40 per cent were peasant proprietors. As in the rest of the monarchy, the peasant proprietors were no more than the occupiers of a tenure burdened with heavy dues: *robot* with draught-animals for ploughmen and taxes in kind (the tithe and the ninth) which accounted for 15-20 per cent of the meagre harvests. In addition to these dues, since 1767 every peasant had been liable to state taxation. Even Széchenyi thought that progress in agriculture would follow from the abolition of the *robot*. The abolition of seigneurial rights, which was the almost universal demand, could not resolve with the stroke of a pen the agrarian question. This important reform did not stop the peasant masses from supporting the revolutionaries.

The revolution of 1848, as important as it was, only affected the ruling classes and the large cities. With the exception of those countries swayed by nationalism, Hungary and northern Italy, it concerned only the politicized sectors, the nobility, bourgeoisie, intellectuals and artisans in the large towns. In the country, the masses were kept in check by the traditional framework, the clergy and landed proprietors, and were little affected by the claims made by the liberal bourgeoisie. Agrarian reforms alone had an echo and brought some comfort to them in their hardship.

EVENTS

The Paris revolution of 22 February 1848 served as the signal for the other movements in Europe by calling the liberal elements to action. In Austria, as

---

* Translator's note: 'historic nations' are those which have or have had states, e.g. the Hungarians, and 'unhistoric nations' are those which are and have been purely cultural entities, e.g. the Kashubi. This imprecise distinction is made all the more so by the capacity of many nations to research and discover for themselves long-forgotten national states.

elsewhere, the mood had been prepared by an economic crisis originating in the failure of the harvest of 1847. As in Western Europe, the rural world was in a state of collapse. Although the famine was not as severe as those in past centuries, the rural market for manufactured goods all but disappeared and this in turn led to failure for manufacturers and unemployment for workers. In addition, the year had begun ominously at Milan where Italian patriots launched the 'cigar strike', refusing to smoke products with state tax and hoping to thwart the Austrian tax collectors.

The first Danubian capital to react to events in Paris was Budapest. On 3 March Kossuth read to the Diet at Pressburg a constitution and secured the unanimous acceptance of a petition to the emperor Ferdinand. On 6 March the guilds of Lower Austria published a proclamation demanding political rights for the people, the suppression of the censorship, the publication of judicial proceedings and the institution of juries. On 11 March there were disturbances around Prague. Czechs and Germans acting in unison adopted a petition demanding constitutional reforms, the autonomy for the lands of the Bohemian crown and respect for the rights of the two nations.

It was, however, in Vienna that revolutionary action first broke out. It began on the morning of 13 March with the siege of the Diet of Lower Austria (*Landhaus*). Students and burghers attempted to win over the deputies while a doctor read out Kossuth's address of 3 March. Others tried to reach the chancellery at the Ballhausplatz to demand Metternich's resignation. Troops were hastily summoned, opened fire and felled some victims, which prompted disturbances in the suburbs. Popular fury was also exercised against factories and the machines which were blamed for causing misery. The government realized that it was no longer master of the situation. Metternich would have to be sacrificed to save the dynasty. The chancellor presented his resignation on 13 March and fled in a laundrywagon to escape the wrath of the crowds. He reached safety without difficulty and took refuge in England while awaiting the course of events.

The enthusiasm of the first hours of the revolution succeeded in securing from the court freedom of the press and the promise of a constitution. A 'bourgeoise committee on security' was organized, a national guard and a university legion. The 'committee of students' and the 'central committee' made up of representatives of the national guard and the university legion formed democratic institutions which took over from the council of ministers led by Kollowrath who had just replaced the traditional councils. For six months, the government authorities would find themselves closely dependent upon the revolutionary forces in the capital.

At Budapest, revolution did not break out until 15 March when what had happened in Vienna two day before became known. Petöfi and his friends organized a demonstration which presented the authorities with a programme of twelve points summarizing the national and liberal claims: liberty of the press, transfer of executive power to a government answerable to parliament, replacing the Diet which met every three years at Pressburg with a national assembly sitting at Pest, the establishment of equality before the law and freedom of worship, the abolition of tax exemptions for the nobility, the ending of peasants' obligations as serfs, the institution of juries, creation of a national Hungarian bank, release of political prisoners, the reunification of Hungary and Transylvania, the departure of 'foreign' troops and the recall to the country of all Hungarian regiments. These twelve points went noticeably beyond the classic programmes of the liberals since they demanded the organization of a national guard and the liberation of the peasantry without the prerequisite of compensation, but they did not exceed the framework of bourgeois reformism and were received enthusiastically. The thousand or so students who in the morning accompanied Petöfi were joined in the evening by 15 000 demonstrators in Buda. As the garrison made up of Italian soldiers was not trustworthy, the council of the lieutenancy capitulated before the crowd. The revolution of 15 March happened, for the moment at least, without bloodshed. The court at Vienna gave the Hungarians permission to attempt parliamentary government and count Batthyány became president of the council of the first answerable ministry in Hungarian history.

At Vienna, baron Pillersdorf, the moderate head of the imperial government, published on 25 April a constitution based on the Belgian model and valid for the hereditary lands alone and which implicity recognized Hungarian autonomy and dualism. The constitution of April 1848 instituted bicameralism, suffrage on the basis of the electoral poll tax and accorded the sovereign the right of absolute veto. The new fundamental law did not please the 'central committee', which demanded universal suffrage and a single assembly. At this juncture a conflict between the Pillersdorf government and the revolutionary forces was inevitable. On 15 and 26 May 1848, the revolutionaries tried to impose their view-point. The building of barricades had unfortunate consequences for the movement. To protect the emperor from the pressures of the street, the court left Vienna for Innsbruck, where it was welcomed by the province which was ever faithful to the dynasty. The Viennese burghers, however, were deeply upset by the situation and began to shy away from a movement which had changed from being liberal to becoming openly democratic. The riot of 26 May had involved the university legion supported by workers from the suburbs. Power passed into the hands of a 'committee of public safety' which did not set out to become an organ of popular dictatorship but rather to safeguard the reforms secured so far. It tried to maintain order and to secure the material needs of the working classes. After Pillersdorf resigned on 8 July, the archduke John, who represented the emperor in the capital, appointed a ministry led by Baron Doblhoff in which Alexander Bach was minister of justice. The new cabinet had the task of granting a constitution to the whole monarchy. The national question soon overtook social questions and the existence of the monarchy was implicitly challenged by the work of the parliament at Frankfurt, by the Italian insurrections and by developments in Hungary.

The question was whether the idea of German unity could be reconciled with the continued existence of an Austrian state. What did the black, red and gold flag on the cathedral of St Stephen signify? Could Austria fight against Italian unity in Milan and support German unity at Frankfurt? How could it restore a federal structure based on the historic rights of some nations without harming the principle of nationalities in so far as numerous nationalities found themselves excluded from the government of the historic states constituting Hungary? The government and the public were becoming increasingly aware of the problems which would eventually be resolved, albeit somewhat imperfectly, by the Austro-Hungarian compromise of 1867 and the achievement of a united Germany and a united Italy in 1870.

At the end of April 1848, the election of deputies to the parliament at Frankfurt took place. A central committee in Vienna declared itself in favour of the creation of a strong and unified free Germany, and for respect for the integrity of Austria. The view from Frankfurt, however, was quite different; Bohemia without question belonged to the German Confederation, but the parliament's treatment of the Czech question was inconsistent with the idea of nationality. Although a legal plan prepared by a deputy at Graz, Marek, recognized the same political rights for minorities as for German citizens, and the use of minority languages in administration, education and justice, the vast majority of deputies thought that, whatever happened, Bohemia would be preserved within the Confederation and they regarded as treasonable the establishment at Prague of a provisional government. They had been embittered by the Austro-Slavism of Palacký who had refused to be elected as a deputy to the Frankfurt parliament, by the development of Czech autonomy and by the refusal of the Slav population of Bohemia to take part in the election of deputies. The first Germano-Czech crisis in Bohemia began in the spring of 1848. The Germans, especially those from the frontier towns, Cheb, Karlovy Vary and Liberec, declared themselves strongly in favour of participating in the elections and for the integration of the kingdom of Bohemia with Germany. Yet more serious was the German bourgeoisie's refusal to accord the Czechs equal rights. The Moravian deputy Giskra caught the mood in his speech of July 1848:

Czechism should be contained and repressed by force. And it will be a crime against all the rights of humanity if in Bohemia, Moravia and Silesia, a civilization resting on German culture is sacrificed to a new venture in political organization. For my part I cannot accept these cosmopolitan ideas and I expect that you sirs, who sit in the German assembly cannot accept them either. It is not just the moral development but also the material prosperity of the German lands which is threatened. I am the spokesman and friend of numerous Moravian industrialists who are aware of the danger which threatens them, if Bohemia, a Slav state encompassing Moravia and Silesia, is isolated by customs barriers.

The message was clear: an independent Bohemian state was contrary to the fundamental interests of the German minority. This thesis was to be repeated tirelessly for almost a century until 1945 when a radical solution was adopted and the Germans were expelled from Bohemia. Giskra's speech was not simply a momentary outburst but represented the deep aspirations which much later moved the Sudeten Germans. The Czech question was raised in the form of German–Slav antagonism and ended in confrontation between the two nations within the one state.

The Hungarian question was yet more complex because the Hungarian nation demanded a status verging on independence but within the state and so clashed with the national minorities, the Croats, Serbs, Romanians and Slovaks.

The position of the Croats was strong in so far as the Croats had kept their historic rights, their own Diet and internal autonomy with respect to the Hungarian state. The Croatian patriots remained loyal to the House of Austria which presented their best guarantee against Hungarian expansion. Some longed to create an Illyrian kingdom quite separate from Hungary but integrated within the Danubian monarchy. On 25 March 1848, the Croatian sabor (Diet) appointed as ban (governor) one of the leaders of the Illyrian movement, colonel Jelačić. Supported by those at court who were hostile to Hungary, he declared Croatia independent and immediately put at the Habsburgs' disposal the crack Croatian soldiers who were to play an important part in crushing the revolutionary forces in Vienna as well as in Hungary.

The Croats were soon followed by other national minorities. The Slovaks met in an assembly at Liptoszentmiklos on 10 May, the Serbs at Karlowitz on 13 May and the Romanians at Balásfalva on 15 May. They all expressed their disquiet at the unitary policy of the Budapest government and declared their autonomy. They addressed the motions on which they voted, directly to Vienna. Once more the court had the chance to play the minorities off against the Hungarian ruling class in order to re-establish its authority over Hungary. This old tactic, though, always provoked lively reaction from the Hungarians and Kossuth's radicals were quick to denounce the court's duplicity. The moderate parliament which was elected in July 1848 voted in favour of a mass levy of troops to defend the imperiled fatherland. This was the signal for a conflict between the Habsburgs and the Hungarian nation which was only provisionally resolved a year later by the defeat of the Hungarian military. On 11 September, Jelačić's army entered Hungary, a development which enabled Kossuth to take power through a committee of national defence which was formed on 22 September 1848. The break with Vienna had placed the revolutionaries in power at Budapest. Batthyány had resigned and the moderates proved to be increasingly reticent.

The revolution of 1848 was not a series of riots followed by the implacable triumph of reaction. During the period from June to November, the liberals had time to put an end to the *ancien régime* on a political and a social level and to vote for reforms which, although sometimes undeniably slow in being implemented, were nonetheless of value as an example and a precedent.

THE REFORMS

Social reforms finally ended the seigneurial regime. The institutional reforms were based on theory and resulted in a neo-absolutist system. The parliament at Kremsier nevertheless showed that the nationalities were ready to listen to each other and that Austria was far from being 'a prison-house of the peoples'.

The elections for the Austrian parliament held in July 1848 were greeted with some indifference and few voted. The parliament met at Vienna on 22

July but in October, when the situation in Vienna had deteriorated, it moved to Kremsier (Kromeriz) in Moravia and the court and imperial government established itself at Olomouc. Unlike the Frankfurt parliament, it brought together deputies sent by all the different nationalities and it was an authentic reflection of 'Austrian society'. Although the Germans insisted heavily upon 'their intellectual superiority', the Slavs did not forget that they were greater in number. The peasant element dominated. Some among them did not even know how to read. Many others did not speak German. Most of the members of this *Reichsrat* did not have any political experience and represented a heavy responsibility for those who wanted to work there. The left was represented by the liberals and the German radicals, Fischhof and Schuselka; the right by the Czechs who were led by Rieger and Palacký; the centre by the conservatives, representatives of the nobility and the bourgeosie loyal to the dynasty and the state.

While the commission charged with preparing a plan for the constitution was lost in fruitless discussion, on 7 September the assembly voted unanimously in favour of the plan presented by H. Kudlich, a Silesian peasant, for abrogating all ties of serfdom and abolishing seigneurial rights. The question of compensation was discussed for several weeks. It was Bach's view which finally prevailed and the estate-owners were recompensed. This decision was of prime importance for social as well as political reasons. The peasant now had full legal ownership of the parcels of land he occupied. The estate-owners, however, still kept important manorial reserves and it was the well-off peasants who benefited the most from the abolition of the seigneurial regime. The end of the *robot* had important symbolic and psychological value. The peasant was now a full citizen. The great landowners received as compensation large indemnities which they invested in industry in Bohemia and elsewhere. The political effect of the law of 7 September was to neutralize the peasant opposition, for the peasants had obtained what they had aspired to, vaguely, for generations. The peasantry was deeply conservative and did not hesitate to side with the dynasty. The Habsburgs had acquired the support of the rural masses who dropped their momentary allies, the middle-class liberals and democratic intellectuals.

In Hungary, the Batthyány cabinet had abolished the bonds of serfdom in March 1848 but the administration in the counties specified that only the tenures subject to tax, about 5.7 million hectares, would be attributed with full ownership to the tenants. Demographic pressure in the countryside was much greater than in Austria and the abolition of serfdom threatened to contribute to the crisis, which had been looming since 1820. In 1848 the national assembly abolished the seigneurial rights over the vineyards, amounting to 1.2 million hectares, in exchange for a state indemnity. It also decided that agricultural labourers established on allodial lands should receive these plots with full ownership. The law, though, was never even promulgated since it was a response to the immediate circumstances, intended to rally the peasants to the national cause which injured the interests of the ruling class. All the same, after the declaration of independence, Ferenc Deák went so far as to propose that the 'vacant' land should be given to the peasants in order to win the rural world to the national cause.

One of the most ardent supporters of Habsburg Austria was the Czech historian Palacký who thought that the monarchy was a guarantee against German nationalism and Russian imperialism. In his reply to Soiron, the president of the commission of the Fifty, Palacký made some comments which have passed down to posterity: 'Indeed, if the Austrian state did not exist we should have to create it in the interests of Europe and of Humanity.'* He meant by this, that it was necessary to preserve the monarchy both to prevent German nationalism from transforming Austria into a province of the new state and to counter pan-Slavism which would turn the Slav lands into a Russian protectorate. In the same letter, Palacký added 'for the health of Europe, Vienna must not decline to the rank of a provincial capital' and he declared himself ready to join others in doing 'everything possible to maintain Austria's independence, integrity and power especially with respect to the east'. In practice, he envisaged the creation of a German national state which would seal a permanent alliance with the monarchy. At the same time, Palacký insisted upon 'the complete equality of all the nationalities and confessions united under the Habsburg sceptre, the equality which would be the legal and moral justification for the existence of the Empire'. Thus he laid the foundations of Austro-Slavism and the Kremsier constitution.

To counter German nationalism, the first pan-Slav congress was called and brought together the Slav intellectual elite in Prague in June 1848. The congress formulated Austro-Slavism. It put forward measures intended to preserve the Empire and to maintain the autonomy of the Slav nationalities. It wanted to reconstruct the monarchy on the basis of a federal state and declared its loyalty to the dynasty. Palacký protested against those who accused the Slavs of conspiracy and of being the harbingers of Russian imperialism and the pan-Slavism represented at the conference by Bakounine. The Czech poet Havlicek added, 'Austria will become what we want it to be or else it will cease to exist.'

At Kremsier, the parliament which was familiar with the general principle of the equality of the nationalities, for the first time touched on the difficulties of putting the principle into practice. In his speech of 23 January 1849, Palacký proposed the creation of eight groups of lands which would be divided into districts. The Slovene deputy Kaucic argued in favour of fourteen provinces not corresponding to any historic state. Palacký's son-in-law, Rieger, tried to defend the maintenance of state-right. Many Czechs would not countenance the partition of Bohemia on national lines. In the end it was the plan of Cajétan Mayer, a Moravian deputy, which served as the basis of the constitution: the historic lands would be maintained but they would be divided into circles according to national character and be given a large measure of political and cultural autonomy, especially with respect to schools, language and tribunals, which would allow the various communities to blossom.

---

* Translator's note: at the Frankfurt Vorparlament in 1848.

The plan for the constitution adapted tradition to national demands without overturning them. Paragraph 21 recognized the equality of the nationalities as well as the equality of languages in education. The fourteen provinces of the 'one and indivisible' monarchy were divided into circles and electoral districts drawn up on national lines. The plan attempted to lay the foundations for the harmonious coexistence of the peoples inhabiting Austria but it did not find favour in the eyes of either Schwarzenberg's government or Francis Joseph. Even before the commission's plan was presented to parliament, it was rejected, and on 4 March 1849 a constitution was bestowed. Paragraph 21 was later incorporated into the Austrian constitution of 1867. The era of reaction had begun. Austria had lost the opportunity to resolve amicably the dispute among the various nationalities.

THE REACTION

From July 1848 onwards, the tide of reaction did not cease to gain ground and triumphed on 2 December when Ferdinand abdicated in favour of his nephew, the archduke Francis Joseph, then aged eighteen. The forces of conservatism had not been crushed by the Viennese revolution. Once the initial troubles had passed, the army was firmly in control. The aristocracy was resigned to accepting some reform but did not want to open the way for a democratic revolution. The masses whether from fear or indifference, were content to let matters take their course. Order was re-established first in Prague, then in Milan, in Vienna, and the following year with some difficulty in Budapest.

In June 1848, general Windischgrätz, the governor of Bohemia, acted decisively when the Czech radicals appeared set to overwhelm the moderate nationalist champions of the integrity of the monarchy. Following a tactic advocated by Thiers, Windischgrätz withdrew all troops from Prague, then besieged, bombarded and forced the city to capitulate. In Lombardy, Radetzky achieved a notable success against the Lombard insurgents and their Piedmontese allies through the support of the Tyroleans and a good army. On 25 July 1848, he defeated Charles Albert's Piedmontese troops at Custozza and so consolidated Austrian authority in Italy.

Meanwhile the government's authority in the imperial capital continued to crumble. On 6 October 1848, the minister for war, Latour, was assassinated in Vienna by a frenzied crowd which would cheerfully have massacred all the ministers. It also seized the arsenal and whatever weapons it found there. It was not simply a riot but a democratic revolution. The masses wanted to come to the aid of the Hungarian revolution and to prevent Jelačić's Croatian troops from joining forces with the imperial regiments. The riot of 6 October helped to harden positions. The government left the capital to rejoin the court at Olomouc in Moravia. The moderate deputies followed but some democrats remained at Vienna where they constituted an executive commitee. There were many idealists among them but not one politician. Vienna, cut off from the country, could not count on the support of Hungary. It was in a position of inferiority in the armed conflict in which it was about to engage. Windischgrätz was appointed commander-in-chief on 16 October and on 26 October 1848 he began operations in liaison with Jelačić. The town was defended by the national guard under the Polish commander, Bem. The mass of Viennese wanted calm and the democrats represented only a minority within the capital. The idea of the republic raised still less enthusiasm. Kossuth's troops were defeated at Schwechat by Jelačić's army. On 31 October, the imperial troops entered Vienna and began a reign of brutal and mindless oppression. The period of reaction which began in the autumn 1848 did not mark the re-establishment, pure and simple, of the old political and social system. The society of orders, or the Josephist state, had passed. The moderate bourgeoisie emerged victorious from the crisis. From now onwards they would be associated with power. After several years of painful reconstruction, they even enjoyed freedom of the press, a parliamentary regime, personal freedom and, in a general fashion, the reforms demanded by the liberal bourgeoisie in 1848. But the process of liberalization, as slow as it was, was in the beginning secondary to the restoration of the dynasty's authority and the reconstruction of the state which had been shaken by centrifugal forces.

On 21 November, the emperor appointed a new government presided over by prince Felix Schwarzenberg whose prime goal was to restore Austria's status as a great power. Schwarzenberg was a conservative aristocrat but he surrounded himself with liberals, including Stadion and Bruck, and from the previous cabinet kept Kraus, the minister for finances, and the minister of the interior, Alexander Bach, whose name has been linked for posterity with reaction.

It seemed of prime importance to secure the emperor Ferdinand's abdication, an issue which had been long debated in Habsburg family councils. On 2 December, the young Francis Joseph ascended the throne and commenced his sixty-year reign, the longest in Austrian history. Recent work, in particular the excellent biography by Jean-Paul Bled[2] and research by Brigitte Hamann,[3] have shed new light on him both as a man and as sovereign.

FRANCIS JOSEPH (1848–1916)

Francis Joseph was born in 1830, ascended to the throne in 1848 and had one of the longest reigns in history. For many of his former subjects, he is synonymous with the *belle époque* when, despite undeniable political difficulties and unquestionable injustices, Austria was rich, prosperous and happy.

Francis Joseph, however, was not the type to rouse mass enthusiasm. He was a dashing figure but far from brilliant and he grew into a dull and dutiful man. He considered himself the first servant of the state and his dedication made up for his want of inspiration. Deeply conservative, after 1870 he raised stagnation to the rank of a political philosophy. When it came to making important decisions, he was rarely equal to the occasion. In December 1848, he had been the choice of the conservative aristocracy and the army after the latter had re-established order in the Empire. At the beginning of his reign, he was subject to the influence of his mother, the archduchess Sophie, who had been born a Wittelsbach, and of his prime minister Schwarzenberg whose achievements were remarkable. The brutality of the suppression brought down upon Hungary in 1849 shows that the young sovereign had decided to follow a questionable but coherent policy, namely absolutism backed by the army and German bureaucracy. For the first time in its history, the Austrian monarchy was tantamount to a centralized state where the provincial notables were obliged to give way to officials appointed by Vienna. It was the disastrous campaign in Italy in 1859 that led the sovereign to reflect. On the battlefield at Solferino, when contrary to the wise traditions of his family he took command of the army, he lost all illusions regarding his own gifts as a strategist. Punctual and physically courageous, he possessed the qualities of an infantry captain but not of a commander-in-chief. Above all, though, he lost any illusion of the efficacy of the neo-absolutist system which he had imposed on his peoples for ten years. The Hungarians resisted Germanization and the Austrian bourgeoisie desired a far more flexible regime.

The emperor himself, in so far as he had such ideas, never believed in liberalism since he heartily disliked those who advocated 'reason'. He was convinced that the only links uniting the different peoples of the monarchy were the dynasty, the army and the Church, but his device *Viribus unitis* ('United in our powers') shows that he was willing to associate them with government. Right to the end of his life, he collaborated loyally with a parliament elected at first by an electorate eligible on the basis of the property qualification, then, after 1907, by universal suffrage. It was, though, only in Hungary that the president of the council represented the parliamentary majority. Even after the Austro-Hungarian compromise of 1867, the emperor continued personally to appoint the members of the Austrian cabinet.

The period 1859–67 was decisive for the monarchy's development, since in 1860 Francis Joseph tried to organize the monarchy as a federation, issuing the constitutional diploma which granted a large measure of autonomy to the former provinces. Faced with opposition from the German bourgeoisie, the bureaucracy and the Hungarian nobility, he quickly returned, by the patent of 1861, to centralized government. In 1866 Austria's defeat at Sadowa made it possible for Bismarck to drive the Habsburgs once and for all from German affairs, just as the defeat at Solferino had driven them from Italy. Francis Joseph, seeing Austria thrown back towards Danubian Europe, restored to Hungary its full rights by the compromise of 1867 which was a victory for the Hungarian ruling class. This solution promised well for Austria, as long as it was not limited to Hungary alone, for other nations had also, until late, constituted autonomous states within the monarchy. Although the Hungarian-Croat compromise in 1868 gave the Croats some satisfaction, in 1871 Francis Joseph refused to ratify an Austro-Bohemian compromise which would have been the counterpart to the Austro-Hungarian compromise. The Czech question was never resolved and the problem of the nationalities did not cease to poison Austrian political life, right until 1914.

In 1871 Francis Joseph took the most serious decisions of his reign. Although after 1866 he envisaged an alliance with France, from 1873 he played 'brilliant second' to the German empire. It was the annexation of Bosnia-Hercego-vina, the Yugoslav question and the rivalry with Russia which in 1914 led him to the act of aggression against Serbia which was the immediate cause of the First World War. The old sovereign without question had a large share of responsibility for starting the conflict in so far as he was incapable of withstanding the pressure from those around him and so launched Austria-Hungary, and Europe, into a conflict from which it never recovered.

This honest and unexceptional man adopted the way of life and tastes of an emperor. He was not a patron of the arts, was not musical and preferred military parades to the pleasures of composing music, in marked contrast to his great forebears.

His undeniable popularity is explained by reasons other than his personality. His reign corresponded to a period of economic development, but above all Francis Joseph had human qualities which appealed to the Austrian Germans. Like them, he loved hunting and nature. He passed the summer at Bad-Ischl in Upper Austria in an unpretentious villa, dressing in regional costume, passing long days in the mountains in the company of his gamekeepers. This proved to everyone that the emperor enjoyed the simple pleasures of his subjects. He was also sincere in his attachment to Catholicism. He respected, in spirit as well as in the letter, Joseph II's legislation and showed especial goodwill towards the Jews. Not only was he regular in his religious observances but, from his youth, he followed assiduously the devotions traditional in his family, the cult of the Virgin Mary and the adoration of the Blessed Sacrament. Finally he was wise enough to flatter the Viennese by combining good nature with a taste for ceremonial; the court was the centre of a brilliant worldly life which flattered the taste of his subjects for theatricality and the external signs of grandeur.

THE HUNGARIAN WAR OF INDEPENDENCE (1849)

The resolution of the Hungarian question and the restoration of the state were the priorities facing Francis Joseph. Although field-marshal Windischgrätz dreamt of re-establishing the old constitutions and Diets, Schwarzenberg, who had no illusions about the political capabilities of the aristocracy, wanted to establish a centralized and unified state. In the constitution of March 1879, all the lands were placed on an equal footing and reduced to the rank of administrative districts. Hungary, dismembered, found itself on the same level as Silesia, Carinthia and Transylvania; all the nationalities were equal in law. The constitution gave the people political rights which took the form of the election of an Austrian parliament, the upper chamber of which was made up of representatives from the provinces (as in the present-day Austrian *Bundesrat*). In the lower chamber, the deputies were elected by voters who paid the electoral tax. The executive power remained the exclusive prerogative of the emperor who appointed the ministers, governors of the province and officials. The sovereign, who possessed absolute veto on the laws voted by the central parliament and the provincial assemblies, was authorized to proclaim a state of emergency. It was a constitution which showed some liberal concessions to the stigma of neo-absolutism and dealt brutally with the Hungarian problem in the manner of Joseph II without taking account of the rights and aspirations of the Hungarian people.

Although Windischgrätz's troops had occupied Budapest in the course of the winter of 1849, the resistence of the insurgents was not completely crushed. The Hungarian parliament which had fled to Debrecen was dominated by the radicals and by Kossuth who, as minister of war, exercised a virtual dictatorship in order to bring the conflict to a head. The Habsburg dynasty was declared deposed and Hungary became an independent republic. Schwarzenberg, conscious of the gravity of the situation, did not dare wait for Radetzky's army to return, victorious, from Italy, and appealed to the tsar Nicholas I, the champion of reaction. The tsar hoped that by crushing Hungary he would deprive the Polish revolutionaries of their refuge. In May 1849, his troops crossed the Hungarian-Polish border and invaded the north of the country while general Haynau led an Austrian army into Transdanubia. Kossuth was isolated. The Church, the moderate nobles and the minorities were hostile to him. The social measures and the law which he managed to have voted in July arrived too late to assure him a popular basis. Kossuth's government had to take refuge at Seged, then at Árád. At the Battle of Segesvár, during which Petöfi was killed, the Hungarians were defeated. Kossuth handed over full powers to general Görgey, the commander-in-chief of the *honvéd*, and took refuge in Turkey from where he passed to Great Britain in order to continue the fight for independence. Like prince Rákóczi in the eighteenth century, he was never reconciled with the Habsburgs, preferring exile to any compromise with the dynasty, and, from abroad, prepared to resume the great struggle. In this, he stood all but alone and historic Hungary never recovered the independence it had lost in 1526.

Görgey quickly became discouraged. Convinced of the pointlessness of continuing the war, on 13 August 1849 he surrendered at Világos, into the hands of general Paskievitch who commanded the Russian army and did not show any animosity towards the Hungarians. Unfortunately, Görgey's calculation proved to be futile since Paskievitch had achieved the mission entrusted to him by Nicholas I. He withdrew and left the country to the Austrian army, drunk with vengeance and led by general Haynau who had already gained notoriety in Lombardy and was known as the 'hyena of Brescia', but only acted with the authorization of the emperor's military cabinet. Francis Joseph proved to be merciless, especially towards Hungarian soldiers who had broken their oath of loyalty to the sovereign and had therefore committed a crime which was in his eyes quite unpardonable. The good emperor began his reign with a bloodbath.

The country was subjected to brutal oppression. Haynau installed courts martial to try the officers and officials who had taken part in the revolution and the war of independence. On 6 October 1849, count Batthyány, who had been invested as president of the council of ministers by the emperor Ferdinand, was assassinated. The same day at Árád, thirteen Hungarian generals who had commanded troops against the imperial army, were shot. They are known in Hungarian history as the 'thirteen Árád martyrs'. Only Görgey escaped the firing squad and was condemned to twenty years in detention. Numerous political leaders were condemned to death *in absentia* and, like count Andrássy, were hung in effigy. There were thousands of arrests and a hundred executions. The repression affected equally the Romanians, Serbs and Slovaks who 'received as recompense what the Hungarians had had as punishment'.

Until 1852, Hungary was treated as a conquered land and was subject to Austrian military authority and it was only at that date that the minister of the interior, Bach, took responsibility for affairs. Hungary found itself integrated into the system of neo-absolutism according to the arrangements of the Austrian constitution of 1849.

The revolution had created more problems than it had resolved. It had prompted great social changes, the past had been swept away with the abolition of the *robot* and the dismantling of the seigneurial system. In this area, the Austrian empire firmly joined the camp of West European countries. The reforms of 1848 made the peasant a complete citizen and skilfully freed him without despoiling the landed proprietors. These social reforms did not settle the question of the proleteriat which was urban in the hereditary lands and agricultural in the Hungarian lands. The fulfilment of peasant claims had allowed the triumph of the traditional conservative forces: the Church, the nobility, and the state apparatus which had been revitalized the previous century. The bureaucracy and the army had remained faithful to the dynasty and the Austrian state. Francis Joseph was convinced that his troops had saved the state, mercilessly crushing the liberal movements in Italy, Prague, Vienna and Hungary and it is one of the reasons he cherished the 'imperial and royal army' throughout his whole reign.

The Habsburgs had triumphed and the 'court camarilla' took its place again behind the archduchess Sophie. Paradoxically, Ferdinand the Debonnaire had spared the dynasty unpopularity during the worst hours of the revolution and his abdication had disassociated them from all the events from March to October 1848. The renunciation of the pious archduke, Francis Charles, had made way for the accession of a young ruler who admired Nicholas I and who, as Bled has shown, dreamt of a Russian-style autocracy in the Austrian empire. Bled has also said much about the intelligence and political education of the new ruler, since absolutism was a departure from the political tradition of the monarchy which had always associated the orders with power.

This at least proved what everyone, in particular Metternich, who was playing the part of the *éminence grise*, believed, namely that there could not be a return to the situation of 1848. Francis Joseph did not become a liberal like the archduke John, but rather a reactionary of the stamp of the archduke Albert, son of the archduke Charles, the hero of Aspern and Wagram. Thus was born an attempt unique in the history of the Habsburg monarchy where Germanization and centralization were practised, making systematic those experiences which in another context had so lamentably failed under Joseph II. From 1849 to 1859, Austria was a caricature of the image portrayed throughout its history in French school-books: Germanizing, centralizing, subject to the reactionary forces of the army and Church, and above all 'prisonhouse of the peoples'.

It remained to be seen whether this experience, sanctioned by the forces of conservatism, would be sufficient to resolve the problems posed by Palacký in June 1848, namely to maintain Austria in Germany and to assure the harmonious development of the nationalities. The future of the monarchy, the happiness of its peoples and the equilibrium in Europe depended on its response to the problem posed by the Czech historian. The honest Francis Joseph was not the most gifted of statesmen, nor the one best fitted for the task.

These political vicissitudes could not hide the basic fact that the seigneurial regime was at an end; its decline, postponed by Maria-Theresa, had continued under Joseph II, but the peasants still had not risen to a condition on a par with that enjoyed by western peasants. The classic socio-political cell, the domain, however, had gone for good. A situation which had persisted for more than four centuries ended to the great benefit of the state and its subjects. The society of orders which, in Danubian Europe, had survived the French Revolution was truly dead and the aristocracy was aware of a page in its history being turned and that the sovereign was more powerful than ever. The revolution of 1848 was a judgement on the history of the Habsburg empire in so far as the old society based on the preponderance of the nobility was destroyed by the assembly at Kremsier and Francis Joseph did nothing to restore it. The monarchy had left the enlightened camp (under Francis I) but now, in marked contrast to the course taken by Russia and the Ottoman empire, it rejoined, becoming, as in the eighteenth century, a leading member.

The revolution, political in character, had positive and immediate social consequences, while the reaction gave way to solutions acceptable to the many partners within the monarchy.

NOTES AND REFERENCES

1. Jacques Droz, *Les Révolutions allemandes de 1848*, Paris, 1957.
2. Jean-Paul Bled, *Francis Joseph*, Oxford, 1992.
3. Brigitte Hamann, *Die Habsburger, ein biographisches Lexikon*, Vienna, 1988. See entries for the empress Elizabeth and the archduke Rudolf.

CHAPTER TWELVE

The Rearguard Fights Back (1849–67)

Francis Joseph was convinced that the French and English constitutional systems were totally inappropriate for Austria. He even saw a council of ministers appointed by himself as a limit on his authority and it was for this reason he did not replace Schwarzenberg who died prematurely in 1851. Following the example of Louis Napoleon, for whom he cared little, he rescinded the constitution which had been established in 1849 and suspended in August 1851. All pretences were abandoned in 1852 when the neo-absolutist phase of his reign began in earnest. In October 1860, the monarchy entered a brief but passionate period of federalism in keeping with its traditions, but this was followed by a phase of renewed centralism in 1861. The famous Austro-Hungarian 'Compromise' of 1867 marked the final period and, in appearance at least, presented a highly original solution which enabled the Habsburgs to try to establish good relations with their subjects within the framework of an empire which was finally limited to Danubian Europe where the majority of the population were Slavs.

THE TRIUMPH OF THE FORCES OF CONSERVATISM[1]

The crushing of the Viennese revolution, the repression in Italy and the brutal rout of the Hungarian political forces after the military victory of 1849 neutralized, at least for a while, the liberal bourgeoisie, students and lesser nobility. Imprisoned, exiled or reduced to a prudent silence, they had all the less influence because the press was again subject to fresh suspicion and control by a vigilant and narrow censorship. Bled has identified three currents within Austrian conservatism in the aftermath of 1848. One was the 'feudal' conservatism which rested on the Bohemian aristocracy and dreams of a federal structure for the monarchy rooted in the historic right of the different kingdoms; embodied by marshal Windischgrätz, it was all but invisible in the new regime. The second current was Austrian romantic conservatism which was inspired by the German writer Schlegel and took the form of conservative Catholicism. Its origins went back to father Diesbach, Francis I's tutor, but above all to the mystic revival inspired by Clemens Hofbauer, a saintly priest of the Biedermeier era who helped the Church to free itself from the rational-ist education dispensed to a whole generation of secular clergy who had been educated in the general seminaries and who thought of themselves less as pastors than as officials in the service of the state. Through Hofbauer, Austrian Cath-olicism revived the traditions of the baroque. This movement provided, after 1860, the great battalions of Catholics who were determined to fight against the liberal policies of the Vienna government. It had its origins in the Catholic conservative party which became one of the essential components of political life to the very end of the Habsburg empire and indeed long afterwards in the successor states.

The third current was the conservatism of the government which, conform-ing to the Josephist tradition, emphasized the primacy of the state and saw rigorous centralization as the only future course for the monarchy, such were the misgivings of the different lands and the different nobilities. It found its greatest support within the bureaucracy and the army which were deeply at-tached to the unitary state as the means to combat the centrifugal forces which had so suddenly emerged in 1848. Francis Joseph, despite his sympathies for the Catholics, was the most notable representative of this current. For all the vicissitudes of his constitutional policy, he remained faithful to centralism; the Austro-Hungarian compromise was simply the juxtaposition of two cen-tralisms, the Hungarian and Cisleithanian. The latter could readily ally with moderate liberalism and important personalities such as Alexander Bach and baron Bruck could easily change camp and remain in the ministry. During the neo-absolutist phase, the liberal Bach became the minister of the interior in Schwarzenberg's cabinet. The economist Bruck, responsible for finances in 1855 in the cabinet of count Buol-Schauenstein, kept his post in 1860 in Schmerling's cabinet, which was liberal in orientation. He conducted the same policy in support of economic development and continued to reduce the army's alloca-tion, to the great horror of archduke Albert who loathed him and went so far as to call into question his honesty.

Austrian conservatism, then, did not take just one form and efforts by Bohe-mian aristocrats to create a unified conservative party were doomed to failure. In fact, as Beck has shown, the end of neo-absolutism provoked a harsh divi-sion in conservatism. Historic and Catholic conservatism entered into conflict with government conservatism which was more than ever tied to the Josephist tradition and allied with the liberals. The age-old division of the modern era was once again manifest. The aristocracy, the partisans of federalism and the renewal of the Diets, were set in opposition to the emperor and the champions of strong central power – in tandem with control of a representative assembly sitting at Vienna.

Government conservatism lay at the heart of the neo-absolutist era. The 'feudal conservatives' were unstinting in their criticisms of Francis Joseph's min-isters, if not of the emperor whose person was above criticism, and of the aged marshal Windischgrätz, who thought of himself as the monarchy's saviour and was outspoken in a way worthy of a grand seigneur of the *ancien régime*. According to Bled, Francis Joseph was the archetypal governmental conservative who profoundly shook conservative circles by his anti-Russian policy, his policy of centralization, which had no respect for the Hungarian constitution, and his policy towards the Church which was close to that of the emperor Francis. Francis Joseph did not love the old aristocracy, 'the most reprehensible and the most harmful party.'

The young emperor at first depended for support on his ministers, who remained in power for a long time but were soon treated as senior officials, just like the politicians. Like his grandfather Francis I, he worked as a bureaucrat, conforming to the Habsburg practice of the past three centuries. After prince Schwarzenberg's death, Francis Joseph became the real head of government. The title of president of the council (*Ministerpraesident*) was carried *pro forma* by a minister, but the council did not meet in the emperor's presence and provided him with reports, as had, in the past, the Privy Conference of the council of state. Francis Joseph carefully annotated these reports which have recently been published on the initiative of the Austrian historian Engel-Janosi.[2] In the course of 1852, the emperor presided at only one meeting of the council but he had read 300 000 pages of reports and so repeated the same mistaken methods as Philip II in the sixteenth century. Count Buol-Schauenstein was in theory Schwarzenberg's successor. In practice he was minister of foreign affairs responsible for no more than carrying out the emperor's policies. The cabinet was dominated by two strong personalities. Alexander Bach would have been prince Schwarzenberg's successor as president of the council if the emperor had not reduced the council's remit. Bach's name nonetheless is associated with neo-absolutism, often referred to pejoratively as the 'Bach system'. It is an irony of history that this Viennese burgher, doctor of law and advocate, began his career during the *Vormärz* in the liberal camp because he was tired of stagnation rooted in doctrine as well as the abuses of the police and the pettiness of the censorship. In favour of reform, he supported the revolutionaries in March 1848 and in July was summoned by Doblhoff to the ministry of justice, a post which he kept in Schwarzenberg's cabinet. After seeing the excesses of the democratic revolution, Bach thought that serious reform could not be achieved without a return to order. Before the regime could be liberalized, the monarchy's power had to be restored by strengthening centralization. Arbitrary policing and repression were, for him, only the means to an end. He let it be thought that his goal was the re-establishment of the constitution, whereas his master saw neo-absolutism as the 'constitutional' regime conforming to his wishes. In 1859, when the sovereign thought that the time was right to change direction, Bach was dismissed since he symbolized the policy of repression. Bach enjoyed a long and peaceful retirement, dying in 1893 at the age of eighty.

The other strong character in the cabinet was count Leo Thun-Hohenstein, the minister of public education and culture. A member of the historic nobility of Bohemia, as grand burgrave, at the beginning of the revolution in 1848 he had taken decisive action authorizing the creation of an autonomous government but the Pentecost uprising had led him to take a more realistic view. In 1849, having become one of the leaders of the Catholic party, he had worked to repeal the Josephist legislation. His name remains associated with the signing of the Concordat of 1855. At the same time, he believed in a unified Empire, or even an Austrian patriotism which could develop into national consciousness. It was in this spirit that he created at the university of Vienna, on the model of the Parisian school for archivists, an institute for research into Austrian history where archivists and historians whose interests extended beyond the Tyrol, Moravia or Transylvania would be trained. After 1860, Thun distanced himself from the government and with his friends from the 'historic nobility' again championed a federalist system within which state-right was respected.

Baron Bruck embodied the rise of the world of business. He was an ennobled member of the bourgeoisie from the Rhineland and founder president in 1832 of the *Österreichischer Lloyd* (Austrian Lloyds). Bruck was a disciple of Friedrich List and as minister for trade in Schwarzenberg's cabinet, he supported an enlarged *Zollverein* or *Mitteleuropa* but he failed in his attempt to break into the *Zollverein* headed by Prussia. He succeeded in abolishing the customs barriers between the hereditary lands and Hungary and so made the Austrian empire, for the first time in its history, a homogenous economic unit. He left the government in May 1851 and carried out various missions before being summoned to the ministry of finance in 1856 to reduce the budgetary deficit which had started to trouble Francis Joseph. He supported the great projects of the day, in particular the Suez canal. This man of money was criticized by the aristocracy, the army and the conservatives who attributed to him, as to Bach, liberal sympathies.

The real reactionaries in Francis Joseph's entourage were to be found among the military, men such as baron Crenneville and general Kempen, the head of police who, on the recommendation of some ministers, opposed Bach over Hungary and over raising the siege. The archduchess Sophie was also too important to be overlooked since she retained her ascendancy over her young son and remained his confidante in all matters. The real *éminence grise* was count Grünne, the head of the *Militärkanzlei*, the emperor's military chancellery. In 1853 he obtained the outright abolition of the ministry of war, created during the war of 1848, a move which marked a return to the time when officers had had to take an oath to the constitution. Even the quartermaster general, general Hess, who directed the headquarters, found himself marginalized by Grünne while the emperor took effective command of his army contrary to the traditional practice of the House of Austria.

Practically all serious matters bypassed the council of ministers which in 1852, to judge from the reports published in the traditional form, the *Votum* of each minister and the conclusions proposed to the emperor, had not dealt with any question concerning defence or foreign relations and was content, in the words of count Buol, 'to thresh straw without grain'.[3] The raising of the sieges at Vienna and Prague, on which the council decided in March, did not become the object of an imperial ordinance until September, six months later.

The emperor was dependent on the support of the bureaucracy, the army and the Church. Although Maria-Theresa and Joseph II had progressively put in place a state apparatus throughout Austro-Bohemia as a whole, with the abolition of the seigneurial regime, a new phase was begun. It was no longer a question of controlling the private administration of the seigneuries but of installing functionaries directly dependent on the crown. In Hungary, it was a matter of starting at the beginning since the nobility controlled everything, even at departmental level. The extension of the task of administration entailed an increase in officials, many of whom were recruited from among the former personnel of the seigneuries, at least in the hereditary lands. In Hungary, Bach's hussars were German-speaking aliens.

The bureaucracy was strongly hierarchical with twelve echelons ranging from the governor of the province to a simple, humble clerk employed in an office. Those working within the bureaucracy might be Czech or Polish by birth, but they all had a good knowledge of German. Salaries were modest at all levels and quite inadequate for minor officials who could not enrich themselves in the employment of their superiors. The corruption which had imparted a certain charm to the Austrian administration during the baroque age, was a thing of the past and servants of the state had renounced corruption. The bureaucracy was a factor in the Germanization of the provincial petite bourgeoisie who, without repudiating their original culture, were proud to master the common tongue of the Empire and came to practise bilingualism entirely naturally. State service was a sign of social advance and provided an outlet for students from the law faculties. Loyalty to the monarchy and sense of the state were great virtues in the administration. Deeply imbued with the values of Josephism, these bureaucrats were committed above all else to the programme of a unitary and centralized Austria.

THE PRIVILEGED ARMY

'The army is naturally called to occupy a privileged place in the neo-absolutist state. The latter has the characteristics of a military as much as a civil dictatorship.' With the same vigour, prince Friedrich Schwarzenberg, the cousin of the president of the council, maintaining the aristocratic opposition, condemned 'the janissaries of the sabre' and 'the janissaries of the pen'. If the bureaucracy was a creation of the age of the Enlightenment and above all of the Metternich era, then the army, the creation of the baroque age, constituted the foremost social and political force controlled by the emperor.

In 1849 the imperial army sensed that it had saved the dynasty and the Empire. In the high-flown style of the age, the old marshal Radetzky who had crushed the Milan revolution and annihilated the Piedmont army addressed his troops 'when everything around your august throne was wavering, you did not waver. As the waves of the sea, let loose by the storm, break against the rocks, treason, perjury, rebellion have been broken against your noble breast.' The Austrian officer was held to be the champion of legitimacy and the counter-revolution. The imperial army, created to fight against an external enemy, the Turks and the French, gradually came to resemble a South American army, a social melting-pot necessary to maintain the state, but a tool ill-fitted for war against a foreign power. After 1849, the army piled up one defeat after another with the exception of the 1878 campaign in Bosnia-Hercegovina, which would prove to be its last victory.

The symbol of this new vocation for the army was the arsenal at Vienna. Until 1848, it had stood in the old city, not far from the Schottenkloster, but during the revolution it was sacked by rioters in search of the firearms they needed. Francis Joseph decided to rebuild the arsenal on a hill dominating the city, not far from the *Südbahnhof*. It is an enormous building, solid, easy to defend and surrounded by barracks built in the same style. This military complex could serve as a redoubt in the event of an uprising in the capital. The Austrian government adopted the same tactic as Thiers in France in 1871: in the event of an uprising in the city, first the town would be evacuated and the troops isolated before they fell back to secure positions and proceeded to the systematic reconquest of the land. In the same way, Schwarzenberg's government created a gendarme corps responsible for surveillance and maintaining order. These gendarmes were hated by the people, especially the Hungarians for whom they symbolized the 'Bach system', and were mistrusted by the rest of the army.

The army kept its privileged links with Francis Joseph who, from the earliest age, had received a military education and dreamt of being a great military commander. He was happier wearing military than civilian dress, increased the number of parades on the rampart which separated the fortifications of the old town from the suburbs, and aspired to forming an army in his own image, firm in his conviction that the army remained the only institution spared the ferments of revolution and modern ideas.

His idea of an officer was old-fashioned. The whole edifice rested on a 'feudal' ethic combining honour, fidelity, obedience, sense of duty and extending to absolute devotion to the emperor. Respect for the letter of the law was absolute and the cult of detail pervaded everything. There was a mistrust of change, even of technology, and an ideology grew up hostile to culture, technical innovations and science. Even in 1866, the *Österreichische militärische Zeitschrift (Austrian Military Review)*, edited by a distinguished officer, colonel Neuber, found few readers and its articles excited little discussion within the army. Francis Joseph summarized his point of view in the following characteristic statement: 'the quality of my army depends less on its educated officers than on those who are loyal and chivalrous'. He opposed adopting the needlegun, which the French and Prussians, his potential enemies, had already embraced, since, he said, 'the strength of my army is based on attack by bayonnet'. A general like Benedek enjoyed his favour because he was a trainer of men and very popular among the troops.

The conservative character of the Austrian army came, not from the aristocracy whose role at the centre of command had declined, but from Francis Joseph and his entourage, the archduke Albert and count Grünne. Bled sees the army under Francis Joseph as an alternative society which carried out its function within the state very well and to the very end guaranteed the cohesion of the monarchy, as a melting-pot for the nationalities and as a means of social rise. Even though in 1906, 80 per cent of the active officers were still German, at a time when Germans represented only 24 per cent of the total population of the monarchy, there were also Hungarian generals, South Slavs, some Czechs, Poles and Germans from the Empire. The aristocracy took refuge in the cavalry regiments and the headquarters. The number of generals of bourgeoise origin continued to grow, rising from 110 in 1848 to 147 in 1859, then dropping to 100 between 1865 and 1880, but they were present at both levels, just as at the general headquarters. A commoner promoted to officer would generally integrate himself within the *zweite Gesellschaft*, the second society which was poorly regarded by the old aristocracy. The offspring of the order of seigneurs made a show of excluding the recently ennobled from their salons and palaces. It was the age-old problem of relations between the *noblesse d'épée* and the *noblesse de robe*. After 1859, there was a campaign against generals of noble origin such as Clam-Gallas and general count Franz Gyulai, who was defeated at Magenta. General Alexander Benedek, on the other hand, was ennobled.

The army was the only school where attachment to the land of one's birth, be it the Tyrol, Bohemia, Hungary or Galicia, took second place to attachment to the common fatherland embodied in the person of the emperor. The House of Habsburg and its head could still unite subjects of different nationalities in a common sentiment. This was why military leaders like Benedek or the archduke Albert were strongly attached to centralism and opposed dualism. They constituted the last bastion of Josephism and did not hide their hostility towards the Catholic conservatives and the concessions made towards the Church. The army was the purest expression of government conservatism.

The same was not true of the old orders, the clergy and the aristocracy. The latter understood that it was on the decline and that it was the great loser in the revolution of 1848. Count Thun confided to Alexis de Tocqueville that the nobility as a body had ceased to play a role. The abandonment of the seigneurial regime, underway since the reign of Maria-Theresa and ratified by the parliament at Kremsier, was ruthlessly continued under neo-absolutism. The nobles lost all their administrative powers and power in local politics to the benefit of the bureaucracy. The Diets were no more than chambers for registration which voted tax without discussing the amount. The agrarian reforms had given the *rustical* to the peasants, and the lesser nobility who only possessed *dominical* land were ruined or impoverished. In Lower Austria where in 1848 there had been 2 000 estates, by 1860 only 600 persons were admitted to the curia of great estate-owners. Often it was members of the bourgeoisie – bankers, dealers, and enriched industrialists – who had bought up the lands belonging to the impoverished nobility. In Styria, the number of estates dropped by more than half, falling from 948 to 399. Nobles, though, who possessed vast *dominical* lands in Bohemia or Hungary quickly took an active interest in agriculture. To exercise political influence over the rich peasants who had become electors in the local assemblies, they were prepared to abandon their palaces in the towns and to stay for long periods on their country estates. They were harsh in their judgements of neo-absolutism and the bureaucracy and they thought that Bach and Felix Schwarzenberg, by bringing about the destruction of the society of orders, had cast themselves as the apostles of democracy. Prince Felix, who understood the circle he lived in, accurately caught their mistrust: a pessimist, or else clear-sighted, he thought that an institution in Vienna similar to the English House of Lords would not yield good results since the Austrian nobles had had too little education and lacked interest in political affairs.

Throughout the nineteenth century, from 1804 to 1918, the role of the aristocracy in the higher administration and in the army was continuously reduced. In thirty years, from 1848 to 1878, the number of officers belonging to the old nobility fell from 55 per cent to 33 per cent of the total strength. The drop in the number of aristocrats employed in the higher administration was yet more dramatic. They occupied 80 per cent of the posts in 1848, but less than half in 1878. To make up the balance, 2 157 officials and twice as many career officers were ennobled between 1804 and 1918. Members of the aristocracy who were not members of the liberal opposition, like the Auerspergs, or federalists, like the Schwarzenbergs, still obtained posts as governors or as head of ministeries, but ministerial portfolios were no longer the preserve of high birth. Posts in the diplomatic service remained in the hands of the aristocracy, for example Richard Metternich in Paris and Trauttmannsdorf at Rome, since, as in the past, 'one lived off one's own' as salaries and allowances always proved inadequate to meet the cost of maintaining Austria's prestige amid the glittering whirlwind of the Second Empire.

The richest and the most dynamic aristocrats had in fact broadened their range of activities. Shrewdly, they had invested the compensation received after the abolition of seigneurial rights, in industry, banking and railways. The Schwarzenbergs had received from the state 2.2 million florins, the Lobkowitz family 1.2, the Liechtensteins 890 000, the Wallensteins 875 000, the Kinskys 600 000 and the Dietrichsteins 550 000 florins. In 1855 prince Johann Adolf Schwarzenberg, head of the senior branch of the family, became president of the board of directors of the Creditanstalt, the great merchant bank founded by the Rothschilds. Members of the Auersperg, Fürstenberg and Chotek families were also directors. The boards of directors of the great banks created at this time, and until the crisis of 1873, counted among their members some twenty-five bearers of aristocratic titles. The interest of the aristocracy in the railways was still more evident since thirteen princes and sixty-four counts were directors of railway companies. Count Harrach was president of the union of brewers in Bohemia which was not inappropriate for 45 per cent of breweries in the country were owned by nobles who were simply continuing the tradition maintained during the previous three centuries.

The most clear-sighted did not see beyond the political struggle in support of federalism and, with the recognition of state-right, restoring the Diets to their former glory. Although clearly in the main conservative, the aristocracy could not support the conservatism of the government. For this reason the great aristocrats of Bohemia who made up the corps of the 'historic nobility', for example the counts Egbert Belcredi, Heinrich Clam-Martinic and Heinrich Harrach and the princes Karl Schwarzenberg and Georg Lobkowitz, engaged resolutely in political action.

The Catholic Church as represented by cardinal Rauscher was unstinting in its support of Francis Joseph and gave its blessing on the defeat of the progressive, minority wing during the 1848 revolution. Joseph Othmar von Rauscher had been tutor to Francis Joseph and retained influence over his former pupil who rewarded him generously in 1853 by appointing him archbishop of Vienna. A renowned theologian and a strong personality, Rauscher was a leading member of the movement for Catholic renewal and, like the archduchess Sophie, supported close union between the throne and altar. After 1848, Rauscher denounced liberalism and proposed a close alliance with the neo-absolutist state. The Church's influence over the rural masses was still a valuable alliance for the state, an alliance which the bishops had decided to exploit by taking this unhoped-for opportunity to secure the repeal of Josephist legislation. Rauscher declared that, 'If the work of salvation and of renewal is to succeed, then spiritual power must be united with the power of the sword.' Even Alexander Bach was ready to give in at the prospect of worse to come. The demands of the Austrian episcopate in June 1849 amounted to the dismantling of the Josephist system and increased control over civil society, in particular in the area of education. The Church found in Thun a willing intermediary. In return, the episcopate would exercise strict control over what the laity did and Catholics would limit their sphere of activity to charitable works. In 1850 the *Wiener Kirchenzeitung* (Vienna Church Times) was authorized on condition that it refrain from all political commentary.

It was only after 1860 that the Catholics organized themselves, and then with some difficulty since they had become used to being defended by the episcopate and by the crown. Under the constitutional system, Francis Joseph let the liberal majority govern and cardinal Rauscher, acting on an old Josephist reflex, respected government decisions, as unpalatable as they might be. After 1870 it was cardinal Schwarzenberg, the archbishop of Prague, who assumed leadership of the Catholic opposition, in order not to allow himself to be marginalized by bishops of bourgeois origin who were much more combative, such as the bishop of Linz, Mgr Rudigier. The first Austrian Catholic congress met in 1875 with 2 300 delegates of whom 13 were bishops and 684 clerics, a proportion which reflects the strength of the conservative element. Francis Joseph, meanwhile, in 1870 had been taken aback by the proclamation of the doctrine of papal infallibility and once again distanced himself from the Church. A large united Catholic party never emerged in the hereditary lands.

THE ACHIEVEMENTS OF NEO-ABSOLUTISM

The most original feature of the period was the short-lived rapprochement between the Church and the state following the realization of the Austrian bishops' programme of 1849. Despite the reservations of some ministers, in

April 1850 Francis Joseph promulgated ordinances which satisfied the demands of the episcopate. By suppressing the *placetum regium*, the direct connection between the Curia and the bishops was re-established. Diocesan synods could now meet without preliminary authorization from the government. Control over primary education and the right to teach catechism in the gymnasiums was granted to the religious authorities and the ecclesiastical courts were re-established. After 1852, there was a move towards negotiating a concordat with Rome where Rauscher represented Austria's interests. Count Thun, lately in favour of the ordinances, denied the Church tight control over higher education. While he was in favour of a Catholic and conservative university, he did not want to recreate the intellectual ghetto which had existed at the time of the Counter-Reformation. Instead he followed the Prussian model of an autonomous establishment where the only means of control was the recruitment of Catholic professors, but he refused to grant the monopoly of university education to the Church. He recognized the Church's right to censorship and the government would forbid the publication and distribution of books on the Index. Finally, he transferred jurisdiction over all issues connected with marriage to ecclesiastical tribunals with the result that divorce was condemned.

The Concordat was signed on 18 August 1855, the emperor's birthday, and was promulgated by imperial patent on 13 November. Francis Joseph saw the Church as an ally in the reconstruction of the state and returned to it the freedom of action and power which it had lost since 1780. The episcopate did not hide its satisfaction and Rauscher obtained a cardinal's hat in return for his good services. The concordat was well received in some conservative circles. The elderly Metternich regarded it as the most important event of the reign. The majority of conservatives in the government, however, did not hide their disquiet over this strengthening of the Church's power and the army and bureaucracy disapproved of this repudiation of Josephist tradition. The liberals saw it as a permanent mark against the new regime. Count Anton Auersperg observed, 'This treaty appeared to me as another Canossa* which was forced upon us and by which the Austria of the nineteenth century would atone for the Josephism of the eighteenth century.' Some liberals later blamed the Concordat for the disaster at Sadowa in 1866.

The policy of centralization was also new. The territorial assemblies, the communes, circles and districts had already been created by the patent of March 1849 and were subsequently extended to Hungary where it was more than a question of simple administrative divisions. Croatia was divided into districts, and the province promised to the Serbs was no more than a simple administrative entity. The elections which had been expected were postponed indefinitely. Court juries were suspended and the ministry of justice exercised close control over magistrates, including the former seigneurial courts which were now 'nationalized'. German remained the sole language of administration

---

* Translator's note: it was at Canossa in 1077 that Henry IV, king of the Germans, submitted to pope Gregory VII and performed his three-days penance, barefoot in the snow.

on the basis of an argument dear to Joseph II, 'efficiency'. Count Thun supported systematic Germanization: 'If any other language, no matter which, were in as favourable a situation as is German, we would recognize the same advantages. Our action is not dictated by favouritism.' The unity of the Empire required all its subjects to possess, in addition to their maternal tongue, at least the rudiments of German so that they could communicate among themselves and with the administration. Primary education was to be bilingual, the emphasis on German would be increased in gymnasiums and universities would be forced to Germanize, with the exception of those in the kingdom of Lombardy-Venetia which were spared this final humiliation. Even Hungary for the first time in its history did not escape systematic Germanization.

At first the bourgeoisie appreciated the return to order and especially the prosperity which accompanied neo-absolutism. There were parallels with the authoritarian Empire of Napoleon III which also experienced police surveillance, the suspension of liberties, the close alliance with the Church and a remarkable growth in wealth in the nascent capitalist world. Only Hungary took refuge in stubborn resistance. The conservative aristocracy could not forgive Francis Joseph for deliberately depriving it of its political rights by suppressing the old constitution. As moderate a man as the baron Joszef Eötvös and as distinguished and original a one as Tocqueville in France, could not but take their place among the opposition to the Habsburgs. The greater part of the population practised passive resistance. It was intimidated by the apparatus of repression and deeply demoralized by the failure of the war of independence. This discontent was sometimes expressed in violence, for example the conspiracy of Gál and Makk in 1851 and Libényi's unsuccessful attempt in 1853 to assassinate Francis Joseph. Intellectual life was stifled by censorship and liberal writers such as Mór Jókai resorted to historical novels. In the course of 1850 there appeared in Pest two novels and nine short stories on the history of Transylvania. The recollection of happier times in the past gave Hungarian patriots hope. The ten years which followed the capitulation at Világos were counted among the blackest in the country's history.

Even so, this was a period of economic development. In 1850, for the first time since 1526, customs barriers between Hungary and the rest of the monarchy were abolished. The economic problem was acute. With their freedom, 15 per cent of peasants had obtained sufficient land, 31 per cent worked a plot to feed their family and 54 per cent had not received any land. The agrarian question had assumed its modern form. Large landed proprietors held concentrated in their hands great estates (*latifundia*) while the only relief presented to the agrarian proletariat was to leave the countryside and emigrate to the New World. This rural exodus had, at first, helped to create industries resting on the processing of local primary materials, such as the food industries which were most important, metallurgy and attempts at textile industries. The first railway lines appeared at this time and the towns grew so that by 1855 Buda and Pest had around 100 000 inhabitants.

The period from 1849 to 1859 for the whole of Austria was a period of political stagnation and undeniable economic growth. It remains to be asked what led Francis Joseph from the neo-absolutism of 1849 to the Austro-Hungarian compromise of 1867.

THE CONSTITUTIONAL REFORMS OF 1860–61[4]

The system put in place by Bach, despite latent opposition to it and internal tensions, was not seriously challenged until the conflict with France in 1859 during which Austria lost Lombardy.

Order had been restored in Milan in 1849, but Austria, despite its positive achievements, had not won over the bourgeoisie. The period of Austrian domination was marked by economic prosperity for those working in agriculture and efficient administration from which everyone benefited, but a fresh attempt at insurrection in 1853 was once again met with brutal repression. In 1857 the arrival of the archduke Maximilian, the future victim of the Mexican débâcle, as governor-general of the kingdom of Lombardy-Venetia did not diffuse the tension, despite the conciliatory attitude of the emperor's younger brother. The Venetian lawyer Manin summed up the situation by declaring that it was not a question of waiting for Austria to become more humane and more understanding but rather that it should quit the country. Vienna was isolated at the diplomatic level. Russia was ready to avenge itself upon Austria for not supporting it during the Crimean War but rather, by its neutrality, forcing Russia to keep part of its army far from Sebastapol. Prussia was waiting for the moment when Austria would be occupied in Italy so that it could bring about German unification in its favour. France supported the ambitions of the Piedmontese, for the House of Savoy dreamt of effecting Italian unification under its aegis.

Austria was no longer in a strong military position. The financial difficulties in which the state found itself had retarded the processes of modernization. The command structure was deficient. Marshal Radetzky had just died and the emperor preferred to entrust responsibility to count Gyulay who was a mediocrity, rather than to Hess who was a bold strategist and pupil of Radetzky. After Magenta, Francis Joseph himself took command and at Solferino he proved that he did not have the gifts of a Bonaparte or the archduke Charles. The war began badly; preparations were inadequate and it was Austria that addressed an ultimatum to Victor Emmanuel, demanding that Piedmont cease its military preparations. The Italian campaign of 1859 was marked by a series of defeats for the Austrian army which, however, was not reduced to capitulation. After a day of bloody but indecisive battle at Solferino, that evening the two emperors Francis Joseph and Napoleon III thought it best to negotiate. Even so, by the terms of the armistice at Villafranca on 11 July 1859, Austria lost Lombardy, the principalities of Modena and Tuscany, and a great deal of prestige. Napoleon III, who feared a prolongation of the campaign, saved for Francis Joseph the Veneto, which remained Austrian until 1866.

Instead of strengthening the monarchy's cohesion, the Bach system had diminished it. Francis Joseph broke off the war partly because he was afraid of what the Hungarians might be intending. Kossuth, in exile, had negotiated with Napoleon III and proposed a combined action aimed at securing independence for Hungary. The emperor risked confronting a Hungarian uprising. The Austrian government felt betrayed by the Germans of the *Reich* who had maintained a neutrality biased against Austria. To regain the sympathies of the liberals, Francis Joseph believed Austria should be given a representative regime. The question of nationalities was no easier to resolve than in 1848 and the Hungarian burden weighed as heavily as ever. As unification and Germanization were no longer possible, the questions were whether there would be a return to the federal system, whether or not to grant the nationalities the place the Kremsier constitution had assigned them, and whether Hungary should enjoy a privileged position as in the early days of the monarchy? Each possibility was tried, but from 1867 onwards it was the last that endured.

By the diploma of October 1860, the Vienna government reinstated the old particular constitutions. It was a major concession to state-right and the conservative aristocracy who were deeply attached to local liberties and hostile to German centralism. The diploma entrusted legislative power to the old provincial Diets while the Hungarian Diet was restored and secured powers more extensive than the others. Hungarian even received back its status as the language of administration, which pleased the Hungarians but alarmed the minorities. The autonomy of the counties was re-established, the Banat and the Vojvodina were rejoined to the kingdom of Hungary, while Transylvania and Croatia-Slavonia-Dalmatia kept their autonomy in relation to Budapest. For the Hungarians, as for the Czechs, the diploma was nevertheless inadequate because it did not make sufficient concessions to the historic nations. For the liberal bourgeoisie, the diploma did not establish a parliamentary regime and posed a threat to centralization. Francis Joseph very quickly realized that the October constitution would not work and turned once more to the liberal Germans. He put Schmerling, a former minister in the Frankfurt government, in charge of preparing a new text, but Schmerling was a liberal in favour of centralism. The patent of February 1861 was presented as a companion to the October diploma of 1860, whereas in fact it amounted to a return to centralism which this time would be controlled by the parliamentary assemblies. It was essentially the regime wished for by the upper bourgeoisie who henceforth constituted the driving elements of political and economic life of the monarchy. The text still made large concessions to the class of large estate-owners.

The electoral system was based on the property qualification, direct taxation and noble property. To qualify to vote, it was necessary to pay at least 10 florins in direct tax. The deputies of the parliament at Vienna were only the representatives of the provincial Diets which were appointed by an electoral body divided into four curias: the great noble estate-owners whose lands were registered in the 'table of the country'; the towns; the corporations; and the rural communities. The aristocracy thus preserved considerable political rights, an echo of their dominance in the Estates before 1848. An elector could vote twice if his title gave him access to two different curias. In Bohemia, the Diet had 241 deputies: five from the clergy and Prague university, seventy from among the great estate-owners, seventy-two from the towns, fifteen from the chambers of commerce and industry, and seventy-nine from the rural communes.

It was still a long way from the application of a democratic system, 'one man, one vote'. The allocation of representation was still more favourable to the German language element than to the Czech language element which was confined mainly to the curia drawn from the countryside.

The patent instituted a federal parliament made up of two chambers: a 'general parliament' which dealt with affairs common to the whole monarchy and a 'limited parliament' which was not concerned with Hungarian affairs. This was the beginning of the dualist solution. The 'limited parliament' was a deliberative assembly which held the initiative in law-making. However, its proposals were examined by the council of state which was the *Reichsrat* of the 1849 constitution. Of course, the ministers were not responsible before parliament and in practice the government sought to limit its jurisdiction, especially in financial matters.

The Hungarians protested as soon as the patent of February 1861 was promulgated because it did not respect state-right, and they refused to send deputies to Vienna with the result that the 'general parliament' never met. The Croats were dissatisfied because they had received only partial autonomy in relation to Hungary and so sent no more deputies, and the Czechs reacted the same way because the patent was a retreat from the federal solution put in place by the October diploma of 1860. The new constitutional law then drew unanimous opposition from all those who were devoted to respecting state-right. The landed aristocracy sensed very well the difficulty posed by the liberal and centralist solution, but now had too little weight in the political game to impose a solution conforming to the deepest aspirations of the peoples brought together within the monarchy.

The Hungarians could not abstain for ever. The demands of the political class were difficult to reconcile with a centralist conception of the monarchy, especially since it imposed as the prerequisite for any negotiation the re-establishment within the monarchy of an autonomous state, corresponding to the historic tradition established in 1527 and maintained, not without difficulty, until 1848. In exchange for this fundamental concession on the part of Vienna, Deák and his friends agreed to renounce complete independence. They had understood that, in the face of Russia and the Slav minorities, secession would swiftly lead to loss of independence. They were no more eager than the Habsburgs to repeat the experiences of 1849, even though Kossuth still had supporters within the country.

This was a unique opportunity for Hungary to have in the 1860s a liberal and patriotic political class capable of drawing lessons from the disaster of 1849. Ferenc Deák had taken an active part in political life during the *Vormärz*.[5] At the age of thirty he was deputy of the county of Zala and quickly acquired a reputation as a liberal reformer opposed to violence. He took his stand in the middle ground between Széchenyi and the radical current of Kossuth. Like Széchenyi, he supported the minorities and was in favour of transforming

Hungary into a multinational state. He favoured the growth of education and the promotion of Hungarian at the expense of Latin, which he thought obsolete, and Germanization. At the Diet where he sat until 1849, he proved a good tactician, capable and wise. A member of the middling nobility who owned 1 250 acres, he did not have the faults of his class. He was not cosmopolitan but an open and tolerant man who dreamt of a genuine collaboration between the Habsburgs and the Diet. In 1848 he kept apart from the conflict and was acquitted by court martial. He refused to collaborate with the Austrian authorities and wanted a return to the laws of April 1848. This was why in 1860 he declined Schmerling's offer of the post of grand judge (*judex curiae*) because he thought the October diploma inadequate. The other head of the liberal party was a magnate, count Gyula Andrássy, who filled the place left vacant after the suicide of count Jozsef Teleki in 1861.

Andrássy was ten years younger than Deák. He was born in 1813 at Košice and belonged to a family who had traditionally championed national liberties. He was very closely linked with Kossuth and, unlike Deák, approved of his radical tendencies. A deputy for the county of Zemplén in the 1847 Diet, he responded favourably to the 1848 revolution but his enthusiasm was tempered by the lessons which he had drawn from touring Western Europe. He very quickly understood that Hungary could not remain isolated and that it was necessary to support the Germans. All his life, he remained a supporter of the Austrian alliance. During the revolution, he played only a marginal role. He was an officer and represented Kossuth's government at Constantinople. These activities earned him a death sentence for contempt of court, since he had gone into exile after Világos. A refugee in London, then in Paris, he kept apart from Jozsef Teleki and Lajos Kossuth while considering how to restore his country's liberty and independence. He became increasingly convinced of the need to reach an agreeement with the Habsburgs. After receiving a pardon, he returned to Hungary in 1858 but, like Deák, considered that the 1860 October diploma was inadequate since he was dedicated to respecting state-right and the reestablishing the constitution but remained firmly opposed to a federalist solution which would grant the same rights to the Czechs. Elected vice-president of the Diet in 1865, Andrássy with Deák conducted negotiations with the government in Vienna. His good faith, his loyalty and competence won over Francis Joseph, while his charm and distinction impressed the empress Elisabeth who intuitively favoured the Hungarians. In this way he began a remarkable political career and soon asserted himself as one of the few eminent statesmen of Francis Joseph's reign.

The tension lifted when an article appeared in the *Pest Gazette* of Easter 1865 in which Deák declared himself ready to negotiate. Schmerling's cabinet distinguished itself by questioning the 1855 Concordat, but its stubborn pursuit of a policy of centralization had alienated the greater part of conservative opinion in the hereditary lands and all the Hungarians, including the bishops who had become as reserved with respect to the crown as the rest of the population. Francis Joseph was well advised by count Móricz Esterházy, minister without portfolio in the Vienna cabinet. He travelled to Buda, dismissed Schmerling and undertook long negotiations on the basis defined by Deák:[6]

Hungary does not wish to imperil in any way the power of the monarchy.... There is no conflict between the hereditary lands and Hungary, they can exist without being absorbed. We do not want to sacrifice our liberty for the sole reason that there exist differences with respect to certain rights between the new constitution of the Cisleithanian peoples and our constitution but we will always be ready to harmonize, by constitutional means, our laws with the demands of the security and cohesion of the monarchy.

Schmerling's successor, count Richard Belcredi, was a Bohemian aristocrat, an influential member of the 'historic nobility' who had already advanced far in the higher administration. He did not hide his sympathies for federalism. On 20 September 1865, Francis Joseph suspended the patent of February 1861. So ended the period of centralized monarchy controlled by a representative assembly, the *Reichsrat*, which was not representative since the kingdoms of Bohemia and Hungary were voluntarily absent from it. There were celebrations in Prague and declarations of satisfaction in Budapest. All that remained was to negotiate a new constitution.

In the autumn of 1865, centralism appeared finally defeated despite the weight carried by the liberals and government conservatives. Although neo-absolutism had not survived the defeat at Solferino, parliamentary centralism had not succeeded in winning over Hungarian public opinion. Since subduing the Hungarians by force was out of the question, Francis Joseph would have to find a compromise before he could be crowned at Buda. Two years passed before the negotiations reached a conclusion, at which point the defeat at Sadowa (1866) gave the Hungarians a clear advantage. After having been chased from Germany, the Habsburgs had to consolidate their power in Danubian Europe or risk seeing themselves driven out as their relatives had been from Tuscany, Modena and Naples after the formation of the kingdom of Italy.

The Austro-Hungarian compromise of 1867, it is often claimed, was a consequence of the Prussian victory of 1866. The reality was a little more complicated since by 1864 everyone was already convinced, like the papal nuncio, that any lasting constitutional solution was impossible without the Hungarians' agreement. The defeat had certainly made the weight of concessions yet heavier and transformed the Hungarians into privileged negotiators, to the detriment of the other historic nations within the monarchy.

Little now remained to be seen of the programme hastily implemented in 1849 after the suspension of the Kremsier constitution. Austria had lost its hegemony in Italy and only kept the Venetia which was coveted by the newly formed kingdom of Italy, ready to re-open hostilities at the first opportunity. Only the old warhorses at the imperial headquarters imagined that Victor Emmanuel's Italy would be short-lived. The following year, Francis Joseph won guarantees of French neutrality in the Austro-Prussian conflict. By the secret agreement of 13 June 1868, the emperor ceded the Venetia to Napoleon III so that the French sovereign could then give it to Italy.

Austria's position in Germany was challenged by Bismarck's Prussia which had not forgiven Schwarzenberg. Hungary had resisted forcefully and the absolutist regime had passed. Austria's preponderance had been challenged and Austria was no longer the great conservative power, the guardian of counter-revolution on the Continent. The crisis of 1866 would lead Austria to lose both Germany and Italy, reducing it to the Danubian region. The Habsburgs' vocation underwent change for the last time. From being a German dynasty, from having pretensions to universal monarchy, and having been a great continental power, the Habsburgs found themselves reduced to governing a multinational state and taking second place to imperial Germany which was then in full rise. Solferino, Sadowa and Sedan marked the three stages in the shuffling of the cards whereby Napoleon III and Francis Joseph lost to the benefit of modern and dynamic Prussia. The decisive moment, though, was in 1866.

NOTES AND REFERENCES

1. Jean-Paul Bled, *Les Fondements du conservatisme autrichien 1859–1870*, Paris, 1988.
2. F. Engel-Janosi (ed.), *Die Protokolle des österreichischen Ministerrates 1848–1867*, Vienna, 1975.
3. *Protokolle III Abteilung. Das Ministerium Buol-Schauenstein*, part 1 (14.4.1852–11.3.1853), Vienna, 1975.
4. György Szabad, 'Hungarian political trends between the Revolution and the Compromise 1849–1867', *Studia Historica*, 128, Budapest, 1977.
5. Béla K. Kiraly, *Ferenc Deák, 1803–1876*, Boston, 1975.
6. Louis Eisenmann, *Le Compromis austro-hongrois de 1867. Études sur de dualisme*, Paris, 1904.

CHAPTER THIRTEEN

1866, The Decisive Year

The Austro-Prussian war was a blitzkrieg which, in the space of a few weeks, put an end to the Habsburgs' German vocation, a vocation which had begun in 1273. Bismarck, by debarring Francis Joseph and the Austrian monarchy from German affairs, had changed the balance of power in Europe and believed that he had solved the problem of German unity. He had broken up the German Confederation, one of the basic provisions of the treaties of Vienna, and in creating the German empire he had debarred his fellow Germans from Austria and Bohemia, leaving them in a state where they formed but a minority, scarcely a quarter of the total population. Perhaps he was giving Danubian Europe an unhoped-for chance to constitute a third power, between the Russian and German empires. Once again it would call for a great effort of will on the monarchy's part not to give in to events. It is necessary to examine how Francis Joseph found himself in such a position that external forces could impose so radical a situation upon him following the resounding military defeat at Sadowa (Königgrätz) on 3 July 1866.

GERMAN POLITICS IN THE NEO-ABSOLUTIST ERA[1]

German politics, under Schwarzenberg's influence, was every bit as reactionary as Austrian domestic politics. The president of the Austrian council proved as energetic as he had on the home-front in erasing the consequences of the revolution and restoring Austrian power, while making use, once again, of the tsar's benevolent complicity.

The Frankfurt parliament, elected in May 1848, was still in session at the end of the year, despite the defeat of the revolutions in Berlin and Vienna. With Heinrich von Gagern as president, it elected the archduke John, the loser at Hohenlinden, as *Reichsverweser* (vicar-general), an old office which gave the *Reich* the pretence of executive power in the event of the emperorship falling vacant. The Habsburgs, like all great families in times of trouble, had members in both camps. The monarchical states lived on in Germany. Besides the Prussia of Frederick William IV, who, like Francis Joseph, was experiencing a period of extreme political reaction, Germany included the kingdoms of Saxony, Bavaria,

Hanover and Württemberg, the grand duchies of Baden, Hesse-Kassel, Hesse-Darmstadt, the duchies of Mecklenburg and of Oldenburg, the free towns of Bremen, Hamburg, Lübeck and other principalities of less importance. The large states, especially Bavaria, Saxony and Württemberg, jealously guarded their independence and did not want to become Prussian or Austrian satellites.

Schwarzenberg thought that there were four possible models for re-building the German world on a firm basis, but he did not favour them all. The first two models which he found wholly unacceptable for the Habsburgs and the Austrian empire were the institution of a national parliament in the light of the experiences of 1848 and the creation of a *Kleindeutschland*, 'a small Germany', under Prussian domination, a model which the French and some scholars understood to mean a united Germany. Schwarzenberg wanted Austria to become part of a revived German Confederation which would go beyond Metternich's objectives since he aimed at creating a single territory with a population of 70 million, all under Habsburg rule. Such a state would not be a German national state because it would include Slavs, Hungarians and Latins as well as Germans. It would represent the realization of Friedrich List's project for a *Mitteleuropa* which would guarantee for Austro-Germany extraordinary weight in continental Europe and exceed the original objective of a Central European customs union.

Prussia, however, was not prepared to accept, at any price, integration within the Austrian empire, within a German Confederation enlarged to include Hungary and northern Italy, since under such conditions it would find itself reduced to the rank of a secondary power within the German world. Nicholas I's Russia, although it was allied to Prussia and Austria, was against such an arrangement and the plan was received with considerable reservation in London and Paris.

The fourth proposal, to which Schwarzenberg gave a lukewarm response, was the re-establishment of the German Confederation within the boundaries set out by the Treaty of Vienna in 1815, on condition that the Habsburgs, as on the eve of the 1848 revolution, were guaranteed its leadership. This solution strengthened Austria's preponderance in Germany but excluded Hungary, Galicia and the kingdom of Lombardy-Venetia. Schwarzenberg accepted the proposal *faute de mieux*. Its fragility, however, was plain in 1866 when it fell apart under the brutal assault from Prussia, backed by Napoleon III.

The conservative governments were in agreement over dissolving the parliament at Frankfurt. It had implicitly declared war on Austria at the end of 1848 by announcing that a member state of the German Confederation could not be linked to non-German lands. Such a solution would obviously entail independence for Hungary and the disappearance of the Habsburg monarchy. The Habsburgs would retain only the Austro-Bohemian lands and the Czechs would be reduced to small islands within a *Grossdeutschland*, a 'great German' state.

For this reason, Schwarzenberg let the Frankfurt parliament know that he envisaged the Austrian empire, with a unitary constitution, entering a revitalized Confederation in which the parliament would be replaced by a chamber drawn from the Estates, with Austria having a majority of seats, thirty-eight out of seventy. This was a deliberate provocation, intended to precipitate the coming clash. The parliament at Frankfurt responded by offering Frederick William IV the imperial crown of a Germany which excluded the Austrian monarchy. This was the *Kleindeutschland* proposal of 28 March 1849. The king of Prussia turned it down, partly out of solidarity with the Habsburgs, but above all because his power would have a democratic origin which, as a Hohenzollern, he could not accept. For Schwarzenberg, this was the worst possible solution since it would mean a Germany under Prussian leadership and one from which the Habsburgs and Austrian Germans would be excluded. Frederick William IV's refusal postponed for twenty years Prussia's triumph and the formation of a German empire which would never be less than a Great Prussia. At the same time, the king of Prussia condemned the Frankfurt parliament. Austria recalled its deputies in April 1849 and Prussia followed suit in May. The rump parliament fled to Stuttgart where it met an inglorious end, scattered by the Württemberg army. Thus ended a brilliant episode in the history of Germany. Despite the errors from lack of experience, the bourgeois liberals of the Frankfurt parliament had almost succeeded in establishing a democratic Germany. It would be another century before democracy could flourish east of the Rhine. The hopes of an entire people had ended and the German patriots suffered their second disappointment of the century. The popular movements of 1813 and 1848 had both been followed in 1814 and 1849 by the restoration of monarchies.

Ambition, however, outlived the parliament at Frankfurt and the following year provoked a serious Austro-Prussian crisis, the Olomouc retreat. Frederick William IV imagined heading a 'limited union' led, not by parliament, but by the other German princes who would offer him its leadership. Austria would then be associated with this enlarged union, even if it meant offering Francis Joseph the presidency of the union in which *Kleindeutschland*, led by Prussia, would deal on equal terms with the Austrian monarchy. The Prussian memorandum of 10 May 1849 which set out this plan, was rejected by Schwarzenberg who was then free to crush the Hungarian revolution. After enjoying tactical successes in the summer of 1849, in the autumn Prussia had to face a coalition of German states, Bavaria, Württemberg, Saxony and Hanover which feared Prussian hegemony. In the spring of 1850, the German world was divided into two camps, between those states which stood behind Prussia and desired the limited union, the *Kleindeutschland* proposed by Frederick William IV, and those states which, with Austria, were prepared to sit in the old-style Frankfurt Diet which had been summoned for 1 May by Francis Joseph, acting as president of the restored German Confederation.

The conflict began over Hesse-Kassel which was a member of the Union. The grand duke appealed to the Confederation for help against the challenge to his position posed by his subjects. The Bavarian army was charged with reinstating the grand duke in his prerogatives at Kassel. Prussia sensed that its vital interests were at stake, since Hesse-Kassel separated Rhineland Prussia from Brandenburg, and denied the Confederation the right to intervene in the affairs of a member state of the limited Union. On 12 October 1850, Francis Joseph met the kings of Bavaria and Württemberg at Bregenz and decided upon a plan of campaign in the event of Prussia taking up arms to prevent the Bavarians from intervening. Five Austrian army corps were concentrated in Bohemia under the orders of marshal Radetzky. The Prussians occupied Hesse-Kassel on 25 October and on the same day Nicholas I met Francis Joseph and agreed to support Austria. War seemed inevitable. The monarchy was in a position of strength which it would never again enjoy. Prussia was diplomatically isolated and had only 50 000 troops while the imperial army had 130 000. The cabinet in Berlin was deeply divided between those in favour of a conclusive war and those who wanted an honourable compromise.

Schwarzenberg through his moderating influence effected a compromise. On 2 November, Frederick William IV decided to dissolve the limited Union and at the same time decreed general mobilization and refused to evacuate Hesse-Kassel. On 28 November, Schwarzenberg sent an ultimatum to Prussia. Frederick William responded by sending the minister president count Manteuffel to negotiate with Schwarzenberg who agreed to meet him at Olomouc in Moravia.

The meeting took place on 27 November and ended the crisis. Francis Joseph and the imperial army were both greatly attached to the Prussian alliance and neither wanted a fratricidal war. The meeting of the two heads of government ended with an agreement which, according to the Austrian historian Heinrich von Srbik, left 'neither victor nor vanquished'. Prussia agreed to allow passage to the Bavarian troops in charge of carrying out the Confederation's policy in Hesse-Kassel. It put its army on a peace-footing and agreed to take part in a conference of German princes which was to meet at Dresden to reorganize the German Confederation.

The Olomouc Proclamation was far from being a retreat and was the Habsburgs last success in Germany. It has, however, been judged in a number of different ways. Prussian patriots resented it as a humiliation and it is this *Kleindeutschland* historiography, which dominated after 1866, which is responsible for the theory that it was a 'retreat'. Schwarzenberg would have preferred a war which would have dispelled all ambiguities, and Beust, the minister president of Saxony, wrote that 'the path from Olomouc led to Sadowa'. The Bavarian minister president drew a pessimistic conclusion: 'the fight for hegemony in Germany has been decided and Austria has lost'. This was a perceptive analysis. Prussia would develop rapidly without renouncing its premier position in Germany.

The Dresden Conference of April 1851 adopted a solution which did little to please Schwarzenberg by advocating the restoration of the German Confederation and a return to the situation before 1848. The *détente* between Vienna and Berlin could scarcely hide the antagonism between the two powers. Frederick William IV was against the Austrian empire entering the *Zollverein* and Francis Joseph refused him co-presidency of the German Confederation. Austria had suffered a partial defeat since opposition from the concert of nations – Russia, Great Britain and France – had prevented it from realizing the *Mitteleuropa* of 70 million inhabitants which would have changed the balance of forces considerably in its favour, making the Germans the national majority

in Central Europe and creating a vast market at the time of the industrial revolution. Felix Schwarzenberg cannot be accused of lacking determination and
ambition for his country. Austria, by patching up the old German Confederation, had settled for an easy solution but one which went against German
national feeling and Prussian imperialism, two forces which continued to grow
after 1850.

After Schwarzenberg's death, Francis Joseph entrusted foreign policy to
count Karl Ferdinand Buol Schauenstein, a worthy but limited man and one
of several officials appointed to high office because the emperor liked them.
Buol wanted to move away from Nicholas I in order to reach a reconciliation
with the western powers, a plan he soon realized when the Crimean War
broke out.

THE CRIMEAN WAR AND THE
EASTERN CRISIS (1853–55)

In October 1853 Nicholas I occupied the Danubian principalities, Moldavia
and Wallachia, which still belonged to the Ottoman empire. The Sublime
Porte, backed by Britain and France, refused to allow itself to be stripped of
its possessions and declared war on Russia. Francis Joseph was not willing to
accept the division of the Balkans which the tsar was proposing and, faithful
to the principles of Metternich, declared his commitment to the integrity of
the Ottoman empire. For this reason in 1854 he chose to remain neutral and
concluded a treaty of alliance with Prussia which put the German Confederation outside the conflict at the time when France and Britain were sending
expeditionary corps to the Crimea. Very quickly, however, Francis Joseph's
position declined into hostile neutrality towards Russia. Buol, Bach, Prokesch-
Osten, an orientalist and Austrian minister at Athens, and baron Hübner, the
ambassador to Paris, urged the emperor to declare war on Russia, its former
ally, contrary to the advice of the imperial army which was shocked at such
ingratitude. In July 1854, Francis Joseph ordered the tsar to evacuate Moldavia
and Wallachia and the Russian troops complied in order to avoid opening a
second front in the Balkans. The ties of friendship between St Petersburg and
Vienna were, however, broken for good. The Austro-Russian alliance was no
more and Francis Joseph was now convinced that Russia was the Habsburg
monarchy's natural enemy in the east. If the Christians of the Balkans were
freed from Ottoman tutelage, they would become satellites of Russia; a division of influence in the Balkans would be an illusion because the Slavs, including those of the monarchy, would look towards Moscow. In the short term,
Austria's prudent policy, as ungrateful as it was, served the interests of the
German Confederation and helped to maintain peace in Europe, for if Francis
Joseph had engaged actively in either camp (he had signed in December 1854
a formal treaty of alliance with the western powers), this would have provoked
the general conflict which Europe was spared from 1815 to 1914.

THE WAR IN ITALY[2]

During the Franco-Austrian war, Prussia was out of favour with Francis Joseph for having abandoned him in the face of Napoleon III and Piedmont. The cabinet in Berlin had concentrated two army corps on the Rhine, but as a precaution, reminded the Austrian government that it was not under any obligation to bring Francis Joseph military assistance if territory outside the Confederation, such as the kingdom of Lombardy-Venetia, were attacked. After Solferino, Francis Joseph sent Windischgrätz, a friend of Prussia, to Berlin where the aged marshal received a polite rejection. The prince-regent, the future William I, set very strict conditions as the price for military aid to Austria, insisting on having command of the Confederal troops or, at the very least, joint command with Austria. In short, he demanded parity with Austria or Austria's relegation to second-place. During the past ten years, Prussia's demands had grown markedly. To save the Italian provinces, Francis Joseph would have had to sacrifice supremacy in Germany. As this was out of the question, he preferred once again to negotiate with Napoleon III at Villafranca and to renounce Lombardy and, with it, Austrian hegemony in Italy.

Francis Joseph was probably surprised by Prussia's reaction because he had not taken into account how the situation had changed and he was unfamiliar with the character of the new Prussian ruler who was dedicated to Prussian state interest. Prussia was experiencing remarkable economic growth, particularly in the Ruhr where the Krupp family was in the process of creating its industrial empire. The German public favoured Prussia, which appeared modern and relatively liberal at a time when neo-absolutism and the Concordat of 1855 had reinforced the monarchy's tarnished image as reactionary, clerical and hostile to any form of progress. Times were turning against the Habsburgs and the idea of *Kleindeutschland* was gaining ground.

Francis Joseph's entourage realized that conflict was unavoidable. Rechberg, who succeeded Buol as minister of foreign affairs, thought that any hostile gesture should be avoided since the monarchy had not rebuilt its army. Schmerling, on the other hand, favoured the idea of a *Grossdeutschland* centred on Austria, and thought that the German princes should be given full support in their stand against Prussian imperialism. He was supported by baron von Biegeleben, a Hessian in the Habsburgs' service, who directed the German section of the ministry of foreign affairs. He advocated a firm approach and was convinced that Prussia would have to be crushed before it was too late and reduced to its 1740 boundaries. It was vital, therefore, to reach an understanding with Napoleon III, regardless of the personal feelings of Francis Joseph who held the French emperor to be a supporter of revolution and an enemy of Austria. To this end, the most would have to be made of the cordial relations which the ambassador to Paris, Richard Metternich, son of the late chancellor, was enjoying with Napoleon III and the empress Eugénie. Unfortunately, Francis Joseph remained undecided, whereas William I had since 1862 enjoyed the support of Bismarck whom he had made a president of the council against the liberal majority of the Prussian *Landtag*. Bismarck was a statesman who directed Prussian policy with as much authority as intelligence and made no secret of his goal, the realization of *Kleindeutschland*.

In 1863 Bismarck dissolved the *Zollverein* in order to force his partners to accept the terms of the Franco-Prussian treaty of commerce. Through a preferential customs tariff, exchanges between France and *Kleindeutschland* were made much easier than between *Kleindeutschland* and the Austrian monarchy. Albert Schaeffle, the future minister of Francis Joseph, thought that this was for Austria an economic Villafranca for which it would have to try to compensate by politically remodelling the German Confederation.

Francis Joseph sought to put an end to the liberal *Nationalverein*'s campaign for an election to a truly federal parliament limited to *Kleindeutschland* and proposed tightening the links between the states of the Confederation by creating an executive directory composed of four members (Prussia, Bavaria and two other states) and presided over by Austria. He was convinced that this was the only chance to unite Germany under Habsburg authority in accordance with the dynasty's secular vocation. In August 1863, he brought together a congress of princes at Frankfurt from which William I quite deliberately stayed away. This boycott, the work of Bismarck, led to a crushing diplomatic defeat. The reform project was buried.

THE DUCHIES

It was easy for Rechberg to convince Francis Joseph that Schmerling's policy was a disaster and that it was essential to cooperate with Prussia over an issue which would provide Bismarck with a pretext for rupture.

In 1863 Denmark had annexed Schleswig and Holstein, duchies which were members of the Confederation and in personal union with the crown of Denmark, for the dukes of Holstein had been kings of Denmark since the fifteenth century. An earlier dispute had been settled by international arbitration in 1852 but Christian IX's unfortunate initiative provoked the Confederation. In 1864 Austria, without much enthusiasm, decided to join Prussia in ousting the duke of Augustenberg* who had been installed in Kiel by the Saxon and Hanoverian troops of the Confederation. The imperial troops and Prussians occupied the duchies and crushed the Danish troops who made, at the most, a gallant last stand. The powers, as guarantors of the 1852 settlement, did not intervene because Britain did not have an expeditionary corps capable of rapid and effective action. The victors divided their spoils according to the terms of the Gastein Convention which was negotiated in August 1865 by Bismarck and count Blome. Prussia annexed Saxe-Lauenberg and Kiel and controlled Schleswig, thus gaining access to the North Sea, while Austria took charge of Holstein which proved no more than a source of trouble.

---

* Translator's note: Frederick of Augustenberg, who enjoyed the support of most German liberals, challenged the claims of Christian of Glücksburg to Denmark and the duchies. Of the two duchies, only Holstein was part of the Confederation.

Rechberg had fallen into the trap which Bismarck had prepared to lure Austria away from the German Confederation and into cahoots with Prussia. Briefly Austria had nurtured the hope of exchanging Holstein for Silesia. Bismarck was evidently playing upon the old dreams of Austrian diplomacy.

Austria was faced with the inevitable choice of either granting Prussia equality within the Confederation or waging war. In 1864 lord Clarendon, secretary to the foreign office in London, confided in Beust, the minister president of Saxony, 'Bismarck is an adventurer fearing neither God nor man and Rechberg is his blackboy'. In more diplomatic terms he confided to count Apponyi, the Austrian ambassador, that he regretted seeing a power like Austria surrendering its role as a great power and its independence to become the plaything and the instrument of its rival's ambitions.

THE ORIGINS OF THE AUSTRO-PRUSSIAN WAR (1866)

Francis Joseph remained no less faithful to the policy outlined by Rechberg. At the beginning of 1866, at the time when Bismarck was unveiling his plan for the reorganization of the Confederation from which Austria was to be excluded, the emperor was openly optimistic about relations with Berlin. A dispute over the administration of the duchies, however, provided Bismarck with the occasion to despatch a threatening note to Rechberg on 28 January 1866.

In October 1865 at Biarritz, Bismarck had already secured Austria's diplomatic isolation by assuring Napoleon III of his concern over the duchies. It was easy to win round Napoleon III since he was already well-disposed towards Prussia and German unification and he hoped for some compensation or, as Bismarck would later say, 'gratuities'. Britain was without an army and after prince Albert's death in 1861 was less interested in continental affairs. Russia was not prepared to forgive the Habsburgs for their stance over the Crimean War and the eastern crisis of 1853. On 8 April, the king of Italy signed an alliance treaty with Prussia and made no secret of his intention of waging war for the sake of liberating Venetia and so presenting Austria with two fronts to defend.

Austria, to end this volatile situation, in mid-April demanded that Prussia draw a halt to arming itself since, at the end of March, the two powers had begun to mass their troops. This snare laid by Bismarck closed fast on the Austrian government. What would be Francis Joseph's reaction?

The emperor responded in a surprising way for a head of state, by giving in to events and waging war against his will for the sake of honour. The debates of the council of ministers are especially revealing; the Austrian ministry was passive and Bismarck kept the initiative, leading public opinion to believe that it was Austria that wanted war.[3]

The monarchy's finances were, as ever, in a parlous condition. Schmerling had allowed the *Reichsrat* to enact large cuts in the military budget and money had to be found quickly to finance preparations for war. Von Beck, the director of the ministry, in response to a summons for consultation, proposed raising a loan of 60 million florins (150 million francs) from Paris, which seemed quite a reasonable proposal since relations between Paris and Vienna were apparently cordial. Bismarck used the occasion to create the impression that the Vienna cabinet was bent on war, whereas in fact Vienna was putting Bohemia and Moravia, which had been all but disarmed for ten years, on the defensive. Bismarck was, in modern terms, practising 'disinformation'.

In May, William I gave orders to mobilize the artillery and cavalry and on 12 May 1866 issued a decree for general mobilization. Napoleon III proposed an international conference which would lead to general disarmament. Prussia, however, responded to the denunciation of the Garstein convention by invading Holstein on 7 June.

On 14 June, the German Confederation responded to this act of hostility by issuing a federal writ against Prussia. Austria was not isolated since Bavaria, Württemberg, Baden, the two Hesses (Hesse-Kassel and Hesse-Darmstadt) and Saxony voted for the writ and joined Austria's side. Their heart, however, was not in it since the military was well aware of its own unpreparedness and still tended to think of the Prussians as comrades-in-arms rather than as 'hereditary enemies', a legacy of the Napoleonic Wars. Lacking in all enthusiasm and out of a sense of duty and loyalty to the emperor, they went to war. Public opinion supported the war in Italy alone, its contempt for Victor Emmanuel's army vying with its feelings of animosity. It was, then, the repudiation of the Gastein convention by Austria and the invasion of Holstein by Prussia that led to the declaration of war on 15 June 1866.

On 11 June, Francis Joseph had secured French neutrality by ceding Venetia, not to Victor Emmanuel, which would have been a humiliation for Austria, but to Napoleon III. He was thus free from the threat of the French army coming to the aid of the young Italian army and of his having to engage with the French on the other side of the Alps. The Austrians had only one adversary on the Italian front. They were certain of losing Venice, whatever the outcome of any engagements, but in the difficult situation in which the monarchy then found itself, Francis Joseph thought that this sacrifice was inevitable and that without it Napoleon III would pass into the enemy camp.

The real reasons for the war of 1866 lay beyond these specific aspects in the application of the principle of nationality and Prussia's desire for power which led it to seek German unification on its terms within the framework of a *Kleindeutschland*. During the war, Bismarck did not hide his goal of driving Austria from the Confederation. As Austria had lost Venice by the secret treaty of 11 June 1866 Italian unification was practically achieved. The only question outstanding was that of Rome, or rather the pope's sovereignty over Rome where French bayonets protected him from the excesses of Italian patriots. Italy was lost for the Habsburgs even though, in June 1866, Francis Joseph supplied the Bourbon king of Naples, Francis II, with a million francs to assist him in rousing his kingdom in revolt against the authorities in Florence. There were further military operations but the game was up in Italy. In Germany a short war, desired and prepared by Prussia, would in six weeks impose the worst solution envisaged by Schwarzenberg and the apparent triumph of the principle of nationalities would deprive the Habsburgs of their main reason for being, the direction of the German body.

THE FORCES CONFRONT EACH OTHER

In mid-June, Austria did not seem to be in a wholly unfavourable position. Following the secret agreement with France, the Italian front became a secondary theatre of war, albeit one which still brought to a standstill on the south side of the Alps an army which could have been more usefully employed in Germany.

In 1866 the imperial army had 528 000 men, of whom 460 000 were ready for combat. Some 94 000 were needed to occupy the fortified towns and as Vienna and Hungary could not be left totally ungarrisoned for political reasons, 25 000 men had to be left there. This meant that the Austrian battle corps was made up of some 300 000 men divided among ten army corps and five cavalry divisions. The war in Italy made it necessary to divide the imperial army into the Northern army of 238 000 men, seven army and cavalry corps under general Benedek, and the Southern army commanded by archduke Albert and consisting of three army corps, some 74 000 men, sufficient to fight the Italians.

Prussia had at its disposal 320 000 men, of whom 30 000 were cavalry divided into four armies with the Guard constituting a strategic reserve corps. Even with the second Italian front, the opposing forces were of almost equal size since the imperial army was joined by the forces of the Confederation, Hanoverians, Hessians and Bavarians. The Northern army was reinforced by 23 000 Saxons so that in the Bohemian campaign two forces of comparable size stood face-to-face – 270 000 Prussians and 270 000 Austrians and Saxons, while the secondary theatres of operation, Italy for the Austrians and north Germany for the Prussians, each occupied 70 000 men.

These troops were not, however, of equal strength. The imperial troops lagged behind the Prussian partly because of lack of money and partly because of the ideology and ossification of those in command who had refused to adopt the technical innovations which had so dramatically transformed the art of war. The Prussian general staff under Moltke with the king and Bismarck's support had forged a formidably efficient fighting machine.

The war of 1866 marked a revolution in tactics. It ended the frontal attack advocated by Guibert in the eighteenth century and used by the Revolutionary armies and for the last time at Solferino in 1859. The bayonet charge had become impossible because of the increased fire-power of the infantry, itself a consequence of the adoption of the needlegun charged by the breachblock. Half the Prussian army used it while the other half still used the Minié rifle with its rifled bore of 17 mm which was muzzle-loaded. The whole Austrian army was equipped with 1854 model Lorenz rifles with rifled muzzles and muzzle-loaded. In addition, in the Prussian army firing practice and instruction were much more developed with Prussian troops using five times as many cartridges a year as the imperial troops. Its soldiers took part in their annual manoeuvres in order to train the commanders to handle great units whereas the imperial army contented itself with parades and regimental exercises and had not taken part in any great manoeuvres since 1861. Attempts at modernization had concentrated on the artillery, which since 1863 had been entirely equipped with cannons with a rifled bore and of superior range to the Prussian cannons, 3 750 metres as against 3 500. More than 60 per cent of the Prussian army's cannons were of traditional design with smooth bores.

These choices reflected the tactical options taken by the Prussian and the imperial general staffs. The Austrian generals had failed to learn from the 1859 campaign and were convinced that victory could only be achieved by reckless bayonet attacks. The 1862 ruling on manoeuvres cost the Austrians thousands of men in 1866 when the Prussians wrought havoc upon them with rapid fire from their needleguns. The Prussian ruling of 1861 had endorsed the primacy of the rifle charged by the breachblock and the superiority of fire over frontal attack. The entire 1866 war and the Austrian defeat rested on the enactment of this idea. The imperial troops were decimated at Sadowa and were demoralized, the leaders more than the soldiers. But at the time when war was declared, the Austrians knew nothing of the Prussians' tactic.

The Prussian commanders were manifestly superior. General Helmut von Moltke was the architect of the victory even though the army commanders were Hohenzollern, the First army being commanded by prince Frederick Charles and the Second by the crown prince of Prussia, the future Frederick III. Moltke was an educated man, an admirer of Clausewitz, passionate about military history and had taken part in archaeological excavations in Anatolia in 1839. He became chief of the Prussian general staff in 1857. Whereas general von Roon, the minister for war in Bismarck's cabinet, increased the power of the army, Moltke was committed to raising the military knowledge of the officers of the general staff and the war academy in order to make them proficient assistants to the generals. After having inculcated in them how to deploy tactically the divisions and the army corps, he turned his attention to the conduct of the troops.

The problem of the Austrian army command was discussed at Vienna on 7 March under the presidency of general Kuhn, the minister of war. It was vital to re-establish this department in Schmerling's cabinet and to entrust it to an officer of liberal tendencies. Out of the 208 generals whom the imperial army then had, only two were kept as army commanders, general Benedek and the archduke Albert, son of the archduke Charles. A good soldier, the archduke Albert certainly did not have his father's genius. To put him in a position where he might be held responsible for a defeat was, however, too great a risk since any unpopularity might rebound on all the Habsburgs and prompt another revolution. For this reason, the archduke who planned an offensive and wanted to march on Berlin with the aid of his Saxon troops, found himself relegated to commanding the Southern army. Command of the Northern army went to Benedek on account of his popularity. He was a 'brave general', but incapable of manoeuvring great masses of men and he did not reckon on victory over the Prussians. He was, however, well-acquainted with the terrain of northern Italy where he had passed almost the whole of his career.

OPERATIONS[4]

There were four theatres of war: three areas of operations on land and one on sea, on the Adriatic where the still raw Italian navy tested itself against the Austrian imperial navy which, though it appeared modest, was very efficient. The Adriatic, Germany and Venetia were secondary theatres where the results had no bearing on the final outcome for it was the brief Bohemian campaign which decided the war, above all the decisive events of 3 July 1866.

In Germany, the Prussian Fourth army, 70 000 strong, was placed under general von Falkenstein whose mission was to neutralize the troops of the German Confederation. On 15 June, he invaded Hanover and on the 27th the Hanoverians surrendered. The Prussians invaded Hesse, then defeated the Bavarians at Bad Kissingen. The Fourth army achieved its objective without great difficulty.

The Italian army had in total 200 000 men who faced 140 000 Austrians of whom half were immobilized in the strongholds of the Quadrilateral.* On 24 June 1866, the First Italian army which numbered some 120 000 men, commanded by general La Marmora, the minister of war, was defeated at Custozza by the archduke Albert's Southern army. The soldiers did not know that whatever happened Venetia was lost for Austria and that in the emperor's mind they were fighting for honour. This tactical victory increased the army's prestige, raised morale in the Austrian camp and made it possible to send to Vienna reinforcements to cover the capital. This was no minor success, not least because the Italians had been rendered incapable of taking part in further combat.

Still more humiliating for the young kingdom was the naval disaster at Lissa,[5] which happened on 20 July following an attempt to land on the island of Lissa on the Dalmatian coast, 130 nautical miles east of Ancona. The Italian navy was the product of a hasty fusion five years earlier of the Neapolitan and Piedmontese fleets. The admirals had little knowledge and the commander-in-chief, count Carlo di Persano, already old, lacked any combative spirit, as did the captains. Persano had at his disposal excellent resources: besides seven steam frigates, of a very old design, he commanded twelve battleships, three of which were new – the *Re d'Italia*, the *Re di Portogallo*, 5 700 tonnes and built in the United States, and the *Affondatore* built in England and armed with turrets. All the battleships were equipped with a ram, a feature of Roman gallies which had been rediscovered during the war of the secession. The armour-plating of modern ships was vulnerable to attack from a ram which could scuttle an iron hull.

The imperial marine was, in theory, inferior to its adversary. It consisted of

---

* Translator's note: the Quadrilateral was the region of north Italy defended by the fortresses of Mantua, Verona, Peschiera and Legnano.

a flagship, the *Kaiser*, with ninety-two cannons, and five steam frigates. The two armoured frigates, the *Habsburg* and the *Ferdinand-Maximilian*, were both new but were still not provided with their permanent artillery. The Austrians had only seventy-four cannons with rifled barrels whereas the Italian navy had 200 modern guns. The Austrian commanders, however, were excellent. The officers had attended Danish naval college and the commander-in-chief, vice-admiral Tegetthoff, had shown his capabilities during the war of the duchies, at the Battle of Heligoland. At thirty-nine, Tegetthoff was an energetic sailor who was well-supported by the flag-captains and did not let himself be demoralized by the mediocrity of his resources for which he compensated with an offensive spirit in marked contrast to the hesitancy of the enemy.

It was some time before there was a naval engagement. The Battle of Lissa took place a month after the Italian defeat at Custoza and two weeks after the Battle of Sadowa. The Italian minister for the navy, the lawyer Depretis, gave the order for the fleet to disembark at Lissa to eliminate the disastrous psychological effect of Custoza and to give much more weight to Italy in the peace negotiations. Admiral Persano, however, committed a serious tactical error in attempting to disembark before having tried to neutralize Tegetthoff's squadron.

The Battle of Lissa took place on 20 July 1866 and was the second engagement with battleships in naval history. Persano positioned his battleships in line and left to one side a mixture of vessels entrusted to vice-admiral Vacca. Tegetthoff had no difficulty in cutting through the line, using a tactic favoured by Nelson. His ships rammed the enemy battleships. The *Ferdinand-Maximilian* scuttled the *Re d'Italia*, while the battleship *Palestro* was put out of combat. At midday, the Italian fleet disappeared. It was a great victory for the Austrian navy and both a tactical and a strategic success for disembarkation had not taken place. The Battle of Lissa had tremendous psychological impact and consoled the Austrians for their defeat in the face of Prussia. For forty years, sailors remained convinced that carrying rams was effective, so that all battleships until the advent of the English *Dreadnought* of 1906 were fitted with gigantic rams.

The victory at Lissa was, however, bittersweet, for it was the Battle of Sadowa that proved decisive in settling the German question to Austria's detriment.

THE BATTLE OF SADOWA (3 JULY 1866)

The Prussians had decided to concentrate their main effort in Bohemia. By 30 May, mobilization was complete and the Austrian army was gathered around Olomouc in northern Moravia with the intention of adopting the defensive strategy recommended by colonel Neuber.

On 15 June, the Prussians invaded Saxony and did not encounter any resistance as the Saxon army fell back to Bohemia, hotly pursued by the Prussians who were opposed only by covering troops. In the end Benedek decided to bring seven army corps to the Jung-Bunzlau-Münchengrätz line. The Austrian battle-plan had been betrayed to the Prussian general staff. From 26 to 29 June, the opponents faced each other in particularly bloody combat where the Austrians took the worst of it and their morale was much diminished. Benedek, in despair on the eve of battle, wanted to retire. Prince Frederick Charles with the First Prussian army then decided to attack the three Austrian army corps at Sadowa, but it was Moltke who took the main decision by ordering the prince royal's Second army to march on Sadowa to join the First army. This decision revealed the military genius of the chief of the Prussian general staff since it saved the First army from a decisive defeat, changing into a victory a situation which might have been disastrous if Moltke had agreed to prince Frederick Charles's battle-plan. The Second army, however, did not receive its marching orders until 5 a.m. and the First corps mobilized at 7 a.m. and the prince royal's army only reached Sadowa at midday. Without the energy of the commandants of the Prussian Guard, the initiative of the heads of division and the ardour which the officers were able to communicate to their men, the attack by Benedek's right flank would have taken place much later. Once again, the prince royal benefited from an error by Benedek who did not use his excellent cavalry to cover himself. He was taken by surprise when the Prussian Second army arrived in the middle of the day.

The first phase of the battle went in the favour of the Austrians who had occupied a triangle of 10 km opposite the First Prussian army. The latter attacked at 8 a.m., after the thick fog had lifted. The Seventh Prussian infantry division crossed the Bistrica but suffered heavy losses. Briefly isolated when four other infantry divisions were immobilized under Austrian artillery fire, it was only saved from annihilation in the afternoon through the intervention of the Guard which had just arrived at 2.30 p.m. At 3 p.m., the First army had only advanced 200 metres. The Austro-Saxon troops counter-attacked but at this point the battle was almost over when Chulmec was captured by guard divisions. The Second army's assault from the side was a success. Benedek was surprised by the rapid fire of the Prussian infantry and the completely unforeseen arrival of the enemy. The element of surprise and the needlegun decided the day. By 8 p.m., 20 000 of the Austrian army were out of combat and 150 of its cannons taken. Nevertheless, it fell back in order and the Prussian cavalry did not pursue. The Austrians used cover of darkness to beat a retreat. Benedek was unanimously held responsible for the defeat. Francis Joseph had lost the battle but it was open to question whether he had lost the war on 3 July. Nothing was yet decided in the days that followed, despite the crushing psychological effect of the defeat at Sadowa.

For all the panic aroused, it would be another three weeks before the Prussians reached Vienna. Two army corps were still at Olomouc and the archduke Albert led back the victorious Southern army to defend the capital. The conduct of the war had a political dimension and depended on the wishes of Francis Joseph, the response of Viennese and Hungarian public opinion and of Napoleon III, who for some days held in his hands the fate of Austria, Germany and Europe.

THE ATTITUDE OF THE FRENCH GOVERNMENT[6]

The French government was riven with differences. Napoleon III, as well-disposed as he was towards Prussia, was taken aback by Austria's defeat and, according to those Austrians and Prussians with whom he spoke, depressed and reticent. The empress Eugénie made energetic pleas for unconditional support for Austria since she now feared the military power which had been revealed at Sadowa. On 19 July 1866, she confided that the Prussians might invade France the next day without encountering any resistance; 'One night, we could go to bed French and wake up the following day Prussians.' She did not, however, manage to convince the government and Drouin de Lhuys who abandoned all resolve in his efforts to keep his post as minister of foreign affairs. Also, the Left in France was hostile to Austria and supported Italy. It was greatly influenced by prince Napoleon, Victor Emmanuel's son-in-law and head of the Italian lobby in Paris. The emperor, like the French army, was afraid to confront the Prussian army.

On 2 July, the day before the Battle of Sadowa, Francis Joseph had asked Napoleon III to secure an armistice in Italy and to sign immediately the treaty ceding Venetia and also requested French troops to occupy at once the fortresses of the Quadrilateral since the authorities in Vienna were afraid that the Italians might attack. On the evening of the battle, Mensdorff-Pouilly, the minister for foreign affairs in Belcredi's government, sent a telegram to Richard Metternich, telling him that Austria accepted French mediation and no longer requested armed intervention against Prussia. Austria thought that surrendering Venetia was a wise move which would pre-empt its having to sacrifice German territory. Napoleon III was less than enthusiastic and told count Fleury, 'We have won Venice for others and have lost the Rhineland'. Fleury replied, 'We have nothing at all to lose, Sir. On the contrary, it is now or never for us to redraw the map of Europe.'

On 7 July 1866, Metternich explained to the sovereign the alternatives facing the French government which was alarmed at the prospect of a war in both Germany and Italy. One course was for France to leave Prussia alone and yield to the charms of William I's diplomacy and the illusion of instant peace, an easy solution which before long would involve France in war with Germany. The other course was to ally immediately with Austria in order to stop Prussia and Italy, and to accept the threat of war. Napoleon III was in a state of complete prostration, weighed down by the wide range of his responsibilities and tried to keep trouble at bay by negotiating against Austria's interests. There would be a Great Prussia and on 9 July the fate of Europe was decided for a century. Napoleon III remarked to the Austrian ambassador, 'My dear prince. Be sure that for the moment it is indispensible for Austria to accept the terms of the armistice since only my mediation can lighten the losses it has suffered.'

Prussia demanded that the armistice be accompanied by preliminary peace negotiations since Moltke feared that the enemy might use the suspension of fighting to reassemble its forces and to try to rectify the situation. The essential condition for the armistice was Austria's leaving the Confederation, the other terms were not so important. Napoleon III was, in fact, ready to buy peace at any price and refused to intervene with arms which alone could have made an impression on Prussia. Despite the urgent approaches of Beust, who was still minister president of Saxony, Napoleon III, on 13 July, refused to concentrate 100 000 men on the Rhine. He agreed readily to the other conditions laid down by Prussia. The first condition was the integrity of Austrian territory, with the exception of Venetia which had already been ceded. This was contrary to the wishes of Prussian public opinion and of the king who wanted to annex the occupied lands, especially Bohemia which once again had been invaded. The second condition was Austria's payment to Prussia of a war indemnity of 20 million florins. French mediation was of some assistance to Austria with respect to these two clauses since Napoleon III had exerted his authority to curb Prussian appetites and had supported Bismarck who, more calculating than his master and mindful for the future, did not want to humiliate the Habsburgs. Napoleon III was sufficiently sensitive to territorial issues. He did, though, allow Prussia to annex 4 million inhabitants of north Germany on condition that it stop at the Main and let Bavaria constitute a South German Confederation, the issue that was to cause contention between France and Germany and the 1870 war.

On 13 July, Napoleon III told Beust that while undertaking to advise Austria to abandon its position in Germany, he had demanded that Austria's territorial integrity be maintained and that this request had been unopposed. With reference to federal reform, he had a free hand and the confidences with which the prince von Reuss, William I's personal envoy, had entrusted him gave him reason to hope for an arrangement which would not excite fears of exaggerated ambitions on the part of Prussia. Finally, Napoleon told him that he wanted to make it perfectly plain that he was not ready to wage war.

Prince Metternich was losing heart and on 17 July he advised the Austrian government to conclude an armistice, and the council of ministers which met on 19 July at Saint Cloud abandoned Francis Joseph to his fate. It is open to question as to whether the emperor could have continued the conflict alone.

AUSTRIAN IRRESOLUTION (JULY 1866)

The day after Sadowa, the mood in Vienna was dire. Trains full of wounded arrived daily at the Nord Bahnhof and the empress Elizabeth worked tirelessly in the military hospitals to bring comfort to the soldiers. Francis Joseph had become very unpopular and there were cries of 'Long live Maximilian', for a rumour was current that the emperor's liberal brother was returning from Mexico to replace him. Benedek's chivalry in taking upon himself the entire responsibility for the defeat deceived no-one and the public searched for someone to blame. It pointed its finger at the emperor who in the last councils of ministers had been won over to the opinion of the majority and ignored Mensdorff-Pouilly who suggested to him ways of gaining time, a policy of delaying tactics with a long record of success among the Habsburgs. The public accused the generals from the nobility, Clam-Gallas and others, of having led their men to slaughter. The liberal Germans made no secret of their admiration for Prussia.

From 10 July onwards, the Viennese expected a great battle outside their city and were seized by panic. The wealthy fled the capital as they had in the days of the Turkish menace, and accompanied the government, not to Linz or Passau as in the past, but to Budapest. On 9 July, the imperial family, with the exception of the archduchess Sophie, settled in the Hungarian capital. As the constitutional problem was still unresolved, there were fears that Bismarck might be engaged in intrigues with the Hungarians. He had revived the Klapka legion which Napoleon III had used in 1859 and a Hungarian rebellion was feared. For this reason, the empress suggested to Francis Joseph that he should receive Andrássy and appoint him minister for foreign affairs in place of Mensdorff-Pouilly and so win the immediate support of the Hungarian liberals. The meeting on 16 July achieved nothing because Francis Joseph was frightened of the idea of a constitutional regime. The mobilization of 100 000 Austrian reservists in the *Landsturm* was cancelled out of fear of insurrection. In the midst of all this agitation, Francis Joseph remained calm and took all the important decisions, his ministers simply carrying out orders.

The archduke Albert advocated organizing resistance in front of Vienna but Francis Joseph feared that a battle lost in the Wagram region would lead to the break-up of the monarchy. Despite what the empress thought, he did not envisage all-out war. On 21 July, when Napoleon III refused him armed mediation, he thought it preferable to request an armistice since the first Prussian divisions had reached Wagram, William I's army had occupied the whole of Bohemia and Moravia, and two corps of the army at Olomouc had fled to Hungary. The Austrian general staff seemed not to know that the enemy had been struck low by a cholera epidemic and was much weakened. Prussia did not have the funds to support a prolonged war. Militarily, nothing had been lost but Francis Joseph, pushed by Napoleon III, fell into the trap laid by Bismarck. He concluded a satisfactory peace after a straightforward defeat. Francis Joseph, for all his martial spirit, hated bloodshed and was not a fighting-man. It was rather lightly that he set the seal on the destiny of his House by agreeing to a treaty. The Habsburgs were no longer the arbiters in Germany and the monarchy no longer administered the land between Germany and Russia.

THE NIKOLSBURG ARMISTICE

On 27 July, the council of ministers ratified the armistice convention which was accompanied by peace negotiations. Since there had been much concern over the possible territorial demands which William I, who wanted to annex Bohemia, might make, there was a sense of having emerged well from the negotiations with no more than the conditions set out above, even if Prussia was left with much latitude to organize a North German Confederation and to annex territory. After long debate, the council preferred to ratify the agreement since to refuse would mean resuming hostilities and that was a turn of events no-one desired. In August, normal relations were resumed with the occupied territories and the Peace of Prague, signed on 13 August, confirmed the Nikolsburg negotiations. The council was preoccupied with quickly finding a war indemnity of 20 million florins which it covered by issuing bank notes to the value of 300 million florins. This concern had probably played no small part in the final decision to stop hostilities. Austria was no more in a position to sustain a long war than was Prussia.

Prussia gained on all sides. It received a war indemnity, annexed Hanover, Hesse-Kassel, Frankfurt, Schleswig and Holstein and organized a North German Confederation whose troops were all placed under the command of the king of Prussia. As Austria was excluded from Germany, Prussia now exercised hegemony. Did the schemes proposed to Napoleon III have any chance of being realized? Metternich had given his answer already, on 11 July: 'In two months, with Austria expelled from Germany, the German nation, united by the spirit of revolution, will be as one and will turn against France.' The war of 1870 was the logical consequence of the Austro-Prussian war and as the armies were unable to learn from Sadowa, Sedan was its continuation.

In the words of Wandruszka, 1866 was Francis Joseph's 'year of destiny'. It was the most serious setback of his reign which wrecked the policy pursued by the Habsburgs since 1700 when they had been obliged to renounce their dreams of universal monarchy. They had been driven from Italy and Germany, the cradle of their House, and their real *raison d'être*. They were left with Ferdinand I's patrimony, but he had busied himself with German affairs whereas Francis Joseph was excluded from them. To solve the Hungarian problem and to settle its constitution was all the more urgent. This would be achieved in the space of a year.

NOTES AND REFERENCES

1. Jean-Paul Bled, *Francis Joseph*, Oxford, 1992.
2. William A. Jenks, *Francis Joseph and the Italians, 1849–1859*, Charlottesville, 1978.
3. Horst Brettner-Messler (ed.), *Protokolle. VI Abteilung. Das Ministerium Belcredi*, part 2 (8.4.1866–6.2.1867), Vienna, 1973.
4. *Der Feldzug von 1866 in Deutschland*, compiled by the history section of the Prussian headquarters, Berlin, 1867.
5. A. E. Sokol, *The Imperial and Royal Austro-Hungarian Navy*, Annapolis, 1972, pp. 30–81.
6. Hermann Oncken, *Die Rheinpolitik Napoleons III von 1863 bis 1870*, 3 vols, Stuttgart, 1926.

CHAPTER FOURTEEN

The Austro-Hungarian Compromise (1867)

The Austro-Hungarian empire lasted half a century, from the Compromise of 1867 to the dissolution of Austria-Hungary in the autumn 1918. It was made up of Cisleithania and the kingdom of Hungary, officially 'the lands and kingdoms represented in the *Reichsrat*'. It was not known as the Austrian empire. It is easier to refer to it as the Danubian monarchy (*Donaumonarchie*), the term used today in Vienna, which shows that the state created in 1526 by the union of the kingdoms of Hungary and Bohemia and the German patrimony of the Habsburgs was essentially a confederation in which each land kept its originality and autonomy.

The Empire had not been created by military conquest but by voluntary union on the basis of contracts between the Czech and Hungarian nations and the Habsburg monarchy, the exceptions to this being Galicia which was annexed in 1772 and Bosnia-Hercegovina which was occupied in 1878. It was an empire because the sovereign was also head of the Holy Roman Empire and thought of himself as heir to the Roman emperors. In 1804, when Napoleon Bonaparte was crowned emperor, the Habsburg sovereign took the title of hereditary emperor of Austria while remaining head of the Holy Roman Empire. It was only in 1806 that he renounced the title of Holy Roman Emperor and formally pronounced the Holy Roman Empire dissolved. In 1815 he refused to restore it. It was only in the nineteenth century that there was an emperor of Austria and a centralized empire existed only for the brief phase of neo-absolutism which lasted from 1849 and the end of the war of Hungarian independence, to 1859 and the defeat at Solferino which drove the Habsburgs from Italy and forced them to reorganize the monarchy on a federal basis.[1]

The judicial foundations of the Empire were outside the Austro-Hungarian Compromise. The constitutional laws of 1860–61 were remodelled from 1868 to 1871 with the result that the Austro-Hungarian empire appeared to be a liberal and parliamentary regime.

THE DIPLOMA OF 1860

The diploma of 1860, the constitutional law passed to end the twelve-year-old neo-absolutist regime and to settle the nationalities question after the defeat at

Solferino, reinstated the old constitutions belonging to the different lands making up the monarchy. It was a major concession to state-right and to the conservative aristocracy, which remained strongly attached to local liberties and hostile to German centralism. The diploma gave legislative power to the old provincial Diets. The Hungarian Diet, which had been restored, obtained far greater extended powers than the other provincial assemblies.

THE COMPROMISE OF 1867[2]

After the brutal suppression of the war of independence, the Hungarians demanded the restoration of state autonomy, in return for which the moderates within the political class, whom the Bach system, the diploma of October 1860 and the patent of February 1861 had left dissatisfied, would renounce independence. The Compromise was an agreement between the House of Austria and the Hungarian nation. Francis Joseph agreed to be crowned at Pest and confirmed the existence of the bicameral Hungarian parliament which had been in operation since March 1848. The upper chamber was for the magnates and the lower chamber was elected by suffrage based on the property qualification. Francis Joseph recognized the parliamentary regime in Hungary and ministerial answerability before parliament. The nobility recovered the power it had lost in 1849 and the Hungarian state got back the provinces which long ago had been separated from it, Transylvania, Croatia and Slavonia. Hungary once again had its own army and customs barriers. It ceased to be a privileged province and became an autonomous state which, under Andrássy, would acquire a modern administration.

The Hungarians recognized that Hungary and Austria had interests in common. From now onwards there would be common ministries for foreign affairs, defence and finance and the officials within these ministeries were appointed by the emperor-king. The Hungarians found an important role in the army and diplomatic service. Parliamentary control was exercised by a delegation made up of representatives appointed by the parliaments in Vienna and Budapest. Each delegation was made up of sixty members, of whom twenty were elected by the upper chamber – in Austria the chamber of seigneurs, in Hungary that of magnates – and forty by the lower chamber. Every law would have to be passed by a majority within each delegation and obtain the sovereign's sanction. There was an annual meeting of the delegations which alternated between Vienna and Budapest, particularly to pass the budget for the common ministeries.

'Dualism' appeared very contrived to most western observers. It was, though, what was demanded by the most moderate Hungarian patriots, Deák and Andrássy, and was grounded in tradition.

THE MODERNIZATION OF THE AUSTRO-HUNGARIAN EMPIRE[3]

In Hungary, the Compromise signalled a return to the parliamentary regime established by the revolution of 1848 when the national assembly of the feudal period had been transformed into a parliament with the bicameral system intact.

The deputies of the lower chamber were no longer elected by assemblies drawn from the nobility of a county (*comitat*), but by suffrage based on the property qualification. The upper chamber of the magnates continued to be composed of members of the old aristocratic families. The ministry appointed by Francis Joseph and presided over by Andrássy was faced with a considerable task. It had to create an administrative apparatus to replace the old system of the noble *comitat* and to secure the passing of the education laws respecting the rights of the Slav and Romanian minorities and find a *modus vivendi* with the Croats who suddenly felt at the mercy of the Budapest government.

In 1868 Andrássy's cabinet reached a compromise based on Croatian state-right and ancient tradition. The Croats had the right to send to the Budapest parliament twenty-nine deputies elected by their sabor (diet) and they would be represented in the Hungarian government by a minister without portfolio. The ban (governor) of Croatia would be appointed by the Habsburg king on the recommendation of the president of the Hungarian council. Croatian would be the official language of the kingdom of Croatia-Slavonia in both the administration and the regiments of the territorial army. Dalmatia remained under the direct authority of Vienna, an arrangement which much later was the cause of contention between Vienna and the South Slavs.

The Austrian constitution of 1867, the 'constitutional laws of December 1867', an inevitable consequence of the Austro-Hungarian Compromise, was applied in the provinces of Austro-Hungary which were not part of the kingdom of Hungary. It was inspired by previous constitutional texts, the Kremsier constitution, the diploma of October 1860 and the patent of February 1861, and finally gave Austria a liberal regime. It declared equal rights for ethnic groups but it did not define clearly who the ethnic groups were, nor how they were recognized, with the consequence that there were untold difficulties in applying the legislation right until 1905. It was not clear whether nationality should be defined by the language used or by the free and willing declaration of the individual. Moreover, if the language used were to be the criterion, the question remained as to whether it should be the language of the district or of the province. The parliament at Vienna established by the patent of February 1861 was confirmed, but right until 1873 the deputies were nominated by the provincial Diets which had been re-established by the diploma of October 1860. The Germans were greatly favoured in comparison to the non-German nationalities in that they were given a system of four curias. The Slavs were discontented in the extreme by the 1867 constitution. In short, the parliamentary regime was established, but in a crisis the emperor could appoint a ministry and dissolve the parliament. This was sufficient for the German bureaucracy to regard the constitution and the Compromise in an ill light.

The question of universal suffrage remained unresolved in Cisleithania as in Hungary.

UNIVERSAL SUFFRAGE

In Cisleithania the right to vote was granted to the whole electorate in stages between 1867 and 1906. To begin with, electors were divided into four curias, one each for the great estate-owners, the towns, chambers of commerce and rural districts. This electorate represented only 60 per cent of the adult male population since only those paying at least 10 florins in direct tax were eligible to vote. In 1882 Taaffe's cabinet lowered the voting qualification from 10 to 5 florins and so enlarged the electoral body to include the petite bourgeoisie. In 1893 the conservatives defeated a projected law which would have made all adult male citizens electors in a fifth curia. It was Badeni's cabinet which passed this reform in 1897. All men aged twenty-four and over were registered in a general curia which elected 72 deputies out of 425. Francis Joseph supported universal suffrage which was adopted by Beck's cabinet in 1906. In 1918 the social democrats granted equal voting rights to women.

In Hungary, the question of universal suffrage was much more contentious since the nobility wanted to conserve the monopoly of power without sharing it with the working classes and the other nationalities. In 1905 the issue provoked a constitutional crisis and in 1913 István Tísza's liberals were forced to grant an electoral reform which increased the number of electors from 1 to 1.9 million. It was only in 1918 that universal suffrage was granted to the adult male population by Károlyi's government.

Despite appearances, Austria-Hungary remained what the Habsburg monarchy had always been, a state resting on the dynasty, the army, the bureaucracy and the Church. The system was really only welcomed by the Germans, with the exception of the pan-Germanist minority, the Polish nobility, a section of the Croats and the Hungarian ruling classes, which were still divided between supporters of the Compromise and the champions of total independence grouped around Kossuth's son. Relations between Vienna and Budapest were often difficult.

Having renounced all ambitions in Germany and Italy, Austria-Hungary found itself driven towards Eastern Europe. Joseph Redlich, the jurist and statesman, defined its vocation in 1914:

How could this empire where no-one had a feeling of empire, preserve its cohesion? How could it maintain itself given the present state of the administration, of domestic policy and diplomacy, the incapacity of the old sovereign, the personality and indescribably difficult position of the heir, the impossibility of the dualism of 1867, the hopeless quantity of problems on all sides, the eagerness of the masses over national, financial and political issues which expressed itself in the travesty of a parliament here [at Vienna] and at Budapest. None of this offers any hope of improvement. However, how and where could all the peoples, all these cultures, all these folk exist if not in this impossible Austria-Hungary which has brought and still brings German culture to the Slavs and Magyars. How is it possible to imagine a Hungary of independent Magyars following the creation of powerful states among the South Slavs? Where could the Czechs or the Poles find themselves better off than in Austria?

It was French pressure which had raised 'the Austrian question' before 1914. Austria-Hungary in August 1914 was still considered a true great power on the economic as well as the military level, but the linguistic diversity, the coexistence of the historic nations and the simple ethno-linguistic groups posed problems almost incomprehensible to the champions of the nation-state.

THE NATIONALITIES QUESTION[4]

The complexity of the situation is best understood by considering the nationalities question, that is the diversity of ethno-linguistic groups and the claims of the 'historic nations' which dominated the states forming the monarchy.

The term 'ethno-linguistic groups' is better than 'nationalities', especially when referring to those classified in the legal and political jargon of the nineteenth century as 'non-historic' for the simple reason that they did not enjoy state-right and had not formed the framework of a nation-state since the Middle Ages. The 1910 census based on citizens' voluntary declarations distinguished twelve groups. Two out of five inhabitants were German or Hungarian. The majority of the population was made up of minorities, 60 per cent in total.

A group was characterized less by an ethnic division, for assimilation and mixing were frequent, than by the originality of its culture and, especially since the sixteenth century, its written and spoken language. Ethno-linguistic groups had translations of the Bible, catechisms and collections of canticles in their own tongue as well as a diverse popular literature in the form of almanacs. The 'cultural re-awakenings' emphasized in historiography came later but these movements in the eighteenth and nineteenth centuries were incomprehensible without this continuity. Finally, the economic revolution of the nineteenth century favoured the rise of the national bourgeoisies and intellectuals. It was their rejection of the protection traditionally afforded by the nobles belonging to a historic nation that led to antagonism between the Slovaks and Hungarians in Upper Hungary and to enmity between the Ruthenians and Poles in Galicia.

The presence of these ethno-linguistic groups greatly complicated the traditional balance of relations between the central powers and the historic nations. Their claims after 1848 lent urgency to the nationalities question which constituted the major political problem for the monarchy from 1848 to 1919.

The geographical distribution of the different groups had its origins in the early Middle Ages and the situation existing in the tenth century had changed in only three respects. The Germans of the *Reich* had been forced by population growth to seek to colonize elsewhere and on a number of occasions they were called upon to populate or re-populate almost deserted regions. The most notable instances of German colonization were the Germans who had settled in Bohemia in the fourteenth century, the Saxons who settled in Transylvania in the thirtenth century and the Swabians in the Hungarian plain in the eighteenth century. In the fifteenth century, Romanians from Moldavia and Romania settled in Transylvania. The third important factor was the Turkish conquest in the sixteenth century which left the Hungarian plain devoid of men so that the Habsburgs could deliberately re-people it with Swabians, Serbs and Romanians and so dominate the Hungarian element. Thus a formerly Hungarian region was 'balkanized'.

Tables 1, 2 and 3, derived from the 1910 census, show the situation.

Table 1: Ethno-linguistic groups within the Austro-Hungarian empire in 1910, including Bosnia-Hercegovina

	Ethno-linguistic group	Percentage
	German-speaking	23.9
	Hungarian-speaking	20.2
	Czech-speaking	12.6
	Slovak-speaking	3.8
	Polish-speaking	10.0
Slavs: 47.2%	Ruthenian-speaking	7.9
	Slovene-speaking	2.6
	Croats (Catholic)	5.3
	Serbs (Orthodox)	3.8
	Bosnian Muslims	1.2
	Romanians	6.4
	Italians	2.0

Table 2: Distribution of population

Area	No.
Cisleithania	28 572 000
Hungary	20 000 000
Bosnia-Hercegovina	1 932 000
Total	51 390 000

STATE-RIGHT AND THE HISTORIC NATIONS

The 'historic nations' dominated the four states making up the monarchy with Galicia. The Austrian Germans thought of the Habsburgs as their natural masters and they alone showed true loyalty to the dynasty. They constituted the majority in all but the southern border-regions, the south Tyrol, Istria and the Trieste region, and they did not question their membership of the monarchy. They tended to think of themselves as masters of the empire which in the nineteenth century became increasingly Germanic. Vienna was a real melting-pot where immigrants from all over the empire became German.

The Czechs were the founding element within the kingdom of Bohemia. The presence of German colonies from the thirteenth century onwards and the Germanization of the ruling classes in the eighteenth century gave rise to rivalry between the Czechs and the Germans.

The Croats of the small kingdom of Croatia-Slavonia had accepted personal union with Hungary in the eleventh century and greatly mistrusted the government in Budapest.

The Hungarians, more than their neighbours, had managed to defend their

Table 3: Distribution of ethno-linguistic groups according to region in 1910 (%)

	Germans	Czechs	Slovenes	Serbs+Croats	Poles	Ruthenians	Italians	Romanians	Hungarians
Vienna	94.0	5.0							
Bohemia	36.8	63.2							
Moravia	27.6	71.7							
Silesia									
Lower Austria without Vienna	100.0								
Upper Austria	100.0								
Salzburg	100.0								
Tyrol	57.0						42.0		
Vorarlburg	100.0								
Styria	70.5		29.4						
Carinthia	78.6		21.2						
Carniola	5.3		94.4						
Istria Goritzia	3.7		32.6	20.7			43.0		
Trieste									
Dalmatia	0.5			96.2			2.8		
Galicia	1.0				58.6	40.2			
Bukovina	21.4					38.4		34.4	1.3
Hungary*	10.4			13.6		2.5		16.1	54.5
Transylvania	8.7					0.1		55.0	34.8
Croatia-Slavonia**	5.1			87.1					4.1

Notes:

* Slovaks made up 10.7 per cent of the population

** 62.5 per cent Croats, 24.6 per cent Serbs

Jews were not recorded as a separate group within the census. They represented 4.5 per cent of the population of Cisleithania (including Galicia) and 4.5 per cent of the lands of the crown of St Stephen. They made up 5–6 per cent of the population of Vienna and 23 per cent of the population of Budapest.

autonomy in the face of the Habsburgs, taking up arms in the seventeenth century and during the 1848–49 war of independence.

The Galician Poles had belonged to Austria since the partition of Poland in 1772. The Habsburg regime introduced reforms but progress was slow. In 1848 a measure of agrarian reform was imposed upon the nobility, and the Habsburgs for the first time depended on the support of the Ruthenian peasantry (Ukrainians). The Polish nobility in Vienna conducted a clever policy while supporting the demands of the Hungarians. After the 1867 Compromise, count Goluchowsky secured complete autonomy for Galicia and a far more extensive measure of liberty than that enjoyed by any other province in Cisleithania. It was the Galician deputies, the *Polenklub*, who enabled Francis Joseph to constitute the parliamentary majorities within the *Reichsrat* and the Poles played a large part in the political life of Cisleithania and in the external policy of the monarchy. Several Austrian chancellors were Poles. In return Polish was recognized as the only official language within Galicia and the Ruthenians were ignored by the government. The Ukrainian movement made slow progress and was stifled by the Poles and Germans of Austria.

The languages of all these nations had been recognized for a long time on the cultural as well as the administrative level. They had acquired the status of literary languages during the Renaissance and in the cases of German and Czech in the early Middle Ages and the fourteenth century respectively. German was not accepted as being pre-eminent. In the sixteenth century, Czech was the official language of the kingdom of Bohemia and it was the 1627 constitution which had imposed German as the second official language. The Hungarians maintained Latin right until 1842 when it was replaced by Hungarian. From the sixteenth century, the Hungarian domestic administration had used the national language alongside Latin to the exclusion of German.

State-right was the body of privileges which maintained a nation's independence in the face of the foreign dynasty. For a long time, the nation was identified with the orders. The feudal system which since the sixteenth century had grown increasingly burdensome, had turned the peasant masses into second-class citizens. The orders, the clergy, aristocracy, nobility and privileged towns were supposed to protect the interests of the whole population but this was far from being the case, especially where the population included different ethnolinguistic groups. After the 1867 Compromise, the question of nationalities took on four basic aspects in the Austro-Hungarian empire.

The non-historic nations did not possess any state-right and constituted non-native groups in Hungary and Austria. A number of these nations had kept a measure of cultural autonomy. Through their clergy and through primary education and as a result of the rise of a bourgeoisie in rural areas who depended on outside support, essentially from Russia or Romania, they gradually became aware of their own existence as nations.

After the successive waves of destruction brought by the Turkish wars, in the eighteenth century numerous non-native colonies, made up especially of Serbs, Romanians and Germans, settled in the Hungarian plain. The Habsburgs, sometimes out of liberalism in cultural matters and sometimes out of political cunning aimed at undermining the cohesion of the Hungarian nation, had not forced linguistic integration but had favoured the coexistence of different languages and national cultures. Following the 1867 Compromise, the Hungarians undertook to impose their national language and to Magyarize all the inhabitants of Hungary. This policy of assimilation was legitimate in itself for those who wanted to advance socially, but it was accompanied, particularly after 1880, by great abuses which coincided with the national awakenings of the non-historic nations. This would lead to conflicts with neighbouring states, with Serbia, Romania and Russia, which championed their protégés.

The Croats who were Catholic and loyal to the dynasty felt frustrated by the Compromise which the Hungarian state had imposed on them in 1868 and which placed them under the tutelage of Budapest. The Czechs were embittered by Francis Joseph's refusal in 1871 to be crowned in Prague as king of Bohemia. They came to the conclusion that the government in Vienna refused to restore the traditional federal structure of the monarchy because it was so greatly under the influence of the Bohemian Germans and the Hungarian aristocracy. They never forgave him for this error.

The Czechs and the Bohemian Germans had, in theory, the same rights but the numerically large German minority, which in 1910 accounted for 36.6 per cent of the population of Bohemia, refused to learn Czech. The Germans rather looked down on the Czechs, their language and culture at the very time the rising classes within the Czech nation were refusing to allow themselves to be Germanized, for in the eighteenth century Czech national consciousness had been weak. As a consequence, the national dream was linked to a social problem, as was the case with relations between the historic nations, the Germans, Hungarians, Czechs, Poles and Croats, and the non-historic nations.

The vicissitudes of the nationalities dispute between 1867 and 1914 in the Austro-Hungarian empire requires more detail than is here appropriate. In brief, in Hungary, the liberalism outlined by Ferenc Deák in 1868 was put into action hardly, if at all, and the government's chauvinist policy was an alibi for postponing vital agrarian reform. In 1914 the Hungarian government, still dominated by the nobility, refused to introduce universal suffrage and the secret ballot. The representation of minorities in the Budapest parliament did not reflect the numerical significance of the non-Hungarian population.

German–Czech rivalry had the most deplorable consequences for the political life of the Austrian part of the Empire. After 1871, the young-Czech opposition led by Rieger, then by Masaryk, became increasingly nationalistic without going so far as to seek secession. It provided the German national opposition with the excuse to disrupt sessions of the *Reichsrat*. In 1896 Francis Joseph again missed the opportunity to mollify the Czechs by not imposing with sufficient authority Badeni's decrees aimed at achieving complete equality between the Czechs and Germans in Bohemia. The Bohemian question remained one of the monarchy's great weaknesses until its disillusion in 1918.

The irredentist movements were the other great weakness at the beginning of the twentieth century.

THE IRREDENTIST MOVEMENTS

Some ethno-linguistic groups actively sought inclusion within nation-states outside the monarchy where their fellow nationals formed the majority. Irredentism was born out of Italian unification and chiefly affected Italians, Romanians, Serbs and some Sudeten Germans. The irredentist movements among these national groups all contributed to the break-up of Austria-Hungary.

The Italians in 1866 did not accept as permanent the exclusion of Trieste and the Trentin from their new kingdom and the Italian population of the Dalmatian littoral, of Julian Venetia and the south Tyrol still wanted to secede despite the formal alliance between the governments of Rome, Vienna and Berlin, the Triple Alliance of 1882–1914. Italy did not fulfil its obligations towards the central powers in 1914 and by the Treaty of London in 1915 was promised annexation of all the 'irredentist lands', including the predominantly Croatian Dalmatian littoral, before it entered on the side of the Entente.

The Romanians of the kingdom of Romania, formerly the principalities of Moldavia and Wallachia, continued to support the claims of the large Romanian minority in Transylvania where, in 1910, it accounted for 55 per cent of the total population. For the Romanian general public, Transylvania had the same emotional significance as Alsace-Lorraine then had for the French. The Romanians wanted Transylvania to be united with their kingdom. The ruling family in Romania, however, was Hohenzollern and so, out of fear of Russian imperialism, Romanian diplomacy showed itself no more antagonistic towards Austria-Hungary than did Rome and the Italians. It was only in 1916 that Romania entered the war on the side of the Entente.

Serbian ambitions to join Bosnia-Hercegovina to the kingdom of Serbia were at odds with 'the Yugoslav idea' which was then gaining ground among the discontented Croats. During the period before the war, hostility towards the monarchy, rather than rivalry between Serbs and Croats, increased even though the Belgrade government tried to maintain good relations with Vienna. Archduke Francis Ferdinand's assassin was armed by a patriotic Serb organization which saw the heir to the monarchy as posing a serious threat to Yugoslav independence.

Some pan-Germanists were dissatisfied with the Vienna government's benevolent policy towards the Czechs and dreamt of realizing German unification by joining the hereditary lands and the Sudeten lands to the *Reich*.

The system established in 1867 and maintained by Francis Joseph left all the different nationalities dissatisfied, with the exception of the Germans, the Polish nobility and, to an extent, the Hungarian nobility, which still preferred the status quo. All the other social and national groups, commencing with the social democrats who in 1914 represented a real political force, demanded, not the dismemberment of the Empire, but reforms which would either confirm the historic nations in their state-right or create a federal state. The conservatives championed the former and the social democrats the latter path of reform.

The emperor's opposition to change, which was respected but challenged even within his own family circle, was disastrous since a measure of bold reform would have satisfied those who were devoted to the idea of a large Danubian state. The sovereign, however, was convinced that it was better to leave everything as it was, since any remedy would be worse than the ill it set out to cure. Foreign observers such as E. Denis saw what they wanted to see and, mistaking troublesome events in political life for a deep crisis within the system, thought that Austria-Hungary was condemned to disappear.

THE CONSEQUENCES OF THE COMPROMISE

The Czechs and the old nobility had every reason to be dissatisfied with the Compromise since they had lost the most by this settlement. The Vienna government had recognized Hungarian state-right and reinstated an arrangement with a long historical precedent. The kingdom of Bohemia was, though, without question one of the constituent elements of the Austrian monarchy. The Battle of the White Mountain had led to its privileges being limited, not suppressed. Even Ferdinand the Benign had gone to Prague to be crowned and had regularly summoned the Bohemian Diet. In 1848 it had been Hungary, not Bohemia, which had seceded, but for all its loyalty Bohemia had been rewarded with incorporation within a unitary state, albeit one where the regime was tempered by a measure of decentralization. By the terms of the 1867 constitution, the Bohemian Diet did not, however, have the same powers as the parliament in Budapest. Palacký sensed the dangers posed by the Austro-Hungarian rapprochement and took issue with the idea of dualism in 1864 in an article in the journal Narod (Nation). The following year, in The Idea of the Austrian State,* he returned to Austro-Slavism and predicted that dualism would give rise to pan-Slavism and consequently to the monarchy's ruin.

Those who had negotiated the Compromise became firmly established in power in Vienna as in Budapest. In October 1866, Francis Joseph had appointed Beust, the minister president of Saxony, as chancellor of Austria, and replaced Belcredi whose cabinet had not survived the summer's defeats. Beust's appointment marked the liberal Germans' return to power and the establishment of liberals in the two capitals. Francis Joseph had chosen Andrássy as president of council within the restored Hungary. Although there was a liberal majority in the Budapest parliament, Andrássy, with the help of his friends Eötvös and Deák, formed a great ministry which created a modern administration in Hungary. He still had to fight against the opposition forces, the die-hard patriots loyal to Lajos Kossuth, and against the national minorities. His success was so swift and so effective that he played a decisive role in the European crisis of summer 1870 in which Francis Joseph, egged on by the archduke Albert and the regulars of the imperial army, briefly imagined taking revenge for Sadowa and entering into war against Prussia on the side of Napoleon III.[5]

Between 1866 and 1870 there was a Franco-Austrian rapprochement.

* Translator's note: Idea státu rakouského.

219

Napoleon III failed in his bids for territorial compensation and, hounded by the French liberal opposition, opened negotiations with Austria with the aim of preventing the south German states from being absorbed into a Great Prussia as a logical consequence of the Peace of Nikolsburg. He wanted to make up for the opportunity lost in July 1867 and, besides, the Austrian constitutional reforms were favourable towards an alliance with the French empire. Francis Joseph's coronation at Pest was reported warmly in the French press. The world of business was attracted by the markets in Danubian Europe and the Franco-Austrian trading agreement of 11 December 1866 spoke of developing exchanges with agrarian Austria; should the French harvest fail, Hungarian wheat would be imported. This rapprochement was made manifest in the meeting which took place at Salzburg when Napoleon III and Eugénie came to express their condolences following the emperor Maximilian's tragic death in Mexico. France proposed forming an offensive alliance against Prussia by the terms of which Austria would be free to deal with Germany as it chose so long as France could be certain of having the left bank of the Rhine. Beust, who was *a priori* in favour of rapprochement, thought simply in terms of a defensive alliance since the monarchy needed to build up its strength again (for two years there had been a plan to equip the army with needleguns). The governments at Vienna and Budapest as well as public opinion needed to be taken into consideration. The liberals would never agree to an offensive action against the North German Confederation and, besides, such action would alienate German sympathies towards the Habsburgs. In October 1867, Francis Joseph visited the Universal Exhibition in Paris. This was his only official visit to France and it marked the beginning of his popularity with the French which continued until 1914. The Parisians were attracted by his courtesy, elegance and refinement.

Nothing positive, however, was concluded between the two governments, although Napoleon III did everything he could to reach an accord. He obtained nothing more than an exchange of letters in which the two sovereigns acknowleged the 'community of interests' existing between Austria-Hungary and France (September 1869). At the beginning of 1870, he tried to give this entente a precise form but the agreement of the staff headquarters remained only at the planning stage because France did not want to commit itself against Russia and Austria-Hungary insisted on obtaining a guarantee from Italy since it did not want to have to fight a war on two fronts. The liberal Austrian press loosed its fury on France and wanted neutrality. The *Neue Freie Presse* went so far as to demand an Austro-Prussian alliance against the French. The French consul at Pest, Pierre de Castellane, summarized count Andrássy's position in five points:

i. it was impossible for Hungary to make war and, moreover, it would never do so on the side of Prussia

ii. an additional year of peace would be necessary for Hungary to organize itself

iii. it would not undertake engagements which could not be kept and all those which it had undertaken were very probably impossible to carry out

iv. there was a desire to reach an understanding with France
v. the Hungarian government's francophile tendencies should be kept secret until the elections.

It was a tactical withdrawal for the Hungarians but the French officials had not understood the subtlety of the Austrian game. They readily turned a blind eye to the realities in Vienna and Budapest and they imagined that the 1867 Compromise, by regenerating the monarchy, had eased the way for an alliance between France and the monarchy, whereas in fact it had done quite the opposite. Francis Joseph could no longer act alone as he had done until recently. The misunderstanding between France and Vienna had disastrous consequences when French public opinion, confident that it had the support of the imperial and royal army, forced war upon Bismarck in July 1870 without realizing that France was isolated.

The Austrian council of ministers meeting on 18 July 1870 settled the monarchy's position. Beust, Andrássy and Francis Joseph reached an agreement on the need to repair fortresses, remount the cavalry and partially mobilize the joint army which, after the 1868 reform, consisted of seven classes of reservists of almost 800 000 men. Austrian neutrality was provisional since Francis Joseph intended declaring war on Prussia. He believed that the destinies of Austria and France were interdependent and at the beginning of August 1870 he thought that 'a French defeat on the Rhine would be a greater misfortune for Austria than Königgrätz'.[6]

Francis Joseph had tremendous confidence in the French army which he had seen in operation ten years earlier, and the first defeats, that of Frossard at Spicheren and those of MacMahon in Alsace, came to him as an immense disappointment. These battles made neutrality the best position for Austria since it was out of the question for Austria-Hungary to risk suffering further defeats. Habsburg diplomacy had reached deadlock and Beust's strategy proved to be a failure in a totally unforeseen way, for no-one in Europe had imagined that the French army would be knocked out of the conquest so swiftly. Napoleon III's army appeared to be a match for the imperial Austrian army and it did not have the excuse of surprise which the army of the North had had in 1866. During the four years which had elapsed since the Bohemian campaign, the French government and military command had not drawn the lessons to be learnt from it, even though the Prussian headquarters had published an accurate and detailed description the year after the event.

The events of the summer of 1870 were the logical consequence of those of the summer of 1866 and marked a major turning-point in the history of Franco-Austrian relations and in the European balance of power. France and Austria-Hungary had a common enemy, Prussian imperialism, which the two great powers together were incapable of defeating. By refusing his armed intervention on 19 July 1866, Napoleon III had given Bismarck his chance to please the French Right and to satisfy the desire for revenge of his compatriots who, fired once more by Girondist ideology, wanted to recover the left bank of the Rhine. After the Compromise, Francis Joseph was no longer able to take such effective action and the chance to stop Prussia's advance was missed. Austria-Hungary was condemned to being a 'brilliant second' to the German empire which was formed on 18 January 1871 as a consequence of the French defeat.

All hope of revenge was now out of the question for the Habsburgs, all the more so since the Hungarian leaders were obsessed by the Russian menace and looked favourably upon the creation of the German empire which needed an alliance with Austro-Hungary in the face of the French 'revisionists'. Only the Hungarian Left, Kossuth's friends, protested against the annexation of Alsace-Lorraine.

Francis Joseph responded to this irreversible change by accepting the resignation of Beust, who had not accepted the defeat of 1866, and on 13 November 1871 appointed count Andrássy as minister for foreign affairs. It was the first time a Hungarian had occupied this post since Ferdinand I's accession and it was a sign that from now onwards the Hungarian political class would carry a great deal of weight in the government of the monarchy to the point where it prevented any internal change in order to defend its own interests.

Although 1870 marked an important change in German policy and in the monarchy's foreign policy, 1871 confirmed the impasse in domestic politics by raising the Czech question in an acute form.

On 7 February 1871, Francis Joseph dismissed Auersperg's cabinet and appointed count Hohenwart as president of the council. It was a conservative cabinet marking a break in the liberal era which lasted from 1867 to 1879. The new ministry was federalist in tendency and tried to find a compromise with the political forces in Bohemia, 'the historic nobility' and the Czech national party led by Palacký and his son-in-law Rieger. Two Czech academics accepted the portfolios of justice and public education. One of the essential tasks was to negotiate a historic compromise with the Bohemians similar to the Compromise between the Habsburgs and the Hungarians. If such a compromise were reached, the Bohemian deputies would cease to boycott the parliament in Vienna and the conservative cabinet would be assured of a comfortable majority. The historic nobility resolutely demanded recognition of state-right as the precondition for any agreement but Francis Joseph did not want to question the dualist structure and any arrangement would have to be within the framework of the 1867 Austrian constitution. The accord would be sealed by Francis Joseph's coronation at Prague, as king of Bohemia and the words of the coronation oath would be a contract between the Habsburg king and his Bohemian subjects, the German *regnicolae* and the Czechs.

There was little room to manoeuvre and the whole summer of 1871 passed in negotiating the fundamental articles while preparations were underway for the coronation celebrations. In the royal ordonnance of 14 September 1871, Francis Joseph recognized the state-right of Bohemia in a text which did full justice to the nation:

Considering the constitutional position of the crown of Bohemia, gauging the place it has assured to our ancestors as to ourselves, conscious of the unshakeable loyalty with which the Bohemian people have always supported our throne, we freely recognize the rights of the kingdom of Bohemia and this we are ready to affirm in our coronation oath.[7]

Unfortunately, the coronation did not take place because of the intransigence of both parties. The historic nobility raised their bid and demanded personal union, whereas the fundamental articles envisaged that the kingdom would simply regain its own executive led by a chancellor responsible before the Diet. The Habsburg king, though, could sanction the re-establishment of federalism only in Cisleithania. The fundamental articles were founded on a genuine and just compromise which caused deep disquiet among Hungarian politicians, the Bohemian Germans and Bismarck. For the Bohemian Germans, the re-establishment of state-right broke the direct ties which linked them with the Austrian Germans and protected them from the Czech majority within Bohemia. They risked losing the privileged position which they still had in the kingdom and which corresponded to that enjoyed by the Hungarian nobility in the lands of the crown of St Stephen. The Hungarian nobility feared that granting the fundamental articles would strengthen the claims of the Slavs, especially the Croats and Serbs. For this reason, Andrássy exerted all the influence he could. As for Beust, he showed Francis Joseph that strengthening the Slavs' political influence compromised the rapprochement between Austro-Hungary and the German empire which had been reached a month earlier during a meeting with William I at Ischl. There was a risk that Francis Joseph's actions would strengthen the German–Russian alliance and again leave the monarchy isolated since France, recently defeated, could not be relied upon as an ally.

The Crown Council of 20 October 1871 was a dark day in the history of the Habsburgs and the Czech people. Francis Joseph allowed himself to be swayed by the opposition and by Beust and Andrássy's arguments and signed a rescript which was unacceptable to the Bohemian Diet. The coronation was cancelled and Hohenwart's cabinet resigned. The blow was especially hard for the 'old Czech party' which supported the Compromise with the Habsburgs. Francis Joseph and his conservative ministers needed a strength of character which they did not possess. The moderate Czechs, of the tendency of Palacký and Rieger, clamoured to know what their place would be in the monarchy since they were denied the position which state-right had assigned them. By refusing to take risks, the sovereign showed that he was adhering to the line set out in 1867 and that he would respect the Austro-Hungarian Compromise as well as the Austrian constitution of the same year.

In this way, the Czech question was posed which poisoned Austrian political life until 1918. The Czechs were embittered by Francis Joseph's climbdown and by his refusal to be crowned king at Prague. Victims of a grave injustice, they drew the conclusion that the Vienna government was under the influence of the German liberals and the Hungarian nobility and would refuse to restore the monarchy's traditional federal structure. They never forgave this mistake which had ruined the chances for Austro-Slavism.

The negotiations which took place during the summer of 1871 were the last challenge to the monarchy's political structures until the emperor Charles I attempted reform at the end of the First World War. Francis Joseph, for the rest of his life, prided himself on the strict application of the terms of the 1867 Compromise.

Few undertakings were as controversial as the Austro-Hungarian Compromise. Many historians of Central Europe have seen it as containing the seeds of the end of the Habsburg monarchy since the Austrian Germans associated the Hungarians with power but more or less excluded the other historic nations.

In this author's opinion, the Compromise would have been no more threatening than any other constitutional arrangement provided that Francis Joseph had had the will and the intelligence to develop his ideas and to realize when necessary a compromise with the other historic nations, re-establishing the old federal structures of the monarchy which in the past had had real strengths, whatever the criticisms made of them by western observers. Count Belcredi's project of 1862 was entirely acceptable: to transform the monarchy into a 'heptarchy' associating the crown of Hungary, Bohemia, the South Slavs, Galicia, Venetia and Austria, i.e. the German-language parts of the hereditary lands. Francis Joseph yielded to German and Hungarian pressure in 1871 and obstinately refused to extend dualism. The Compromise of 1867 was only a partial and mongrel solution which still left the problem of the nationalities. It was a chronic malady which did much to bring about the monarchy's death in 1918.

NOTES AND REFERENCES

1. Jean Bérenger, 'L'Empire austro-hongrois', in Maurice Duverger (ed.), *Le Concept d'Empire*, Paris, 1980, pp. 311–32.
2. Louis Eisenmann, *Le Compromis austro-hongrois de 1867. Études sur le dualisme*, Paris, 1904.
3. Adam Wandruszka (ed.), *Die Habsburger Monarchie 1848–1918*, part II *Verwaltung und Rechtswesen*, Vienna, 1975.
4. Hugo Hantsch, *Die Nationalitätenfrage im alten Österreich*, Graz, 1951. Adam Wandruszka, ed., *Die Habsburger Monarchie 1848–1918*, part III, Vienna, 1980.
5. André Lorant, *Le Compromis austro-hongrois et l'opinion française*, Paris, 1967.
6. Istvan Dioszegi, *Der deutsch-französische Krieg und Österreich Ungarn*, Budapest, 1973.
7. Jean-Paul Bled, *Les fondements du Conservatisme autrichien, 1859–1879*, Paris, 1988.

CHAPTER FIFTEEN

Economic Expansion During the Reign of Francis Joseph

Francis Joseph's subjects in general, but especially the German bourgeoisie, had borne the rigours of neo-absolutism well and although economic growth had been modest, the monarchy was in a situation comparable to that of France under the authoritarian empire.

The American historian Komlos claims that the whole Austro-Bohemian complex experienced regular growth from the reign of Maria-Theresa to the First World War, with a period of recession during the Napoleonic Wars and after the 1873 stock-exchange crash.[1] The industrial expansion of the Biedermeier period, after a brief pause from 1847 to 1848, picked up again markedly and reached real growth during the period from 1867 to 1873. The wars of 1859 and 1866 had little effect on economic life and the rise of capitalism. The Compromise acted as a stimulant.

The 1867 Compromise favoured the development of Hungary, not only the traditional areas of agriculture and the agro-alimentary industries, but also the processing industries as a consequence of the re-establishment of customs barriers between Cisleithania and the lands of the crown of St Stephen. According to Komlos, Hungary even profited from the 1873 crash because Viennese investors were keen to place their capital in secure investments such as the bonds issued by the Hungarian authorities. The monarchy had been excluded from the *Zollverein* and represented a vast market of 40 million inhabitants which Cisleithania supplied with manufactured products and Hungary with food products. There were great regional differences within the monarchy between the poor regions, Galicia, Slovakia, Transylvania and the Bukovina, and the prosperous regions, Bohemia, Silesia, Moravia, the Vienna basin and the Hungarian Great Plain. As demographic growth was general throughout the monarchy, many thousands from the poor regions emigrated to the cities of the New World. In the United States, the Czechs, Slovaks, Poles and Jews could find a place for themselves within communities where they left behind the frustrations of their homeland.[2] Vienna, Budapest and the regional capitals experienced remarkable growth, even though the poor were crowded together in over-priced and unhealthy living conditions.

The history of Francis Joseph's reign and of Austria during his rule is more than a history of political combats, diplomatic and military defeats and, as it was portrayed in the French press of the period, the nationalities question. Economic and cultural development, even though it was accompanied by appalling inequalities, had a profound effect upon the collective mentality. For today's Viennese, as republican as they may be, their national past is represented by two sovereigns, Maria-Theresa and Francis Joseph. The harshness of neo-absolutism and the reactionary politics of Francis Joseph's reign have been conflated with an age of well-being, peace and the blossoming of culture which has become idealized through comparison with the catastrophes which have touched Danubian Europe in the twentieth century. Tapié has shown that while the nationalities question exercised the political classes, the journalists and some intellectuals at home and abroad, economic prosperity affected the whole population and had a profound effect upon the social structures and traditional equilibrium of a society which in 1850 was still predominantly rural. The industrialized regions, Bohemia, Lower Austria and Upper Silesia, strengthened their production capacity while the other regions, Budapest and some of the Hungarian counties, became industrialized. Through Trieste, the monarchy finally expanded into large-scale maritime trade.

Vienna rivalled the other great European capitals, London, Berlin, Paris and St Petersburg, but especially so after Francis Joseph gave orders for the old fortifications to be destroyed. By the imperial rescript of 25 December 1875, the emperor ordered the demolition of the old bastions encircling the capital. They were replaced by the famous Ringstrasse, the grand boulevard which symbolized Vienna before 1914. Until Francis Joseph's intervention, the town proper had been separated from the suburbs by a featureless expanse of ground which was used by the regiments in the garrison for manoeuvres and was often churned into a quagmire. The decision to undertake the project was reached after long discussions and was generally well-received. Work began immediately and after two months the first bastions were blown up. On 31 December 1858, the plans for rebuilding, the work of the architects Siccarsburg, Van der Nüll and Förster, were published. It was the latter, who came from Saxony, who had the idea of putting the Ring in the middle of the old glacis and so giving the new zone spacious proportions. The imperial administration completed a great property deal by selling the vast expanses of ground to capitalists who then built apartment blocks. The treasury received from this venture 220 million florins which was then spent on public buildings. The success of this prestigious project is explained by the progress made by the Austrian economy after 1849.

At this time, the monarchy acquired a network of railways radiating out from Vienna. From 300 km of line in 1849, the network grew to reach 4 000 km ten years later. The most spectacular achievement was the railway to the south, the Südbahn, which linked Vienna, via Graz, to the Adriatic and crossed the Alps through an impressive series of viaducts and tunnels. The Semmering line was finished in 1854 and was the first transalpine line, soon to be followed in 1867 by the Brenner line. In 1860 the Vienna–Linz–Salzburg line came into service and in 1882 extended to Zurich via Arlberg. Most of the railways belonged to the state which in 1896 created the ministry of railways. After the

1867 Compromise, Hungary also developed a rail network radiating around its capital. At the time of the Compromise, Hungary had no more than 4 700 km of line but by 1900 this had grown to 17 500 km and in 1914 the Hungarian network extended to 22 000 km of track. The Danube still served to link the monarchy together even though there was need for regulation, and the link betweeen the Danube and the Oder remained at the planning stage.

With the development of the railways, the neo-absolutist era experienced the mobilization of transferable capital. The Creditanstalt, the bank for trade and industry, was founded in 1855. It dealt especially with Austria and its administration included not only middle-class businessmen but also great estate-owners and members of the aristocracy, which inspired the public's confidence. The Rothschilds found themselves in competition with the Fürstenbergs, Auerspergs and Schwarzenbergs. These members of the nobility were following a time-honoured local tradition and had no reason to disdain participation in active economic life, all the more so as they were investing the capital they had gained from the peasants buying the seigneurial rights. After 1850 there was an alliance between the aristocracy by birth and the aristocracy by fortune whose power was manifest in the Bourse. The *nouveaux riches* appeared at a time when daring and entrepreneurial spirit enabled some individuals to make a fortune quickly. Merchants, bankers and industrialists felt obliged to build along the Ring, even though a square metre of land cost 100 florins at a time when a senior official earnt no more than 1 000 florins a year. Besides, the specifications were very exacting: the first building had to be complete within a year and the whole site of a concession had to be finished within four years. In return, the most illustrious businessmen were ennobled according to tradition, including the 'king of brick', Drasche, who supplied Vienna and Budapest with building materials and opened ten building sites on the Ringstrasse in his own name.

Vienna quickly changed its appearance in 1860 as it had after 1683. As well as the prestigious houses where apartments were let to the well-to-do, the Ringstrasse was also the site of public monuments and private mansions which, unlike those in the old city, were occupied, not by the aristocracy, but businessmen such as the bankers Wiener, Todesco and Königswarter. The latter was head of the Jewish community in Vienna and owned his own banking house as well as directing three railway companies and the Danube navigation company. Further along lived the industrialists Wertheim and Skene, who was one of the principal suppliers of the imperial army. The archdukes also settled along the Ring, including the emperor's youngest brother, Louis Victor, as well as such bona fide aristocrats as a prince Colloredo and a count Kinsky. Of the fifty-five buildings built by private individuals during the 1860s, two belonged to archdukes, seven to nobles, eight to members of the bourgeoisie and thirty-eight to representatives of the new monied aristocracy, bankers and industrialists. Some of these palaces have since been turned into hotels and others into administrative buildings. The Ring's monumental appearance was emphasized by the construction of public buildings, a barracks, the votive church and especially the opera house which was opened to the public in 1869 and was inspired by the Paris opera house. The neighbourhood of the Opera remained, until the First World War, the centre of social life.

Vienna was still more important from a social than a cultural point of view. It gave rise to a 'human type', 'the Austrian notable' who was often of Slav origin and had made his career in the administration, as a *Hofrat* (Aulic councillor), or in the army as a *Rittmeister* (captain of cavalry). Regardless of national origin, he had received a higher education in a law faculty or military academy, was partially Germanized and in the course of his career had been sent to all four corners of the empire. While acknowledging his ancestry, he felt first and foremost a servant of the state and of the dynasty. Ennoblement marked the end of a successful career, whether in finance, the army, or administration. Vienna, faithful to its old tradition, welcomed all foreigners, Jews and Germans from the *Reich* especially. This cosmopolitanism bore fruit in the city's rich contribution to science and to music. The surgeon Billroth was a Prussian, as was the composer Brahms, who came originally from Hamburg and received constant support from the formidable music critic, Hanslick. The Opera and the philharmonic orchestra helped make Vienna the European capital for music, even though Richard Wagner was given a bad reception. In the next generation, Gustav Mahler brought great glory to the Opera. After 1900, the music school in Budapest with the young composers Bártok and Kodály started to compete with the Viennese school where the young Schönberg struggled to gain a foothold.

The defeat at Sadowa did not affect the general level of prosperity or the construction of the Ringstrasse. The Viennese thought that politics were best left to the dynasty, the government and the army, and that it was for them to work and amuse themselves with the tunes of Johann Strauss. News of the Prussian victory in Bohemia did not stop them from crowding into the cafés and the Prater and 1867 was a record year. A bad harvest in the west forced France and north Germany to import large quantities of cereals and wheat became one of the principal articles of export from the monarchy thanks to the surplus from Hungarian agriculture. Before the arrival of American cereals, the Danubian plain served as the granary for industrial Europe. The Hungarian mills began by flooding the whole monarchy with flour, then neo-absolutism removed the customs barriers between Austria and Hungary and made the monarchy a single market. Hungarian cattle furnished meat for the industrial regions of Bohemia and Austria since the great noble estates, more than ever, were given over to producing marketable goods for export.

The most enterprising aristocrats applied for credit so that they could modernize their farming and so increase productivity. The 1848 legislation strictly applied enabled them to recover a share of the common and reclaimed lands which in many cases estate-owners had ceded to their peasants with precarious title. There was no shortage of manual labour for hire, even after the abolition of the *robot*. The Great Plain accordingly underwent an agricultural revolution which greatly benefited the large noble estate-owners. In Bohemia, the great landowners also embarked on large-scale farming, combining the production of cereals with beet, cattle-breeding and the sugar industry. The use of fertilizer and more complicated rotation made it possible to increase yield and the food industries, milling, brewing and sugar-refining, remained among the prime industries of the monarchy.

Economic growth was also apparent in industry, where considerable progress was made. Coal production made a particularly significant leap, growing from 800 000 tonnes in 1848 to almost 34 million in 1904. The main region of production was the Moravia-Silesia basin where the Rothschild and Gutmann banks invested. Even so, it was necessary to import German coal because the increase of operations in the Alpine lands was still insufficient, just 12 per cent of the total production, which constituted a drawback for the iron and steel industry. Styria was rich in good quality iron but lacked coke for metallurgy, whereas Bohemia which was better provided with coal had only a small seam of iron at Nurčič. The Thomas process, which facilitated the use of phosphorous minerals, was not adopted until 1879. The ironmasters used the Bessemer convertor from 1863 onwards and subsequently Styrian industry could compete because the Siemens blast-furnace made it possible to use the local lignite. These technical innovations were accompanied by financial restructuring. In 1868 the state ceded the old corporatist association of Innerberg to the Rothschilds and their Creditanstalt and in 1881 they concentrated all Styrian iron and steel in an incorporated Austro-Alpine metallurgical company which constituted the largest business in the Alpine lands. It specialized in steel production and in 1914 the Donawitz factories were the premier steelworks on the Continent.

Metal-working expanded in conjunction with the iron and steel industry. The Styrian cutlery industry exported two-thirds of its production of sickles and scythes and the state railways were equipped with Austrian rolling-stock. In 1860 the Prussian engineer Engerth invented a mountain engine which had four motor axles coupled, for use on the Semmering line. Workshops producing locomotives were established in Vienna (the Simmering and Florisdorf works), Graz, Wiener Neustadt, Prague (the Smicho works) and Budapest, and a factory for rails was established at Ternitz. Steyr, through Joseph Werndl, became the capital of light armaments. His company manufactured hunting guns and hand guns for the infantry. At Plzěn, Emil Škoda developed the largest arms manufactury in Central Europe, starting in 1886 to manufacture armour-plate. The small family-run forges which had been in decline since 1840 disappeared in the face of competition from capitalist companies. Only those that specialized survived, such as the factory at Krems belonging to the Wertheim family which specialized in manufacturing safes.

Austria acquired a leading position in the world market for porcelain with the most important manufacturing centres in the German regions of Bohemia. The monarchy exported ten times as much glassware as it imported. The factories at Jablonec produced mirrors, crystal, glassware for tables and chandeliers and the manufacturers worked closely with Viennese decorators. The glassworks in the Tyrol, Styria and Lower Austria continued to operate but chose to keep their registered offices in Vienna, which made it easier for them to compete with Bohemian manufactures. Viennese porcelain manufacture bowed before Czech production which benefited from the kaolin deposits at

Karlový Váry, and in 1865 even state manufacture gave in. Two-thirds of the total production were exported.

The paper industry modernized at the right time, using the raw materials supplied by the Alpine forests. The great factories faced a growing demand and increasingly replaced the traditional mills. Paper-paste and prepared products played an important role in the exports from the Alpine lands.

The textile industry adapted well to changes in the second half of the nineteenth century. Viennese silk manufacture lost ground after 1850 when customs barriers were lowered, but many firms settled in Bohemia and Moravia and were able to compete with foreign competition. Cloth manufacture had difficulties adapting but Austria became an exporter of high-quality fabrics. The wool industry underwent a noticeable change. Australian wool came increasingly to replace home-grown wool, while carded wool was abandoned in favour of combed wool. Some workshops continued in Carinthia but cloth manufacture was concentrated in Moravia. The cotton industry expanded most dramatically in Bohemia and the other principal centres in the Vorarlberg, the Linz and Saint-Pölten regions.

The rapid rise of these factories marked, as everywhere else in Europe, the decline of the craftsman. The old-style practitioners of these trades took refuge in a narrow conservatism, turning their backs on modern methods of production and sale, and producing goods of inferior quality. After 1890 they found an outlet for their discontent in anti-Semitism and the Christian social party whereas in many cases they should have blamed themselves. The problem posed by these self-employed craftsmen was not new and had been encountered two centuries earlier by the mercantilists. Some types of production were not suited to large-scale manufacture and for a long time Vienna kept a large number of small furniture, clothing and building businesses.

The period 1867–73 was characterized by particularly intense economic activity. Political uncertainties had been dispelled, although the crises of 1859 and 1866 had been resolved to the monarchy's detriment and the 1867 Compromise drew forth lively criticism at Prague, Vienna and Budapest. New businesses were started. In 1850 the monarchy had 35 incorporated companies but by 1867 this had risen to 154. In 1869 alone, 141 new companies were founded with an authorized capital of 517 million florins and in 1872, 376 companies mobilized capital of almost 2 billion florins. In the space of six years, 682 incorporated societies came into being, an average of around 114 a year.

The triumph of 'rampant' capitalism was accompanied by profound social changes. The bourgeoisie became increasingly rich and distant from the world of the working class which never ceased to grow. This period saw the birth of a true proleteriat drawn from the world of ruined craftsmen as much as from the peasants who had joined the rural exodus. The agrarian reforms of 1848–49 and demographic pressure made a reasonable life in the villages no longer possible and numerous young peasants went to the towns in search of work. At this stage, the national question was not a factor and migrations contributed to the intermixing of ethno-linguistic groups. Czechs from Bohemia looked for work in the industrial zones of the Sudetenland and Czechs from Moravia emigrated *en masse* to Vienna. Political questions were of little interest to the proleteriat whose lot was precarious and whose prime concern was securing work, wages and somewhere decent to live.

The workers' movement at this time was still weak. After 1869, social democrat groups appeared which managed to organize mass demonstrations and demanded universal suffrage as well as the right to form coalitions. They had close links with the German social democrats and rejected the nationalities question since all workers, regardless of origin, were subject to the same constraints in the workplace and the same economic conditions. In Bohemia, the perception was somewhat different among Czech workers who found themselves employed under German management.

The stock-exchange crisis of 1873 marked a break in economic expansion. Vienna had, that year, organized a universal exhibition like those in Paris and London. A wave of foolish speculation swept the city and prices tripled in a few months. Suddenly, on 9 May, the stock-exchange crashed and speculators and small depositors who had invested their savings in the hope of getting rich quickly, were ruined. Some firms went bankrupt, others had to lay off workers and all but a few had to lower wages when only a short while before, managers had agreed to raise them. It was not only the dubious financiers but all levels of society that were affected by bankruptcy. More than a thousand committed suicide and, although the exhibition was not cancelled, it was lifeless. The monarchy's vitality, however, was not extinguished and the market recovered after 1880.

It was at this time that the Ringstrasse was completed. Work was finished on the monumental *Rathaus*, standing on the field where manoeuvres used to be held, the parliament, the university and, opposite, the Hofburg theatre, the Viennese equivalent of the Parisian Comédie-Française. These mighty edifices were deliberately eclectic in style. The architects and developers could not be limited to the monumental style based on the baroque which had been used for the new Hofburg and at Berlin, but, imbued with a thoroughgoing historicism, adopted for each institution the style associated with its golden age. Thus the parliament building resembles a classical Greek monument, the *Rathaus* is Gothic in style, the university inspired by the Italian renaissance and the votive church is an imitation of a Gothic cathedral in northern France.

The other capitals of the empire, Budapest and Prague, were also transformed, as were the large provincial towns where gymnasia, barracks, townhalls and theatres were erected, and the great apartment blocks took on a monumental apearance characterized by their neo-classical architecture. The centres of these cities and towns were cut across by great avenues down which, after 1900, ran trams. Here lived the officials, officers and merchants while the suburbs were crowded with workshops and poor lodgings, a chaotic mass of low, dilapidated buildings served, if at all, by an inadequate rubbish collection service. The spectacular growth of Budapest deserves special comment. The two towns of Buda and Pest were joined in 1873 and the population rose from a combined total of 270 000 in 1870 to more than a million in 1914. Buda kept its aristocratic and residential character. It was dominated by the royal palace and the palaces of the nobility, some administrative buildings and numerous villas. Pest assumed the appearance of a nineteenth-century city with large buildings, boulevards, including its own version of the Ringstrasse, the Körut, the avenue Andrássy, theatres and, dominating it all, the parliament. This was rebuilt in 1896 by the architect Steindl and is both a copy of the palace of Westminster and a monument to the glory of Hungarian liberty in the face of the Habsburgs. For the Millenial Exhibition of 1896, Budapest acquired an urban railway, the first city on the Continent to do so. It was an electric tramway which circled under the avenue Andrássy. The Millenial Exhibition gave the world the opportunity to gauge the progress made by Hungary and its capital.

THE SITUATION IN 1913

On the eve of the First World War, Austria-Hungary was one of the great industrial powers of the world and was responsible for 6 per cent of Europe's total industrial production. It ranked fourth among the European industrial powers, coming after Britain, Germany and France, but was some little way ahead of Russia. It ranked third among coal producers and fifth among iron and textile manufacturers, having just been passed by the Russian empire.

It produced 2.7 million tonnes of steel, or 6.3 per cent of European production, but the 1873 crisis and the change in the direction of investment in favour of government bonds put it behind in the 'second industrial revolution'. The chemical and electric industries were far less developed than in the German empire. Even though the Ganz factories established at Györ made the most of the Kando patent and manufactured excellent trains, they could not rival the Siemens company. Like all the great industrial lands, Austria-Hungary produced its own rolling-stock adapted to the constraints of uneven tracks and given a style of its own by the great engineers who worked on it. There was no question of buying locomotives from Britain. The motor industry began in the workshops of Johann Puch in Steyr where there had been a metal-working industry since the Middle Ages, and Daimler installed a motor-car factory at Wiener Neustadt.

The principal weakness of the Austro-Hungarian economy was its continued dependence on foreign capital. Foreign investments rose to 10 billion crown, of which 60 per cent came from Germany and 30 per cent from France. This was why Vienna's role as the great financial centre of Danubian Europe was an illusion. Despite the existence of the stock-exchange founded during Maria-Theresa's reign, the market essentially ran on foreign capital. Austria-Hungary could not aspire to being a dominant economic power like Britain and France.

There were great disparities among the different regions. Industrialization had advanced without making any noticeable difference to the distribution of economic activity. Hungary's share of the total quantity of exports did not change between 1880 and 1913, remaining constant at 38 per cent, with

Cisleithania responsible for the remaining 62 per cent. The degree of industrialization remained proportionately the same: the Czech lands 36 per cent, Lower Austria and the Alpine lands 40 per cent and Hungary 18 per cent, although during the period the latter's total horsepower rose from 10 000 to 300 000. Despite the 1867 Compromise and the unquestionable growth which resulted, the contrast between the Austro-Bohemian lands and Hungary remained consistent with the long-established tradition: the hereditary lands, Austria and Bohemia, had industries, whereas Hungary remained an agricultural land in the process of industrialization.

The advances made by Hungarian agriculture were plain to see. The production of wheat tripled between 1973 and 1913, rising from 1.3 to 4.1 million tonnes, while that of oats rose from 0.55 to 1.25 million tonnes in 1913 and maize production quadrupled, rising from 1.15 million tonnes in 1873 to 4.2 million tonnes in 1913. The annual harvest of barley and rye almost doubled. The most spectacular increases were evident in the potato crop which rose from 0.85 to 5.15 million tonnes and the sugar-beet crop, which grew exponentially from 0.24 million tonnes to 3.8 million tonnes on the eve of the war. This was proof that the great estates adopted more complex systems of crop rotation and chemical fertilizers. Cereal production, however, lost its importance in relation to the benefits from stock-rearing. The customs tariffs raised from 1906 onwards guaranteed almost a monopoly for Hungarian agricultural produce within the expanding market of the dual monarchy. The conflict with Serbia and the retaliatory measures taken against the kingdom benefited the farmers on the Great Plain and substantially increased their profits.

Heavy industry was concentrated on the northern fringe of the monarchy. After 1880 the main centre for cast-iron moved northwards to the centres of coal production and to be closer to the mines of German Silesia. In 1913 the Moravska Ostrava basin produced 2.5 million tonnes of coke for the metallurgical industry. There was no real combination of coal and steel as there was in Britain and Germany. The Styrian mines supplied 64 per cent of the iron used and 30 per cent was imported from Hungary and Sweden, and later, Algeria and Spain. In 1868 the Alpine lands were responsible for 57 per cent of the total cast-iron production but by 1913 their share had dropped to 40 per cent. Meanwhile, Bohemian and Moravian cast-iron increased its share of the total production from 42 per cent in 1868 to 60 per cent in 1913.

From 1880 onwards, industrial activity was concentrated in the coal basins but this pattern of development declined after 1900 with the advance of electric power. The mechanical engineering industries grouped together at Steyr (the centre for weapons manufacture for the imperial army), Vienna and its suburbs, Prague (where the Skoda factories founded in 1868 employed 6 000), Brno and Trieste. Coal production increased by 40 per cent between 1848 and 1914 but was insufficient to satisfy demand and was balanced by the production of Bohemian lignite at Most, Teplice and Chomutov. The secondary industries in these regions provided employment for more than 15 per cent of the active population, accounting for 2.5 million workers in Cisleithania and 3.5 million industrial workers within the whole monarchy. The pattern of industrialization within Cisleithania in 1913 was very uneven. Galicia and the Bukovina were essentially still agricultural lands, even more so than numerous Hungarian counties.

The progress made by Hungarian industry was, in relative terms, quite dramatic. The traditional industries, flour-milling and textiles, tended to decline while heavy industry made a leap forwards. Coal production rose from 6.2 million tonnes in 1874 to 13 million tonnes in 1913 and the metallurgical industries were in full expansion, the three principal centres being the island of Csepel in Budapest, Győr and Miskolc.

Half the active population in 1913 still derived its living from agriculture and the great estates were still growing. There were 6 000 estate-owners with more than 500 hectares who held between them 40 per cent of the land, while some 2.5 million smallholders had only 30 per cent with the result that most landholdings were too small for a family to live off. Smallholders, though, considered themselves considerably better-off than the agricultural labourers who were badly paid and subject to endemic unemployment and who in 1914 made up the greater part of the Hungarian proleteriat. It was they who posed the real social question and caused disquiet among the wealthy and the authorities. In 1898 the government forbade strikes by agricultural labourers after the violent agrarian unrest of 1891, 1892 and 1897 which had raised so much fear among the small landowners. The agricultural proleteriat, as uncontrolled and potentially disruptive as it was, posed more of a threat than any organized political force. The electoral law had carefully excluded them from any consultations of the electorate and they were without the right to vote.

THE POPULATION

One of the great strengths of Austria-Hungary in 1914 was its large population. In 1900 it had 47 million inhabitants and by 1910 this had risen to 51.4 million, an increase accounted for in part by the annexation in 1908 of Bosnia-Hercegovina. On the eve of the First World War, Austria-Hungary had a much larger population than France. The population density in Cisleithania was 95 inhabitants per square kilometre. In forty years, the population of the monarchy had grown by 35 per cent, more so in Cisleithania than Hungary where the low level of industrial development had forced many landless peasants to emigrate for good to the United States.

The German portion of the population was numerically weak. In the 1910 census, it represented just 24 per cent of the total population even though German-speakers constituted the ruling class. Three-quarters of the ministerial bureaucracy were German at a time when there were as many Slav students as there were German, 18 000 in both groups in 1913. At the level of secondary education, 38 per cent of German pupils attended high schools and 65 per cent business schools. The Germans still had economic superiority since they paid 65 per cent of direct taxes. They also enjoyed a cultural hegemony which was evident in the press and publishing. On the eve of the First World War in

Cisleithania there were 2 190 newspapers and periodicals in German and 1 630 Slav publications.

This German hegemony was in part counterbalanced by the large measure of decentralization and the Empire's great capacity to assimilate; anyone who wanted a career in the army or in administration would have to accept Germanization, at least in Cisleithania. The position of the Hungarian ruling class in Hungary was just as precarious since it represented only 55 per cent of the population of the lands of the crown of St Stephen and only 20 per cent of the monarchy as a whole. The Slav element had an absolute majority but it was made up of different nations and was really a heterogeneous population. Even the South Slavs (the Slovenes, Serbs and Croats) represented no more than 12 per cent of the whole, no more than the Czechs.

Despite the regional differences and undeniably archaic features of life in Galicia and Hungary, the economy and population continued to grow, giving proof of the healthy situation within the monarchy on the eve of the First World War. This was expressed in the linking-up with the gold standard and the creation of a new unit of currency, the crown, which was worth half the traditional florin. It was worth almost the same as the gold-mark or 1.20 francs. The good health of the economy is explained above all by the range of the internal market. Cisleithania exported its industrial products to Germany and Hungary, and a small quantity to Western Europe, and in the Balkans it experienced fierce competition from Germany. For Hungary, the system of protective customs made the Austrian market a virtual monopoly for its food products and also benefited the development of fledgling industries. The excellent rail network radiating out from Vienna and Budapest favoured trade.

The economy was rich with potential opportunities as long as the unity of the monarchy remained unbroken. It could, perhaps, have expanded into a vast Central European market which would have united Germany and Austria-Hungary. The German allies, who appealed to this idea at the beginning of the First World War, rejected the idea of a *Mitteleuropa* as imagined by F. List and advocated by prince Schwarzenberg. It remained to be seen whether this thriving economy would be sufficiently powerful and well-structured to turn itself into a war economy. The First World War would show that the economy of Austria-Hungary was less capable than the other great powers of supporting the strain of a long war.

NOTES AND REFERENCES

1. John Komlos, 'The process of industrialisation in Austria: a longrun view', *Etudes danubiennnes*, 2, 1988, pp. 167–74.
2. John Komlos, *Die Habsburgermonarchie als Zollunion: die Wirtschaftsentwicklung Österreich-Ungarns im 19 Jahrhundert*, Vienna, 1986.

CHAPTER SIXTEEN

Political Life from 1867 to 1914

The constitutional framework set out in the 1867 Compromise became final by will of the sovereign, the Hungarians and, secondarily, the Austrian Germans. Cisleithania, though, still remained without a constitution for the organic laws of 1860 and 1861 had been suspended since 1865, much to general approval. On 21 December 1867, new laws were sanctioned and it was these 'December laws' which continued to serve as the Austrian constitution until the end of the monarchy. The laws recognized the Compromise and organized national representation in two chambers based on the Hungarian and, more generally, the western model. The upper chamber, the *Herrenhaus* (house of lords), where members of the aristocracy appointed by the emperor sat, served as a debating chamber. The lower chamber, the *Reichsrat* (imperial chamber), was filled by deputies elected by suffrage on the basis of the property qualification. A further law confirmed the fundamental rights of a citizen to equality before the law, freedom of conscience and the right to property. Article 19 of this law recognized the complete equality of all ethno-linguistic groups and the right to free practice of one's mother tongue.

Whether this was indeed a parliamentary regime, as was now the case at Budapest, has been the subject of much discussion. Article 14 of the patent of February 1861, which had authorized the emperor to rule without his ministers having the express confidence of the *Reichsrat*, was abrogated by the December laws. A final clause of the 1867 laws, however, made the army and diplomacy the sole responsibility of the emperor and so instituted a 'private domain' which for Francis Joseph was a fundamental guarantee in keeping with the monarchy's tradition. In practice, though, Francis Joseph was not inclined to rule against the wishes of the Vienna and Budapest cabinets.

Cisleithania was not governed entirely by a parliamentary system. The Austrian cabinet was answerable first and foremost to the emperor, who appointed the ministers and the *Ministerpräsident* (president of the council), and it also needed a majority in the *Reichsrat*. If the cabinet did not have the parliament's trust, it could still operate and govern by article 14 which had been enacted in anticipation of any occasion of *force majeure*. Francis Joseph continued to appoint as deputies to the *Reichsrat* 'technical' ministers, drawn from high public office, in preference to politicians.

Francis Joseph recognized the monarchy's fragility and that it needed institutions capable of facing up to the centrifugal forces within it, represented by the Slav and pan-Germanist nationalist parties. The conservatives, liberals and Polish aristocrats were loyal collaborators.

THE LIBERAL ERA (1867–79)

Apart from the short-lived conservative Hohenwart-Schaeffle cabinet in 1871, the liberal majority in the *Reichsrat* dominated political life in the period following the Compromise. Francis Joseph collaborated loyally with the liberals, all the more so since they were wedded to centralism and espoused other values dear to the emperor.

In January 1868, he appointed a cabinet led by Karl Auersperg which promptly set about abolishing the main part of the dispositions of the 1855 Concordat, much to the despair of the nuncio Falcinelli who could not stop the emperor authorizing civil marriage and sanctioning the new laws on schooling. Control of civil status and of schools again passed into the hands of the state and the Church was driven back to its position during the *Vormärz*.[1]

The new Austrian legislation established eight years of compulsory, secular elementary education and teaching the catechism was entrusted to priests in local schools. Pius IX condemned these 'abominable laws', all the more so when the Hungarian parliament voted similar legislation with the blessing of the primate Simor and the whole Hungarian episcopate.

Auersperg's cabinet granted the Galician Poles a small measure of liberty at the time Russian Poland lost all autonomy as punishment for the 1863 insurrection. The universities of Kraków and L'vov were to have only Polish professors and the academy at Kraków was free to pursue its own independent line of historical research. This policy of openness and the support given to Catholicism made the Poles loyal supporters of the Habsburgs to the monarchy's very end.

As president of the Hungarian council, Andrássy accomplished a great deal for his country. The Compromise recognized the constitution of April 1848 which established a true parliamentary regime even though executive power was divided between the crown and a cabinet answerable to the king, Francis Joseph, and parliament. As was the tradition, the parliament was bicameral, consisting of a chamber for the magnates made up of hereditary peers and bishops, and a chamber of deputies elected by suffrage based on the property qualification.

Faithful to the ideal of the founding fathers, in 1868 the Andrássy cabinet introduced liberal legislation which, however, was only imperfectly applied. The 'nationalities law' of 1868 recognized the primacy of Hungarian as the language of state but offered many possibilities to the other languages which could be used, as was traditional, at the local level, in the administration and in primary schools. Hungarian remained the language of instruction in secondary schools and universities where the tradition of Latinity remained strong and theses were still defended in the language of Cicero. At secondary level, Romanian, Slovak and German were taught for only a few hours a week. All social advancement in Hungary depended on Magyarization, just as in Cisleithania the elites were Germanized.

The Croats, the only historic nation incorporated within the kingdom of Hungary, received in 1868 a 'compromise' which was modelled on the Hungarian Compromise and is sometimes referred to as the Hungarian-Croat Accord.* The Croatian sabor sat in Zagreb and debated in Croatian, which was the language of administration, the railways and education. In principle, Croatia enjoyed a large measure of autonomy since only the ban was appointed by the council of ministers in Budapest where a minister without portfolio was charged with protecting Croatian interests. The Croats wanted Dalmatia to be reincorporated into their kingdom. Following the Treaty of Campo-Formio in 1797, Dalmatia had been attached to Austria and, like the Military Frontier in Slavonia, was still part of Cisleithania. Croatian state-right was recognized in principle but the legislation of 1868 was applied in a restricted way.

Hungary and Cisleithania did not have a ministry for foreign affairs since this role devolved upon a minister of state appointed by the emperor. The ministers for common finances and the minister for war charged with administering the common army were also appointed by the emperor and an Austrian and a Hungarian minister for war ran the two territorial armies, the *Landwehr* in Cisleithania and the *Honvéd* in Hungary. To begin with, these armies were of little importance but they grew once the reserves became important in the plans for mobilization. The imperial and royal army, where German remained the language of command, was reorganized in 1868 on the Prussian model and remained a tremendous cohesive force for the whole monarchy as was Francis Joseph's wish. It was financed by a common budget which was administered by the common finance ministry. The contribution was fixed at 30 per cent for Hungary and 70 per cent for Cisleithania according to the long-standing tradition whereby the Hungarian contribution to overall military expenditure was proportionately markedly small. The ratio of 70 per cent to 30 per cent could be renegotiated every ten years, as could the customs rates between the two parts of the monarchy. The budget for operations, essentially military expenses, was voted each year by the 'delegations', the 'deaf and dumb' common parliament where each part of the monarchy was represented in strictly equal manner. To respect the equality between the two parts of the monarchy, the delegations met alternately in Vienna and Budapest for the annual session which was usually very brief on account of their limited jurisdiction.

The common ministeries based in Vienna had a quota of Hungarian officials. In 1914, 56 per cent of high officials were German and 44 per cent Hungarian, and Hungarian aristocrats readily occupied ambassadorial posts.

Karl Auersperg's cabinet was toppled by the question of electoral reform.

---

* Translator's note: in histories of Croatia, the Accord is known as the *Ugodba*.

Francis Joseph appointed count Alfred Potocki as president of the council in April 1870. Acting on the 1868 laws, Potocki made a straightforward denunciation of the 1855 Concordat at the time when relations with the Vatican were deteriorating. The emperor and the episcopate, especially cardinal Rauscher, were unhappy about accepting the doctrine of papal infallibility which had been adopted in 1870 at the first Vatican Council. The pretext used for the denunciation was that as the nature of the partners in the Concordat had changed, the contractual agreement had become null and void. Francis Joseph gave his approval to this position in the Crown Council of 30 August 1870. The Habsburgs regained their liberty and returned to the tradition of Maria-Theresa's day. The sovereign and many of his subjects' solid devotion to Catholicism spared the monarchy the kind of *Kulturkampf* waged in the German empire.

Potocki's government did not reach a compromise with the Bohemian opposition and in February 1871 the emperor summoned to power the Hohenwart-Schaeffle cabinet. This, in turn, failed in its principal task of reaching an agreement with the Bohemian opposition represented by the historic nobility and the 'old Czech' party.

The defeat of the Hohenwart cabinet and the consolidation of the 1867 Compromise returned the liberals to power. Francis Joseph appointed prince Adolph Auersperg who, like his brother, was a liberal. The minister for the interior was baron Lasser, for public education, doctor Stremayer, for justice, doctor Gaser, for war, baron Horst and for trade, Banhans. The liberals remained in power for eight years until 1879 when, after failing to gain a majority in the elections, they were replaced by the conservatives.

The Auersperg ministry had passed an electoral reform by which the imperial council ceased to be merely a manifestation of the Diets and was composed of deputies elected in the four curias. The elections of 1873 confirmed the falling away of support for the liberals who had hoped to strengthen their hold through the new electoral law. Instead, the federalist conservatives consolidated their position. From this point onwards, the liberals went into a long slow decline which was assisted by the stock-exchange crash on 9 May 1873. 'Black Thursday' caused the crash of several industrial and banking firms which had been founded rather too hastily during the years of prosperity, and the resulting scandal affected a number of liberal politicians who were members of the boards of directors of these firms. Some small depositors were ruined by the crash and the philosophy of free enterprise suffered a severe blow. The crash favoured the propaganda peddled by the social democrats and various Catholic and anti-Semitic groups. Reactionary circles within the government and army cheerfully contemplated the collapse of the government and the return to authoritarian power. That suffrage was based on the property qualification meant that the shock was absorbed by the time of the elections to the imperial council. The general election, however, was ruined.

The 1879 elections put an end to the liberal era. The liberals gained a derisory majority in the imperial council with 172 seats as against the conservatives' 168. As the Bohemian deputies continued to boycott the Vienna parliament, Francis Joseph entrusted power to count Taaffe who enjoyed the support of the Hohenwart club, the Polish club and the Bohemian deputies belonging to the national party and to the historic nobility. Taaffe maintained power for fifteen years. The emperor distanced himself from the liberals who had greatly annoyed him by refusing to take a risk in Bosnia-Hercegovina, caution which was later proved quite justified. The liberals thought that for the time being there were enough Slavs in the monarchy. Francis Joseph, however, thought that it was his right to follow the foreign policy of his own choosing and that the Austrian cabinet had overstepped the mark. Count Andrássy, who was still minister for foreign affairs, had received the emperor's approval, happy at the prospect of enlarging the empire after the successive defeats in his foreign policy.

THE HUNGARIAN LIBERALS IN POWER

After the Compromise, administrative reform occupied the middle ground between the tradition of the autonomous county and centralization, with the latter directed in favour of the Hungarian national government, now answerable to parliament rather than the authorities in Vienna who were traditionally regarded as foreigners. The prefect was appointed by the government in Budapest, but by the law of 1870 the counties lived on with their own elected dignitaries. The judiciary was separated from the departmental administration and was given a code for civil procedure, magistrates appointed by the government and an independent public prosecutor's department.

Confessional policy was marked, as in Cisleithania, by a break with the spirit of the Concordat. The exercise of the *placetum regium* was re-established and confessional matters were taken away from the ministry for religion. The emancipation of the Jews which had been rejected by the Diet during the reform era, was established by law. In 1868 primary education from the age of six to twelve was declared compulsory. Civil status and judgement in matrimonial affairs were entrusted to the different churches.

The liberal party suffered a setback from the loss of its great leaders. Andrássy was promoted to the Balhausplatz and was no longer occupied with Hungarian internal policy. The great minister Eötvös had died before he could supervise the implementation of the education laws of 1868. Deák was disheartened by the prevailing atmosphere of conservatism and corruption within his entourage. He retired from public life and remained steadfast in his withdrawal. He died suddenly in 1876.

The liberal party was hampered by the obligations imposed upon it by the Compromise, obligations which the general public regarded as insufficient. In the general elections of 1869, they lost sixty votes. Andrássy's successor as president of the council was Lonyay, the former minister for the common finances, who was authoritarian, stiff and lacking in character. He was content to draw support from the conservative aristocracy and proved to have little sympathy for the nationalities. He announced the dissolution of the Croatian sabor and the synod of the Serbian orthodox church, but he failed in his plans for an electoral law which would have reduced the electoral body once more to a narrow basis. He used the administration to put pressure on the electors and to win the elections in 1872. Accused of corruption, he resigned and handed power to count Kálmán Tísza, the new strongman in Hungary.

Following the 1872 elections, there was a movement towards a rapprochement between the liberal party which had signed the Compromise, and the independence party made up of the liberals and radicals who had never accepted it. For three years, Tísza sustained the government and 'transitional' liberal cabinets. The 1873 crash affected the Budapest liberals as much as those in Vienna. A loan of 150 million florins had to be taken out on unfavourable terms with the Rothschild bank. This enabled the state to avoid bankruptcy but it cost the government the last of its already compromised prestige. Tísza only accepted the merger after the vote of a restrictive electoral law. At the beginning of 1875, he judged that the moment had come to join with the liberal party which was on its last legs. A few months later, Tísza became president of the council. Although some elements rejected the merger, the new party possessed an enlarged electoral base. The policy of compromise was consolidated within the country while any hope of change or constitutional reform was postponed for the distant future.

THE CABINET OF KÁLMÁN TÍSZA (1875-90)

Tísza remained in power for fifteen years. He came from the Calvinist gentry and was a sly politician, clever at manipulating parliament, rather than a charismatic leader animated by strong ideals. He was the man of the moment, suited to consolidating the power of the Hungarian ruling class within the constitutional framework. He was endowed with undeniable political flair, subtlety and intuition. He was a liberal, anxious to maintain legal forms, and despite his indifference to the minorities he possessed the qualities necessary to govern for a long time during a period of calm when conflicts remained latent.

Tísza managed to solve the main problems by legal means, even though the electorate remained extremely small in relation to the number of potential electors who were excluded from polling stations and greatly under-represented in the parliament at Budapest. The right to vote was enjoyed by no more than 6 per cent of the population; because of the high property qualification, it was denied to the poor peasants, the workers, part of the petite bourgeoisie, clerks and servants. Even so, the guarantees offered by this rigorous selection process were insufficient to guard against the whims of the opposition drawn from the peasant proprietors, middle-classes and bourgeois members of the minorities. The electoral wards were drawn up with great care. In the non-Hungarian regions, the number of deputies was far smaller than elsewhere. Voting in the country continued to be in public. Promises, bribes and threats enabled the government party machine to win free elections. The full arsenal of tricks was used and, as in the twentieth century, Hungary experienced serious abuses.

Tísza was equally clever at manipulating his parliamentary majority, the disciplined and grateful members of which were dubbed 'the Mamelukes'. The liberal party was led by the great estate-owners who proved solicitous for the impoverished minor nobility, the gentry. Tísza found them posts in the public administration. The bourgeoisie, in many cases of German or Jewish origin, competed for economic power which during this period of economic expansion was considerable. It was dependent upon the aristocracy.

It is debatable as to whether Tísza's government was truly liberal, for it had succeeded in basing its power on a single party which was virtually irremovable. He had strengthened centralization by enlarging the powers of prefects and the administrative commissions over which they presided to the detriment of the departments' autonomy. In 1881, while pretending to modernize, he took control of the authorities charged with public order. He did away with the pandours who were obsolete, and replaced them with gendarmes who recalled the gendarmes of the absolutist era and had extensive powers in the countryside. In 1882 the police were reorganized in the capital which had only officially existed as Budapest since 1873 when Buda, Obuda (Old Buda), and Pest were united.

A new penal code was passed in 1878 which punished severely those spreading socialist and nationalist propaganda or taking part in a strike. In 1870 servants were placed under the 'tutelage' of their master who had the right to use corporal punishment against them, a practice which was widespread among the bourgeoisie.

The treatment meted out to the nationalities was likewise hardly liberal. Many Slovak secondary schools were closed between 1875 and 1876 and the Slovak cultural association Matica slovenska was suppressed. The Serbian deputy Svetozar Miletic was arrested. In 1879, the 1868 law on public education was modified. Instruction in Hungarian was made obligatory in all primary and training colleges, including those in Slav and Romanian districts. Every teacher had to know sufficient Hungarian to be able to teach it. Instruction in Hungarian was extended to the secondary schools and in 1891 it was made obligatory even in nursery schools. This was far from the policy of respect for minority languages which until 1840 had allowed the different ethnic groups to live together harmoniously in the kingdom of Hungary. The cultural policy of the baroque age was discarded in favour of the policy of integration after the French model.

The close surveillance by the police was oppressive and weighed especially heavily on the workers' movement, which after 1875 grew steadily with the help of the movement in Cisleithania. In 1876 Leo Frankel, the former commissar of the Paris Commune, returned to Hungary and infiltrated the mutual aid associations to create a socialist party. In 1878, with permission from the police, he founded the Party of Disenfranchised Citizens which in 1880 changed into a United Hungarian Workers Party (*Magyarországi általános munkáspárt*), which the police regarded with mistrust since its programme was Marxist in inspiration. Frankel was arrested and sentenced to eighteen months in prison. He left leadership of the party to the employees of the mutual aid associations and followed the path into exile.

The liberals' governmental apparatus functioned smoothly throughout the 1880s. The conservative opposition in 1875 formed an autonomous party and in 1881 named itself the Moderate Opposition Party. It professed its roots to be in the 1867 Compromise, did not publicly espouse any precise programme and rallied to the aristocracy's defence. Its members proved open to the anti-liberal currents coming from Austria and Germany. On the left, the national opposition was divided between many tendencies and did not come together until 1884 when the Party of Independence and of 1848 was formed, which drew its support from across the social classes, from the minor peasantry as much as from the landowners and members of the liberal professions. It wanted the democratic programme of 1848 to be applied and the Compromise to be turned into the straightforward personal union of Austria and Hungary. There were numerous currents within the party since the right wing was as close to the liberals as to champions of outright independence of the stamp of Daniel Iranyi and Károly Eötvös. Lajos Mocsary, who favoured openness with respect to the nationalities, was excluded from the party. Although the independence party enjoyed a large following among the masses, unlike the radical socialists in France, it did not have any social programme and was part of a large consensus in Hungary which supported the 1867 Compromise. With its goal of strengthening domination over Cisleithania no less than over the nationalities, it was a common platform for all shades of opposition and for the government party. Tactics might vary but the goal remained the same. For this reason, the imperial and royal army which was common to the whole monarchy and loyal to the dynasty was utterly alien to Hungary, and the numerous Hungarians who served in it with such skill and devotion were a permanent embarrassment to the cause of Hungarian nationalism. It had been the emperor's express wish that saved the joint army. Francis Joseph saw it as the means of ensuring the monarchy's survival and he had made it a *sine qua non* of the Compromise. While the liberal governments developed the *Honvéd* (territorial army), the joint army represented a permanent outrage to Hungarian national sentiment. German as the language of command, the respect for vernacular languages within each regiment, which took the French military attachés by surprise, the Hungarophobe sentiments of many of the officers and their ignorance of Hungarian traditions gave rise to many points of friction. In 1888 the pressure of public opinion forced Tísza to contemplate an overhaul of the army. The army legislation presented to parliament was intended to modernize recruitment and also to impose German on officers in the reserve. The debate that followed unleashed nationalist agitation in the streets as well as in parliament. The fray within parliament wore away Tísza's authority and his skill at handling parliament proved unequal to the task. He called up strong characters, was joined by Sándor Wekerle as minister of finance, then in March 1890 resigned.

His government did not fall prey to parliamentary manoeuvring but rather was confronted by yet more serious political and social problems. The development of industry, the continuation of the system of great estates, the impoverishment of the gentry and the growth of an industrial and agricultural proleteriat raised urgent social and political questions. In 1892 Francis Joseph entrusted power to Sándor Werkele, a champion of reforms. He was the only president of the Hungarian council before 1918 whose origins were bourgeoise. The need for such an energetic and intelligent man was great since during the 1880s Hungary, like Cisleithania, was experiencing the emergence of new political forces.

THE NEW POLITICAL FORCES

The liberals and conservatives, the traditional parties stemming from the 1848 revolution, and the national parties in Cisleithania and the independence party in Hungary found themselves having to reckon with new political forces: a social democratic party and in Austria, a Christian social party and a pan-Germanist movement. The pan-Germanist programme was in favour of a *Grossdeutschland* which would challenge the very existence of the monarchy and incorporate the Austrian and Bohemian Germans within a national state under Prussian direction.

The Young Czechs probably gave more cause for alarm than the other national parties in Cisleithania.[2] The National-Liberal Party (*Narodni strana svobodomyslna*) dominated Bohemian political life from its foundation in 1874 until 1914. It was a classic nineteenth-century liberal party, strengthening the links between anticlericalism, liberalism and Czech nationalism. It trained and moulded the men who in 1918 realized Czechoslovak independence. Its relations were somewhat tempestuous with the Czech national party, the Old Czechs led by Rieger, Palacký's son-in-law, which became the government party and supported Taaffe's cabinet. The difference between the two parties was similar to that between the independence party and the liberal party in Hungary; in both cases, tactical divergences obscured deep underlying agreement over long-term goals. Both Czech national parties wanted to advance their compatriots' material and intellectual well-being and to secure complete autonomy for Bohemia, Moravia and Austrian Silesia, while rebuilding the kingdom of Bohemia within the framework of the monarchy. These goals overrode all pan-Slavist tendencies, although the Czech patriots recognized that the nation's progress was linked to the emancipation of the other Slav peoples within the monarchy. Francophile and Russophile, they did not receive any assistance from the governments in Paris and St Petersburg. They thought of themselves as representing the whole nation, although the electoral colleges which elected them had a very narrow basis because suffrage was based on the property qualification. Their authority rested mainly in the local and provincial institutions which they controlled.

The Young Czechs were rather more anticlerical and nationalist than the Old Czechs. It was from among the urban upper middle class, the great landowners and Prague intellectuals, that the Old Czechs drew their support, whereas the Young Czechs attracted voters from the more modest social levels from among the traders, prosperous farmers and schoolteachers. A difference in tactics led to schism in 1874 when the Young Czechs favoured a policy of open opposition to the German liberals in the Vienna government while the Old Czechs took refuge in passive resistance, boycotting the *Reichsrat* and allying with the federalist and conservative historic nobility. The two parties joined forces once more in 1879 and collaborated with the Taaffe cabinet until 1887 when the government's conservative measures provoked differences between them. The elections of 1891 sanctioned the erosion of the Old Czechs' influence. The Young Czechs tried to represent the national interests of the whole of Bohemia while the people's party attempted to end the Old Czechs' hegemony in Moravia. The failure of the Badeni cabinet in 1897 and of the Thun cabinet in 1899 brought the moderate wing of the Young Czechs into disrepute. The introduction of universal suffrage reduced their audience to the benefit of the popular parties but in 1914 with their leader Karél Kramar they still represented the interests of the Czech upper middle class. Western historiography too often presents caricatures of the Young Czechs as radicals when they were in fact pragmatic lawyers who tried to realize their goals within the framework of the constitution, as did their Hungarian counterparts.

All these parties were deeply wedded to suffrage based on the property qualification. They did not address the working classes and ignored their specific problems with the result that the workers rapidly turned to socialism.

The first workers' associations were more influenced by the ideas of Lassalls than Marx. In 1869 they organized a meeting at Wiener Neustadt and sent a number of delegates to the congress at Eisenach. After a dramatic demonstration, in 1870 they received the right to form a coalition and, in Cisleithania, the right to strike. The workers' movements soon split into a moderate tendency and a radical tendency, Marxist in inspiration. This schism lasted until the Hainfeld congress in 1888 when Victor Adler brought the workers' movement together, after which the social democratic party became a force in the political game. The extension of the right to vote in 1893 enabled it to strengthen its position in the industrial lands of Lower Austria, Styria, Bohemia and Moravia. It accepted the theses of Marxism and was strongly influenced by Kautsky.

The Pressburg Congress of autumn 1889 gave a fresh impulse to the Hungarian workers' party. In the presence of Victor Adler, a new leadership was elected which decided to resume agitation and 1 May 1890 was celebrated by 60 000 workers in Hungary. At the end of the year, the workers' party was reorganized to become the Hungarian social democratic party, distinct from the Austrian social democratic party. It adopted the Hainfeld programme and made a similar declaration of principle; the final goal was the common ownership of the means of production and the emancipation of the working class. It also demanded universal suffrage and wanted to develop unions, especially in the countryside. The leadership headed by Paul Engelmann encouraged agitation among agricultural labourers and in June 1891 there were bloody confrontations between striking day labourers and the forces of law and order. In 1892 the moderate elements within the party responsible for the mutual aid associations, pursued a new direction, excluded Engelmann and provoked schism within the social democratic party. Although the party came together in 1894 under the leadership of Ignacs Silberberg, it remained deeply divided and seriously weakened. This crisis, though, had forced it to consider the agrarian problem in Hungary as well as in general.

The 1894 congress adopted an agrarian programme and, departing from Marxist tenets, proposed the socialization of the great estates. It made it clear that social democracy could not save the peasantry, condemned in theory to pauperization, and the idea of sharing out the land was abandoned. This programme, which was in accordance with the Second International, did not, however, coincide with the desires of the mass of peasants.

The Austrian social democratic party was internationalist in tendency and added its voice to the nationalities question. The socialists in principle defended class rather than national interests. At the Brno congress in 1889, there was approval for the proposition that nationalism was a means for the bourgeoisie to defend class interests and obscure the real problems. Marx and Engels were convinced that it was for the German working class to lead the way and that the Slavs presented a serious obstacle to the rise of social democracy. Otto Bauer made no secret of his view that German was the expression of a higher culture and should be the unifying language of the monarchy. His work of 1907 on the nationalities question was a celebration of German culture.[3] He believed that the best solution for the working class would be the break-up of the monarchy, but he confined this idea to his correspondence with Kautsky.

Each nationality in Cisleithania set up its own social democratic party, contrary to the unitary thinking of the party leadership. The Brno congress had called for universal suffrage as the best way of hastening reform and had stressed the desirability of preserving a unitary state in the best interests of the workers' movement. It especially wanted the maintenance of a vast unified economic space. The working class would take part in political life and demand a radical transformation of the state on a federal basis. Each nationality would enjoy a large measure of political and cultural autonomy while retaining German as the language of communication.

Karl Renner, the future chancellor of the Austrian republic, put forward the theory of national autonomy for the individual, tied to the person not to the territory. The state would be divided into different national territories corresponding to the historic lands. Each *Land* would be home on average to two or three nationalities, and in the towns national communities would be formed. Every inhabitant would be included in a *Kataster* (land register), in which he would be free to declare the nationality of his choice. He would elect his representatives and for cultural affairs the monarchy would be a federation of communities while common economic and military concerns would be the responsibility of a unitary state.

The Austrian social democrats were able to appear objective allies of the Habsburgs as long as the Habsburgs followed a policy of openness, bypassing any obstacles raised by the German liberals.

Social democracy became a representative political force, as in the German empire, once universal suffrage was introduced. In the 1897 elections it received only fifteen mandates for the *Reichsrat* but was considerably more successful in the elections of 1907, winning eighty-seven mandates and in 1911 it lost the elections only because the Czech social democrats split away. Social democracy in Germany appeared, by contrast, much more successful where it carried considerable weight within the Berlin *Reichsrat*, but industrialization in Austria was far less developed and the petite bourgeoisie, like the peasantry, was attracted to the Christian social party of Karl Lueger.

THE CHRISTIAN SOCIAL PHENOMENON

Rarely has a political group gone under so misleading a name. It was anything but social in the social democratic sense. Christian too was a misnomer since its success was due in no small part to anti-Semitism, which it fostered, fanning the age-old rancour of the Austrian lower classes, egged on by the Church and traditional abhorrence of the 'Deicide'.

It was a Catholic party fundamentally opposed to the liberals and the recent changes in Austrian society. In 1900 it replaced the conservative party which until then had been favoured by the Catholic hierarchy. It formed a true populist party in the Alpine regions whereas Lueger's Christian social movement in Vienna and Lower Austria attracted popular forces hostile to liberalism and progress.

Lueger was a demagogue who could speak to the artisans and lower middle-class of Vienna, who were victims of the 1873 crash, the economic crisis and the decline of the artisan class in the face of large-scale industry. He based his agitation on anti-Semitism. Many of the upper classes who inhabited the Ringstrasse, the bankers and industrialists, were of Jewish origin and it was not difficult to convince the embittered victims of economic transformation that the Jews were to blame. As 'bosses', Jewish managers attracted the opprobrium of their Christian employees. Lueger found it easy to arouse 'the old demon' and to make himself the champion of the *kleiner Mann*.

The movement had its beginnings in 1875 in the Catholic circle of baron Vogelsang to which Lueger belonged. The baron brought together groups of Catholics and alerted them to social problems, poverty and the crisis in housing. This circle of 'united Christians' was the foremost movement opposed to the liberals and their *laissez-faire* philosophy. In 1888 Lueger transformed this elitist movement into a popular party which would compete with the social democrats and oust the liberals while attracting conservative Catholic votes. He won the support of the nuncio in Vienna and of pope Leo XIII as well as the 'benevolent neutrality' of some government quarters. However, his violent criticisms alienated military circles, high church dignitaries and the emperor. Franz Joseph did not like Lueger and his demagogy fired with hatred. Leopold Kunschak, a fellow-traveller, went recruiting in popular circles. The extension of suffrage benefited the Christian socials who became an important political force in Cisleithania.

Lueger with some difficulty became mayor of Vienna in 1897 and accomplished valuable work bringing gas, electricity and the tramways under the city's control. The system of curias worked to the Christian socials' disadvantage and in the general elections of the same year they secured only six mandates. In 1907, though, they obtained almost 100 and in 1911, 74 mandates.

In the years before the First World War, the Christian socials and Christian democrats showed their strength in the elections and in parliament, even though they did not take direct part in government since count Stürgkh's cabinet which lasted from 1911 to 1918 enjoyed the support of national groups and of the conservatives.

Social democracy made a break-through in Hungary where industrialization had brought about the development of the working class. In 1880 Leo Frankel, a refugee from the Paris commune, created a workers' party and spread its message through its newspaper *Népsava* (Voice of the People). The party quickly fell apart but was reorganized in December 1890 and called itself the social democratic party. The movement grew in size after 1900 and the number of strikes increased. The general strikes and the riots in Budapest in May 1912 made the government aware of social questions, but the system of suffrage based on the property qualification prevented the social democrats from obtaining seats in the parliament. In 1907 Giesswein founded a Christian social party directed towards social issues but it never came to play the same role in Hungarian life as the Christian socials did in Austria since the general public was preoccupied with national questions.

THE NATIONALITIES QUESTION

In Cisleithania, the most serious problem was the conflict between the Germans and Czechs in Bohemia. In 1882, ten years after the abandonment of trialism, Taaffe enacted measures greatly in the Czechs' favour. The whole administration was made bilingual, even in those cantons where the majority was German-speaking. As the Germans refused to learn Czech and most Czechs were practically bilingual once they had received some instruction, the decree opened a way into the administration for thousands of lower middle-class Slavs. The German-speakers became increasingly defensive, but it was the Young Czechs who caused the failure of the 1890 negotiations which would have made the administration of Bohemia entirely bilingual. In 1897, when count Badeni took steps which were tantamount to requiring German officials to know Czech, he precipitated a crisis for the regime since the president of the council had reached an agreement with the Czechs without consulting the Germans of Bohemia. The parliament in Vienna was the scene of indescribable uproar while 'German nationals' stirred up riots in the city as well as in Eger, Prague and even Graz. Francis Joseph lost his nerve, dismissed Badeni and formed a government under Gautsch who governed according to article 14 while the parliament remained provisionally closed after the stormy sessions of the autumn 1896. Until the end of the monarchy, the central government abstained from any move towards applying article 19 of the constitution. A compromise was reached in 1905 in Moravia whereby everyone declared to which group he belonged and the old constituencies based on geography were replaced by constituencies based on ethnicity. The results of this agreement were good and in 1913 were adapted to fit circumstances in the Bukovina. As a system, it was close to the principal of 'personal autonomy' espoused by the socialists Karl Renner and Otto Bauer whose theoretical writings made a great contribution to the Leninist exposition of the principle of nationalities.

The Galician Poles adapted very well to the conditions of internal autonomy granted to them in 1868. The Croats and Serbs of Dalmatia, governed directly from Vienna, demanded that their language enjoy parity with Italian and wanted the province of Fiume (Rijeka) to be joined to the kingdom of Croatia. It was, however, for the government in Budapest that the national question posed the most difficulties.

In Croatia, despite the 1868 Accord, agitation began again in 1873 with the formation of a party advocating the union of all the South Slavs within a 'Yugoslavia' which would be linked to the monarchy. The clumsy policy followed by Khuen-Héderváry, who was ban from 1883 to 1893, made the situation worse at a time when Croatian cultural life was blossoming under the influence of Josip Juraj Strossmayer, the bishop of Djakovo. The advocates of Yugoslav union set out their programme at Fiume in 1905 and were supported at Vienna by the heir presumptive, the archduke Francis Ferdinand. When the Hungarian minister for trade Ferenc Kossuth, the son of Lajos, wanted to impose Hungarian on the railways in contempt of the Compromise, the Croatian sabor protested and there were demonstrations in Croatia.

The Romanians in Transylvania were afraid of Magyarization. They resumed agitation when an education act imposed six hours a week of Hungarian instruction in the minority schools, despite the guarantees provided by the law of 1868. A Romanian national party was founded in 1881 which demanded autonomy for Transylvania and a Romanian administration in those districts inhabited by Romanians, essentially the centre of the country. The Romanian national party received encouragement from Budapest and presented Francis Joseph with a memorandum. It gained fourteen seats in the Budapest parliament during the 1905 elections. The question of the Romanians in Transylvania was serious because those who favoured autonomy received strong support from Bucharest and also a sympathetic ear within Francis Ferdinand's entourage at Vienna.

THE WORK OF THE CONSERVATIVES (1879–1914)

It is easy to criticize the Taaffe cabinet of 1879–94 for its opposition to change. Taaffe came from an Irish noble family and enjoyed the trust and friendship of Francis Joseph. He was supported by the Slav parliamentary groups in the *Reichsrat*, by the Czech national party, the Polish club and the conservatives in the Hohenwart club. A skilful tactician like his Hungarian counterpart Kálmán Tísza, he remained in power for fifteen years and pursued a policy of cautious reform.

The government, in a departure from what had been the case for many years with the liberals, took an interest in social questions. It was in part copying Bismarck, but unlike the Prussian chancellor, attached greater importance to the protection of the workers than to national insurance and social security. Victor Adler, at the conference of social democrats held at Brussels in 1891, acknowledged that Austria with Britain and Switzerland possessed the best legislation safeguarding the workforce. From 1879 onwards, the government considered fresh labour legislation, but it was Belcredi's plan for a corps of labour inspectors with extensive powers and under the trade ministry which was debated and adopted by the *Reichsrat* in 1883. The liberal deputies were divided, and although some supported the law, it came under fierce attack in the *Neue Freie Presse*, the great Viennese newspaper which invoked the principles of Adam Smith. Workplaces were subject to controls, the working day limited, the *Trucksystem* (payment in kind) formally forbidden. In 1887 and 1888 the government passed legislation concerning accidents at work and health insurance, which no longer came under the sole domain of the mutual benefit associations.

The president of the Austrian council saw this legislation as essential for rescuing the members of the proleteriat from the lamentable conditions in which they found themselves and for guaranteeing them the dignity to which every citizen, and every Christian, had a right. He thought that the legislation would have to be accompanied by measures extending the right to vote. In 1882 he achieved the lowering of the property qualification from 10 to 5 florins, but in 1893 abandoned plans for a law which would have made all adult citizens electors in a system of curias. This proposal roused indignation among the conservatives and led to the dissolution of the government coalition. The Taaffe cabinet was brought down by plans for electoral reform.

Taaffe's immediate successor, Windischgrätz, was supported by a coalition of conservatives, liberals and Poles but remained in power only briefly. The real successor to Taaffe was count Badeni, the governor of Galicia. He formed a firm and energetic government which enjoyed Francis Joseph's support. Agenor Goluchowski, a Polish aristocrat, served as minister for foreign affairs. Badeni brought electoral reform to a successful conclusion by creating a fifth or 'general' curia in which all men aged twenty-four and over were enrolled and elected 72 deputies out of a total of 425. Badeni was brought down in 1897 by his policy on nationalities which favoured the Slav groups. It was only after the defeat of the second Gautsch cabinet that baron Beck, former tutor to the archduke Francis Ferdinand, secured the adoption of universal suffrage in December 1906. Many groups, not least the German liberals, were opposed, but the newly emerged forces as well as the conservatives and the emperor supported it. Francis Joseph thought that by strengthening the social democrats, universal suffrage would marginalize the nationalities question and work against the interests of such parties as the Czech radicals. A compromise was reached by shrewdly trimming the electoral wards. The Germans who paid 63 per cent of taxes in Cisleithania but made up only 35 per cent of the population, held 43 per cent of the seats. The Italians and Romanians enjoyed a similar advantage. In the general elections of 1907, for the first time parliament was elected by universal suffrage.

THE AUSTRO-HUNGARIAN CONSTITUTIONAL CONFLICT OF 1905

In Hungary, the question of universal suffrage was much more acute and resulted in the first confrontation since 1867. The Hungarian nobility, which had defended the country's liberties and restored its independence, wanted to keep the monopoly of power without associating it with either the labouring masses or the minorities. The question was raised much later than in Cisleithania and in a way which made it appear as though Francis Joseph was using backmail. The results of the 1905 election had been a condemnation of the liberal policy of Tísza who enjoyed the emperor's trust. The liberal party, the party of Deák and Andrássy and the cornerstone of the Compromise, gained 159 seats as against the 244 won by the opposition consisting of an amalgamation of the anti-Austrian nationalist party of 1848, conservatives, social democrats and deputies representing national minorities. Francis Joseph counter-attacked by appointing an extra-parliamentary ministry which he entrusted to marshal Fejérváry, the bold and daring general. The socialists organized demonstrations in support of universal suffrage which were supported by the minister for the interior, Kristóffy, as a means to ending the political hegemony of the Hungarian nobility. Parliament was emptied by armed force in February 1906, then dissolved. The new chamber abandoned all plans for an independent Hungarian army and a compromise was reached. The elections of 1912 restored Tísza to power and in 1913 he passed an electoral reform which raised the number of voters from 1 to 1.9 million.

CHANGES IN MENTALITY: PAN-GERMANISM

Carl Schorske, in his pioneering work, *Vienna fin de siècle*, has shown very clearly the changes which took place within the political outlook of the Austrian capital with the emergence of Schönerer, who under cover of pan-Germanist ideology introduced violence as a means of expression within the *Rechtstaat*.[4]

Pan-Germanism from the outset denoted the desire to realize the political and cultural unity of Germany and of making the Germans alive to the necessity of working together towards unification, scattered as they were among so many states; before 1848, Prussia, Austria and the numerous parts of the German Confederation. Following the creation of the German empire in 1871, pan-Germanism was synonymous with German nationalism. Its followers dreamt of a single state embracing all the German-speaking states and provinces of Central Europe, a feeling which found expression in 1841 in the poetry of Ernst Moritz Arndt.

After Bismarck's success, pan-Germanism took on a different complexion and it was distinguished in some of its objectives from classic German nationalism. Pan-Germanism in Germany was different from Austrian pan-Germanism. In the *Reich*, it was shaped by the *Alldeutscher Verband* (Pan-Germanist League), which was founded in 1890 to promote German economic interests overseas. The League quickly extended the range of its activities, elaborating patriotic propaganda, extolling the grandeur of the *Reich* and strengthening solidarity among the Germans outside the state. More than anything, though, it encouraged the leaders in Berlin to pursue an aggressive foreign policy. It was less a voice supporting German unification and more a pressure group in favour of imperialism. It became increasingly racist and anti-Semitic, supported the idea of annexing territory in Europe and was opposed to the continued existence of Austria-Hungary. Right until the outbreak of the First World War, it was in principle loyal to the policy of Bismarck and did not interfere with the internal affairs of the Danubian monarchy. Most of its members came from the national liberal party, were very conservative and basically wanted to maintain social order within the framework of the Bismarckian state. Naumann breathed new life into pan-Germanism with the idea of *Mitteleuropa*, according to which the *Reich* and Austria constituted the kernel of a confederation which embraced the Dutch, Flemish and Scandinavians and even the Turks and Balkan peoples. Until the war, these ideas remained the preserve of a small group of intellectuals, as did Gustav Schmoller's ideas on the 'Great German space'.

Pan-Germanism within the Danubian monarchy first affected a small number of Austrian Germans who after 1866 refused to be separated from the Germans of the *Reich*, even at the cost of their country's destruction. The Austrian pan-Germanists were a group distinct from the champions of *Grossdeutschland* who wanted the south German states and Austria to be enveloped within one great state enjoying the same rights as Prussia. The pan-Germanists repudiated traditional values and envisaged a German paradise on earth from which all 'modern corruption' would be banished. They renounced all the great nineteenth-century values: parliamentary government, liberalism, socialism, liberty and civil equality. They found an audience among the working classes. Taking its position outside the classic political framework, the movement advocated direct action and violence, force being the only argument it knew. In this sense, it heralded the political methods of the twentieth century. It was dominated by Georg von Schönerer, the son of an industrialist enobled for his success during the neo-absolutist era. He professed a yet more violent anti-Semitism than Lueger who took him as a model. In 1888 Schönerer was excluded from political life but found imitators not only for his methods, the systematic use of violence, direct action, mass demonstrations, but also for his goals, the unification of all Germans within one state and the stamping out of liberal democracy. Later Adolf Hitler would take Schönerer and Lueger as his two intellectual mentors.

The parliamentary agitation of 1897 and the malfunctions within the 1867 constitution gave justified cause for concern. They were not, however, sufficient reason to raise 'the Austrian question' as the apostles of doom in the French press began to do, deliberately creating a problem which did not exist. There was no question of destroying this *Völkerkerker* but rather of modifying the existing system to allow swifter development in the more backward provinces and giving justice to those ethno-linguistic groups which were perhaps treated less well than some others, but without undermining the cohesion of the whole. Almost everyone in a position of authority supported reform. No-one wanted an end to Austria-Hungary which offered its peoples, including the Slavs, considerable opportunities for material and moral advance.

It was the emperor himself who posed a serious threat to the monarchy, contrary to the view expounded in the foreign press that he was the only link among the disparate elements and that with his death the monarchy fell apart. Francis Joseph, as he grew older, became an ardent supporter of the status quo and of dualism to the point where it was a double centralism and Austria-Hungary was sustained by the dynasty, army, administration and Church. The emperor was less afraid of social democracy than of the excesses of the liberal bourgeoisie. He favoured universal suffrage in the hope of crushing fanaticism of any kind, be it of Schönerer's pangermanists or of the Czech and Hungarian radicals. It is however, true to say that the death of the aged emperor who had been universally respected, without as within the monarchy, led to necessary changes. The archduke and heir, Francis Ferdinand, is attributed with great plans which changed often and perhaps never even had the slightest chance of being put into action. He wanted to do away with dualism and to return to a centralized monarchy, but the situation was very different from that in 1849.[5] His assassination in Sarajevo on 28 June 1914, cut short all speculation.

The period from 1867 to 1914 was not as inglorious as has been claimed. The monarchy enjoyed a constitutional regime, was a state based on the rule of law and had undergone considerable modernization. The press and elections were free, universal male suffrage had been introduced in Cisleithania and that this was not the case in Hungary before 1914 was not the fault of Francis Joseph but rather of the Hungarian political classes which mounted a strong and steadfast resistance. The agreements reached over language at the beginning of the twentieth century showed that there was a movement towards reconciliation among those nations long at odds with each other. In this sense social democracy advanced. The emancipation of the Jews stirred anti-Semitism, but no more so than the Dreyfus affair in France, and provided the monarchy with an economic and cultural elite. *Fin de siècle* Vienna boasted the founder of psychoanalysis, Sigmund Freud, and Gustav Mahler as director of the Vienna opera. Those Jews who had assimilated were the staunchest supporters of Germanism in the face of the demands made by the nationalities.

The threat to the monarchy did not come from internal tensions but from international politics, its own ambitions in the Balkans and the German alliance. For more than forty years, Francis Joseph used all his authority and all his prestige to prevent the empire from becoming embroiled in war and he could count the benefits of his wise policy: Austria-Hungary in 1914 was a rich and prosperous great power. With age, though, the clarity of his vision blurred and he allowed the clan of warmongers to impose upon him a war from which the Habsburgs would never recover. The ultimatum to Serbia was a suicidal step and uncharacteristic of a man as cautious as Francis Joseph.

Why was an emperor who in 1870 had been wise enough to forego a vengeful attack on Prussia now so reckless as to engage in a war of vengeance for a nephew whom he heartily detested?

NOTES AND REFERENCES

1. Jean-Paul Bled, *Les fondements du conservatisme autrichien, 1859–1879*, Paris, 1988.
2. Bruce M. Carver, *The Young Czech Party and the Emergence of a Multi-party System 1874–1901*, Yale, 1978.
3. Otto Bauer, *Die Nationalitätenfrage*, Vienna, 1907.
4. Carl E. Schorske, *Vienna, fin de siècle*, Cambridge, 1981.
5. Robert Kann, *Erherzog Franz Ferdinand – Studien*, Vienna, 1976.

CHAPTER SEVENTEEN

The Monarchy During the First World War

Francis Joseph resigned himself, after the events of 1870, to playing a prominent, but nonetheless secondary role to Prussia which had realized, at least partially, German unification. After being driven from Italy in 1859 and from Germany in 1866, the House of Habsburg devoted itself to building a strong corridor against Russia and uniting under its protection the various nationalities of Danubian Europe. Francis Joseph appointed Andrássy, a Hungarian, as minister for foreign affairs, which under the dualist system meant that he was responsible for the foreign policy of the dual monarchy. This appointment showed that the emperor had turned his back on any prospect of vengeance on Prussia in order to leave himself free to become involved in the Balkans. Hungarian public opinion favoured Turkey and was hostile towards Russia but Andrássy and the emperor, at the time of the 1876 eastern crisis, abandoned the principle of upholding the integrity of the Ottoman empire. The Congress of Berlin in 1878 marked the high point of this policy but also the beginning of setbacks. Without waging war, Austria-Hungary received the right to occupy Bosnia-Hercegovina whereas Russia, the victor, was forced to give up its conquests. The Near East presented the Viennese bankers and Bohemian industrialists with a considerable market and at the time when the great powers were endeavouring to acquire a colonial empire, Austria rediscovered its traditional sphere of economic interest. In the heyday of imperialism, nothing serious would have happened if Austria had not become weighed down in the Bosnian mire.

The Ottoman province of Bosnia was inhabited by Orthodox Serbs and Slav converts to Islam and was coveted by the kingdom of Serbia which was then still quite small. Until 1878, relations between Austria and Serbia were good. In 1848 the Serbs had turned towards Austria to oppose Hungarian independence. After the Austrian occupation of Bosnia, however, the Serbs saw Austria as a major obstacle to their national aspirations. From this evolved the South Slav question which played a significant part in launching the First World War.

The military occupation of Bosnia-Hercegovina met fierce resistance from the Bosnian Serbs. Andrássy was severely criticized for having become involved in such a sensitive area and, going against the emperor's advice, resigned. Bosnia was occupied and placed under an administration which acted in the sultan's name but which was dependent on the joint ministry of finance. Bosnia-Hercegovina was treated as a *Reichsland*. Hungary opposed the construction of a standard-gauge rail network and linked Sarajevo and Dubrovnik with a narrow-gauge track which was of strategic importance but severely hampered the country's economic development. Austria bided time for thirty years, administering but not annexing Bosnia. Then, suddenly in 1908, the minister for foreign affairs, baron Ährenthal, decided to annex unilaterally the province for the emperor's jubilee, thereby rousing the latent conflict with Serbia and its protector, Russia, and provoking an international crisis.

The heir presumptive, the archduke Ferdinand, detested the Hungarians and wanted to save the monarchy by instituting a thoroughgoing programme of reform. He dreamt of a 'trialist solution' in the South Slavs' favour. He became the target for Serbian nationalists because it seemed likely that he would create a 'Yugoslavia' to the Habsburgs' advantage.

The assassination of the archduke at Sarajevo on 28 June 1914 was the work of Serbian nationalists whose plans were unknown to the Serbian government in Belgrade. A party within the Austrian staff headquarters led by a friend of the late archduke, Conrad von Hötzendorf, saw the assassination as providing the long-awaited opportunity to crush Serbia and settle the Yugoslav question to Austria's advantage once and for all. Count Berchtold, the minister for foreign affairs, and public opinion in Vienna were in favour of the war, but Tísza, the president of the Hungarian council, was against it. The emperor, who had lost his appetite for war after the defeats at the beginning of his reign, allowed himself to be persuaded that the assassination was an attack on the army and dynasty, all that he held most dear. Those around him promised only a small-scale confrontation and thus it was that he came to explain in a long *Proclamation to his peoples* that the honour of the army demanded that it seek reparation by force of arms.

Francis Joseph had, however, underestimated the threat posed by the diplomatic configuration which then divided Europe into two blocks; the Entente of France, Britain and Russia, and the Triple Alliance of Germany, Austro-Hungary and Italy. In 1908, at the time of the annexation of Bosnia-Hercegovina, these alliances had not come into play because France had refused to support Russia. In 1914, however, the alliances worked perfectly. Russia refused to allow Serbia to be crushed and France honoured its obligations, while Germany, which had pushed Austro-Hungary towards war, mobilized. The personal decision of Francis Joseph thus played a crucial part in launching the war.

The power which had the least to gain from provoking a conflict was the very one that lit the touch-paper. The monarchy was kept together by a fragile equilibrium of which the emperor had only lately become conscious; he told president Theodore Roosevelt that he was 'the last European monarch of the old school'. Why did he fail to recognize that this fragile equilibrium could not survive the strain of the war? The hunger and misery provoked by the world conflict would shake the monarchy much more than the question of nationalities which so concerned the politicians and journalists.

Austro-Hungary in August 1914 was held to be a great power in terms of both its economic and its military strength. The forces which kept it together were still there even though they appeared strangely archaic.

AUSTRIA-HUNGARY IN 1914, AN ECONOMIC POWER

Austria-Hungary covered 677 000 square kilometres and stretched from the Adriatic to the Russian frontier, from Saxony to the Balkans, and in the west extended as far as Lake Constance. Its centre of gravity was the Danubian basin encircled by mountains which joined the eastern Alps and the massifs of Bohemia. It had direct access to the sea through the port of Trieste and along the Elbe valley to the port of Hamburg. The two capitals, Vienna and Budapest, were linked to the provinces by a network of roads and especially by the railways which were constructed in a star on the French pattern, while the Danube remained a useful and cheap route of communication. The famous Berlin–Baghdad railway project, the *Baghdad-Bahn* of the chancelleries, engaged the attention of financiers and diplomats at the beginning of the twentieth century. Via Vienna, Budapest, Belgrade and Constantinople it opened the Near Eastern markets to Austrian manufactured goods.

The Austro-Hungarian economy on the eve of the Great War was prosperous and had recovered from the break in industrial expansion and capital growth following the 1873 stock-exchange crash. Industrial production had grown according to natural resources and along specialist lines already tentatively established in the eighteenth century. Heavy industry was concentrated in Vienna and Prague and throughout Bohemia. In the Czech lands, the wool and cotton textile industries, adapted to the new conditions, were in a position to supply the markets of the Near East. The cloth factories at Litoměřice in Bohemia supplied felt for the fezes and tarbooshes worn by the Ottoman army and administration. Within the empire the less industrialized regions, Hungary and Bosnia, were also natural outlets. The coal mines of Bohemia and Lower Silesia suited the development of heavy industry. The Skoda factories at Plzeň (Pilsen) in Bohemia manufactured artillery equipment for the imperial army and engineering works for the railways were installed in the suburbs of Vienna and Prague. There were numerous small workshops in Vienna and its outlying districts which produced furniture, clothing, shoes and luxury goods. The city provided an enormous market for these products and set the fashion for the whole monarchy. Vienna prided itself on being a rival to Paris.

The customs system between the Austrian and Hungarian parts of the Empire favoured Hungarian agriculture and made it possible for a certain amount of industry to develop. Until the very end of the century, investment, usually from Austria and France, continued to be directed towards the primary sector and food industries, mines, mills and distilleries. At the beginning of the twentieth century, the Hungarian textile and metallurgical industries grew rapidly, especially in Budapest which experienced an increase in its working population as the rural world suffered a serious crisis in development. The great estate-owners

had improved production by mechanizing agriculture and using chemical fertilizers, but also by developing direct farming and extending the scale of operation. The dramatic advances made in agriculture were, however, accompanied
by a marked deterioration in the condition of the peasantry. The whole rural
world, but especially Hungary, suffered a serious crisis exacerbated by the
concentration of capital in agricultural land and the rise in population. The
revolution of 1848 had abolished the manorial regime and the *robot* as part of
the domain economy, but legislation had carefully maintained the distinction
between *Dominikalländer* (seigneurial lands) and *Rustikalländer* (peasant lands).
The peasants had only received outright ownership of the *Rustikalländer* even
though, prior to 1848, they had for various reasons cultivated a share of the
seigneurial lands. All parties had gained from this arrangement since the landowners had benefited from having part of their lands brought under cultivation on advantageous terms and the peasants had escaped taxes. After 1848,
however, the landowners recovered all the lands which belonged to them and
the imbalance between the large-scale farming operations and the *microfundia*
became more pronounced and this happened at a time when the population
was rapidly expanding. Towards 1900, Austria had 232 and Hungary 175 estates of more than 5 000 hectares. Less than 1 per cent of landowners possessed
40 per cent of the cultivable land while 99 per cent had to make do with the
remaining 60 per cent of land which could be farmed. In Transylvania, the
average area of a *latifundium* was 1 900 hectares, whilst the average peasant
smallholding was less than 2 hectares. At the end of the nineteenth century,
capital was concentrated in property since the aristocracy used the banks to
finance the development of their estates. In the Hungarian plain and some other
parts of the monarchy well before 1910 there was the threat of a revolutionary
outburst by the agricultural proleteriat for whom the only natural release was
to join the exodus from the countryside and to emigrate to the United States.

This picture should be modified to take account of the differences between
regions. Agriculture in Bosnia-Hercegovina, for example, was still at the subsistence level with poor harvests and was organized on the basis of family
smallholdings. By contrast, in the Bukovina, the average holding was 50–100
hectares directly farmed by the owner. The census of 1910 shows that with the
exception of Bohemia where only 38.1 per cent of the working population was
engaged in agriculture, Austria-Hungary was predominantly rural with 56.5
per cent of the working population employed on the land. These families
depended on agriculture for their livelihood and provided an inadequate outlet
for manufactured goods so that factory-owners had to search for export markets.

In 1914 capitalist industry was clearly thriving but it was also threatened
by long-term developments since Austria-Hungary's place in international trade
had diminished. German investments in the Balkans and Near East continued
to increase and Austrian industry ran up against German competition in the
regions which hitherto had constituted its traditional zone of influence. Serbia
increasingly asked for German and French capital for armaments and for its
railways and imported from Germany a quantity of manufactured goods. When
in 1905 Austria-Hungary came to renew its trade treaties, it wanted to impose

tougher conditions in order to forestall a flood of agricultural goods from the Balkans and to protect the living standards of its mass of peasants. Austria-Hungary wanted to defend its agriculture and at the same time fought to preserve the foreign markets for its industry. In these circumstances, the development of a railway network in the Balkans became a burning issue. The Russians wanted to construct a line which would stretch from the North Sea to the Adriatic and pass through Serbia and so divert traffic from Austria-Hungary. For this reason, the Austrians were anxious to join their railway network to that of the Turks and to open a line to Thessaloniki which would link Bosnia via the Sandžak of Novi Pazar to the Aegean and so provide the shortest route from Central Europe to Egypt and India. Industrialists and bankers in Bohemia were excited at the thought of Ottoman and Balkan markets. An Austro-Oriental commercial society established branches in Smyrna and Alexandria and enjoyed support from the government in Vienna. This was an old dream which the Austrian government and capitalists wanted to realize at last on a large scale. The extent to which the economic interests of the Central European empires were linked to their policy of expansion became clear. In this, however, Germany and Austria-Hungary were competitors, not allies.

At the political level, Austria-Hungary still appeared as the best ally of pan-Germanism and as a growing threat to the recently freed Slav peoples of the Balkans. The publication in 1915 of a book by Friedrich Naumann did nothing to reassure international opinion. In the midst of the Great War, he took up the title and thesis of Friedrich List's work *Mitteleuropa* and argued that Germany and Austria-Hungary should join their economies in order to dominate the European markets. The rest of the world understood that if the central empires were victorious, Berlin would exercise hegemony over the European economy. A theoretical work, Naumann's book was unpopular with German businessmen and with the Prussian junkers who did not want to compete with Hungarian agriculture. Soutou has recently shown that these projects for a customs union were rejected by the German negotiators but even so they caused disquiet in many.[1]

THE ELEMENTS OF COHESION

The nationalities question in 1914 was a source of weakness within the monarchy. Romanian and Italian irredentism, Hungarian hegemony over the Slav minorities and tensions between the Germans and Czechs posed a threat to stability. The monarchy's basis, though, was solid and this was demonstrated by its cohesion during the first months of the war. Its principal error was to rely on essentially conservative forces, the dynasty, the army, the bureaucracy and the Catholic Church, forces which still had a great deal of prestige in a society which was essentially rural.

The Habsburgs were a link between the different nationalities which quite often hated each other and quarrelled. This link was all the stronger because Francis Joseph who had ruled since 1848 was universally respected for his sense of duty and the benevolence which he showed to all his subjects, without exception. The politicians were anxious to know who might be his successor and viewed the heirs presumptive with some concern. The archduke Francis Ferdinand was authoritarian and did not hide his wish to enact a great pro- gramme of reforms after his uncle's death. His assassination on 28 June 1914 at Sarajevo put an end to the prospect of his grandiose and disquieting plans being realized. His place was taken by the archduke Charles, who after 1916 faced an enormously difficult task.

The Church had always been an ally of the House of Austria. In the past the Habsburgs had given their full support to the Counter-Reformation. Lib- eral in cultural matters, tolerant in politics, they had wished only that their subjects be good Catholics. Since the time of Joseph II, the state had allowed the existence of religious minorities and the Empire included Protestants, Orthodox, Jews and Muslims. Even so, Austria-Hungary still remained a great Catholic country where the rural masses were fervent in their piety, the elites remained attached to religion and the clergy promised loyal support for the dynasty. Austrian Catholicism was not fanatical. It was marked by two cen- turies of baroque piety and attached much importance to the external forms of worship and certain devotions characteristic of Counter-Reformation Cath- olicism, for example the adoration of the Blessed Sacrament and the cult of St Jan Nepomucki. It was little affected by intellectualism and rationalism. The link between religion and the dynasty was demonstrated in 1912 by the extra- ordinary success of the Eucharistic congress. Crowds of people from all walks of life came to pay homage to the old system and reaffirmed the old alliance between the throne and altar.

The imperial and royal army was for a long time the only institution which depended directly and personally on the sovereign. Through the recruitment of its regulars, especially those trained at the Military Academy at Wiener Neustadt, and by compulsory military service, it served as a social melting-pot and as a force devoted to the sovereign and the state. Francis Joseph had had to struggle with the Hungarian nationalists to maintain a joint command and one language, German, as the language of command, and to preserve intact the army as a force common to the whole monarchy. As for Francis Ferdinand, he rested his great hopes for the state's salvation on the army and its sense of loyalty.

The bureaucracy also played a part in maintaining unity. Since Joseph II, it had been famed for its competence and its loyalty to the sovereign. At the level of central government, it represented an integrating and Germanizing element within the monarchy, since at Vienna 76 per cent of ministry personnel were German and 24 per cent were drawn from other nationalities. Regional and local administration by contrast was in the hands of the predominant nation- alities. In Bohemia in 1914, 94.54 per cent of functionaries were Czech and 5.46 per cent German.

Fierce opponents were aware of the strength of the system before the declaration of war. In 1913 Masaryk declared to the parliament at Vienna, where he represented Bohemia: 'It is precisely because I have not let myself entertain dreams of the fall of Austria, because I know that Austria must, for better or worse, endure, that I see it as my task to do something. Our projects for the reform of public law and administrative reform should not tend towards weakening the rest but strengthening the whole.'

Four years later, Austria-Hungary collapsed without having experienced a resounding military defeat but rather because it had been undermined by internal political conflicts and economic crisis.

MILITARY CATASTROPHE

At the time of the declaration of war in 1914, the Empire was one of the great military powers. The regular army, cherished by the regime, enjoyed great social prestige. It consisted of sixty infantry and eleven cavalry divisions. The Allies expected that the reserve units made up predominantly of Slavs would defect or fight badly, but these troops acquitted themselves as well as the other combatants. The South Slavs, the Croats and Bosnians showed great fighting spirit and in the first months of the war the masses exhibited the same enthusiasm as elsewhere in Europe. It is true that they, like the chiefs-of-staff, thought they were embarking on a brief war as in 1866 or 1870.

Following the system of two-years' military service adopted in 1912, the infantry was well-trained but poorly equipped with modern armaments, especially the machine guns which were to play so important a part at the beginning of the war. It seems that contrary to its inflated reputation in the west, the artillery was second-rate, especially the field artillery. Only the heavy artillery made in the Skoda factories at Plzeň was superior to the other belligerents' because of the howitzer with its high trajectory and low muzzle velocity. The cavalry had good mounts and like the Hungarian hussars and Polish lancers came from a solid tradition, but its tactics, like the French army's, were out-of-date because its officers had not learnt from the lessons of the Boer War. The best troops were the battalions of *Kaiserjäger* where the elite officers and highly motivated and well-trained soldiers served. The imperial army should not be judged by such satirical works as *The Good Soldier Svejk* which was written at the end of the war and is both anti-Habsburg and anti-militarist. This work, like *Les Gaietés de l'escadron* in France, lampoons certain officials and sections of an army which attached great importance to strict respect for discipline. The French military attachés, though, had for a long time noted the unique and solid character of an army which had drawn lessons from the defeat in 1866. Conrad von Hötzendorf, the chief of the general staff, although he was fiercely criticized in Austria and in Germany, nonetheless appears as a courageous leader. Since 1899, when he was in the garrison at Trieste, he had observed Italian irredentism and had begun to mistrust the Italians as allies. Through his friendship with the archduke Francis Ferdinand, he had enjoyed a brilliant career combining political and military functions. Appointed head of the general staff in 1906, he tried to recover the ground lost by the imperial army under his predecessor general Beck. He modernized the armaments and reorganized the artillery, but he came into conflict with the German liberals, Slavs and Hungarians and with the emperor.

Conrad assumed the role of head of the war party and champion of a preventive war against Serbia or even Italy. In 1912 Ährenthal, the minister of foreign affairs, secured his departure, but he returned as head of the general staff and actively prepared for war against Serbia in collaboration with the German general staff. He pushed Francis Joseph into sending the ultimatum to Serbia in July 1914 because he believed that a limited and preventive war would bring the South Slavs to their senses. He underestimated the Serbian enemy, spread his forces too far and suffered defeats on the Russian and Serbian fronts. In 1917 the emperor Charles demanded his resignation and sent him to command a group of armies on the Italian front.

Austria-Hungary also possessed a strong navy at the start of the Great War. In addition to the traditional flotilla on the Danube made up of gunboats and 'monitors', Austria had developed an ocean-going fleet which weighed 264 000 tonnes. It included among its twelve battleships, four dreadnoughts (*Saint Istvan, Viribus Unitis, der Tegetthoff* and *Prinz Eugen*) and possessed seven cruisers, fifty-five torpedo boats and six submarines.[2] Based on the Dalmatian coast at Pula and Kotor, it was manned mainly by Croats with officers drawn from all the different nationalities; in 1914 Miklós Horty, the future regent of Hungary, was captain of a flagship. Conrad also supported the development of military aeronautics which were more advanced in Austria than Prussia.

THE CONDUCT OF THE WAR

The imperial army was engaged in three main fields of operation: in the Balkans in Serbia, Macedonia and Romania, on the Russian front in the Ukraine, and on the Italian front after 1915, when the Rome government abandoned its neutrality and joined the Allies after being promised by the terms of the Treaty of London the lands coveted by the irredentists, including Dalmatia and the Tyrol, as well as many other rewards. That the first campaigns on the Russian and Serbian fronts were not mere military excursions was partly because general Conrad had not been wise enough to decide which enemy was the priority at the moment of mobilization. He employed on the Russian front an army prepared for war against the Serbs and failed in both the campaign to take Belgrade and in the offensive in Galicia which ended in early October when the territory was occupied by the Russians. A more serious failing was that the railways remained the Achilles' heal of the Austrian war effort. The weaknesses apparent at the time of mobilization became more pronounced with 40 per cent of locomotives under repair. In 1918, during the June offensive on the Italian front, the Austro-Hungarian army lacked munitions at the decisive moment for want of means of transport.

The monarchy, no less than the other belligerents, saw its active divisions decimated during the campaign of the summer of 1914. If the warring sides had followed the reasoning which had prevailed during the nineteenth century, they would quickly have made peace on the basis of compromise, but instead they rebuilt their armies with reservists. Even with the industrial problems which the monarchy was facing, the imperial army in 1916 was better than it had been at the time of going to war in 1914. Besides the celebrated defection of the 28th infantry regiment, the Prague regiment, it had fewer deserters than the German armies which lost mainly Alsatian and Polish troops, and unlike the Russian and French armies, it did not experience any mutinies.[3] The good behaviour of the troops is explained by the traditions of discipline and the humane character of those in command who listened carefully to their men. The army maintained the unique character it had acquired when it adopted conscription in 1868 and created reserve officers who served for a year as volunteers. It was neither a purely professional nor a purely national army. This is why the Germans' harsh criticisms of their Austrian allies as inefficient, have swayed military historians. Conrad certainly made mistakes during preparations for the war but he was not alone in failing to take account of the most recent conflicts. Good discipline was essential, just as the British officers believed, and patriotism played only a secondary role in maintaining an army's cohesion.

It should come as no surprise that after 1915 the Austrian army experienced tactical successes. After a successful offensive in Bukovina, the army occupied the whole of Serbia and Montenegro. The Serbian army, though, escaped complete annihilation and struggled its way to the Adriatic coast whence it was evacuated to Corfu. It re-assembled, underwent reorganization and straightaway joined the Allied army in the east at Thessaloniki and played a decisive role during the last months of the war. Conrad and the strategists of the Ballhausplatz had overlooked the fact that the Serbs had a seasoned army which had been fighting continuously since 1912 and the first Balkan war.

In 1916 Romania's entry into the war on the side of the Entente gave the Austrian troops the chance to win a brilliant victory. The Romanian army was well-equipped and well-motivated. The nation was pro-French and had forced the war upon its Hohenzollern king who was pro-German and an ally of the central powers. Unfortunately, the army lacked experience. After launching an offensive in Transylvania which was swiftly blocked, it found itself isolated by 600 000 Austro-Germans backed by the Turks and Bulgarians. Bucharest fell in autumn 1916 and Romania concluded an armistice.

The Tyroleans and Croats were excited by the war against Italy and took part in the defensive action against the Italians whose commanders launched a succession of useless attacks. From June 1915 to October 1917, the twelve battles fought over Isonzo entailed for the two adversaries an enormous loss of men, equipment and supplies. The war of attrition was such that the Austrian staff headquarters feared the front would be breached, but it was their adversaries who capitulated. On 24 October 1917, the final offensive began and turned into a catastrophe for the Italians. The imperial army crossed the Tagliamento, reached the Piave and took 300 000 prisoners. For a while, Venice seemed threatened but the new front which was fixed at the Piave was easier to hold. The victory at Caporetto brought the Austrians vast food supplies and was also a great boost to their morale. The Allies, meanwhile, were obliged to come to the assistance of the Italians.

These undeniable victories, crowned by the Austro-Hungarian navy's success over the French fleet, were thrilling for soldiers and civilians alike but did not have any decisive effect since the 'war of movement' for which the belligerents had prepared had turned into a 'war of position'. The only strategy left was to wear down the enemy forces. The economy of the central powers was severely affected by blockades and was much more vulnerable than that of the Entente. The civilians and the military were discouraged and weighed the vast sacrifices that had been made against the poor results obtained.

THE EVOLUTION OF MENTALITIES

The way the peoples of the monarchy responded to the war has been studied by Kann and little corresponds to the popular version propagated after 1920 by those who had changed sides and thought it vital to fly to the aid of victory.[4] In 1918 the Czech political leaders created a historiographical tradition which portrayed them as patriots and resistance fighters. Apart from Masaryk, who had fled from Austria to fight in the west for the Czechoslovak cause, the leaders of the large parties were content to constitute a secret committee, 'the Mafia', since with the proclamation of the state of siege all parliamentary life had been suspended and the *Reichsrat* was closed. They dreamt of restoring a Bohemian state. Kramar, the most radical, had wanted in 1914 to put a grand duke, a Romanov, at the head of the kingdom of Bohemia. The social democrats, on the other hand, for tactical reasons remained faithful to the monarchy. They were hostile in principle to tsarist Russia, seeing it as too reactionary, and thought that socialism had a better chance of triumphing in an Austro-Hungarian state that was industrialized and far more developed than the Russian empire.

The pan-Slav dream vanished in 1915 with the defeat of the Russians but was reborn in 1916 after the Russian general Broussilov led a successful offensive against Mackenson's German forces to relieve pressure on the French front. The accession of the emperor Charles made possible a return to normal political life. The *Reichsrat* was re-opened and the Czech deputies constituted the united Czech club in Vienna and a national Czech committee in Prague. The new government, contrary to what might be expected when the president of the council, Clam-Martinic, and the minister of foreign affairs, Czernin, were Bohemian aristocrats, was especially well-disposed towards the Germans in Bohemia. The Czech Union did not, however, welcome president Wilson's promise, made on 10 January 1917, that Bohemia would be set free. In May 1918, it was still content to demand respect for Czech state-right within a federal framework and the recognition of the Czechoslovak union which immediately roused the anger of the Sudeten Germans and the Hungarians, since Slovakia, an integral part of the kingdom of Hungary, did not have any juridical existence. It was only in October 1918 that the National Committee, sensing that the currents were changing, radically altered its position and proclaimed the independence of Czechoslovakia.

In Hungary, the political class continued to oppose universal suffrage which would grant the right to vote to the poor and to non-Hungarians. King Charles, conscious of the stakes, obliged the president of the council, István Tísza, who in 1914 had made a mark by opposing the sending of the ultimatum to Serbia, to dismiss his cabinet although it had always enjoyed the confidence of the parliament in Budapest. In July 1918 the cabinet of Sándor Wekerle, who only had a minority, voted through, not without some difficulty, a reform which extended the right to vote to 13 per cent of the population. Even those who had fought in the war did not obtain this right which was thought basic everywhere else in Europe.

Public opinion changed very quickly in the course of the war. The collective hysteria of the summer of 1914 waned the following year and by 1916 gave way to a genuine desire for peace which was expressed in demonstrations but also by the opening of negotiations. The intelligentsia exercised moderate influence, especially after the re-opening of the *Reichsrat* in 1916. Almost all of them, with the exception of the Salzburg poet Trakl, did not take part in active service. Although Robert Musil and Franz Werfel went to the front, Rilke spent the war in the archives, Franz Kafka was given a special assignment and Hugo von Hofmannsthal found refuge in staff headquarters. This did not stop them from pouring out their hatred for the Welsches and the Slavs. It was to their credit that they refused to associate with the anti-English campaign orchestrated by the Germans when the rest of the world remained anglophile.

In Hungary, the intellectuals were even more divided. In 1914 all the peoples of the monarchy seemed reconciled to the point where Hungarians sang the hymn *Gott erhalte den Kaiser*. Progressive writers expounded the theme of the fraternity of arms and regeneration through combat. Endre Ady, the greatest poet of his generation, who had spent much time in Paris, did not hide his misgivings and understood that if the monarchy was to survive, it would have to be victorious. Many Hungarian intellectuals were committed to defending the liberties of the west in the face of the tsarist empire and Juhasz called resolutely for revenge upon Russia for 1849. At the same time, the revue *Nyugat (The West)*, to which Ady contributed and which since its foundation had been francophile, abandoned its Parisian orientation. Even among the progressives, enthusiasm for all things French had been eclipsed by a new-found Germanomania. Deeply affected by the sufferings of the people, in 1916 they appealed to the king to end the conflict. After the defeat of the negotiations for a separate peace, they no longer had any faith in him nor in the existing system and rallied to a more radical line inspired by the Bolshevik revolution.

The revolution and the separate peace concluded by Lenin with the central empires at Brest-Litovsk in March 1918 excited great expectations among the masses. The prisoners of war in Russia who were now free, were won over by Bolshevik propaganda and helped to demoralize the people by spreading pacifist and communist ideas.

Towards the middle of 1918, the prevailing economic crisis meant that the hinterland faced catastrophe. Cisleithania was suffering from famine, at least in the cities, and even Hungary was struggling with food shortages because of the fall in agricultural productivity, and was short of coal and raw materials. Workers' real income had fallen to 53 per cent below the pre-war level and those who were struggling were open to revolutionary propaganda. The most dramatic action occurred on 20 June 1918 in the state railway workshops in Budapest. The military command gave orders to open fire on strikers. All the factories of the capital walked out in the space of a few hours, followed the next day by workers in the provinces and 500 000 workers demanded an immediate end to the war and the resignation of the government. The strike lasted nine days and was finally quelled, not so much by repressive measures as by the intervention of the Hungarian social democrat party which existed legally but did not have any representation in parliament.

To avoid similar incidents in Vienna, on 30 April 1918 general Ottokar Landwehr, president of the commission for food supplies, confiscated German grain convoys to supply the capital.

ECONOMIC CATASTROPHE

The change in outlook is explained by the turn in the monarchy's economic situation, especially in Vienna, which by autumn 1918 had become dramatic. The blockades and the crisis caused by the management of the war economy combined to bring the inhabitants of Vienna and Cisleithania to the brink of famine.

The harvest in 1918 was less than half that of 1913 and industrial production, excluding manufacturing connected with the war, had fallen to 40 per cent of the level in 1913. At the start of the war, the mobilization of 8 million men had more than any other factor prompted a drop in production. The call to arms had appealed mainly to manual workers who were plentiful and cheap. By 1917, the production of cereals had halved and in Cisleithania had not even reached a third of the 1913 level. The Hungarians refused to deliver grain to their famished neighbours. For the first time, the specialization of the two parts of the monarchy resulted in a serious failure to function but nothing, in the system born of the 1867 Compromise, could force the Hungarians to carry out these deliveries against their will. The industrial regions of Cisleithania and the working population found themselves severely affected by rationing since the allied blockades prevented all imports from overseas, mostly strategic materials and food.

Between August and October 1914, Britain imposed a restrictive interpretation on the 1909 London declaration. The British government included food supplies and raw materials in the list of goods which could not be exported and raw materials related to arms and munitions were seized even on neutral ships. It was a severe blow to the central powers facing commitment to a long war. The allied blockade proved to be a formidable weapon. The United States provided the Allies with raw materials, foodstuffs and manufactured goods but

Table 4: Cereal production in millions of kilogrammes

	Austria	Hungary	Total
1913	9 100	14 600	23 700
1916	4 900	7 800	12 700
1917	2 810	9 800	12 610

Table 5: Industrial production

	Coal (millions of tonnes)	Blankets (millions)
1914	57.0	9.5
1916	7.0	7.0
1917	2.7	2.9

the central powers were without outside assistance apart from receiving iron from Sweden. Germany experienced the same difficulties as Austria and could not aid its allies. These problems without doubt played an important part in the defeat of the central powers, which were unable to feed properly their soldiers and civilian population.

Industrial production underwent the same changes. The production of coal, which was almost the only source of energy, declined sharply. In three years it dropped by 95 per cent with the result that those living in cities experienced not only hunger but also cold and darkness. Every effort was directed towards the manufactures needed by war, but in 1917 even these declined rapidly. The case of blankets intended for the army illustrates this well (see Table 5).

As Austro-Hungary remained a market economy, the catastrophic drop in production was accompanied by a dramatic rise in prices, fed by inflation which the government maintained to finance the cost of the war. In order to face up to an interminable conflict, the government, like the other belligerents, had recourse to credit, to loans, but especially to advances from the Austro-Hungarian bank, in other words to the wholesale issuing of bank notes in the tradition of the Revolutionary Wars. It seemed that the monarchy, as in 1811, would have to resort to bankruptcy.

Mobilization had been financed by a loan of 2.5 million crowns,* a sum equal to 75 per cent of the total budget of the monarchy in 1913. The expenses of the last fiscal year during the war, 1917/18, rose to 24 million crowns, six times the budget in 1913.

The effects were soon felt. Prices rose sharply and there was a rapid depreciation of the currency which reached its lowest point once the war was over.

---

* Translator's note: the crown replaced the florin in 1891, was linked to the gold standard and worth 1.5 francs.

In spite of rationing, the cost of living multiplied fifteen times in four years while nominal salaries increased only slightly. With an index of 100 in 1914, the expenditure of a Viennese family rose to 382 in 1916, 616 in 1917 and 1 560 in 1918.

The result was a dramatic drop in spending power among wage-earners, industrial workers, clerks and civil servants, and disturbances started in the spring 1918. The war and the regime were held responsible for everyone's ills and the masses were no longer willing to pursue an endeavour which they saw as futile, nor to support a system which had led to such catastrophe.

The people, hitherto loyal, had suffered too much to defend a regime which had brought them, instead of the predicted war lasting three months, an interminable conflict which had lasted four years and entailed innumerable losses. Of the 8 million men mobilized since the declaration of war, 4.2 million had served continuously under the colours, 1.2 million had been killed and almost 3 million wounded, while many were crippled for the rest of their lives.

1918, THE YEAR OF DEFEAT[5]

After the Peace of Brest-Litovsk, the imperial army finished on the Russian front and could direct all its efforts towards the Venetian front. The authorities in Vienna expected much from the great offensive of the summer of 1918 after the German attacks on the French front had failed. Burian, the minister for foreign affairs, noted in his diary, dated 6 June, that in the event of the offensive succeeding, his government would be in a position to offer an honourable peace; failing that, the people would force a settlement in the autumn. The Austrian offensive on the Piave failed. As on the western front, the central powers lost the initiative at the moment when American troops started to swing the balance in the Entente's favour.

The decisive event from the military standpoint was the collapse of the Bulgarian front in September. The French Eastern army based at Thessaloniki had wiped out all resistance in Macedonia and entered Serbia. Austrian and German reinforcements sent in haste were unable to restore the situation and the Bulgarian government signed the armistice on 26 September 1918, while Romania entered the war on the side of the Entente. Three weeks later, on 18 October, the Ottoman empire laid down its arms and signed the Moudros armistice. Marshal Kövess made desperate efforts but nothing could stop Franchet d'Esperey at the head of the Eastern army as he advanced victoriously towards southern Hungary.

The Italians in October 1918 launched a general offensive against the Austro-Hungarian army which was weakened by serious political tensions. When the united Anglo-Italian forces had broken the Austrian lines at Vittorio Veneto on 24 October, many non-German troops refused to join the line. The front began to disintegrate because many soldiers did not want to die for a state in which they no longer believed. For four years the Allies had waited in vain for the troops on the opposite side to disobey orders for national and political reasons. In the last week of the war, this happened. At this point, provisional governments were already in existence. The political collapse was already a *fait accompli* but the imperial and royal army still existed, justifying the confidence which the Habsburgs had placed in it since the seventeenth century.

In these circumstances, all that was left was to draw a halt to the bloodshed and negotiate an armistice which was signed on 3 November 1918 at Padua. A misunderstanding in the signal corps led to 300 000 men surrendering to the Italians while the other soldiers returned home, some by train, others by their own means. The terms of the armistice at Padua were very severe. The Trentin and the south Tyrol as far as the Brenner had to be abandonned, as did Istria, the Kvarner and north Dalmatia. The Allies ordered the imperial and royal army to demobilize at once and demanded that the German troops withdraw immediately, although in fact 180 000 Germans were made prisoners on 4 November. Allied troops were to have absolute freedom of movement over the whole of the Austro-Hungarian monarchy.

In just a few days, the military might of Austria was annihilated, not for strategic, but for political reasons. The retreat under orders of two Hungarian divisions had contributed to the Allied victory at Vittorio Veneto. The Austrian socialist leader Otto Bauer summed up the situation very well: 'In the interior, the Empire was already fully in decay. At the front it still seemed to live in the unity of an army which embraced every nation. The situation of the summer of 1848 [...] was, however, only a façade since the army could no longer remain unreceptive to revolutionary contagion.'

Austria-Hungary was conquered and disarmed because the different peoples who made it up had, from the summer of 1918, withdrawn their confidence from the Habsburgs and the monarchy, despite the proposals for reform made *in extremis* by the emperor Charles. Suddenly, they had decided to pursue an independent existence.

After the proclamation of the German Republic of Austria (Deutsch-Österreich), Charles withdrew to his castle at Eckartsau in the Marchfeld not far from the place where in 1278 Rudolph I had based the power of his House in the mark of Austria, and defeated Otokar of Bohemia. The emperor did not abdicate formally but 'put a provisional end to his activities' before taking the road into exile. Two tentative attempts at restoration in Hungary were opposed by the successor states, a section of Hungarian public opinion and the Entente. The emperor left power in Vienna to a council of state of twenty-three members who appointed the secretaries of state to direct the ministerial departments.

In the space of a month, one of the oldest monarchies in Europe collapsed. It had been unique among European states, achieving the coexistence of Slavs, Hungarians, Germans and Latins and, more precisely, the association through state-right of historical nations as dissimilar as Germany, Hungary and Bohemia.

Francis Joseph had foreseen that the monarchy would not be able to weather a crisis on the scale of the 1848 revolution. It seems, then, reasonable, since the grand old man was one of those chiefly responsible for the catastophe, to ask why he precipitated his peoples into war. Conrad, who roused considerable reservations in Francis Joseph, based his arguments on the idea that the war with Serbia was without risk and believed that Serbia was isolated, an enormous error of judgement which was shared by others at Vienna and was based on the situation at the time of the Bosnian crisis of 1908. Then, despite the press campaign financed by Russia, the French government had refused to support Nicholas II who subsequently did not dare declare war to prevent the monarchy formally annexing Bosnia-Hercegovina.

In 1914 Poincaré did not want to risk breaking the Franco-Russian alliance which was the basis of French strategy and national security in the face of a Germany perceived to be threatening. The system of alliances was ready to come into play and Serbia was not isolated, a fact which totally discredits the thesis still defended by Hugo Hantsch, that the monarchy had not wanted a European war but rather a limited conflict. Even so, Conrad the warmonger had not considered that Austria-Hungary might confront a war lasting longer than three months. No plans, not even financial ones, had been made for that eventuality.

Europe in 1914 was divided into two systems of alliances opposed to each other, the Entente made up of France, Russia and Great Britain and the Triple Alliance of Germany, Italy and Austro-Hungary which, after Italy's defection, was presently reduced to the central powers, Germany and Austria. It was a dangerous situation which Bismarck had foreseen and dreaded. The slightest incident could degenerate into a crisis beyond the control of any government. This was the situation in the last week of July 1914 when the powers began to mobilize their reserves. The assassination at Sarajevo and the response from Vienna created precisely this volatile situation. After having avoided any risky venture since 1866, Francis Joseph, according to his biographer Jean-Paul Bled, was largely responsible for letting his hand be forced. By agreeing to send the ultimatum to Serbia, he signed the monarchy's death sentence and condemned the House of Habsburg to being a dynasty in exile.[6] Defeat allowed the triumph of the principle of nationality against which the Habsburgs had fought since 1789, thinking, with good reason, that the French idea of the nation was a nonsense in Danubian Europe. The emperor who had the least to gain from declaring war, rushed in and so provoked a catastrophe which still has repercussions today.

The fate of Austro-Hungary was not predetermined. The Habsburg empire in its fourth incarnation, the dual monarchy of 1867, could, with federalist reforms carried out in peacetime, have done much to benefit Europe.

NOTES AND REFERENCES

1. Georges-Henri Soutou, *L'Or et le Sang. Les buts de guerre économiques de la Première Guerre mondiale*, Paris, 1989.
2. A. E. Sokol, *The Imperial and Royal Austro-Hungarian Navy*, Annapolis, 1972.
3. Guy Pedroncini, *Les Mutineries de 1917*, Paris, 1972.

4. Robert Kann and Béla Kiraly (eds), *The Habsburg Empire in World War I. Essays on the Intellectual, Military, Political and Economic Aspects of the Habsburg War Effort*, New York, 1977.
5. Leo Valiani, *La Dissoluzione dell'Austria-Ungeria*, Milan, 1961.
6. Jean-Paul Bled, *Francis Joseph*, Oxford, 1992.

CHAPTER EIGHTEEN

Finis Austriae: Dissolved or Put to Death?[1]

Fin de siècle Vienna, a decadent capital filled with a presentiment of catastrophe, a city of 2 million inhabitants at the head of a rump state of 6.5 million, is a fiction. Robert Musil and other authors of this scenario were writing after the collapse. The aesthetes of the Vienna of 1900 were not the chroniclers of a society enjoying its last days. Cultural life in the 1880s was, as Carl Schorske has shown, so intense that the sons of the businessmen of the Ringstrasse and *Gründerzeit* generation who made up the *Zweite Gesellschaft* devoted themselves to the arts and culture. This younger generation was particularly active in the Secession movement, in the plastic arts and a little later in music when 'the second Viennese school' which included Alban Berg and Arnold Schönberg searched for and found a highly sophisticated new musical language which had nothing in common with the waltzes of the Strauss family or even the operas of Wagner but responded to a need for renewal and found a voice in the works which have become the classics of the second half of the twentieth century.

There are two ways of interpreting the catastrophe which led to the emperor Charles's departure on 12 November 1918. Either it was the 'dissolution' of Austro-Hungary, as the Italian historian Leo Valiani has shown so brilliantly, or else forces hostile to the monarchy quite simply conspired to destroy and replace it with successor states which fell short of being nation-states, as François Fejtö argued in 1988 in his remarkable and convincing book. A third hypothesis, the official version of Malet-Isaac and Czechoslovak historiography, can be discounted entirely. This argues that the *Völkerkerker* finally met the end it deserved as the Habsburgs had enslaved the peoples of Central Europe.

THE DEATH OF FRANCIS JOSEPH

The old emperor lived on for a further two years after war had been declared and persisted in carrying out his duties to the very end. On the eve of his death, he was still working in his office at Schönbrunn although he was already suffering from the pneumonia which finally carried him off. His private life had been marked by a series of bereavements which he had borne with a stoicism that superficial observers might have mistaken for indifference.

The first Habsburg to die tragically was the archduke Ferdinand Maximilian, who was much better intellectually endowed than the emperor, his elder brother by two years. As a liberal, he did not have any political future in the monarchy. While governor-general of Lombardy in 1857, he had tried to make himself popular with the Italians. After the defeat at Solferino, he retired with his young wife Charlotte to the castle of Miramar near Trieste where he idled away his time. When in 1864 leading Mexican conservatives offered him the imperial crown, he accepted and so entered into Napoleon III's scheme for creating a Latin and Catholic monarchy in America to put a check on the United States which were then torn apart by civil war. The young emperor had little support from France and none at all from Francis Joseph. He soon realized that he was called upon to rule a country split by civil war and where president Juarez and the republicans held the power. He would have to conquer his empire by force of arms.

The venture quickly turned to disaster. Ferdinand Maximilian, a liberal, quarelled with the Church and with the conservatives. Juarez was still supported by the United States which was then free of civil war. Napoleon III, unhappy about the changes in European politics, stopped sending money and recalled his expeditionary corps. Ferdinand Maximilian found himself abandoned, was taken prisoner and shot at Queretaro on 19 June 1867, the tragic scene immortalized by Édouard Manet as *The Execution of Maximilian*. Napoleon III and Eugénie went to Strasbourg in August 1867 to express official condolences but also to try to seek forgiveness for the venture in which they had involved the unfortunate Ferdinand Maximilian.

Francis Joseph had forced his brother to renounce all his dynastic rights before embarking for Mexico. He did not support him and was anxious not to involve the monarchy in a distant venture, especially after the defeat at Sadowa. He restored him to his full rights, hoping that the Mexican war council would not dare to shoot an archduke, but Juarez, the son of a peasant, had no respect for the House of Austria. Maximilian's death was felt keenly, especially by his mother the archduchess Sophie, who refused to receive Napoleon III at Salzburg, regarding him as her son's assassin.

The second tragedy of Francis Joseph's life was the death of his only son, the archduke Rudolf, at Mayerling on 30 January 1889. There can be no doubt that the archduke committed suicide, but the scandalous nature of his death in the company of his sixteen-year-old mistress, Maria Vetsera, led the government and the emperor to try to hide the truth. This has given birth to a whole body of romantic literature fed from time to time by 'revelations', the most recent being those made by the empress Zita shortly before her death. The archduke's death has been attributed in turn to the Hungarians, the Jews, the freemasons, Bismarck and Clemenceau, even though the latter was one of the archduke's friends.

The loss of the heir apparent, the *Kronprinz*, was a catastrophe for the monarchy. Rudolf was an amiable figure. He belonged to that generation of liberal princes who in the 1880s for various reasons were unable to show their capabilities but who dreamt of reform and European peace. The archduke's most recent serious biographer, Brigitte Hamann, considers the suicide at Mayerling tantamount to a political defeat. Like his forefather and model Joseph II, the archduke was ill-starred. He had the best of intentions and great qualities but had failed in everything. His birth in 1858 had been welcomed as a great success for the House of Habsburg. Francis Joseph wanted to turn him into a soldier and at an early age imposed on him a military education which left the young Rudolf in the clutches of superannuated warhorses. The result was such a disaster that his father finally appointed as tutor count Latour, an aristocratic liberal whose influence on the young crown prince was decisive. He was, perhaps, the only child of his generation to escape the clerical stamp which the 1855 Concordat gave to the Austrian education system. Latour recruited teachers from among the leading scholars of the monarchy, including Gindely and Arneth, and the only cleric among them was a Hungarian Benedictine and freemason. Unbeknown to his father, Rudolf seems himself to have been initiated through the intermediary of a Hungarian lodge, for freemasonry was forbidden in Austria but permitted in Hungary. His liberal orientation was always criticized by the Church and the aristocracy. Very much under the influence of his mother, the empress Elizabeth, he favoured the bourgeoisie, the Hungarians and all the many nationalities of the Empire. Pro-Slav, he criticized the Compromise of 1867. A supporter of the Jews with close ties to the journalist Moritz Szeps, he was the target of the earliest anti-Semitic campaigns by Schönerer's pan-Germanists. He did not believe that the federalist system of the 'historic nobility' was the best guarantee of the interests of the minorities but rather favoured centralism tied to genuine liberalism. He was disappointed that neo-absolutism had not been pursued further and for longer. With respect to the army, he was as uncompromising as his father and was convinced that it was a powerful cohesive element.

The army was the only area in which Francis Joseph entrusted him with any responsibility. A major-general, the young man was appointed inspector-general of the infantry in 1889. Otherwise, the sovereign and the government kept him at arms length, refusing to keep him informed as an heir presumptive might expect. He tried to act indirectly, inspiring articles in the press in Vienna and Paris and often using the columns of the *Figaro* to express his point of view. Francis Joseph, who loved him dearly, refused to discuss politics and only ever talked to him about hunting.

The major disagreement between the government and the archduke was over foreign policy. As a good liberal, Rudolf detested and feared Russia, but also had no sympathy for Prussia and the German empire. He considered the Austro-German alliance, which since 1879 had been the cornerstone of the monarchy's foreign policy, to be contrary to the best interests of the dynasty and the state. He feared a general war in which Austro-Hungary would have to support a large-scale military effort against Russia. He suspected Bismarck of harbouring ambitions to annex the German provinces of Cisleithania and supported Francis Joseph's great project, post-Sadowa, for a French alliance aimed at revenge. Like the conservative circles at Vienna and his great-uncle Albert, he had not forgotten the humiliation of the defeat in 1866 and did not want to find himself on Germany's side in a war against the republican regime in France which he admired. He was leader of the 'French party' at Vienna. Bismarck and the young William II, king of Prussia and, since 1888, emperor of Germany, detested him and spied on him. They believed that if Rudolf reigned at Vienna, the system of alliances put in place in 1873, confirmed in 1879 and strengthened in 1882 by the Triple Alliance, would be at an end. Rudolf was on good terms with the prince of Wales and supported an alliance with Great Britain. He wanted Austria to pursue an active policy in the Balkans, even going so far as to advocate the cession of Bosnia to the kingdom of Serbia and territorial concessions to Romania at Hungary's expense with the intention of making Austrian influence outweigh that of Russia and Germany at Bucharest and Belgrade.

But as brilliant as he was, the archduke was highly strung. In January 1889, he was worn out by work and dissolute living. He had pursued a life of pleasure, attending the theatre, carrying out his military duties and occupying himself with various intellectual activities. Wasting away with venereal disease, he was depressed and saw himself as finished. The tragedy at Mayerling came as no surprise.

The third tragedy in Francis Joseph's life was the assassination of the empress Elizabeth by Luigi Lucheni, an Italian anarchist, on 9 September at Geneva. The emperor had deeply loved his wife whom he had chosen when very young and whom he had married at sixteen, despite the protests of the archduchess Sophie who had understood that the young girl, who was also her niece, would not always conform to the constraints of the court. From 1859 onwards the empress embarked upon a life of voyages and exotic sojourns on Madeira and Corfu, hunting in England and Ireland, neglecting her children, with the exception of the youngest, Maria-Valeria, and abandoning her husband who addressed to her increasingly desperate letters. She only used her influence over Francis Joseph on two occasions. In 1865 she rescued the archduke Rudolph from the hands of the elderly soldiers who were in the process of driving him insane and secured a liberal education for him. In 1867 she supported the Compromise, a move which brought her a popularity in Hungary comparable to that enjoyed by Maria-Theresa, although the Magyars found it difficult to forgive their brutal repression in 1849.

She tried to make a reputation for herself as a horsewoman, then, as a great admirer of Heinrich Heine, turned her hand to poetry. Her contempt for the monarchy was profound. She considered it 'a ruin' and benefited from the advantages of the system without wishing to accept its constraints. Sporting, a feminist, anorexic, egocentric, a tyrant over her entourage, she was very modern in outlook. Her radiant beauty and character seduced many of her contemporaries, as it has posterity. She was broken by the suicide of her son and passed the last years of her life in perpetual wandering, having eased the way for Francis Joseph to enjoy intimate relations with Katarina Schratt, an actress from the Burgtheater who brought the emperor a measure of the bourgeois comfort in which his life had been so lacking. He wept sincerely at his wife's death.

Francis Joseph certainly wept far less for the archduke Francis Ferdinand who, after the tragic events of 1889, had been groomed as his successor. The emperor's younger brother Victor Louis would, like Ferdinand the Benign, have been incapable of exercising power. Robert Kann has shed new light on the character of the archduke who was as conservative as his cousin was liberal. A man of character, Francis Ferdinand was stubborn. Suffering from the consequences of pulmonary tuberculosis, he married late and persisted in his choice of wife even though the emperor refused him permission to marry. The countess Sophie Chotek belonged to a good and long-established Bohemian family but the Choteks were not connected to the empire and did not belong to a sovereign house. Neither the emperor nor Francis Ferdinand would move and the archduke had to be content with a morganatic marriage. His wife became duchess of Hohenberg and his three children were without any rights to the throne. The emperor appealed to the famous ruling of 1839 but Francis Ferdinand never forgave his uncle who had appointed him inspector-general of the army and the navy in 1898. He devoted himself to the navy and to aeronautics but he neglected the artillery and ignored the lessons in trench-warfare to be learnt from the Russian-Japanese war. From 1906 he became actively involved in politics and formed his own cabinet at the Belvedere which served as a shadow government or rather a shadow cabinet.

His politics were the opposite of those of his cousin Rudolf whom he visited often and of whom he was very fond. He corresponded with William II but kept his distance from Germany since he had not forgotten Sadowa and found it difficult to tolerate the role Berlin had assigned to Vienna. In short, he reacted the same way as the archduke Albert who had moulded him into a true Habsburg. Like the emperor he had wanted universal suffrage to be introduced in Hungary and believed it essential to maintain the unity of the army. Brusque, incapable of mastering his speech, he was seen, probably mistakenly, as the head of the war party which earnt him the hatred of the South Slav nationalists and provoked his assassination on 28 June 1914. His physical courage was his undoing. After the first attempt upon his life with a bomb, he should have left the town, but he recrossed Sarajevo in an open car only to fall victim to the bullets of the terrorist, Gavrilo Princip. He shared the indecisiveness characteristic of so many of the Habsburgs and was very sensitive to the influence of those in his entourage. Despite Kann's research among the archduke's personal papers, the mystery surrounding Francis Ferdinand remains unresolved.

THE EMPEROR CHARLES I (1916–18)

The emperor Charles, the last Habsburg to reign over the monarchy, was born in 1887. His reign, like that of Leopold II, was brief, lasting just two years from November 1916 to November 1918. He was the son of Otto, 'the fine archduke', and Maria Josepha of Saxony and became heir apparent after his father's death in 1906. Otto, the younger brother of Francis Ferdinand, led a dissolute life, even more scandalous than that of the future Edward VII. Maria Josepha, pious and long-suffering, took great care over her children's education. The archduke Charles attended the *Schottengymnasium*, a prestigious school run by Benedictines in the centre of Vienna, and then at eighteen followed his father, uncle and cousin Rudolf into the army. As a cavalry officer, he expressed interest in his uncle's projects, but carefully kept his distance from political life, devoting himself to the army and his family. In 1911 he married Zita of Bourbon-Parma who died in 1989. The couple had six children of whom the archduke Otto is the eldest. Promoted to major in 1912, he settled in the castle of Hetzendorf near Schönbrunn.

After the assassination of Francis Ferdinand, Charles remained far removed from the decisions of government and took an active part in the conflict, first as a staff officer in the general headquarters at Teschen. Then in 1916 he was promoted to lieutenant-general and took part in the offensive on the Italian front at the head of the 20th corps before being sent to Galicia to raise the morale of the troops on the eve of their assault on Broussilov. After his accession, he became commander-in-chief of his armies, installed the general headquarters at Baden and dismissed Conrad in a gesture designed to show that the army would no longer dictate the policy of the monarchy. He had less success with Tísza than with Conrad since the president of the Hungarian council lost no time in forcing upon him a coronation which entailed his swearing to uphold the constitution and prevented him from introducing any changes to the 1867 Compromise. The coronation of king Charles IV of Hungary and of his queen Zita was the monarchy's final magnificent ceremonial flourish and reinforced the Habsburgs' links with Hungary.

Charles I was convinced that the monarchy needed reforming and that it had much to gain from concluding peace, even at the price of breaking with Germany which, as a good military man, he realized would mean losing the war. In his address 'to his peoples' before his coronation, he set out his strategy:

I wish to do everything to banish the horrors and sacrifices of war as quickly as possible and as soon as military honour, the best interests of my states and of their loyal allies and the stubborness of the enemy allow, to restore to my peoples the blessings of peace. I wish to uphold constitutional liberties and other rights and to safeguard legal equality for everyone. Stirred by a deep love for my peoples, I want to consecrate my life and all my strength to this lofty task.

The margin for manoeuvre was slight. The emperor could count on the support of his wife, Zita, whose brothers were officers in the Belgian army fighting on the side of the Entente, and who made no attempt to hide her hostility towards Germany. He appointed as minister for foreign affairs count Czernin, a member of the Bohemian aristocracy who was hostile to the Hungarian political class and who had formerly served in the Belvedere circle of the archduke Francis Ferdinand. The sovereign wanted to make concessions to the Serbs, Czechs and Slovaks but his hands were tied after the coronation at Budapest.

William II greatly mistrusted his new ally but in August 1917 he resumed negotiations over customs union between the two central empires. The two sides were not in favour of complete customs union and were only concerned with negotiating preferential tariffs on certain products since Austria wanted to protect its industry from German competition.

The two allies, however, were profoundly at odds over the fate of Poland in the event of victory. The staff headquarters of the *Reich* wanted Congress Poland to become a German protectorate. The other proposal was for all the Poles, including those in Galicia and Russian Poland, to be brought together within a Habsburg protectorate and for Austria-Hungary be transformed into a triple monarchy. This new Poland would of course be integrated within *Mitteleuropa*.

The Austrian social democrats clamoured for immediate peace without annexations or indemnity. The emperor found himself conducting a two-fold policy which combined the official diplomacy pursued by count Czernin and the secret diplomacy in which he himself was directly engaged.

ATTEMPTS AT A SEPARATE PEACE

After his accession, Charles I's only intention was to bring his country out of the war unharmed. It is probable that he lay behind certain steps taken by the French government, and stressed the urgency of the mission sent from France to Berne in 1915–16. In the event of the *Reich* restoring Alsace-Lorraine, France would be prepared to sign a separate peace.

At the beginning of 1917, the conditions seemed to him right for negotiations. According to the Austrian embassy to Berne, the moment had come to negotiate with France and the sovereign knew that he would benefit from having a good image with the Allies. At the time of the Austro-German conference at Kreuznach in April 1917, he had even tried to break the impasse by offering to cede Galicia to Poland on condition that Germany restore Alsace-Lorraine to France. This proposal was rejected outright by the German chancellor Michaelis, who was completely under the thumbs of the militarist party of Hindenburg and Ludendorff and by the pan-Germanists. Charles I then entrusted his brother-in-law, prince Sixtus of Bourbon-Parma, with a secret mission. For a long time these talks were taken as being far-fetched, without any serious chance of success, but in fact it seems that if Briand had remained president of the council in Paris, 1917 might have been the year of a peace based on compromise, a result which would have displeased militarist parties on both sides of the Rhine. Fejtö has shown that those who wanted an out-and-out victory, by various underhand moves, prevented the war from ending in conditions which, in Briand's words, 'would have made it possible to save Europe and to prevent future catastrophes'.

Prince Sixtus made many discreet journeys between Paris and Vienna on the pretext of visiting his mother in Switzerland. In a letter to his brother-in-law, the emperor undertook to support France's 'just claims' to Alsace-Lorraine. The prince was well received by Poincaré but it was essential for him to make contact with the Allies. The British government proved in favour of negotiations but no further progress was made because Italy was dissatisfied at the propect of receiving nothing more than the Trentino. Peace would only have been possible if France had renounced Alsace-Lorraine and Italy had renounced Trieste, losses which after so many other sacrifices, public opinion in neither country would countenance. Count Czernin, who was kept informed of the negotiations, was opposed to the idea of a separate peace, as is evident from the letter he sent prince Sixtus in March 1917, tempered by an accompanying letter from the emperor. As for how the German headquarters would have responded to Austria-Hungary laying down its arms, that can only be guessed at.

The emperor Charles's subsequent attempts at negotiations failed for similar reasons. Matters were made worse in November 1917 by the appointment as president of the council of Clemenceau, whose one plan was to continue fighting until final victory was reached. The emperor also tried to start negotiations with the king of Spain, Alphonso XIII, who had remained neutral, as mediator. He also tried to use as mediators the Holy See, for pope Benedict XV genuinely wanted to see an end to the war, and the queen of Belgium who was a Wittelsbach. These efforts were all in vain since the Allies increasingly saw the monarchy as serving German interests and as a puppet of Berlin.

The French headquarters, disappointed by the politicians' indecisiveness, also tried to approach those in authority in Austria-Hungary. The Second Bureau, responsible for counter-espionage and more generally for military intelligence, was convinced that it was possible and desirable to detach the monarchy from the German alliance. In the event of peace, Austria-Hungary would try to preserve its influence in Eastern Europe and the Balkans with the purpose of controlling the Hamburg-Baghdad line, the famous *Baghdad-Bahn* project of the beginning of the century. The report sent to the high command stated that the monarchy was still powerful and that it was not in the Allies' interest to support its break-up. Rather, it would be far more expedient to break the direct links which under the influence of Hungary had been established with Germany since 1879. The monarchy for its part would have to give as compensation some of its territory – Transylvania, the Bukovina and Galicia – and agree to the founding of a South Slav state. In return for internal reforms, which Charles I wanted, the Habsburgs could remain at the head of a Danubian monarchy which was essential for the equilibrium of Europe. It is evident from this that the French military was well-informed and not swayed by any ideology. It wanted in practice to conclude an armistice with Austria-Hungary.

The Armand-Revertera negotiations took place in Switzerland in the course of the summer of 1917. These were a continuation of the discussions begun in March 1917 by Painlevé, the French minister of war, and held through the mediation of Madam Zuckerkandl, the daughter of Moritz Szeps and a friend of the archduke Rudolph, and her sister, Sophie Clemenceau, the sister-in-law of 'the Tiger'. Clemenceau's friendship with the archduke had come about through the Szeps family and it was through Szeps's daughters that attempts had been made to renew negotiations with Vienna, negotiations which met a blunt refusal from Czernin. Painlevé had become president of the council and used the report of the Second Bureau to renew the link. In August, he commissioned major Armand with the task and he met count Revertera who had the emperor's confidence. Negotiations continued with the backing of the new president of the council, Clemenceau, until February 1918. The fate of Alsace-Lorraine, which was a matter of honour for Germany, remained a stumbling-block. To return it to France would be a sign of defeat and the emperor Charles could not impose a humiliating defeat on his ally. He saw Berlin's refusal as justified and he did not see himself as being in a position to conclude a separate peace with the Entente. Revertera sent a note on 25 February 1918 in which Austria-Hungary expressed its readiness to resume discussions once the French government renounced all plans to annex territory and took as the basis for negotiations the *status quo ante bellum* because Germany could not be forced to surrender provinces which belonged to it legitimately. The Austrian concessions had diminished in a year; at the beginning of 1917 peace negotiations had run aground on the issue of Trieste, at the beginning of 1918 they stumbled over the question of Alsace-Lorraine.

There had been substantial changes within the central empires' camp. In 1917 the German crown prince William favoured an accord and even seemed to support the steps taken by the Habsburgs. In 1918 Hindenburg was dismissed and Ludendorff led the army and government while the Hohenzollerns obediently followed the bidding of the militarist party. The Russian Revolution of October 1917 and the Peace of Brest-Litovsk concluded on 3 March 1918 made it possible to believe that victory was to hand and that with additional effort on the western front, before the Americans arrived in force, victory was possible and peace could be imposed on the Entente. All this might have happened if Czernin, who apparently believed in the superiority of the German army, had not caused the emperor to be rather more circumspect.

It was at this point that Clemenceau, who was not hostile towards Austria-Hungary and distinguished between German imperialism and the interests of the Habsburgs, decided to abandon the emperor to his fate and to support the sworn enemies of the monarchy by promising the Czechs, Serbs and Croats what they demanded. As Charles I had decided against disassociating himself from Germany, Vienna appeared a satellite of Berlin. It would have been better for him to support the national committees and to obtain the cooperation of the Czechoslovak Legion made up of former Austro-Hungarian prisoners of war who, even before the Russian Revolution, had decided to fight on the side of the Entente. Ribot, the minister for foreign affairs, who was close to Clemenceau, had doubts as to whether Charles I's policy could succeed, doubting whether a young and inexperienced ruler could succeed when Francis Joseph with all his prestige and experience had been incapable of securing a straightforward peace. An enormous blunder broke the tenuous links between Paris and Vienna. On 2 April 1918, Czernin, in front of the municipal council of Vienna, praised the virtues of the Austro-German alliance and implied that shortly before the success of Ludendorff's offensive, Clemenceau had offered to negotiate with Austria. The Tiger's response was scathing, 'count Czernin has lied'. He published a letter of 24 March 1917 in which the emperor announced that 'if Germany refuses to enter upon the path of reason, he will be obliged to abandon the alliance in order to make a separate peace with the Entente'.

This incident provoked a serious crisis in Vienna where Czernin dared to suggest to the emperor that he should abdicate. Charles I, supported by the empress, refused and got rid of his minister, replacing him with Burian who had been minister for foreign affairs at the time of his accession. Czernin had developed his ideas after the Austrian victory at Caporetto and would have been prepared to turn the monarchy into a satellite of Germany. This was the impression he gave at the time of the peace negotiations with Bolshevik Russia when he agreed to occupy the Ukraine with Austro-Hungarian units. With Czernin out the way, William II forced the Habsburgs to reinforce their alliance and imposed plans for the economy and for bringing into line the royal and imperial army which the German headquarters had always mistrusted. The Allies thought that Austria would become like Bavaria, autonomous militarily but in practice at the disposal of the Prussian cabinet and heaquarters.

Czernin was Charles I's evil genius and Austria-Hungary was condemned to sharing the same fate as the *Reich*. It was Charles I's tragedy that he wanted to save the monarchy without betraying his allies in Berlin, a policy which Czernin later characterized for Tísza as 'flirtation without betrayal, the most foolish course of all'.

In October 1918 when military defeat seemed inevitable, Charles I tried to save the monarchy by implementing reforms in the spirit of president Wilson's fourteen points. The president was not hostile towards Austria-Hungary and the Habsburgs and had shown reservations over the national committees, not so much with respect to their legality but as to whether the committees of émigrés represented any but themselves. The tenth point of the famous declaration of 8 January 1918 was not intended to destroy Austria-Hungary but simply 'to accord the peoples of Austria-Hungary the greatest latitude for the development of their autonomy'. Wilson changed his mind at the end of May 1918 and on 3 September accepted the principle of an independent Czechoslovakia and Yugoslavia. Nothing could halt the collapse.

POLITICAL CATASTROPHE

In October 1918 a series of purely political events preceded military defeat which to a great extent was the consequence of the formation of independent states whose citizens no longer had any reason to fight for a lost cause.

On 4 October the *Reichsrat* recognized the right to self-determination of all the peoples of the empire, agreeing a resolution made by the socialist Victor Adler, the father of the Adler who in 1916 had assassinated Stürgkh, the president of the council. On 31 October, Lammasch, president of the acting council, transferred his powers to a provisional government of German Austria.

The emperor, though, had published on 17 October a manifesto transforming the monarchy into a federation of nation-states. Had this step been taken a year earlier, it would, perhaps, have satisfied most of his subjects' quite legitimate claims. Promulgated as it was through force of circumstance, it could only appear as further proof of the weakness of a prince who had never been able to control destiny. When in spring 1918 he decided to be crowned king of Bohemia, he consulted the Hungarian government which refused to give its approval. Like Francis Joseph, Charles I did not dare defy the interdicts of the Hungarian political class.

These measures were hopelessly in vain because the Allies had determined to disband Austria-Hungary. The negotiations between Charles I and president Wilson on how to restructure the monarchy came to nothing. During the winter of 1918, the emperor had tried to show the American president that they were in agreement on many points and that their objectives could be reconciled. It was a waste of time and effort. The American declaration of 3 September showed that Wilson had been won over to Clemenceau and Lloyd George's position and was not opposed to the break-up of Austria-Hungary.

At this stage, the national committees were a considerable political force and in them the Allies possessed the means to act. The first and second generation Slav immigrants to the United States provided them with money and ran newspapers. In Paris, the French historian Ernest Denis and his Czech friend Tomáš Masaryk, who had fled from Austria, edited *La Nation tchèque*. Most important of all, the Czechs were a military force. In 1918 the Czech legions appeared to Allied headquarters as a useful additional force now that the Germans were launching potentially decisive offensives on the western front, just prior to the large-scale engagement of American troops. The governments of the Entente were consequently inclined to listen favourably to the claims of the national committees.

In May a meeting was held at Rome of nations which considered themselves oppressed by the Habsburgs. A few weeks later, Clemenceau's cabinet recognized the Czech national council as 'the future basis for an independent government and the representative of the Czechoslovak interests'.

As early as 20 July 1917, the basis for the future Yugoslavia had been laid by the agreement reached between the president of the Serb council, Nikola Pašić, and the president of the South Slav committee in London, Trumbić. The South Slavs of Austria-Hungary agreed to tie their future to that of Serbia. Finally, in Hungary, the social democrats and the liberal left, the heirs of the party of 1848, under the leadership of the francophile Mihály Károlyi, seized the opportunity to declare Hungary independent. Károlyi had preferred to return home in 1915 rather than to spend the war in exile and the Hungarians were without a national committee to represent them before the Allies.

Until the summer of 1918, the national opposition groups which quietly maintained relations with the émigrés remained very unadventurous, but after the front in Serbia was broken and the armistice signed between Bulgaria and the Entente, the representatives of the national groups flew to the aid of victory.

The Poles were already confidently expressing their wish to rebuild an independent state and their declaration of 17 October hastened the process of disintegration. On 21 October 1918, the Germans of Austria declared their right to self-determination. The following week there was an uprising in Prague which gave power to the Czech national council, a body which was made up of notables and which was far from representative. Two days later, on 30 October, the council called a national assembly. On the same day, the Germans in Austria constituted a provisional government and Charles I, over the telephone, recognized the appointment of count Károlyi who had just constituted a provisional government in Budapest and made clear his intention of declaring Hungarian independence in accordance with the programme of the democratic left and the Hungarian national council. On 25 October, the council had adopted a twelve-point programme which demanded universal suffrage and recognized the nation-states of Poland, Yugoslavia and of the Czechs. It hoped that adherence to the Wilson principles would guarantee the territorial integrity of Hungary.

The threat that Hungary might lose territory became real when the Slovak national council followed the Czechs two days later and on 30 October announced the creation of an independent Czechoslovak state. The Croatian Diet on 29 October declared that Croatia's links with Hungary and Austria were at an end and rallied to a united South Slav state. On 27 October, the Romanian national council proclaimed the union of Transylvania and Romania and on 31 October the Ukrainians of Galicia seceded.

The break-up of the monarchy took place extraordinarily quickly. With the Allies' support, it was irreversible. The treaties which later accompanied the Versailles Treaty merely gave judicial sanction to a new system which was neither able nor willing to respect the rights of some peoples to self-determination, as the Germans of Bohemia and the Hungarians of Slovakia and Transylvania learnt to their cost. For the new government in Prague it was out of the question for the Germans of the Sudeten to join their fellow Germans in the Austrian republic because such an arrangement would have compromised the economic and strategic interests of the new state. Among the Czechs, both the conservatives and the radicals like Beneš, there was a strong movement in support of maintaining the integrity of the kingdom of Bohemia. The provisional government was resolved to see its point of view triumph. In December 1918, the Sudeten Germans organized demonstrations in favour of returning under the Vienna government. Masaryk did not hesitate to bring in the army and so kept almost 3 million Germans within the new state. The feelings of these involuntary Czech citizens towards Czechoslovakia were always, at the best, lukewarm.

The borders of the new Austria were fixed in the victors' interests despite the grandiose declarations made before the world and president Wilson's twelve-point programme. The Austrian Germans' new state was reduced to no more than the middle valley of the Danube and the alpine lands. It corresponded to the German-speaking hereditary lands of the Habsburg patrimony and covered up to 84 000 square kilometres, with 6.5 million inhabitants unevenly divided between the country and the capital of about 2 million and still greatly swollen with refugee officials from throughout the monarchy. The Austrian republic was almost ethnically and linguistically homogenous. It was forbidden by the terms of the Treaty of Saint-Germain from declaring union with Germany, which was what the social democrats and the nationalist right wanted. Such a union would be contrary to the interests of France, which as victor was not going to make a gift to its neighbour of 6.5 million inhabitants and so promote German unity to an extent exceeding even Bismarck's wishes.

At the time the armistice was signed at Padua, the Austro-Hungarian army was still in existence but Austria-Hungary had been replaced by a string of successor states, 'the good' and 'the bad'. The peace treaties singled out two states as responsible for the war: German Austria led by the social democrat Renner, and Hungary, now a kingdom without a king, for Charles IV was carefully kept out of the way. Hungary was now governed by the regent Horthy, formerly admiral in the imperial navy which had been handed over to the Yugoslavs. Harsh terms were imposed upon the two countries because it was they that had declared war in August 1914. The rest of Francis Joseph's subjects found themselves in the victor's camp, in the new state of Czechoslovakia which no-one in 1914 had foreseen, and in the South Slav or Yugoslav state, tantamount to a greater Serbia, into which the Croats to their great misfortune found themselves suddenly integrated, bereft of the state-right which had protected them since the Middle Ages.

On 3 November, the Habsburg empire came to an end and its disappearance was a catastrophe for Danubian Europe and for Europe as a whole. The new settlement created more problems than it solved. It was the result of deliberate action and was not solely produced by the weariness of the monarchy's peoples and the quite justified grievances of certain national groups.

THE REASONS FOR THE BREAK-UP

Without going as far as Fejtö in his harsh indictment of the French politicians, it must be said that the governments of the Entente undertook a fight to the death with the Kaiser's Germany and did little to help Germany's 'second in command'. They thought, unlike the military, that a host of successor states, potential clients of the Entente, would be the easiest way of saving Central Europe from German domination. These successor states would also serve as a *cordon sanitaire* against the Bolshevik revolution. This shows a serious failure to understand the situation but explains the course taken by Austro-Hungarian diplomacy after 1873 when Francis Joseph sealed the reconciliation between the Habsburgs and the Hohenzollerns by concluding the 'alliance of the three emperors', Germany, Austria and Russia. This approach is understandable in the light of Bismarck's relative moderation in the aftermath of Sadowa.

Moderation was certainly not a characteristic of the First World War, especially when it is seen as two very different conflicts intertwined. The war unleashed by Francis Joseph's ultimatum was a traditional, imperialist conflict. It had been imagined that the war would be limited to a campaign lasting the summer of 1914. Depending on what happened on the ground, it would not be long before negotiations were begun, territory exchanged and, perhaps, indemnities exacted. The balance of power in Europe would be adjusted, not overthrown. According to these traditional expectations, it would be possible at any moment to start negotiations for a peace based on compromise.

During the autumn of 1914, the nature of the war underwent a profound change and all-out victory became the objective. The goal was not simply to undermine but to destroy the enemy. This change in strategy was linked to changes in the composition of the armies engaged in combat. Active units of young conscripts were replaced by legions made up of reservists, family men torn from their hearth and home, and trained mainly by reserve officers. These nations-in-arms needed a reason to fight and respect for discipline was insufficient to maintain morale. Propaganda offered them the goal of total victory, an end to war through the war to end all wars, the elimination of imperialism and German militarism. The war became an ideological war and so intensified. It changed both quantitatively and qualitatively. The enemy became the devil, the personification of evil.

It was not difficult in France to revive the idea of revolution, of bringing happiness to those peoples oppressed by tyranny, even against their will, and imposing liberty upon them. For the First Republic, the Habsburgs had been its prime enemy and in due course became so for the Third Republic also. It was held against them that as the allies of German imperialism, they had become satellites of Berlin. The discussions concerning *Mitteleuropa*, as Soutou has shown, could scarcely reassure the French authorities. The emperor Charles, for all his demonstrations of good will towards the Entente, exposed himself to such criticisms by allowing Czernin to act as he did and by signing the Spa convention. Austria-Hungary was seen as a Catholic, even a clerical power, for the Habsburgs had never hidden their attachment to the faith of their fathers. For all the display of gestural piety and despite the signing of a short-lived concordat, they were certainly less subject to the will of the Holy See than most of the French clergy, especially after the law separating the Church and the state. The old accusations of obscurantism, however, remained very much alive. The intellectual developments under Joseph II and during the liberal era were readily overlooked. For the intelligentsia of the Left, which was, it is true, very narcissistic, it was as though the intellectual ferment of *fin de siècle* Vienna had never happened. The final accusation against Austria in the eyes of its enemies was that the monarchy was not a nation-state and Austria-Hungary was not a republic. The war provided the opportunity to overthrow the monarchies of Europe and to create a series of sister-republics, clients of the French republic. This, more or less, was the inspiration behind the foreign policy of the Directoire.

The radicals who had been in power since the beginning of the century and had won the elections in 1914, wanted to republicanize Europe. They knew that Germany was a Catholic power but was also home to Protestants and freemasons, whereas Austria was the embodiment of Catholicism and monarchy. It would be impossible to republicanize Europe without destroying the Habsburg monarchy. Fejtö, in his essay *Requiem pour un empire défunt*, analysed the great plan of the French political class and explained why no-one was really prepared to offer help to the emperor Charles. Fejtö wrote:

To recover Alsace-Lorraine and to be avenged for Sedan were insufficient objectives. The great project the political and intellectual elites presented to the soldiers in the trenches was to rid Europe of the last traces of clericalism and monarchy, a project they chose to present regardless of the process of liberalization which had gathered pace in Germany and Austria since the turn of the century, liberalization they ignored or pretended to ignore although they had been witness to the process. It was this great plan which brought the radical republicans into sacred union with nationalist elements, the advocates of revenge on the right, and offered an ear to émigrés from the nations and nationalities of the Austro-Hungarian monarchy who bore 'expert' witness to the state of quasi-colonial oppression to which their compatriots were subjected by the Austrians, Hungarians, Germans and others.

In 1916 the *Comité nationale d'études*, a group led by Léon Bourgeois, a moderate and pluralist, reflected on French objectives in the war and inclined towards a peace with Germany based on compromise. After Ernest Denis's suggestion, however, the *Comité* moved in favour of destroying Austria-Hungary, despite François Wendel's energetic support for the Danubian monarchy. The leading figures in this movement, Louis Léger, Ernest Denis and Louis Eisenmann, were part of a small group drawn from the French universities and supported by their friends Masaryk and Beneš. Léger, a professor of slavistics, had travelled in Bohemia in 1864 and gave substance to the thesis that 8 million Germans and 8 million Hungarians governed a state of 35 million, that the monarchy's *raison d'être* was to resist Ottoman imperialism and that pan-Slavism alone could constitute an effective barrier against pan-Germanism. Since he was convinced that the Slovaks and Slovenes, the non-historic nations, did not have any political significance, he gave the main role to the Serbs and Croats, developing the Illyrian thesis of Ljudevit Gaj which in its modernized form became the 'Yugoslav idea'. Léger was equally enraptured by the Czechs and felt that the 1867 Compromise had dealt them a grave injustice.

The Czechs' greatest champion was the historian Ernest Denis. He was active on their behalf at two levels. His academic writings, albeit somewhat biased, at least had the merit of informing the French about Bohemian history and after the declaration of war he became politically active. A republican and Protestant, he exaggerated the significance of the Hussite tradition and darkened the history of Catholic Bohemia, accorded little weight to the patriotism of the Bohemians of German origin and distorted the Germans' actions. Most important, though, with Louis Eisenmann, the author of *Compromis austro-hongrois*, he became the favoured representative of the Czech emigration and its leaders Masaryk and Beneš. For a long time, Denis had been a supporter of Austro-Slavism and recommended moderation to his friends in Prague who gave vent to their grievances against the Hungarians, pan-Germanists and the German liberals.

It was the journalist André Chéradame who, at the beginning of the century, posed the 'Austrian question' and declared confidently that the dissolution of Austria-Hungary was inevitable. The Habsburgs' empire would be divided between Berlin and St Petersburg.

When Masaryk arrived in Paris in 1915, he brought together the small groups of émigrés and separated them from the other subjects of the Habsburgs in France. In 1916 he was elected president of the Czech national council and the following year in Rome formed a Czech legion from among the prisoners on the Italian front. Masaryk was an academic who had taught at Vienna before being elected deputy to the *Reichsrat* in 1891. In 1900 he founded the 'moderate party' which he represented in the parliament in Vienna while continuing to publish his philosophical works. Masaryk was not attracted by the archduke Francis Ferdinand's proposals and wanted to turn the monarchy into a confederation on the Swiss model. He changed his mind considerably in the course of 1915 and was convinced that the only way to present an obstacle to pan-Germanism was to surround Germany with small independent states allied to the Entente and fundamentally anti-German. For this to be achieved, not only Austria-Hungary would have to be dismantled but also the Ottoman empire which with Mustapha Kemal and the Young Turks had renounced its traditional alliances in order to become a satellite of the kaiser. Masaryk, an intelligent and cultured man, with the support of the freemasons was able to win over those he spoke to in Paris. The role played by freemasonry, although important, has been exaggerated by Fejtö. Poincaré, who was not a freemason but a patriot and russophile, as far back as 1912 had put a stop to the tentative diplomatic rapprochement between Paris and Vienna and Budapest which had Clemenceau's support. He recalled Crozier, the ambassador to Vienna, and prevented Hungary from having access to French loans. Ährenthal, however, was in favour of a rapprochement because he wanted to be free of Berlin's financial and diplomatic protection.

Masaryk, more than anyone else, invented Czechoslovakia, which was without any historical basis and, through the victors, became a miniature Austria-Hungary. Its sole justification was geo-strategic for it brought together the Czechs and Slovaks who were related linguistically but had had separate histories since the tenth century. The other pillar of Masaryk's programme was Yugoslavia where the coexistence of the Croats and Serbs, two related nations who had been separated by history, had to be achieved; it became clear shortly after the victory that neither nation was capable of living peacefully with the other. Masaryk, with the help of the young and brilliant Edvard Beneš, employed his remarkable powers of persuasion first in Paris, then in Rome and London. The prolonged war gave him the time he needed and the Slav émigrés in the United States supplied him with the necessary money. On 21 July 1918, his party was victorious. Clemenceau's cabinet recognized the national council as the provisional government of the future Czechoslovak republic and the destiny of the Habsburg monarchy was finally sealed. France, soon followed by the Entente and the United States, for strategic and ideological reasons favoured the 'Balkanization' of Central Europe in order to contain German imperialism and, if need be, the Bolshevik revolution.

The response came twenty years later at the Munich conference. The Danubian monarchy, in the form it assumed under Ferdinand I, had lasted for four centuries, from 1526 to 1918. The system of successor states and the Little Entente, made up of Czechoslovakia, Romania and the kingdom of Serbs, Croats and Slovenes, lasted two decades and did nothing to impede the outbreak of the Second World War.

The dissolution of Austria-Hungary is not explained by the question of nationalities, the oppression of the Slavs and the Romanians, or even the tremendous tensions created during the war which might have brought the Bolshevic revolution into Europe. The risk was real but revolution only broke out in Budapest where Béla Kun and the republic of councils remained in power for ten days during 1919.

The national conflicts and injustices suffered by the Czechs were of themselves insufficient to destroy Austria-Hungary. Universal suffrage, positive action by the social democrats and the emperor Charles's willingness to embark on reform would have been sufficient to bring about a new stage in transforming the monarchy into a federal state. The Allies, especially those on the Left in France, did not have any sympathy for the Habsburgs, were prepared to listen to Masaryk and were willing to allow the map of Europe to be completely redrawn in the belief that this would establish peace and draw a halt to German imperialism.

The political catastrophe is largely explained by external factors and, after a conflict lasting many years, by the triumph of the principles of the French Revolution. It was a disastrous choice, even for French interests, and one which only the imperatives of total war could justify, namely the promises made to the Allies whose cooperation was essential for the defeat of the central empires. Austria-Hungary was still viable after being stripped of Transylvania, the Trentino and Bosnia-Hercegovina. The successor states fell far short of the treaties which Beneš had inspired. They prevented economic union, fixed the frontiers in an illogical fashion and kept alive regional conflicts by giving rise to a Hungarian irredentist movement.

If it is agreed that Danubian Europe consisted of various genuine nation-states, Poland, Hungary, Bohemia, Croatia, Serbia, Romania and Transylvania, then it would seem that there were four possible ways in which it could be structured.

The first way was that offered by the Habsburgs and entailed gathering the different lands together to form a great power. This arrangement had its faults but it worked and its finest spokesman was Palacký, a Czech patriot whom no-one could accuse of being in the Habsburgs' pay.

Certain foreigners who thought of themselves as well-informed, believed in another solution which allowed for the existence of successor states. These states, though, were only versions of Austro-Hungary in miniature and could do no more than create an illusion at the time of the brief eclipse of German and Russian imperialism. The French republic was the self-appointed protector of its Central European friends. It did not have the military means to come to their aid. The defensive strategy of the Maginot Line was a straightforward negation of such a system of alliances.

The third solution was German expansion. The Third Reich took advantage of French weakness and from 1936 onwards realized its Central European programme with the aid of the German-speakers of *Mitteleuropa* who felt excluded from the successor states. In 1940 the map was remodelled on pan-German principles; Austria was annexed, Bohemia-Moravia became a protectorate, Poland was occupied, Slovakia and Romania reduced to satellites, while Hungary was an ally and Yugoslavia was soon to be carved up.

The fourth solution was presented by the Allied victory and liberation by the Red Army. This was the *pax sovietica*. The successor states were reinstated, with modifications to their 1920 borders in the case of Poland, Czechoslovakia and Romania. They appeared as independent states but, with the exception of Austria which remained neutral, were controlled by Communist governments. Until 1989, the presence of the Red Army and integration within the Warsaw Pact allowed them only formal independence. Yugoslavia was Communist but independent of Moscow. The other successor states, though, formed a formidiable bulwark for the Soviet Union which under Stalin had realized one of the pan-Slavist dreams. Russian imperialism, under a cover of ideology, had made an extraordinary advance into Europe. The hereditary lands which recovered their independence in 1955 were relieved to have escaped the fate of Bohemia and Hungary. The misfortunes they had suffered since 1914 had served to forge their national consciousness.

What purpose did the destruction of Austria-Hungary serve? Its peoples had been much freer before 1914 than they were under the system put in place after 1938.

At the end of 1989, Russian imperialism surrendered its hold over its East European defences. Its abandonment of its eastern bulwark posed a question for the whole of Europe. Would it be replaced by a new form of German imperialism or would the nations freed from Communism be joined together in a European confederation?

NOTE AND REFERENCE

1. François Fejtö, *Requiem pour un Empire défunt. Histoire de la destruction de l'Autriche-Hongrie*, Paris, 1988.

Conclusion

'The House of Austria, a European dynasty', the subtitle of Adam Wandruszka's work, appears, at the end of this survey of the history of the Habsburgs, especially appropriate. Herein lay its grandeur and strength in an age when patriotism had not yet degenerated into disruptive nationalism, but also its weakness when the nation-state became the magic formula of political science and propaganda. The Habsburgs had never wanted to be identified with any one nation and seldom was a nation identified with them. There were perhaps two exceptions. The Castilians truly made the *Casa de Austria* a national dynasty but not to the extent of sacrificing Castilian national interests to those of the German branch of the Habsburgs. At the end of the nineteenth century, Francis Joseph perhaps went too far in favouring centralism and the German alliance, thereby clouding the image of the Habsburgs as sovereigns set apart, an image which the Habsburgs had always cultivated. Be that as it may, the destiny of the sovereign house remained prodigious. The Capetians had had only one vocation, to create French unity, the Habsburgs in the end had had four.

A GERMAN DYNASTY (1273–1555)

The Habsburgs became associated with a particular nation in 1273 when Rudolf was elected king of Germany. An Alemmanic Swiss lord, he used his position to install himself in Austria and in the Alpine regions. The Habsburgs were then excluded from royal power for a century and a half by electors who envied them their success. They used this 'interregnum' to establish themselves in their new domains and to constitute the 'hereditary lands' which correspond to modern Austria. At the same time, they increased their domains in Danubian Europe while the Swiss cantons rejected their tutelage. The hereditary lands served Frederick III, who was elected king of the Romans in 1440, as a territorial base from which to set about satisfying his imperial ambitions. Even though the imperial title remained elective, with the exception of the brief period from 1740 to 1745, the Habsburgs held it continuously until the very end of the Holy Roman Empire in 1806.

UNIVERSAL MONARCHY AND THE EMPIRE OF CHARLES V (1519–55)

Universal monarchy, dominion over the known world, or at least Christendom, was the long-term goal which Frederick III had set for the House of Austria, a goal which was explicit in his device, AEIOU, *Austria est imperare orbi universo*. He amassed defeats but his tenacity and obstinacy enabled him to triumph in the most desperate situations and over the most brilliant enemies. By his death in 1493, the essential elements were all in place. The threat from Hungary had all but vanished following the defeat of Matthias Corvinus in 1490. In 1477 the marriage of his son Maximilian to Maria of Burgundy, the only daughter of Charles the Bold, had sealed the dynasty's European destiny. It was through the Burgundian inheritance that the Habsburgs with a single bound leapt beyond the German and Danubian lands and took possession of the Netherlands, one of the richest and finest countries in Europe. Still more important, the process of dynastic unions had begun and Maximilian triumphed by arranging a double marriage with the children of the Catholic kings, Ferdinand of Aragon and Isabella of Castille, while the Treaty of Vienna prepared the way for the Habsburgs to take hold of Bohemia and Hungary. This matrimonial policy, summed up in the formula *Bella gerant alii, Tu, felix Austria, nube*, was accompanied by some remarkably fortunate turns of fate. The premature death of Philip the Fair, the *infanta* Juana's inability to exercise power in Castile, the discovery of the New World and the unforeseen death of Louis Jagiellon I at the Battle of Mohács in 1526 placed the princely family of German origin at the head of a world empire. The Habsburgs' success had come not through wars of conquest but by contracting marriages, through inheritance and elections. In every case, their subjects felt them to be their legitimate sovereigns or their 'natural seigneurs' as they were known in the Netherlands where the House of Austria was seen as the natural continuation of the House of Burgundy. The Habsburgs embodied legal authority and it was proper to obey them as the continuation of the dynasty. As long as Charles V reigned, no one nation dominated the rest and the privileges of each land were carefully respected. The empire was in reality a vast confederation of lands and kingdoms.

Gerhard Herm, in his work published in 1988, claims that Charles V's reign was the apogee of the House of Austria. As master of the hereditary lands, Spain, the New World, the Netherlands and a good part of Italy, Charles V wanted to make the imperial dignity a reality, to become head of Latin Christendom and to act as the heir of Caesar, Augustus and Charlemagne. This universalist conception of power, inspired by the chancellor Gattinara, clashed with too many interests to be realized without rousing conflict and Charles V's reign was marked by a long series of short-lived victories and lasting defeats. The values which the emperor wanted to impose were ones in which his contemporaries no longer believed: Christianity, universal monarchy and the unity of the Catholic faith. He felt Burgundian but was not attached to any particular nationality and ran up against the nascent national movements and the hostility of France which, like Henry VIII in England, refused to be integrated into his system. He stood by, powerless, as the Lutheran Reformation advanced in Germany and, by the Peace of Augsburg of 1555, recognized the existence of the two Christian confessions while looking forward to the far-off day when they might be reunited. Sick at heart, in an unusual move for a sovereign of the *ancien régime*, he abdicated and retired to a monastery at Yuste where he ended his days in prayer and contemplation, as a good Christian conscious of the vanity of this world.

Charles V's abdication was more than a simple admission of personal defeat, it also marked the end of all claims to universal monarchy. The emperor divided the Habsburg patrimony between his brother Ferdinand and his son Philip and so deliberately created a German branch distinct from the Spanish branch. In 1522 he entrusted the hereditary lands to the archduke Ferdinand who lost no time in taking over from him in Germany. The Danubian monarchy was born in 1527 with the death of Louis Jagiellon. The Habsburgs had dreamt of such a monarchy for two centuries but at their moment of triumph found themselves under grave threat from the Turks and from a section of the Hungarian nobility. The hereditary lands, Bohemia, Hungary and Croatia were brought together under the same ruler, Ferdinand, whose title at Vienna was archduke and at Prague and Pressburg, king. This complex of states and nations, known by many names but finally as Austria-Hungary, lasted until 1918 and has been the central subject of this study. The Habsburgs' Spanish empire, which at the accession of Philip II had seemed certain of a glorious future, was long outlasted by the Danubian monarchy.

THE EMPIRE DIVIDED (1556–1700)

Charles V left the greater part of his inheritance to his only son, Philip II. He would have liked also to have left him the imperial crown but was prevented from doing so by the German princes and the archduke Ferdinand. The people of the Empire did not want to become involved in a costly programme of world conquest. It was enough for them to defend Christendom against the constant threat of Ottoman imperialism in Hungary. Philip II was the most powerful European sovereign but from 1559 onwards he chose to settle in Castile and to give the monarchy its Spanish character. In his imperial policy he suffered serious defeats, in France, England and especially the Netherlands which revolted in 1566, but he also experienced some successes, most notably the victory at Lepanto and the annexation of Portugal.

At the time of Philip II's death in 1598, the Spanish monarchy was still a formidable power, despite the failures of its imperialist policy and its relative economic decline. *La Prépondérance espagnole*, the title of Hauser's magisterial work, fits perfectly the situation in Europe at the end of the sixteenth century. The German branch of the Habsburgs meanwhile were eclipsed for want of sufficient resources and their inability to pursue a grand policy. The separation of Vienna and Madrid was not real but only apparent since the patrimony of the House of Austria remained the joint property of the illustrious dynasty whose head was the king of Spain. The visible sign of this preeminence was the Order of the Golden Fleece which was founded in 1429 by Philip the Good and had as its grand master the king of Spain. It was also he who regulated marriages of family members and multiplied the number of marriages between close relatives in order to tighten the links between the two branches of the House of Habsburg.

After the fratricidal quarrels and the brief eclipse of the German branch of the Habsburgs, it was the collateral line, the Styrian branch based in Graz, which came to the rescue. Philip III had surrendered his rights to his cousin, Ferdinand of Styria, a confirmed champion of the Counter-Reformation. Educated by Jesuits at Ingolstadt in Bavaria, Ferdinand II could countenance only two options for his Lutheran subjects, conversion to Catholicism or exile. He was an odd character whose obstinacy to the point of fanaticism is most unsympathetic to modern eyes. He became the champion of the Catholic cause within the Empire. When the Bohemian estates revolted, he used the occasion to put into action his programme and to suppress the confessional privileges which he had confirmed very much against his will. The revolt of 1618 began a European war which brought the two branches of the House of Austria tightly together with the common and undeclared purpose of imposing their hegemony in Germany and Europe while openly acting to re-establish Catholicism in its former glory. The union between Vienna and Madrid took the form of financial and military aid to the cadet line which was perpetually short of money.

Spain, under the guidance of Olivares, tried to establish its dominance over the Rhineland and northern Italy in order to strengthen its lines of communication between Brussels and Milan and sought to extend its hold over the Baltic. This provoked Richelieu who feared that France would be isolated and encircled. The cardinal was quick to renew alliances with the German Protestant princes and Gustavus Adolphus of Sweden. In 1635 France declared war on Spain and so entered the Thirty Years War. Compromise was out of the question for Louis XIII and his minister who were alarmed by Philip II's claims to universal monarchy.

Events turned to France and its allies' favour and Germany was turned into one vast battlefield. By the Treaty of Westphalia of 1648, the emperor Ferdinand III was obliged to yield Upper Alsace to France and to compensate Sweden. More serious yet, he was forced to extend the provisions of the Peace of Augsburg to the Calvinists. The German liberties, the real issue at stake in the conflict, were guaranteed by the powers. In future, any attempt by the Habsburgs to seize hold of Germany was certain to fail and they could only govern with the Imperial Diet's agreement. Any move by Vienna in the direction of absolutism was remote.

The rout of Spain, confirmed by the Treaty of the Pyrenees, made the defeat yet worse for the House of Austria. It was now clear that it would never realize universal monarchy to its advantage. It would even have to fight to retain the basic elements of its patrimony.

The House of Austria found its very existence brought into question following the death of Philip IV in 1665. At the end of the seventeenth century, the policy of marriage between close relatives led to the extinction of the senior male line. The birth of the *infante* Charles in 1661 had brought the Madrid Habsburgs an unexpected respite but did not solve the problem of the Spanish succession which preoccupied the chancelleries of Europe for almost half a century and led to a general European war. Force of arms was insufficient for Leopold I to persuade the other powers of the indivisibility of the patrimony of the House of Austria. He agreed to cede his rights to the Spanish crown to his younger son, the archduke Charles, but refused to grant all or part of the inheritance to the other pretenders. The Castilians refused to allow the Spanish monarchy to be divided and preferred to support the Bourbon candidate who was a great-grandson of Philip IV and the grandson of Louis XIV and Maria Theresa. Charles II, nearing death, acted as a Castilian and made his will in favour of the duke of Anjou who in November 1700 became Philip IV of Spain. By this single, decisive act, he had curtailed the Habsburgs' European vocation. The archduke Charles, supported by the Maritime Powers and the Catalans, did not succeed in conquering his new kingdom.

The unexpected death of the archduke Charles's elder brother Joseph I in 1711 changed the nature of the problem. The Maritime Powers did not wish to see the empire of Charles V reconstituted and Great Britain was opposed in particular to any power exercising hegemony over the Continent, be it Austria or France. Charles VI found himself abandoned by his allies but managed to obtain some territory, besides the Southern Netherlands, as compensation, keeping Naples, Milan and Sardinia which enabled him to establish a large part of Italy as an Austrian protectorate.

Spain had enjoyed two centuries of glory under the House of Austria and the Madrid Habsburgs had come to identify with the Castilian nation. The Habsburgs' world vocation was at an end but the German branch still had an important role to play in Central Europe. After 1715, the Austrian monarchy was regarded as a great power on account of the vast extent of its possessions and the importance of its army. The structure of the state, however, remained fragile and Charles VI was unable to proceed with essential reforms, or rather was indifferent to the problem.

HABSBURG-LORRAINE (1740–1918)

The death of Charles VI was followed by a serious crisis over the succession. There was no direct male heir and, despite the solemn promises which had been made earlier, the rights of his daughter, the archduchess Maria-Theresa, were contested by the king of Prussia, the elector of Saxony and, most vigorously, by the elector of Bavaria, Charles Albert. An impressive coalition led by France tried to dismember the Austrian monarchy. The electors supported Charles Albert of Bavaria and refused to give the imperial crown to Francis Stephen of Lorraine, the husband of Maria-Theresa and, since 1738, the grand duke of Tuscany. The coalition, though, did no more than play along with Frederick II, who coveted Silesia, a rich and densely populated province which later became the basis of Prussia's power. As for the imperial title, it fell in 1745 to Maria-Theresa's husband who became the emperor Francis I.

Once this crisis had passed, the reign of Maria-Theresa became one of the most brilliant eras in the history of the Austrian monarchy. The empress respected national languages, regional cultures and the privileges of the orders and turned to the Catholic faith, the army and loyalty to the dynasty to provide the basis of her support. She also created a competent administration and a corps of civil servants who were endowed with a sense of state. It remained open to question as to whether this was sufficient to overcome every particularism. Greatly loved by her subjects, including the Hungarians, Maria-Theresa used her large family of children to found a new dynasty, the House of Habsburg-Lorraine. Arranging marriages and finding places for her many sons and daughters was an important element in her foreign policy. She married her favourite daughter Marie-Antoinette to the future Louis XVI in order to consolidate the Franco-Austrian alliance of 1756 which was to be the new fulcrum for the European balance of power and a visible sign of the reconciliation of the Houses of Bourbon and Habsburg.

THE HABSBURGS AND THE FRENCH REVOLUTION

The Habsburgs proved to be implacable enemies of the Revolution, its principles and its achievements. Joseph II, with his bold reform programme, had shown that the House of Austria was not closed to the philosophy of the Enlightenment but his experiences had also shown that it was only with great difficulty that the new ideas could be introduced to such a heterogeneous group of peoples. The attempts to unify through language had stopped short. Joseph II managed no more than to reduce the extensive powers of the Catholic Church and to grant freedom of worship to the Protestants. He improved the legal position of the peasants by abolishing serfdom in 1781 but it would not be until the 1848 revolution that they gained real freedom. From 1792 onwards the nobility and the clergy closed ranks behind the emperor Francis II who showed no leniency in repressing the Jacobin conspiracies in Vienna and Hungary. Censorship and the police prevented the new ideas from spreading and the freemasons wisely drew a halt to their activities. Having terminated Joseph II's bold experiment, the Habsburgs, in line with the governing classes and the peasant masses fanaticized by the clergy, were undisputably the champions of reaction and the counter-revolution. Metternich did not encounter any great difficulty in imposing this policy on his master and on Austria from 1809 to 1848.

The cohesion of the Austrian empire, to use the official name of the monarchy after 1806, was rooted in a system of values completely inimical to the principles propagated by the French Revolution, the sovereignty of the people, the secularization of the state and the independence of the nation-state. Conscious of the mortal threat posed by this ideological revolution, to the very end, the Habsburgs wavered between inaction, brutal reaction, as during the neo-absolutist era 1849–60, and wise reform adapted to the needs of Danubian Europe. Driven from Italy in 1859 and Germany in 1866, the Habsburgs continued to have a role to play in Central Europe where they had reigned since 1527. The peoples of the monarchy realized that it was in their interests to remain united in the face of German imperialism and the pan-Slavism of tsarist Russia, even if they would have to struggle to obtain internal reforms. The 1867 Compromise formally created Austria-Hungary but it left dissatisfied the Slavs within the Empire, who still in 1914 remained convinced that improvement was possible and that it was against their best interests to break up the monarchy. The social democrats likewise were in favour of maintaining the monarchy following a thoroughgoing programme of reform.

THE BREAK-UP OF AUSTRIA-HUNGARY

The emperor Francis Joseph, old and frail, committed a tragic error when, in July 1914, he declared war on Serbia following the assassination on 28 June in Sarajevo of the archduke Ferdinand. He believed that a restricted war would save the monarchy and gave in to the pressure from staff headquarters and the war party. The ultimatum provoked a chain reaction and let loose a conflict from which neither the Austro-Hungarian monarchy nor Europe could extricate itself. The monarchy could not withstand the terrible tensions engendered by a long war which ruined the Austrian economy and revived antagonisms among the different nations.

The emperor Charles courageously tried to negotiate a separate peace with the Entente after 1916 but the monarchy no longer had control of its destiny, buffeted by its powerful ally, Germany, and the nationalities who were negotiating with the governments of the Entente. The military defeats during autumn 1918 enabled the different nations, including the Germans of Austria, to form provisional governments and, with recognition from the Allies, to form successor states.

The emperor Charles abdicated on 12 November 1918 and, after two attempts at restoration in Hungary which were thwarted by the regent Horthy and the governments of the Petite Entente, died in exile on the island of Madeira.

Since then, the descendants of the emperor Charles have lived the lives of the many other European sovereign houses without hope of restoration. Faithful to the House of Austria's European vocation, the archduke Otto of Habsburg sits in the parliament at Strasbourg as deputy for Bavaria. The son of Charles I has shown himself to be interested in the structure of Europe and demonstrates that the Habsburgs remain true to their supranational vocation.

The powers which made up the Entente, though, by supporting the destruction of Austria-Hungary, created a void in Eastern Europe and the problem posed in 1918 still lacks a satisfactory resolution in the 1990s.

Chronology

1700	Charles II of Spain makes his will in favour of the Bourbons (2 October) and dies. Louis XIV accepts this will (November).
1701	Grand Alliance of the Hague. Beginning of the War of the Spanish Succession.
1702	Beginning of the Hungarian war of independence.
1703	Franco-Bavarian victory at Hochstadt.
1704	Defeat of the Franco-Bavarian army at Blenheim. Ferenc II Rákóczi becomes prince of Transylvania. Habsburg *pactum mutuae successionis*.
1705	Death of Leopold I and succession of Joseph I as emperor. The archduke Charles attempts to conquer Spain with the help of the allies. French defeat before Turin.
1707	The imperial troops besiege Toulon and occupy the kingdom of Naples. The Diet of Ónod. Ferenc II Rákóczi elected king of Hungary.
1709	Gertruydenberg peace talks.
1711	Death of Joseph I. Accession of Charles VI. Peace of Szatmár. Ferenc II Rákóczi goes into exile.
1712	French victory at Denain.
1713	Peace of Utrecht. The emperor Charles VI issues the Pragmatic Sanction.
1714	Treaty of Rastadt; the end of the War of the Spanish Succession. The Peace of Baden.
1716–18	Austro-Turkish war.
1717	Birth of the archduchess Maria-Theresa. Belgrade captured from the Turks.
1718	Treaty of Passarowitz; the Turks cede the Banat of Temesvár.
1719	Ostend Company founded.
1722	The Hungarian Diet accepts the Pragmatic Sanction.
1733	Beginning of the War of the Polish Succession.
1736	Marriage of the archduchess Maria-Theresa to Francis Stephen of Lorraine.

1738	Francis Stephen becomes grand duke of Tuscany. Beginning of war with Turkey. Belgrade lost to the Turks.
1739	End of the war with Turkey.
1740	Death of Charles VI. Accession of Maria-Theresa. Accession of Frederick II 'the Great' in Prussia.
1741	Frederick II occupies Silesia. Beginning of the War of the Austrian Succession. Birth of the archduke Joseph, the future Joseph II.
1742	End of the first Silesian war. Charles Albert, elector of Bavaria, elected emperor.
1744–45	Second Silesian war.
1745	Francis Stephen elected emperor, Francis I.
1748	Peace of Aix-la-Chapelle.
1749	Haugwitz's reforms.
1753	Kaunitz becomes chancellor.
1756	Beginning of the Seven Years War.
1761	The council of state (*Staatsrat*) created. Reform of censorship.
1763	Treaty of Hubertusburg. Treaty of Paris; Prussia retains Silesia.
1764	Joseph II elected king of the Romans.
1765	Death of emperor Francis I. Joseph II becomes co-regent.
1767	*Regulatio urbariale* in Hungary.
1770	Marriage of the archduchess Marie-Antoinette to the dauphin Louis.
1772	First Partition of Poland; annexation of Galicia.
1773	Education reforms in Austria.
1775	Acquisition of the Bukovina.
1776	Education reform in Hungary.
1777	Joseph II tours France.
1778–79	War of the Bavarian Succession.
1780	Death of Maria-Theresa. Joseph II sole ruler.
1781	Abolition of serfdom in Austria. Patent of toleration.
1783	American War of Independence.
1786	First performance of Mozart's *The Marriage of Figaro*.
1788–91	Austro-Turkish war.
1789	Revolt of the Austrian Netherlands.
1790	Death of Joseph II. Accession of Leopold II.
1791	Meeting of the Hungarian Diet. First performance of *The Magic Flute*. Death of Mozart.
1792	Death of Leopold II. Accession of Francis II. Beginning of the French Revolutionary Wars.
1793–97	First Coalition against France.
1793	Second Partition of Poland.
1794	Repression of the Jacobin Conspiracy.
1796	Napoleon's victories in Italy.
1797	Treaty of Campo-Formio; Austria annexes Venice.
1798	Napoleon in Egypt. The Second Coalition against France.
1800	Defeat of the archduke John at Hohenlinden.

1801	Peace of Lunéville; end of the Second Coalition.
1802	Signing of the Peace of Amiens.
1803	Recess of the Diet of Ratisbon.
1804	Napoleon becomes emperor of the French.
1805	Third Coalition against France. Defeat of the French at Trafalgar. French army occupies Vienna.
1806	The Peace of Pressburg. Beginning of the Continental Blockade. Defeat of the Prussians at Jena. Francis II renounces the title of Holy Roman Emperor and assumes the title of emperor of Austria.
1807	Peace of Tilsit.
1808	Establishment of Austrian national militia.
1809	Fourth Coalition. Second occupation of Vienna by the French army. Battles of Aspern and Wagram. Uprising in the Tyrol led by Andreas Hofer. Treaty of Schönbrunn; Austria loses its access to the Adriatic. Metternich becomes chancellor of Austria.
1810	Marriage of the archduchess Maria Louisa to Napoleon.
1811	Austrian state bankruptcy. Birth of the king of Rome.
1812	Invasion of Russia by the Grande Armée which includes a corps of the Austrian army.
1813	Austria rejoins the Allies and the Fifth Coalition against France. The 'Battle of the Nations' at Leipzig.
1814	The French campaign. Schwarzenberg enters Paris. Congress of Vienna. First Treaty of Paris.
1815	The Hundred Days. Battle of Waterloo, 18 June. Second Treaty of Paris. Final act of the Congress of Vienna. Adoption of the constitution of the German Confederation. Conclusion of the Holy Alliance.
1816	Economic crisis.
1819	Carlsbad decrees.
1820	Adoption of the definitive constitution of the German Confederation.
1821–48	Metternich chancellor of state.
1831	Polish uprising.
1832	Session of the Hungarian Diet.
1835	Death of Francis I. Accession of Ferdinand I, 'the Benign'.
1846	Uprising in Galicia. Annexation of Kraków.
1847	General economic crisis.
1848	24 February: revolution in Paris.
	13 March: revolution in Vienna; Metternich flees.
	15 March: revolution in Budapest.
	7 April: Lájos Batthyány president of the council in Hungary.
	May: opening of the parliament at Frankfurt.
	June: pan-Slav congress at Prague; Windischgrätz occupies the city. Opening of the *Reichstag* (Parliament) at Vienna (July).
	August: the Piedmontese leave Lombardy.

September: abolition of serfdom by the Austrian parliament; democratic revolution in Vienna; the minister for war, Count Theodor Latour, lynched by Viennese mob.

October: Hungary secedes.

November: Austrian parliament meets at Kremsier in Moravia; prince Felix Schwarzenberg becomes president of the Austrian council.

2 December: abdication of Ferdinand I. Accession of Francis Joseph.

1849 March: resumption of hostilities with Piedmont-Sardinia.

April: Hungary declares the Habsburgs deposed.

May: Russian military intervention in Hungary.

August: surrender of the Hungarian army at Vilagos; Kossuth goes into exile.

October: execution of thirteen Hungarian generals at Árád.

1850 Customs union between Austria and Hungary. The beginning of neo-absolutism. The Olomouc 'retreat'. Prussia gives in to Austria.

1851 31 December: patent suspending the constitution.

1852 The death of prince Felix Schwarzenberg.

1853–56 Crimean War.

1855 Concordat with the Holy See.

1859 Battles of Magenta and Solferino. Armistice of Villafranca; Milan secedes. The October Diploma.

1860 The end of neo-absolutism.

1861 February patent; return to centralism.

1864 The war of the duchies of Schleswig-Holstein.

1865 Convention of Gastein between Prussia and Austria.

1866 The Austro-Prussian war. The battle of Sadowa, 2 July. Italian defeats at Custozza and Lissa. Venice cecedes.

August: the Peace of Prague; the end of the German Confederation and the constitution of the North German Confederation.

1867 The Austro-Hungarian Compromise. The beginning of the parliamentary regime in Cisleithania.

1868 Liberal reforms in Hungary.

1870 Abolition of the Concordat. Austro-Hungarian neutrality in the Franco-Prussian war.

1871 18 January: proclamation of the German empire, Second Reich.

October: collapse of the Austro-Bohemian compromise. Andrássy minister of foreign affairs.

1877 War in the east.

1878 Congress of Berlin. Occupation of Bosnia-Hercegovina.

1879 End of the liberal era. Withdrawal of Andrássy. Austro-German alliance.

1881 Alliance of the three emperors: Austro-Hungary, Germany and Russia.

1882	Conclusion of the Triple Alliance. Founding of the pan-German League.
1887	The Christian social Union founded at Vienna.
1889	Death of the archduke Rudolf. The social democrat party founded.
1897	Karl Lueger confirmed as burgermeister of Vienna. Constitutional crisis surrounding the laws passed by the government of count Badeni.
1905	Austro-Hungarian constitutional crisis.
1907	Introduction of universal suffrage in Cisleithania.
1908	Annexation of Bosnia-Hercegovina.
1913	Balkan war.
1914	28 June: assassination of the archduke Francis Ferdinand at Sarajevo.
	2 August: beginning of the First World War.
1916	Death of Francis Joseph. Accession of the emperor Charles I.
1918	12 November: abdication of Charles I.

Glossary of German Terms

Afterkönig: the 'false-king' of Bohemia, Charles Albert, the elector of Bavaria, who imposed his authority in Prague (1741–42) through the assistance of the French army of occupation.

Alldeutscher Verband: the pan-German league which inspired Schönerer with its ideology during the 1880s.

Allgemeines Krankenhaus: the general hospital in Vienna rebuilt by Joseph II in the *Alserstadt*; it marked the beginning of the rapid expansion of the faculty of medicine in the city.

Aufklärung: the Enlightenment, the philosophical movement which posed as the antithesis of the 'obscurantist' Counter-Reformation.

Ballhausplatz: the palace in Vienna where the state chancellors from Kaunitz onwards held office; situated opposite the Hofburg, it was the seat of the ministry of foreign affairs under the dual monarchy.

Bundesstaat: federal state; the status of the Austrian republic since 1918.

Burgtheater: since 1918, the name given to the theatre, formerly the Hofburgtheater.

Deputation: the government executive commissions in Vienna made up of representatives of several councils.

Dominikalland: the manorial reserve in the system of land-holding prevalent before 1848; it was farmed directly and was exempt from tax.

Geheimer Rat: the privy council linked to the person of the ruler; it was created in 1527 by Ferdinand I and survived in various forms until the revolution of 1848 when it was replaced by a council of ministers.

Gütig: 'benign'; the epithet given to Ferdinand I, emperor of Austria 1835–48 who abdicated in favour of his nephew Francis Joseph and died in Prague in 1875.

Hanswurst: the Viennese Punchinello, originally from Salzburg and an important character in popular dialect comedy.

Herrenhaus: the house of lords or upper chamber in Cisleithania under the bi-cameral system set out in the 1867 constitution; made up of members nominated by the emperor it corresponded to the chamber of magnates in Hungary.

Hochbarock: the high point of baroque art reached between 1680 and 1740 and during the reigns of Leopold I, Joseph I and Charles VI.

Hofburg: the imperial palace in Vienna consisting of a collection of buildings constructed from the fifteenth century (the chapel) to the beginning of the twentieth century (the *Neue Hofburg*) in the neo-baroque style; the main parts are the Stallburg, the Schweizer Hof, the Reichskanzlei and the Library.

Hofburgtheater: the court theatre in the Hofburg which in accordance with the wishes of Joseph II became the German national theatre specializing in drama; originally housed in the Hofburg, in 1888 it reopened in magnificent new premises on the Ringstrasse.

Hofkammer: literally 'the court chamber', the chamber of accounts; it was created in 1527 by Ferdinand I to control the chambers of accounts of the different Estates within the monarchy; it acted as the ministry of finance in the monarchy until 1848.

Hofkriegsrat: the Aulic Council of War created in 1556 by Ferdinand I to administer the army; its powers were similar to those enjoyed by the Council of War under the *ancien régime* in France; it continued to operate until 1848.

Hofrechnungskammer: chamber of accounts at the court created by Kaunitz in 1762 to oversee public finance.

Hofstaat: collective term for all the imperial aulic institutions.

Hofstelle: executive commission with the status of a ministry under Maria-Theresa.

Kaiser: emperor; the Germanized form of Caesar, until 1806 and the dissolution of the Holy Roman Empire it was used of the Holy Roman Emperor.

Kaiserjäger: the imperial chasseurs; elite troops recruited mainly in the Tyrol and the Alpine provinces.

Kataster: a register of properties belonging to the nobility.

Kavaliertour: a tour undertaken by young nobles for the purposes of education; the itinerary typically included Italy and Germany and later France and the Netherlands and might entail periods of attendance at universities.

Kleindeutsch: the conception of German unification as it was realized by Bismarck in 1871; it excluded the German provinces of Austria and conflicted with the concept of German unification defined in 1848 by the Frankfurt parliament.

Kriegszahlmeister: literally 'war treasurer'; the functionary responsible for the financial management of wars.

Kreis: 'circle'; an administrative district within the Empire and in the kingdom of Bohemia, in Czech, *kreš*.

Kreistag: the Diet of a circle which administered a *Kreis* within the Empire.

Kronprinz: the crown prince; a title only occasionally given to the heir apparent in Austria, most notably to the archduke Rudolf who died in 1889.

Landeshauptmann: literally the 'captain of a country'; the head of the executive within one of the hereditary lands.

Landeshoheit: territorial sovereignty limited only by imperial authority.

Landesmutter: 'mother of the country' or of her subjects, a title freely given to Maria-Theresa.

Landhaus: the palace where the Diet and provincial administration were housed.

Landmarschall: the marshal of the Diet and head of the administration of the provincial Estates.

Landrobot: compulsory labour demanded of peasants for public works, for example the repair of roads and fortification; the equivalent of the *corvée royale* in France.

Landschaft: the body of the Estates and orders who made up the *Land* and found political expression in the provincial Diet.

Landtag: a provincial Diet; in Bohemia the Diet of the kingdom.

Landtagsproposition: the list of royal demands presented at the beginning of a session of the Diet; once debated and approved they had the force of law within a country.

Landwehr: territorial army made up of reservists.

Meierhof: manorial farm which worked the *Dominikalland*.

Militärgrenze: the military frontier between the Habsburg and Ottoman empires which protected the borders of the monarchy; it was created in 1522 to protect Inner Austria and was finally broken up in 1878 after the imperial army created Bosnia-Hercegovina; those soldiers serving in its garrisons had the special status of *Grenzer*.

Militärkanzlei: the military cabinet of the emperor Francis Joseph and later of the archduke Francis Ferdinand.

Mitregenschaft: the regency exercised within the monarchy from 1765 to 1780 by Maria-Theresa and Joseph II, the latter being head of the Holy Roman Empire while his mother remained sovereign of the hereditary lands.

Mitteleuropa: Central Europe; the term carries associations with the dream of German hegemony and should be used with caution.

Nordbahn: the Northern railway company which linked Vienna with Moravia and Bohemia.

Oberstburggraf: the grand burgrave of Bohemia, the first of the grand officers of the crown and president of the council of lieutenancy; the governor of Bohemia from 1620 to 1848.

Oberstkämmer: grand chamberlain, a grand officer of the kingdom of Bohemia.

Oberstlandrichter: the supreme judge in Bohemia, one of the grand officers of the crown who made up the council of lieutenancy.

Rechtsstaat: state-right.

Reformkatholizismus: 'Reform Catholicism', an intellectual and spiritual movement inspired by Jansenism which grew during the latter part of the reign of Maria-Theresa (1760–80).

Reich: the Holy Roman Empire of the German nation which was dissolved in 1806; the term was taken up and misused by Prussia in the belief that by creating *Kleindeutschland* in 1871 it had revived the Empire.

Reichsfürst: prince of the Empire; the princes of the Empire made up the second college of the German Diet and ranked immediately after the college of electors, the *Kurfürsten*.

Reichshofrat: the Aulic Council of the Empire; created by Ferdinand I, it was reorganized in 1648 by the Treaty of Osnabrück; it was the supreme court of appeal for the whole Empire and its judges were appointed by the emperor.

Reichsrat: literally 'council of the empire'; it was the lower chamber organized by the 1867 Austrian constitution.

Reichsstadt: a free town in the Empire; the free towns made up the third college of the Imperial Diet.

Reichstag: Diet of the Holy Roman Empire until its dissolution in 1806; after 1871 its name was given to the lower chamber in Bismarck's German empire.

Reichsverweser: administrator of the Empire; in 1848, the office held by the archduke John.

Ringstrasse: the Ring, the circular boulevard in Vienna constructed after the demolition of the old fortifications in the 1860s; a series of magnificent public buildings grew up along the Ring which is the location of the Opera, Parliament, museums, the university and the Burgtheater.

Rustikalland: the lands given to the peasants in return for the payment of taxes in money, kind and labour (*robot*); they were subject to state taxation.

Schatzmann: treasurer.

Sektionschef: director of a ministry at Vienna.

Staatenbund: confederation of sovereign states; this was the status of the German Confederation, the *Deutscher Bund*, from 1815 to 1866 and of the Swiss confederation after 1815.

Stände: the orders or Estates within old European society. The term was extended to the assemblies of the Estates and the Diets.

Statthalter: literally the lieutenant to a sovereign and so the governor of a province or country; in the Netherlands, the term *Stadhouder* was used.

Statthalterei: government, all the offices answerable to the *Statthalter*.

Stolageld: the 'casual', money paid to the curate of a parish in return for certain services.

Studienhofkommission: the aulic commission for education; established by Maria-Theresa and responsible for the school reforms during the 1770s, it had the status of a ministry.

Südbahn: the Southern railway company intended to link together Vienna, Graz and Trieste.

Taiding: a village community.

Türkenlouis: the name given to the margrave Louis of Baden (1655–1707), general of the imperial army, following his victories over the Turks in Hungary.

Vormärz: the period before the revolution in March 1848 and roughly corresponding to the reign of Louis-Philippe in France.

Wiener Stadtbank: bank of the city of Vienna founded in 1705 to guarantee the public debt.

Zollverein: customs union created by Prussia within the German Confederation. The Austrian empire was excluded on the wishes of the cabinet in Berlin.

Zweite Gesellschaft: the 'second society' composed of those whom the aristocracy excluded from their salons as *parvenus*.

Bibliography

It is not possible to cite all the books and learned articles which have been used in preparing this study; the following bibliography simply serves to direct readers to supplementary texts.

PRINTED SOURCES

Aus den Tagebüchern des Grafen Karl von Zinzendorf, selection and translation by Hans Wagner, Vienna, 1972.

Briefe Maria-Theresias an Ihre Kinder und Freunde, 4 vols, Alfred von Arneth (ed.), Vienna, 1881.

Correspondance secrète entre Marie-Thérèse et le comte de Mercy-Argenteau, 3 vols, Alfred von Arneth and M. A. Geoffroy (eds), Paris, 1874–75.

Feldzugerzählung 1809 des Erzherzogs Johannes, Aloïs Veltze, Vienna 1909.

Feldzug von 1866, Deutschland, edited by the history department of the Prussian high command, Berlin, 1867.

Instructions aux ambassadeurs et ministres de France (1648–1789): in particular vol. 1 *Autriche*, A. Sorel (ed.), Paris, 1884, and vol. 22 *Turquie*, P. Duparc (ed.), Paris, 1974.

Magyar törveny tár (Corpus juris Hungarici), 14 vols, Dezsö Markus (ed.), Budapest, 1897.

Materialien zur Geschichte der Löhne und Preise in Österreich, A. F. Pribram and Rudolf Geyer (eds), Vienna, 1938.

Négociations relatives à la succession d'Espagne, 4 vols, A. Mignet (ed.), Paris, 1847.

Pramatische Sanktion, die, Gustav Truba (ed.), Vienna, 1924.

Protokolle des Österreichischen Ministerrats 1848–1867, 6 vols, Friedrich Engel-Janosi (ed.), Vienna, 1977.

The Vatican and Hungary 1846–1878: Reports and Correspondence on Hungary of the Apostolic Nuncios in Vienna, L. Lukacs (ed.), Budapest, 1981.

GENERAL WORKS

Bosl, Karl, *Handbuch der Geschichte der böhmischen Länder*, 4 vols, Stuttgart, 1967–73.

Bruckmuller, Ernst, *Nation Österreich: Sozialhistorische Aspekte ihrer Entwicklung*, Vienna, 1984.

Gonda, Imre and Niederhauser, Emil, *Die Habsburger, ein europäisches Phaenomen*, Budapest, 1978.

Hantsch, Hugo, *Die Geschichte Österreichs*, 2 vols, Graz and Vienna, 1955.

Hoensch, Jörg K., *Geschichte Böhmens: von der slawischen Landnahme bis ins 20 Jahrhundert*, Munich, 1987.

Homan, Balínt and Szekfü, Gyulá, *Magyar Történet*, 7 vols, Budapest, 1935.

Kann, Robert, *A History of the Habsburg Empire, 1526–1918*, Berkeley, Calif., 1974.

Kann, Robert and David, Zdenek, *The Peoples of the Eastern Habsburg Lands, 1526–1918*, Seattle and London, 1984.

Lichnowsky, Prince, *Geschichte des Hauses Habsburg*, Vienna, 1839.

Macartney, C. A., *The Habsburg Empire, 1790–1918*, London, 1969.

Macek, Josef, *Histoire de la Bohême des origines á 1918*, with preface by Robert Mandrou, Paris, 1984.

Pamlenyi, Ervin et al., *Histoire de la Hongrie des origines à nos jours*, Budapest, 1974.

Purs, Jaroslav and Kropilak, Miroslav, *Prehled dějin Češkoslovenska*, 2 vols, Prague, 1980–82.

Wandruszka, Adam, *Das Haus Habsburg: Die Geschichte einer europäischen Dynastie*, Vienna, 1956 (English translation, *The House of Habsburg: Six Hundred Years of a European Dynasty*, New York, 1964).

Wandruszka, Adam and Urbanitsch, Peter, *Die Habsburger Monarchie 1848–1918*, 8 vols; vol. I, *Die wirtschaftliche Entwicklung*, Vienna, 1973.

Zollner, Erich, *Geschichte Österreichs*, 2nd edn, Vienna, 1961.

BIOGRAPHIES

Allgemeine Deutsche Biographie, 54 vols, Leipzig, 1887–1910.

Arneth, Alfred von, *Geschichte Maria-Theresias*, 12 vols, Vienna, 1863–79.

Beales, Derek, *Joseph II: In the Shadow of Maria Theresa*, Cambridge, 1987.

Bertier de Sauvigny, Guillaume de, *Metternich*, Paris, 1986.

Bibl, Viktor, *Kaiser Franz, der letzte römisch-deutsche Kaiser*, Leipzig and Vienna, 1938.

Bled, Jean-Paul, *Franz Joseph*, translated by Teresa Bridgeman, Oxford, 1992.

Braubach, Max, *Prinz Eugen von Savoyen*, 5 vols, Munich and Vienna, 1963–65.

Corti, Egon César, *Kaiser Franz Joseph*, Graz and Vienna, 1960.

Fejtö, François, *Josef II, un Habsburg révolutionnaire*, Paris, 1949.

Hamann, Brigitte, *Rudolf, Kronprinz und Rebell*, Vienna, 1978.

Hamann, Brigitte, *Elisabeth, Kaiserin ohne Willen*, Vienna, 1982.

Hamann, Brigitte, *Die Habsburger: ein biographisches Lexikon*, Vienna, 1988.

Hertenberger, Helmut and Wiltscher, Franz, *Erzherzog Karl, der Sieger von Aspaern*, Graz, 1983.

Ingrao, Charles, *Emperor Leopold I and the Habsburg Monarchy*, West Lafayette, 1979.

Kann, Robert, *Erzherzog Franz Ferdinand Studien*, Vienna, 1976.

McKay, Derek, *Prince Eugene of Savoy*, London, 1977.

Mitrofanov, Paul von, *Josef II, seine politische und kulturelle Tätigkeit*, 2 vols, Vienna, 1910.

Otruba, Gustav, *Joseph II*, 2 vols, Vienna, 1988.

Pickl, Othmar, *Erzherzog Johann von Österreich, sein Wirken in seiner Zeit von Aspärn*, Graz, 1983.

Redlich, Joseph, *Kaiser Franz-Joseph von Österreich*, Berlin, 1928.

Spielman, John, *Emperor Leopold I*, London, 1977.

Tapié, Victor-Lucien, *L'Europe de Marie-Thérèse*, Paris, 1973.

Wandruszka, Adam, *Leopold II, Erzherzog von Österriech, Grossherzog von Toskana, König von Ungarn und Böhmen, Römischer Kaiser*, 2 vols, Vienna, 1963–65.

Wurzbach, Constant von, *Biographisches Lexikon des Kaisertumes Österreich, 1750–1850*, 60 vols, Vienna, 1856–91.

INSTITUTIONS AND POLITICAL LIFE

Beer, Adolf, *Die Finanzen Österreichs im 19 Jahrhundert*, Prague, 1877.

Bidermann, Hermann Ignaz, *Geschichte der österreichischen Gesamtstaatsidee 1526–1804*, Innsbruck, 1867.

Bled, Jean-Paul, *Les Fondements du conservatisme autrichien, 1859–1879*, Paris, 1988.

Csaky, Moritz, *Von der Aufklärung zum Liberalismus. Studien zum Frühliberalismus in Ungarn*, Vienna, 1981.

Dickson, P. G. M., *Finance and Government under Maria-Theresa, 1740–1780*, 2 vols, Oxford, 1987.

Eder, Karl, *Der Liberalismus in Altösterreich: Geisteshaltung, Politik und Kultur*, Vienna and Munich, 1955.

Eisenmann, Louis, *Le Compromis austro-hongrois de 1867: Études sur le dualisme*, Paris, 1904.

Fellner, Thomas and Kretschmayr, Heinrich, *Die Österreichische Zentralverwaltung 1526–1848*, 2 vols, Vienna, 1925.

Hantsch, Hugo, *Das Nationalitätenproblem im alten Österreich*, Graz, 1951.

Hellbling, Ernst, *Österreichische Verfassungs- und Verwaltungsgeschichte*, Vienna, 1956.

Kann, Robert, *The Multinational Empire. Nationalities and National Reform in the Habsburg Monarchy*, 2 vols, New York, 1950.

Kecskemeti, Charles, *La Hongrie et le réformisme libéral*, Rome, 1989.

Wandruszka, Adam and Urbanitsch, Peter, *Geschichte der österreichisch-ungarischen Monarchie*, Vienna, 1980.

ECONOMY

Benedikt, Heinrich, *Die wirtschaftliche Entwicklung in der Franz-Joseph Zeit*, Vienna, 1959.

Berend, Ivan and Ranki, György, *Economic Development in East-Central Europe in the 19th and 20th Centuries*, New York, 1974.

Berend, Ivan, *Hungary, A Century of Economic Development*, Newton Abbot, 1974.

Blum, Jerome, *Noble Landowners and Agriculture in Austria, 1815–1848: A Study of the Origins of the Peasant Emancipation of 1848*, Baltimore, 1848.

Brusatti, A. et al., *Die wirtschaftliche Entwickelung*, part 1 of *Geschichte der österreichisch-ungarischen Monarchie*, Vienna, 1973.

Good, David F., *The Economic Rise of the Habsburg Empire, 1750–1914*, Berkeley, Calif., 1984.

Klima, Arnost, 'Mercantilism in the Habsburg Monarchy', *Historica* II, Prague, 1965, pp. 93–119.

Klima, Arnost, 'Industrial growth and entrepreneurship in the early stages of industrialisation in the Czech lands', *Journal of European Economic History*, 4, 1973.

Komlos, J., *Die Habsburgermonarchie als Zollunion: die Wirtschaftsentwicklung Österreich-Ungarns im 19 Jahrhundert*, Vienna, 1986.

Matis, Herbert, *Österreichs Wirtschaft, 1848–1913*, Berlin, 1972.

Marczali, Henri, *Hungary in the Eighteenth Century*, Cambridge, 1910.

Michel, Bernard, *Banques et banquiers en Autriche au début du xxe siècle*, Paris, 1976.

Paget, John, *Hungaria and Transylvania with Remarks on their Social, Political and Economical Conditions*, London, 1855.

Slokar, Johann, *Geschichte der österreichischen Industrie und ihrer Förderung unter Kaiser Franz I*, Vienna, 1914.

Tremel, Ferdinand, *Wirtschafts und Sozialgeschichte Österreichs*, Vienna, 1969.

RELIGIOUS AND CULTURAL LIFE

Bohemia Sacra: Das Christentum in Böhmen, 973–1973, Ferdinand Seibt (ed.), Düsseldorf, 1974.

Bucsay, Mihaly, *A protestantizmus története Magyarorszagon, 1521–1945*, Budapest, 1985.

Kann, Robert, *A Study in Austrian Intellectual History. From Late Baroque to Romanticism*, New York, 1960.

Klingenstein, Grete (ed.), *Österreich in Europa der Aufklärung: Kontinuität und Zäsur in Europa zur Zeit Maria-Theresias und Joseph II*, 2 vols, Vienna, 1985.

Kopeczi, Béla and le Goff, Jacques (eds), *Intellectuels français, intellectuels hongrois*, Budapest and Paris, 1985.

Kopeczi, Béla and le Goff, Jacques, 'Université et cultures dans la monarchie des Habsbourg 1815–1918', *Études danubiennes*, 4, 1988.
Kovacs, Elisabeth (ed.), *Katholische Aufklärung und Josephinismus*, Vienna, 1979.
Schorske, Carl E., *Fin de Siècle Vienna: Politics and Culture*, Cambridge, 1981.
Tomek, Ernst, *Kirchengeschichte Österreichs*, 3 vols, Innsbruck, 1937.
Wodka, Josef, *Kirche in Österreich. Wegweiser durch ihre Geschichte*, Vienna, 1959.
Ziak, Karl (ed.), *Unvergängliches Wien*, Vienna, 1964.

INTERNATIONAL RELATIONS

Bridge, Francis, *From Sadowa to Sarajevo: the Foreign Policy of Austria-Hungary 1866–1914*, London, 1972.
Dioszegi, Istvan, *Österreich-Ungarn und der französisch-preussische Krieg 1870–1871*, Budapest, 1974.
Elliott, J. H., *Imperial Spain, 1469–1716*, London, 1963.
Fejtö, François, *Requiem pour un empire défunt*, Paris, 1988.
Gagliardo, John, *Reich and Nation: The Holy Roman Empire as Idea and Reality 1763–1806*, Indiana, 1980.
Kopeczi, Béla, *La France et la Hongrie au début du xviiie siècle: Études d'histoire diplomatique et d'histoire des idées*, Budapest, 1971.
Lutz, Heinrich, *Österreich-Ungarn und die Gründung des deutschen Reiches: Europäische Entscheidungen 1866–1871*, Frankfurt, 1979.
Muller, Klaus, *Das kaiserliche Gesandtschaftwesen im Jahrhundert nach dem westfälischen Frieden 1648–1740*, Bonn, 1976.
Renouvin, Pierre (ed.), *Histoire des relations internationales*, 8 vols, in particular G. Zeller, vols 2–3, A. Fugier, vol. 4, P. Renouvin, vols 5–7, Paris, 1949–53.
Soutou, Georges-Henri, *L'Or et le sang: les buts de guerre économiques de la Première Guerre mondiale*, Paris, 1989.
Valiani, Leo, *La Dissoluzione dell'Austria-Ungheria*, Milan, 1966.
Wandruszka, Adam, *Schicksaljahr 1866*, Vienna, 1966.
Wandruszka, Adam and Urbanitsch, P., *Geschichte der österreuchisch-ungarischen Monarchie*, vol. 5 *Die bewaffnete Macht*, Vienna, 1987.

Guide to Further Reading in English

by C. A. Simpson

POLITICAL AND DIPLOMATIC HISTORY

There is an excellent recent account of the Habsburg monarchy from the outbreak of the Thirty Years War to the end of the Napoleonic Wars by Charles Ingrao, *The Habsburg Monarchy 1618–1815* (Cambridge, 1994).

The response to the Pragmatic Sanction is examined by Charles Ingrao, 'The Pragmatic Sanction and the Theresian Succession: A Re-evaluation' in a useful collection of essays edited by William McGill, *The Habsburg Dominions under Maria-Theresa* (Washington, 1980). Two histories offer a fresh interpretation of the War of the Austrian Succession: M. S. Anderson, *The War of the Austrian Succession 1740–1748* (Harlow, 1995); Reed Browning, *The War of the Austrian Succession* (Stroud, 1994).

On the reception of the French Revolution within the monarchy, there are: Kinley Brauer and William Wright (eds), *Austria in the Age of the French Revolution* (Minneapolis, 1991); Ernst Wangermann, *From Joseph II to the Jacobin Trials* (Second edition, London, 1969).

The diplomat Harold Nicolson attended the Paris Peace Conference and his experience there and at the end of the Second World War inform his highly readable account of the settlement at the end of the Napoleonic wars, *The Congress of Vienna; a Study in Allied Unity, 1815–1822* (London, 1946). Barbara Jelavich, *The Habsburg Empire in European Affairs, 1814–1918* (Hamden, Conn., 1975) is a good general diplomatic history.

Many more historians have focused on the Monarchy's decline than have been concerned to chart its rise. The internal changes with the Habsburg monarchy and its break-up at the end of the First World War are set out in two recent and welcome surveys: Alan Sked, *The Decline and Fall of the Habsburg Empire 1815–1918* (Harlow, 1989) and John W. Mason, *The Dissolution of the Austro-Hungarian Empire 1867–1918* (Harlow, 1996). Still of interest are C. A. Macartney, *The Habsburg Empire, 1790–1918* (London, 1968), which is a thorough and pedantic general history, and A. J. P. Taylor, *The Habsburg Monarchy 1809–1918, A History of the Austrian Empire and Austria Hungary* (London, 1948) which is a lively, if at times imprecise, account.

Ernst C. Helmreich, *The Diplomacy of the Balkan Wars, 1912–1913* (Cambridge Mass., 1938) is recommended as a guide to the shifts in alliances on the eve of the First World War.

The literature concerning the First World War is vast. The following are a few of the books which might be recommended: a stimulating and welcome reassessment is Samuel R. Williamson Jr, *Austria-Hungary and the Origins of the First World War* (London, 1991) in which it is argued that Austria rather than Germany took the steps leading towards war; R. J. W. Evans and Hartmut Pogge von Strandmann (eds), *The Coming of the First World War* (Oxford, 1988); Vladimir Dedijer, *The Road to Sarajevo* (New York, 1966). It is appropriate to commend in this context R. W. Seton-Watson, *The Southern Slav Question and the Habsburg Monarchy* (London, 1911) and H. Seton Watson and C. Seton Watson, *The Making of New Europe: R. W. Seton Watson and the Last Years of Austria-Hungary* (Seattle, 1981). Readers might also find interesting Joachim Remak, *Sarajevo: The Origins of a Political Murder* (New York, 1959).

MILITARY HISTORY

There are good studies of the military strengths and weaknesses of the Monarchy: Gunther Rothenberg, *The Army of Francis Joseph* (West Lafayette, 1976); István Deák, 'Defeat at Solferino: The Nationality Question and the Habsburg Army in the War of 1859' in Béla K. Király (ed.), *The Crucial Decade: European Society and National Defence, 1859–1870* (New York, 1984); Alan Sked, *The Survival of the Habsburg Empire; Radetzky, the Imperial Army and the Class War, 1848* (New York and London, 1979).

That the armed forces were free of discrimination on ethnic grounds and transcended nationalism is demonstrated by István Deák's, *Beyond Nationalism, A Social and Political History of the Habsburg Officer Corps 1848–1918* (Oxford, 1990), a scholarly and elegantly-written account of one of the most important institutions within the Monarchy. Three books by Lawrence Sondhaus are highly recommended: *In the Service of the Emperor; Italians in the Austrian Armed Forces 1814–1918* (Boulder, 1990); *The Naval Policy of Austria-Hungary 1867–1918: Navalism, Industrial Development and the Politics of Dualism* (West Lafayette, 1994) shows that the navy too was free of discrimination; *The Habsburg Empire and the Sea: Austrian Naval Policy 1797–1866* (West Lafayette, 1989).

ECONOMIC AND SOCIAL

Economic and social histories of the monarchy available in English include John Komlos, *Nutrition and Economic Development in the Eighteenth-Century Habsburg Monarchy* (Princeton, 1990); Jerome Blum, *The End of the Old Order in Rural Europe* (Princeton, 1978) and *Noble Landowners and Agriculture in*

Austria, 1815–1848 (Baltimore, 1948) and also David Good, *The Economic Rise of the Habsburg Empire, 1750–1914* (Berkeley, Los Angeles and London, 1984).

The essays in H. M. Scott (ed.), *The European Nobilities in the Seventeenth and Eighteenth Centuries, Northern, Central and Eastern Europe* (Harlow, 1994) focus specifically on the individual national nobilities of Eastern Europe.

There are several good studies of Vienna and its culture: Ilsa Barea, *Vienna, Legend and Reality* (Pimlico, London, 1992); S. Beller, *Vienna and the Jews, 1867–1938: A Cultural History* (Cambridge, 1989); Robert Waissenberger, *Vienna in the Biedermeier Era, 1815–1848* (New York, 1986) and, most remarkable of all for its contribution to intellectual history, Carl E. Schorske's *Fin de Siècle Vienna* (New York, 1961 and Cambridge, 1981).

An enjoyable and evocative account of the Hungarian capital and the way of life of its people is John Lukacs's *Budapest 1900, a Historical Portrait of a City and its Culture* (London, 1993).

Three novels of those available in translation give especial insight into the Monarchy during its final years: Robert Musil, *The Man without Qualities*, translated by Eithne Wilkins and Ernst Kaiser (London, 1954 and 1979); Joszef Roth, *The Radetzkymarsch*, translated by Eva Tucker (New York, 1974); Jaroslav Hasek, *The Good Soldier Schweik*, translated by Paul Server (New York, 1962).

THE HABSBURGS AND THEIR MINISTERS

Charles Ingaro, *In Quest and Crisis: Emperor Joseph I and the Habsburg Monarchy* (West Lafayette, 1979) is a thorough and useful survey. For Charles VI, to be recommended is John Stoye, 'Emperor Charles VI: The early years of the Reign', *Royal Historical Society Transactions*, 12, 1962.

Maria-Theresa is the subject of several useful historical biographies: the best is perhaps C. A. Macartney, *Maria Theresa and the House of Austria* (New York, 1972). Others include Edward Crankshaw, *Maria Theresa* (London, 1969) and William McGill, *Maria Theresa* (New York, 1972). A more detailed and scholarly account of the empress which sheds light on the limits of her modernity and her relationship with her son and her minsiters is to be found amid the wealth of information in the first volume of Derek Beales's exhaustive study of her eldest son and co-regent, *Joseph II, in the Shadow of Maria Theresa* (Cambridge, 1987). This and the keenly awaited second volume will furnish the definitive scholarly history of Joseph II, both the man and his world. Strongly recommended is the now expanded and revised edition of T. C. W. Blanning's study, *Joseph II* (Harlow, 1994). It is concise and comprehensive and shows how the emperor sought to transform the multinational empire.

The Enlightenment dominates discussion of Maria-Theresa and Joseph II. H. M. Scott (ed.), *Enlightened Absolutism; Reform and Reformers in Later Eighteenth-Century Europe* (London, 1990) is an important collection of essays by the leading English-language specialists on the Habsburg monarchy. Of particular interest are: Derek Beales, 'Social forces and Enlightened Policies'; M. S. Anderson, 'The Italian Reformers'; H. M. Scott, 'Reform in the Habsburg Monarchy, 1740–1790'; and R. J. W. Evans, 'Maria Theresa and Hungary' and 'Joseph II and Nationality in the Habsburg Lands'.

To be recommended in this context is P. G. M. Dickson's masterly *Finance and Government under Maria Theresia, 1740–1780* (2 vols, Oxford, 1987). Wenzel Anton von Kaunitz is the subject of a thorough multi-volume scholarly biography which raises the importance of Kaunitz above that of the emperor as the advocate of the Enlightenment within the Habsburg lands; Franz A. J. Szabo, *Kaunitz and Enlightened Absolutism, 1753–1780* (Cambridge, 1994). Also excellent are Paul Bernard, *From the Enlightenment to the Police State: The Public Life of Johann Anton Pergen* (Urbana, 1991), and Frank Brechka, *Gerhard van Swieten and his World 1700–1772* (The Hague, 1970).

The ministers around Francis I and Ferdinand I, rather than the emperors themselves, are the subject of several scholarly studies: Karl Roider, *Baron Thugut and Austria's Response to the French Revolution* (Princeton, 1987); Gunther E. Rothenberg, *Napoleon's Great Adversaries: The Archduke Charles and the Austrian Army, 1792–1814* (Bloomington, 1982). Three valuable studies of Metternich's policies are Enno Kraehe's *Metternich's German Policy* (Princeton, 1963–1983); Henry Kissinger, *A World Restored: Metternich, Castlereagh, and the Problems of Peace 1812–1822* (Boston, 1973) and A. G. Haas, *Metternich, Reorganization and Nationality* (Wiesbaden, 1963).

Francis Joseph and in particular the nature of the emperor's power are the subject of an excellent new reappraisal by Steven Beller, *Francis Joseph* (Harlow, 1996). Rather more bland than Beller's biography is Jean-Paul Bled, *Francis Joseph* (Oxford, 1992) which presents the emperor as a dedicated and dull ruler, determined to fulfil his duty to maintain the integrity of the empire. Joseph Redlich, *The Emperor Francis Joseph of Austria: a Biography* (New York, 1929) is a good political history of the age and is still respected. Also of interest is A. Palmer, *Twilight of the Habsburgs; the Life and Times of Emperor Francis Joseph* (London, 1994).

M. Tanner, *The Last Descendant of Aeneas: the Habsburgs and the Mythic Image of the Emperor* (New Haven, 1993) examines how the Habsburgs were surrounded by and supported by mythology. Andrew Wheatcroft, *The Habsburgs; Embodying Empire* (London, 1995) is a lively study of how dynasty and empire were identified with each other.

THE CONSTITUENT NATIONS

National movements within the Monarchy and within Central Europe have become the focus of much recent scholarship. Of especial importance are the essays in Hagen Schulze (ed.), *Nationbuilding in Central Europe* (Leamington Spa, 1987) and R. Robertson and E. Timms (eds), *The Habsburg Legacy;*

National Identity in Historical Perspective, Austrian Studies 5 (Edinburgh, 1994). Robert Kann and Zdenek David, *The Peoples of the Eastern Habsburg Lands, 1526–1918* (Seattle, 1984) gives detailed and comprehensive accounts of the nations within the Monarchy's east European lands. Roy Porter and Mikláus Teich (eds) *Romanticism in National Context* (Cambridge, 1988) includes a survey of romanticism in Germany by Dietrich von Engelhardt, and in Hungary by Mihály Szegedy-Maszák. Roy Porter and Mikláus Teich (eds) *The National Question in Europe in Historical Context* (Cambridge, 1993) has the following relevent and informative essays: Walter Schmidt, 'The nation in German history'; Heinrich August Winkler, 'Nationalism and nation-state in Germany'; Ernst Bruckmüller, 'The national identity of the Austrians'; Arnost Klima, 'The Czechs'; Emil Niederhauser, 'The national question in Hungary' and Mirjana Gross, 'The union of Dalmatia with northern Croatia: a crucial question of the Croatian national integration in the nineteenth century'.

A good general survey of national movements is to be found in R. A. Kann, *The Multinational Empire: Nationalism and National Reform in the Habsburg Monarchy 1848–1918* 2 vols (New York, 1977).

Also to be recommended are: P. F. Sugar and Ivo J. Lederer (eds), *Nationalism in Eastern Europe* (Seattle, Washington and London, 1969); Miroslav Hroch, *Social Preconditions of National Revival in Europe* (Cambridge, 1985) which identifies phases in the development of national consciousness linked to the emergence of particular types of social structure; Józef Chlebowczyk, *On Small and Young Nations in Europe: Nation-Forming processes in Ethnic Borderlands in East-Central Europe* (Warsaw, 1980). Peter Broch, *Folk Cultures and Little Peoples: Aspects of National Awakening in East Central Europe*, East European Monographs, No. CCCXLVI (Boulder and New York, 1992) shows how the growth of national consciousness could depend on the efforts of two or three passionate individuals and includes Broch's essays on Jan Ernst Smoler and the Czech and Slovak 'awakeners'.

A most valuable scholarly study of the roots of the Czech nation revival in the eighteenth century is Hugh LeCaine Agnew's *Origins of the Czech National Renascence* (University of Pittsburgh, 1993). Agnew discusses at length the importance of the Enlightenment and the reforms of Maria-Theresa and Joseph II for the Czech national revival. Also of interest are Agnew's earlier essays: 'Josephinism and the Patriotic Intelligentsia in Bohemia' in Ivo Banac and F. Sysyn (eds), *Concepts of Nationhood in Early Modern Eastern Europe, Harvard Ukrainian Studies*, volume X, Number 3/4, December 1986, pp. 577–97 (Cambridge Mass.) and 'Enlightenment and National Consciousness: Three Czech "Popular Awakeners" in Ivo Banac, John G. Ackerman and Roman Sporluk (eds), *Nations and Ideology: essays in Honor of Wayne S. Vucinich* (Boulder, 1981), pp. 201–26. For comparison there is Joseph Frederick Zacek, 'The Czech Enlightenment and the Czech National Revival', *Canadian Review of Studies in Nationalism*, 10, 1983.

For the Czechs in the nineteenth century, to be recommended are Peter Brock and H. Gordon Skilling (eds), *The Czech Renascence of the Nineteenth Century* (Toronto and Buffalo, 1972); Stanley Pech, *The Czech Revolution of*

1848 (Chapel Hill, 1969); Lawrence Orton, *The Prague Slav Congress of 1848* (Boulder, 1978).

Good histories of Hungary are: Peter Sugar (et al. eds), *A History of Hungary* (Indiana U.P., 1990), a collection of essays which together provide a complete chronological history; C. A. Macartney, *Hungary: A Short History* (Edinburgh, 1962) and E. Palmenyi (ed.), *A History of Hungary* (London, 1975).

Hungary from the Compromise to the post-communist era is the subject of Jorg K. Hoensch's expert and recently updated book, *History of Modern Hungary 1867–1994* (Harlow, 1995). Andrew Janos, *The Politics of Backwardness in Hungary 1825–1914* (Princeton, 1982) is a substantial work of scholarship.

There is an extensive body of literature for the Hungarian national revival and the events of 1848. Available in English and strongly recommended is György Spira, *The Nationality in the Hungary of 1848–1849* (Budapest, 1992), the publication of which stirred old passions in Hungary. Spira examines the position of the non-Magyar nations in Hungary and how their national aspirations conflicted with those of the Magyars.

The extent to which national movements begin as the creation of one or two zealous patriots is illustrated by: George Barany, *Stephen Szechenyi and the Awakening of Hungarian Nationalism, 1791–1841* (Princeton, 1968); István Deák, *The Lawful Revolution; Louis Kossuth and the Hungarians, 1848–1849* (New York, 1979); for the Croats and their national rebirth, see Elinor Murray Despalatovic, *Ljudevit Gaj and the Illyrian Movement, East European Monographs*, 12. (Boulder, 1975).

The following are good introductions to the condition of the different South Slav nations under Habsburg rule: Ivo Banac, *The National Question in Yugoslavia, Origins, History, Politics* (Ithaca and London, 1984); Barbara Jelavich, *History of the Balkans*, 2 vols (Cambridge, 1983); G. E. Rothenberg, *The Austrian Military Border in Croatia, 1522–1747* (Urbana, 1960) and *The Military Border in Croatia, 1740–1881* (Chicago, 1966); Noel Malcolm, *Bosnia, A Short History* (London, 1994) and Peter Sugar, *Industrialization of Bosnia-Hercegovina, 1878–1918* (Seattle, 1963).

The Germans and the German-speaking world are best served of all national groups in the Habsburg monarchy. A bibliography of this length can only mention a few works and the reader is directed towards the excellent bibliographies provided with the following recommendations. First-rate general histories covering politics, culture and economics are James J. Sheehan, *German History 1770–1866* (Oxford, 1989) and Gordon A. Craig, *Germany 1866–1945* (Oxford, 1978). There is a general history of Austria: Barbara Jelavich, *Modern Austria: Empire and Republic 1800–1986* (Cambridge, 1987).

The Austrian Enlightenment is the subject of Paul P. Bernard's *Jesuits and Jacobins: Enlightenment and Enlightened Despotism in Austria* (Urbana, 1971). To be recommended is William C. Langsam, *The Napoleonic Wars and German Nationalism in Austria* (New York, 1930).

An admirable and concise history of nationalism with a chronology is Hagen

Schulze, *The Course of German Nationalism, from Frederick the Great to Bismarck 1763–1867* (Cambridge, 1991); the bibliographical essay by T. C. W. Blanning is an excellent guide to further reading and makes redundant further entries here. Stimulating and controversial is David Blackbourn and G. Elley's, *The Peculiarities of German History. Bourgeois Society and Politics in Nineteenth-Century Germany* (Oxford, 1984).

Insight into the Italians' experience of Habsburg rule is offered by the following: Eric Cochrane, *Florence in the Forgotten Centuries, 1527–1800* (Chicago, 1973); Miriam Levy, *Governance and Grievance: Habsburg Policy and Italian Tyrol in the Eighteenth Century* (West Lafayette, 1988).

The best introduction to the history of Italian unification is still Derek Beales, *The Risorgimento and the Unification of Italy* (re-issued, Harlow, 1981). One of the many strengths of Frank J. Coppa's *The Origins of the Italian Wars of Independence* (Harlow, 1992) is the clarity with which the author shows how rivalries among the European great powers dictated the course of the wars.

Maps and Genealogical Tables

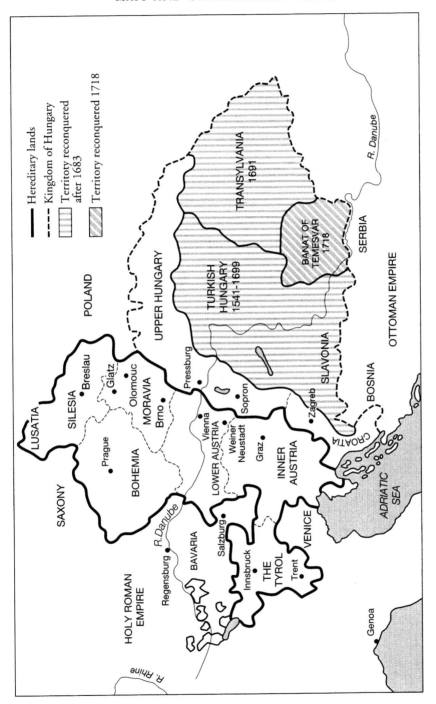

1. The Austrian Monarchy under Charles VI

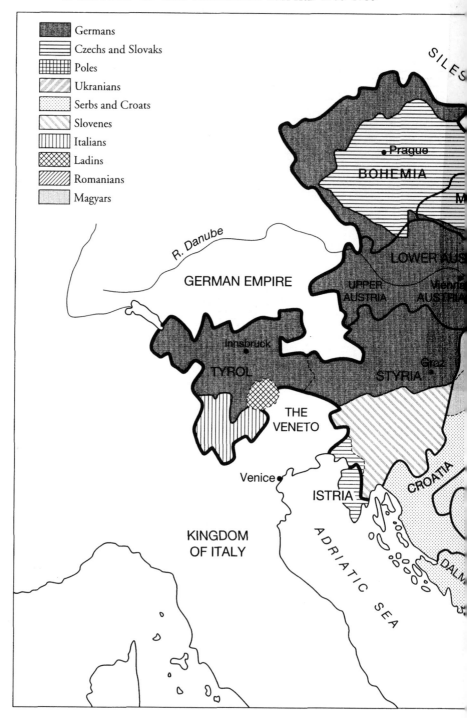

2. The ethno-linguistic composition of the Monarchy up to 1720

3. The German Confederation, 1815–1866

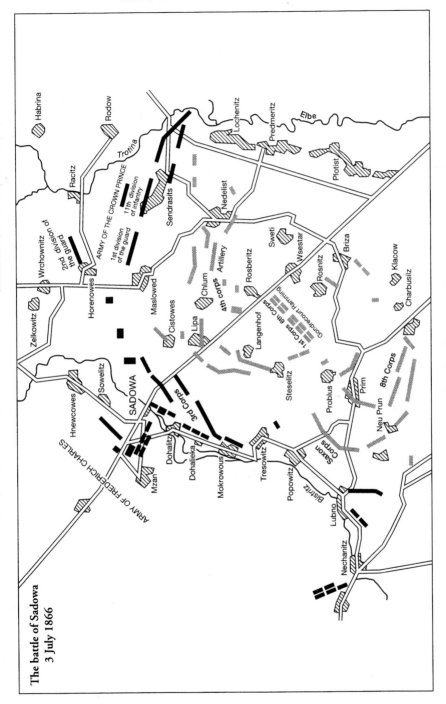

The battle of Sadowa
3 July 1866

4. The Battle of Sadowa, 3 July 1866

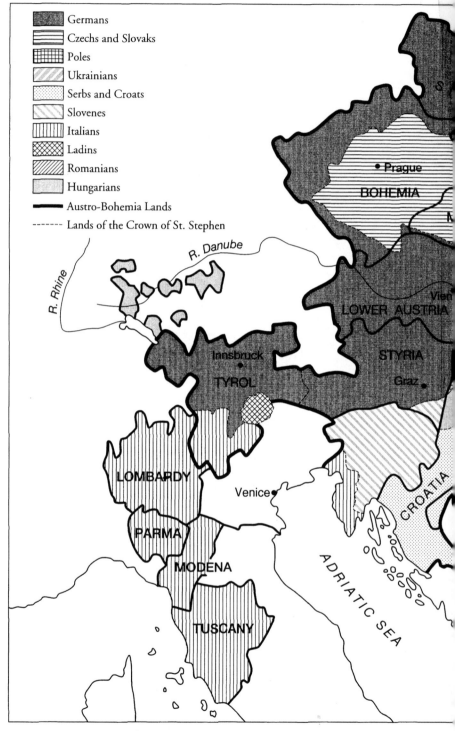

5. Nationalities of the Austro-Hungarian Empire, 1878–1918

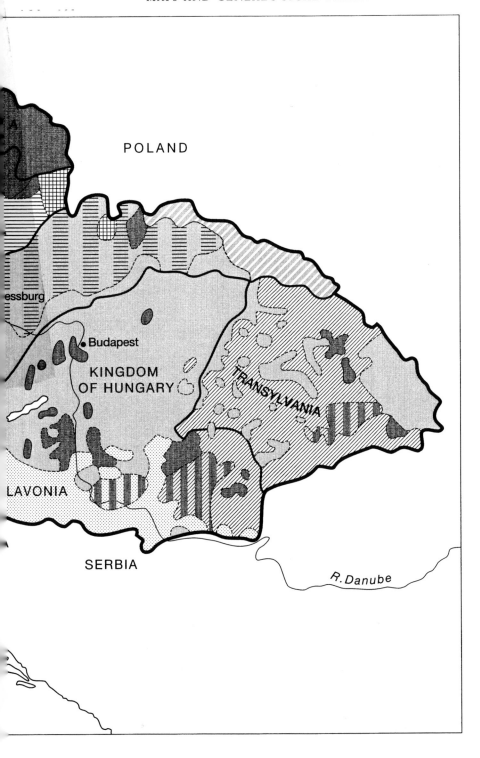

POLAND

essburg

Budapest

KINGDOM
OF HUNGARY

TRANSYLVANIA

LAVONIA

SERBIA

R. Danube

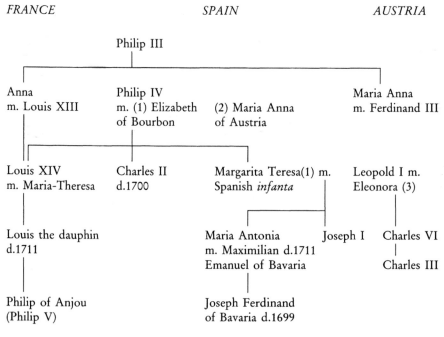

1. The Habsburgs and the War of the Spanish Succession

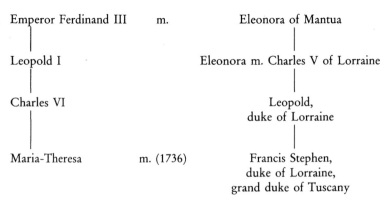

2. Kinship of Maria-Theresa and Francis Stephen of Lorraine

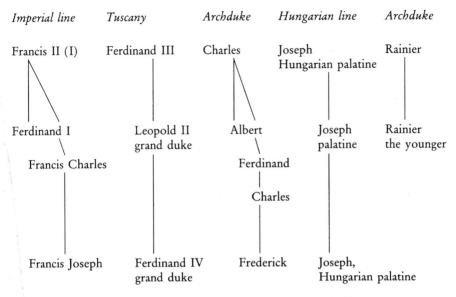

3. The five branches descended from Leopold II

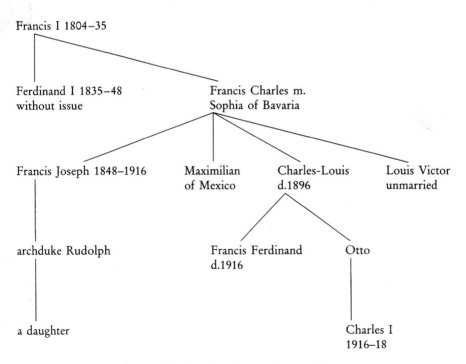

4. The family of Francis Joseph

Index

INDEX